Crossing Boundaries
Knowledge, Disciplinarities,
and Interdisciplinarities

KNOWLEDGE:

Disciplinarity and Beyond

SERIES EDITORS

Ellen Messer-Davidow · David R. Shumway · David J. Sylvan

KNOWLEDGE:

Disciplinarity and Beyond

Crossing Boundaries
Knowledge, Disciplinarities,
and Interdisciplinarities

JULIE THOMPSON KLEIN

UNIVERSITY PRESS OF VIRGINIA

Charlottesville and London

THE UNIVERSITY PRESS OF VIRGINIA

© 1996 by the Rector and Visitors of the University of Virginia

Acknowledgments for previously published material appear on pages ix–x.

First published 1996

♾ The paper used in this publication meets the minimum requirements of the American National Standard for Information Sciences—Permanence of Paper for Printed Library Materials, ANSI Z39.48-1984.

Library of Congress Cataloging-in-Publication Data
Klein, Julie Thompson.
    Crossing boundaries : knowledge, disciplinarities, and
interdisciplinarities / Julie Thompson Klein.
      p.   cm. — (Knowledge, disciplinarity and beyond)
    Includes bibliographical references and index.
    ISBN 0-8139-1678-X (cloth : alk. paper). — ISBN 0-8139-1679-8
(pbk. : alk. paper)
    1. Interdisciplinary approach to knowledge.   I. Title.
II. Series.
BD255.K538'   1996
001.2—dc20   96-7615
                                          CIP

Printed in the United States of America

We are now come to a period of rational knowledges; wherein if I have made the divisions other than those that are received, yet I would not be thought to disallow all those divisions which I do not use.

Francis Bacon, *The Advancement of Learning*, 1605

Now one of the chief errors of thought is to continue to think in one set of forms, categories, ideas, etc., when the object, the content, has moved on, has created or laid premises for an extension, a development of thought.

C. L. R. James, *Notes on Dialectics*, 1981

CONTENTS

ACKNOWLEDGMENTS

 book is only as vital as the conversations that nurture it. I am especially indebted to the following people:

About boundary work: Tom Gieryn
About disciplinarities: Ludwig Huber, Tony Becher, and William Doty
About interdisciplinarities: Stan Bailis and Ray Miller
About interdisciplinary studies: Robert Warren, Daniel Rich, and Ellwyn Stoddard
About literary studies: Jerry Herron
About problem-focused research: Daryl Chubin, Paul Hoch, Renee Friedman, and Don Baldwin
About knowledge description: Katherine Hayles and Joan Fiscella
About strategies and format: David Shumway, George Klein, and Thomas Moeller

I am also grateful to Alice Bennett and Deborah Oliver, for their diligent work on preparing the manuscript for publication.

Most of all, I thank Bill Newell and Ellen Messer-Davidow for never ceasing to question and to challenge as they read several versions of the manuscript.

Portions of the manuscript have been published elsewhere in other forms.

Portions of part 1 appeared in "Interdisciplinarity and Problem-Centered Inquiry," *Library Trends* (fall 1996). Special issue on The Library and Interdisciplinary Inquiry.

Portions of chapters 2 and 3 were published in "Blurring, Cracking, and Crossing: Permeation and the Fracturing of Discipline," in *Knowledges: His-*

torical and Critical Studies of Disciplinarity, ed. Ellen Messer-Davidow, David Sylvan, and David Shumway. Charlottesville: Univ. Press of Virginia, 1993.

Portions of chapter 3 appeared in "TEXT/CONTEXT: Textuality and Rhetoric in the Social Sciences," in *Writing the Social Text; Poetics and Politics in Social Science Discourse,* ed. Richard Harvey Brown. Hawthorne NY: Aldine DeGruyter, 1992.

Parts of the conclusion are adapted from "Finding Knowledge and Information" (*Interdisciplinary Studies Today,* 1994), "Interdisciplinary Studies" (with William Newell, *Handbook on the Undergraduate Curriculum,* 1996), "Interdisciplinary Studies in the 21st Century" (with William Newell, *Journal of General Education,* 1996), "Interdisciplinarity and Adult Learners" (*Journal of Graduate Liberal Studies,* 1995), and "Toward an Interdisciplinary Theory of Adult Learning" (*Options,* 1995).

Crossing Boundaries
Knowledge, Disciplinarities,
and Interdisciplinarities

INTRODUCTION:

Interdisciplinary Claims

Two claims about knowledge appear widely today. The first claim is that knowledge is increasingly interdisciplinary. The reasons cited for this change vary, but the results are similar. The pressing weight of social and technological problems, breakthroughs in research, new scholarship, and new demands on the curriculum have put a slogan of the 1960s and 1970s back on the academic agenda—"Interdisciplinarity has come of age" (Schütze 1985, 9). The second and related claim is that boundary crossing has become a defining characteristic of the age. Definitions of a boundary differ, ranging from demarcations of science from nonscience to divisions of geographical land and political power. Nevertheless, over time and specialist domains, "boundary" has become a new keyword in discussions of knowledge.

Boundary Work

The rhetoric of boundaries is signified by spatial metaphors of turf, territory, and domain. Metaphors of place call attention to the ways categories and classifications stake out differences. Boundary work is the composite set of claims, activities, and institutional structures that define and protect knowledge practices. People work directly and through institutions to create, maintain, break down, and reformulate boundaries between knowledge units. As legitimacy and authority are attached to ideas, reputational systems are created, and knowledge becomes hierarchically stratified (Fisher 1993, 13–14; Shapin 1992, 335).

In studies of science, where the concept of boundary work arose, the primary focus has been disciplinary formations (Gieryn 1983, 1995; Shapin

1992). In studying the Social Science Research Council, Donald Fisher applied the concept to interdisciplinary activities (1990, 1993). Boundary work occurs in all knowledge fields though, because the problem of boundaries is universal. This book further develops the concept of boundary work by investigating an important but understudied example. In emphasizing boundary formation and maintenance, previous studies have tended to treat boundary crossing as an anomaly, a peripheral event, or a developmental stage. At this historical point, however, the interactions and reorganizations that boundary crossing creates are as central to the production and organization of knowledge as boundary formation and maintenance.

The introduction and part 1 explore the reasons. The introduction defines interdisciplinary claims and the ways they are theorized. Part 1 examines the institutional contexts of interdisciplinary activity, the reasons for boundary permeation, and the boundary work that occurs in interdisciplinary practices. Boundary crossing stimulates the formation of trading zones of interaction, interlanguages, hybrid communities and professional roles, new institutional structures, and new categories of knowledge. Interdisciplinary activities, though, do not escape the boundary work of defining and legitimating claims. Part 2 applies the conceptual framework developed in part 1 in case studies at three levels: interdisciplinary fields, an individual discipline, and a national research system. The book concludes with a discussion of three issues that are crucial to the future prospects of interdisciplinary activity: integrative process, criteria of judgment, and institutional strategies.

The intended audience is wide, like that of my two earlier books. It includes anyone who is contemplating, engaging in, evaluating, or reflecting on interdisciplinary activity. It differs from the earlier books in several respects. *Interdisciplinarity: History, Theory, and Practice* (Klein 1990b) was a descriptive overview, intended to provide a basis for common discourse. The focus was definition and description. *Interdisciplinary Studies Today* (Klein and Doty 1994) was a handbook, intended to provide a guide to interdisciplinary curriculum by leading experts. The focus was educational practice. This work takes the next step by developing a conceptual framework for understanding, studying, and supporting interdisciplinary practices. The focus is the production and organization of interdisciplinary knowledge.

This focus places the book at the intersection of several converging inquiries. Over the past two decades, the growing field of knowledge studies has produced a fuller picture of disciplinary, professional, and interdisciplinary knowledges. The methodology of studying knowledge has also expanded beyond traditional questions of epistemology to include interviews and surveys, ethnographic studies, conversation and discourse analysis, citation analysis, critical historiography, archival research, and empirical analysis of research groups and sites as well as organizational analysis of the higher education system. Studying interdisciplinary activities places a greater onus on archival research. The discourse of interdisciplinarity is dispersed across an expanse of disconnected literatures. It must be collected and rendered visible. The task of collecting, though, is not separate from critical historiography and discourse analysis. The origins of claims must be reconstructed and the relation between discourse about interdisciplinarity and what happens in everyday practice assessed.

Location is an important theme in this analysis. All knowledge is located, whether, to echo Michel de Certeau, the space of inquiry is a routine, practiced place or a negotiated, contested space (1984, 139). The question of knowledge space is not unlike the question of cartography, an analogy reinforced by the metaphor of mapping knowledge. Historical European cartography produced a system of mapping geographical and political space that symbolically segmented the world by lines of longitude and latitude forming territorial quadrangles. These divisions were further subdivided into smaller measurements of degrees, hours, minutes, and seconds. Taken together, they formed a mosaic of reference points. Although they were handy for dividing up sovereign territory, their accuracy was problematic, and disputes over territorial lines inevitably arose. The 1884 partitioning of Africa illustrates why. Of the colonial borders that dissected the continent, 44 percent originated from map parallels and meridians. An additional 30 percent were arbitrary curves and straight lines. Yet only one-fourth of them corresponded to defined topographical features such as lakes, rivers, mountains, or valleys. This system of demarcations also ignored the presence of frontier systems and zones (Stoddard 1991, 6).

Comparably, traditional studies of disciplinarity have produced a misleadingly simple account of knowledge fields and their associated academic communities. Extending the metaphor of mapping knowledge, Tony Becher highlights the variety of forms and practices. The earth comprises many *topographical patterns* (tropical versus temperate, mountainous versus maritime); *cross-national connections* (ethnic origins, political creeds, religious affiliations); *economic, functional, and occupational similarities* (concentrations of industrialized zones, areas producing raw materials or providing service activities); *and broad social and cultural features* (urban as opposed to rural ways of life). Their counterparts in knowledge territories include *basic characteristics* (hard, quantitative, and cumulative or soft, qualitative, and reiterative, pure or applied), *shared theories or ideologies* (catastrophe theory, Marxism), *common techniques* (electron microscopy, computer modeling), and *sociocultural characteristics* (the people-to-problem ratio, frequency and form of publication, incidence of collaborative work, nature of competition) (Becher 1990, 335–36, 343–44).

The remapping of knowledge to include this variety and new interdisciplinary fields has highlighted the current extent of boundary crossing. The long-term structural trend of academic institutions has been in the direction of greater specialization, professionalization, departmentalization, and fragmentation. Yet, cross-fertilizations, overlaps, and exchanges are proliferating (Dogan and Pahre 1990, 85). This development has two implications. The first implication is academic structure. For much of the twentieth century, the surface structure of academic institutions has been dominated by disciplinarities. Interdisciplinarities tended to be located in the "shadow structure," to borrow Charles Lemert's term for the composite set of structures and strategies that challenge the prevailing metaphor of disciplinary depth (1990, 6). In the latter half of the twentieth century, the balance of surface and shadow structure is changing as heterogeneity, hybridity, complexity, and interdisciplinarity become characterizing traits of knowledge.

The second implication is the relationship between disciplinarity and interdisciplinarity. The relationship is often depicted as an opposition, a paradox, or a dichotomy (Roederer 1988, 659; Klein 1990b, 106). Close inspection of boundary crossing reveals that disciplinarity and interdisciplinarity are productive tensions in a dynamic of supplement, complement, and critique. New macromodels of knowledge and microanalyses of knowledge cultures dispute the validity of standard models. Standard models posit a uniformity of disciplines that is belied by the heterogeneity of practices and disputes over what constitutes the discipline "proper." Standard models of disciplinarity have tended, in turn, to promote standard models of interdisciplinarity as relating or integrating existing theories, models, and contents through collaboration. These activities occur, but in failing to situate disciplinarity and interdisciplinarity historically and socially, standard models have minimized historical change and the diversity of rationales, forms, outcomes, and problems (Squires 1992, 202, 204).

Mapping interdisciplinary activities is not easy. The task of understanding is complicated by the "jungle of phenomena" (Huber 1992a, 195). Interdisciplinary activities compose a complex and contradictory set of practices located along shifting coordinates. The inevitable result of much interdisciplinary study, if not its ostensible purpose, Giles Gunn rightly notes, has been to dispute and disorder conventional understandings of relations between the most fundamental concepts of knowledge description—origin and terminus, center and periphery, focus and margin, inside and outside (1992a, 249). Mapping is also complicated by the multiple boundaries being crossed in interdisciplinary activities. They are not strictly disciplinary or academic.

The boundaries include demarcations of academic and popular knowledge (in esoteric knowledge versus everyday life), science versus nonscience (pseudoscience and applications of science), disciplines (physics versus chemistry or biology), subdisciplinary specialties (economic, social, and political history), hybrid fields (social psychology, environmental studies, and materials science), disciplinary clusters (science, technology, social science, and humanities), taxonomic categories (hard versus soft knowledge, basic versus applied research), learning skills (integrative thinking, literacy, comparative methodology, and the ability to deal with diversity), knowledge activities (transmission versus discovery, explanation versus interpretation), knowledge forms (quantitative versus qualitative, objective versus subjective and normative), and sectors of society (industry, academe, government, and the public).

Even in a single area a boundary complex exists. Feminist practices, for example, engage the multiple boundaries of knowing and doing; subjective and objectified consciousness; gender, race, class, and culture; disciplinary, professional, and interdisciplinary affiliations. Comparably, in different realms, research in molecular biology and in computer sciences crosses the boundaries of academic disciplines, pure and applied research, sanctioned and de-sanctioned roles of scientists, and assumptions about what constitute proper divisions of academic, government, and industrial work. To understand a single boundary crossing, we must untangle a complex set of interests, actions, and structures.

Whether implicit or explicit, arguments about knowledge are often guided by metaphors (Becher 1990, 333). Over the past several decades, metaphors of knowledge description have shifted from the static logic of foundation and structure to the dynamic properties of network, web, system, field, and topological metaphors that describe relations among elements, such as joints, points of connection, boundedness, overlaps, interconnections, interpenetrations, breaks, and cracks (Goldman 1995, 222–23). Of these metaphors, field is the most powerful. In defining field (*champ*) as a separate social universe with its own laws of functioning and specific relations of force, Pierre Bourdieu (1993) provided a model for understanding academic knowledge. In everyday language the word "field" denotes any set of recurring activities, whether aerobics, comparative literature, or as Bourdieu used the term, artistic, cultural, religious, juridical, and university fields (Posner 1988). The university field, like any other, is the locus of struggles to determine the conditions and criteria of legitimate membership and hierarchy. Interdisciplinarity is a contested concept that enters the university field in the form of diverse claims.

Arguing Knowledge

The claims that prompt this inquiry—that knowledge is increasingly interdisciplinary and boundary crossing commonplace—imply an equally prominent claim even as they cast doubt on it. Burton Clark framed the argument in his 1983 book *The Higher Education System:* "In short, the discipline rather than the institution tends to become the dominant force in the working lives of academics. To stress the primacy of discipline is to change our perception of enterprises and systems: we see the university or college as a collection of local chapters of national and international disciplines, chapters that import and implant the orientations to knowledge, the norms, and the customs of the larger fields. The control of work shifts toward the internal controls of the disciplines, whatever their nature" (16).

Disciplinarity in its present form is the result of a relatively recent development, little more than a century old. Nevertheless, its effects are visible throughout the knowledge system, from the organization of research and curriculum to criteria of excellence in the decisions of editorial boards, funding agencies, and tenure and promotion committees. Disciplinarity is so powerful, Clark adds, that it constitutes a "first principle." Knowledge specialties are the "fundaments on which all else is constructed." Patterns of academic specialization are especially strong in the United States, but their effects are visible worldwide: "No developed or semi-developed country is without organized academic disciplines, reflected nationally in such a common form as the learned society" (35). As a dominant principle, disciplinarity has the force of necessity, implying that the academic institution could hardly be structured otherwise and emplotting knowledge in a narrative of increasingly specialized material.

Interdisciplinary claims highlight other developments. The National Research Council (NRC), a private advisory body in the United States, called attention to these developments in a 1986 report on the discipline of physics:

> The interface between physics and chemistry has been crossed so often in both directions that its exact location is obscure; its passage is signaled more by gradual changes in language and approach than by any sharp demarcation in content. It has been a source of continual advances in concept and application all across the science of molecules and atoms, surfaces and interfaces, and fluids and solids. Yet, in spite of this, the degree of direct, collaborative interaction between physicists and chemists in the United States, especially at universities, has remained surprisingly limited. These relationships have recently begun to grow, especially in the region of interdisciplinary overlap. (*Scientific Interfaces and Technological Applications* 1986, 53)

Although they are not restricted to science and technology, the changes highlighted in the NRC's description of physics are dramatically evident in the emergence of materials science as a hybrid discipline, the cross-fertilizations stimulated by new computational machinery and concepts, the integration of physical methods into biological research, and widespread crossing of the traditional boundaries separating basic science from engineering. Yet even as the cultures of physicists and chemists are merging at major synchrotron facilities, even as the boundaries between chemistry, physics, and to an extent biology have blurred in macromolecular research, academic reward systems continue to favor institutionalized disciplinary categories. Consequently, interdisciplinary research remains circumscribed. Although positing a different picture than Clark does, the NRC's account is still framed by the power of disciplinarity, emplotting knowledge in a narrative of bridge building and accommodation.

In remapping German studies, Jeffrey Peck presents a different claim:

> As a model for interdisciplinary study, German Studies, as a discursive formation, becomes that site or strategic location where the discipline reflects on itself and its practices, both critical and academic, where the variety of discourses about Germany—the literary, political, sociological—converge or diverge. As the in-between-space where the clash of multiple subjectivities can foreground difference, it stimulates reflection on how such a new object is constituted. It is at this in-between level where Germany is constructed, talked about, and represented by the practitioners of the fields that make up the more differentiated practice of German Studies. (1989, 184)

Peck redefines discipline as a new and differentiated site. This argument is advanced in feminism, cultural studies, and many poststructuralist practices. It critiques the way disciplines and even many interdisciplinary programs divide rather than connect. It is a decidedly plural claim. Some, like Peck, argue that boundaries should not be dissolved but should be continually crossed, enabling alternative structures and new inquiries to emerge. Others argue, more radically, that nothing less than a dedisciplining of knowledge has occurred. Disciplines, they contend, are archaic structures. Academic departments, in Charles Lemert's words, are "organizational resting places for professionally committed scholars, many of whom do intellectual work so far beyond being even inter- or multidisciplinary as to be postdisciplinary" (1989, 13). In all oppositional critique, though, the site of inquiry is reconstituted as objects are unbounded, emplotting knowledge in a narrative of decentered paradigms and structural transformation.

All three claims are valid depictions of knowledge, because the forces that shape them operate simultaneously. Clark reaffirms the prominence of disciplinarity. The NRC highlights activities that range from borrowing methods and concepts to forming new hybrid fields. Peck calls attention to new critical practices. Even these examples, though, do not account for the entire range of forces that have fostered the belief that knowledge is "increasingly interdisciplinary." Several refrains punctuate the chant of interdisciplinary ferment. Breakthroughs at the "frontier" and the "cutting edge" of research and scholarship are often deemed interdisciplinary. The complexity of modern intellectual, social, technological, and economic problems also requires integrative approaches and collaborative skills. In a more diffuse, subtle, and slower way, the daily flow of influence and techniques across subjects creates an interdisciplinary presence even in the heart of disciplinary domains (Squires 1992, 202, 209).

Claims differ not only across fields but also within them. Members of humanities disciplines, for instance, invoke a range of authorities from Plato, the Renaissance humanists, and Hegel to Geertz, Derrida, and Fish. Ancient ideas of unified science, general knowledge, synthesis, and integration of knowledge remain powerful warrants for interdisciplinary thought in the humanities and in general and liberal education. Yet poststructuralist practices and disciplinary critique create conflicting claims that oppose traditional notions of unity and organic relation. These claims are linked with new practices and fields that seek to transform existing disciplinary structures and modes of inquiry.

Educators also have a range of precedents, from Plato's Academy to the general education movement in the early decades of the twentieth century and the core curriculum movement in the 1930s and 1940s. The strongest association is with the 1960s and 1970s, a time when the idea of interdisciplinarity was closely entwined with worldwide calls for restructuring knowledge and society. So strong is the connection that in calling an international conference on the concept, the Organization for Economic Cooperation and Development treated it as an innovation of the era, born of the need for universities to renew themselves (Schütze 1985, 9).

Claims in social science are equally plural. The idea that social science disciplines were originally interdisciplinary echoes a widespread belief about all disciplines. In psychology, for example, the work of eminent late nineteenth-century pioneers of psychology—William James, Harry S. Sullivan, and Fritz Heider—is characterized as "interdisciplinary" (Harvey 1981, xv). More accurately, the early disciplines of today's academy were "predisciplinary" and their members "predisciplinarians," not "multi-" or "interdisciplinarians" in the modern sense (Swoboda 1979, 60). Reclamation of an interdisciplinary past is a common strategy in legitimating interdisciplinary work. In disciplinary histories, though, interdisciplinary origin tends to invoke a prehistory of knowledge. In interdisciplinary histories it tends to authorize a foundation or a competing epistemology.

Roberta Frank suggests that the concept of interdisciplinarity was probably born in New York City in the mid-1920s at the corner of Forty-second Street and Madison Avenue—surely a record for genealogical specificity. The offices of the Social Science Research Council (SSRC) were at Forty-second and Madison. During the 1930s the term was used in the SSRC as a kind of "bureaucratic shorthand" for research involving two or more of the several professional societies of the Council. The first citation of "interdisciplinary" in *Webster's Ninth New Collegiate Dictionary* and *A Supplement to the Oxford*

English Dictionary is, in fact, a reference to a December 1937 issue of the *Journal of Educational Sociology* and a subsequent notice regarding post-doctoral fellowships of the Social Science Research Council (Frank 1988, 91, 94–95). Yet interdisciplinary claims are also anchored on other ground, from the earlier movements known as unity of science, culture-personality, and behavioralism to new hybrid domains such as social psychology and new practices of interpretive social science.

One particular claim caught the attention of an unusually wide audience, stirring interest well beyond the social sciences. In 1980 Clifford Geertz commented on the enormous amount of genre mixing in the social sciences and humanities. Society is less often represented as an elaborate machine or quasi organism—explained in terms of covering laws, unified science, and operationalism—than as a game, a drama, a text, or in terms of cognitive aesthetics, discourse, and speech-act analysis. These are not isolated events. They are part of a cultural shift from explanations based on physical processes to symbolic forms. This shift has been occurring among an important segment of social scientists. Conventions of interpretation remain, yet they are more than ever built to accommodate a situation that Geertz described as "fluid, plural, uncentered, and ineradicably untidy." The resulting destabilization has reinforced challenges to some of the central assumptions of mainstream social science.

Claims in science likewise vary. In the geological sciences, plate tectonics has the stature of precedent. In the life sciences, biochemistry and molecular biology enjoy pride of place. Problem-focused researchers, engineers, and many scientists locate historical origins in the 1940s and 1950s, citing the Manhattan Project, operations research, and the mission orientation of the United States Department of Agriculture. By the 1960s interdisciplinarity had become a recognized force in space research. By the 1970s and 1980s the idea was linked with research in areas of keen international economic competition, especially manufacturing, computer sciences, and biotechnology. As the NRC's report suggests, it was also becoming part of disciplinary description.

As the scope of examples demonstrates, interdisciplinarity is both a permanent and a transient issue (Squires 1992, 201). Yet the rhetoric of the new is accentuated in the dispersed scholarship on the subject, the reports of learned societies, the recommendations of educational commissions, and even the public media. The *New York Times* periodically heralds new research developments under the banner of interdisciplinarity. In a recent special issue on graduate schools, *U.S. News and World Report* characterized interdisciplinarity as "the buzzword of the moment" and interdisciplinary studies as the new fashion in the "trendy world of American higher education." The news story correctly notes the contemporary examples of gerontology, cognitive sciences, cultural studies, comparative arts, women's studies, science and technology, and environmental policy (Henderson 1994, 73). It is, though, historically short-sighted. Interdisciplinary claims usually have a deeper history, and older thematics are often redeployed under new names.

By the time the word appeared on a banner at the barricades of student strikes in the Paris of May 1968—"pluridisciplinarité et interdisciplinarité: deux termes barbares, même s'ils sont d'actualité"—it was already regarded in some quarters as a familiar, even overworked slogan. During the 1960s it changed from scattered occurrences into "a kind of weather." From that point forward "the stretching out of syllables" moved hand in hand with extensions of meaning. Little wonder then that by 1977 "interdisciplinary" had made it into *The Dictionary of Diseased English* (Frank 1988, 98–99), or that Dogan and Pahre recently proposed that the word be banished from the language as "virtually devoid of real meaning today" (1990, 65).

The problem is not that the word is devoid of meaning. It is replete with meaning—conflicting meaning. The concept is plural, because the idea of interaction between disciplines involves differing tasks on numerous human and categorical levels (Broido 1979, 246). These differences surface in disputes over terminology. Calling a given boundary crossing a subdisciplinary exchange, a multidisciplinary affiliation, an interdisciplinary solution, an integrative approach, a collaborative project, a transdisciplinary paradigm, or a cross-disciplinary critique is itself a form of boundary work. The claims codified in terminology reflect differing notions of what constitutes a discipline, philosophical and sociopolitical viewpoints, and opinions about whether interdisciplinarity is primarily an issue of research, education, or administration (Kockelmans 1979a, 125).

These differences are not exclusively academic. The possibilities and limits of interaction are embedded in the society at large (Kann 1979, 186). Theories about interdisciplinarity are also theories about knowledge and culture.

Theorizing Claims

Interdisciplinary claims are theorized in many ways, though claims and related activities may be viewed in terms of where they lie along a spectrum of argument. At one end, *instrumentalism* posits interdisciplinarity as an empirical problem (Eisel 1992, 243). At the other end, *epistemology* posits interdisciplinarity as a theoretical problem. Solving social and technological problems and borrowing tools and methods exemplify instrumentalism. The search for unified knowledge and critique exemplify the other end of the spectrum. The difference is embodied in two metaphors identified by the Nuffield Foundation: bridge building and restructuring.

Bridge building is more common. It takes place between complete and firm disciplines and frequently has an applied orientation (*Interdisciplinarity*

1975, 42–47). Most instrumental projects are forms of bridge building. The first major interdisciplinary movement in the social sciences, dating from the close of World War I to the 1930s, was also a form of bridge building. Quantitative methods were borrowed from the sciences. Bridge builders do not tend to engage in critical reflection on problem choice, the epistemology of the disciplines being used, or the logic of disciplinary structure.

In contrast, restructuring changes parts of disciplines. It often embodies, as well, a critique of the state of the disciplines being restructured and, either implicitly or explicitly, the prevailing structure of knowledge. Restructuring is less common and more radical. In transgressing boundaries and generating new visions, feminist practices constitute a form of restructuring (Peterson 1993, 260). The second interdisciplinary movement in the social sciences, dating from the close of World War II, was also a form of restructuring. Developments in logic and in philosophy and sociology of science stimulated a search for new integrative categories. This search was manifested in new integrated social science courses and programs, the concept of behavioral science, and crosscutting concepts such as area, information, communication, decision making, role, and status (Landau, Proshansky, and Ittelson 1962, 11–15).

Bryan Turner's (1990) analysis of the medical curriculum illustrates the difference between bridge building and restructuring. Interdisciplinarity in social medicine and sociology of health emerged as an epistemological goal. Researchers focus on the complex causality of illness and disease and the corresponding assertion that any valid therapeutics must be based in a holistic view of the patient. In contrast, in research centers based on teamwork and solving social and technological problems, interdisciplinarity has been an unintended consequence of economic necessity, not scientific theory. A pragmatic stance renders universities instruments for the production of skills, replacing questions of epistemology with the pragmatics of reliability, efficiency, and commercial value. An epistemologically creative and critical stance toward disciplinarity holds out the promise of a coherent map of knowledge. Yet even postmodernism in social theory, which challenges monodisciplinarity and professional autonomy, may exacerbate fragmentation by creating even more units of knowledge production (Turner 1990).

The Nuffield Foundation identified a third, less common possibility— transdisciplinary integration around an overarching concept or theory. The term "transdisciplinary" usually labels a paradigm or vision that transcends narrow disciplinary worldviews through overarching synthesis (Miller 1982, 20–22). Transdisciplinary schemata are based in older notions of unity and simplicity as well as new searches for coherence and connection in the modern world. The modern paradigms of general systems theory, structuralism, and Marxism have attempted to organize knowledge at a higher, more comprehensive level. Similarly, Erich Jantsch's vision of the entire system of education and innovation was a proposal to reorder knowledge and institutional structure (1972, 104). At present, the Centre International de Recherches et Etudes Transdisciplinaires in Paris has adapted the term to distinguish older forms of interdisciplinary cooperation from a new search for unity of knowledge and culture shaped by the worldview of complexity in science (UNESCO 1994).

The pressing weight of instrumental claims has led to a skewed picture of interdisciplinarity. In 1982 the Organization for Economic Cooperation and Development (OECD) declared that interdisciplinarity *exogenous* to the university now takes priority over *endogenous* university interdisciplinarity. The exogenous originates in the continuous momentum created by "real" problems of the community and the demand that universities perform their full social mission. In the OECD formulation, the endogenous is based on production of new knowledge with the aim of realizing unity of science. Exogenous interdisciplinarity forever questions the disciplines on the validity of demarcations they apply to life. If health, for instance, is the starting point for interrogating biological science, no boundaries can be accepted between physiology and ethnology or between biology and psychology. If the starting point is education, the interaction of sociological and psychological aspects or the functions of an institution and teaching practices is perceived as necessary. Similarly, industrial practice is no longer viewed as simply applied physics or applied economics. Each time, "reality" must be approached from different angles and a vital role accorded to relations among them. The moment universities organize their activities around such problems, not disciplines, interdisciplinarity ceases to be a mere teaching device or vision. It becomes an organizational need (*University and the Community* 1982, 130).

The OECD's claim that exogenous interdisciplinarity now takes priority is valid to the extent that demands for social and economic relevance have heightened the legitimacy of problem-solving projects, many of them funded by public money. Moreover, the broad trend in interdisciplinarity has been in the direction of methodology, not conceptual commonality or transcendence (Reiger 1978, 46). Interdisciplinarity in this sense has taken a pronounced empirical turn. The exogenous claim, though, is oversimplified on two counts. The first oversimplification is the popular notion that "real life" is naturally interdisciplinary. This truism is enshrined in the chapter title in which the OECD's claim appears, "Communities Have Problems, Universities Have Departments" (*University and the Community* 1982, 127). In similar fashion, the original heterogeneity of professional fields such as landscape planning supposedly mitigates the difficulties of interdisciplinary communication common in academic settings. The required knowledge is presumably integrated through contact with "the real world" (Eisel 1992, 240).

Life, however, is not naturally interdisciplinary. It is a neutral assortment of phenomena that are ordered through human thought and action. The naturalizing of "real life" sidesteps tenacious problems of organizational management and communication that undercut the claim. Industrialists are quick to deplore academic myopia, boasting that industrial research is "naturally" interdisciplinary. Project structures and problem orientation do favor integrated approaches, but the literature on interdisciplinary research in industry and government is rife with complaints about gaps between industrial departments and functional divisions. Likewise, symptoms of fragmentation abound in public life. The traditional building blocks of the university are the disciplines: history, physics, and economics. In city government they are units of basic service delivery: police, fire, and sanitation. When crises requiring an integrated response arise—homelessness, neighborhood revitalization, and drug addiction—the appropriate city departments—housing, welfare, and job training—are constrained by their own organizational structures (Hershberg 1988, 14).

The second oversimplification is the narrow equation of "endogenous" with unity of science. A variety of transdisciplinary schemata promote holistic views of knowledge. The ideological problem of interdisciplinarity is laid bare in the idea of holism. Holism and interdisciplinarity begin in the same place. The earliest recorded citation for "interdisciplinary" in the social sciences occurred, in fact, in 1926, the year Jan Christian Smuts gave the term "holism" currency in his book *Holism and Evolution* (Frank 1988, 101). Holism and interdisciplinarity are linked by a common assumption. Any metaphor, theme, theory, or conceptual scheme—whether a material object, a social phenomenon, or an ecosystem—implies a totality that cannot be adequately explained by reduction to the properties of its parts. Holistic thinking privileges study of a system over analysis of its parts (Craige 1992, 5). The main theses and applications of holism have developed since the mid–nineteenth century in philosophy, biology, psychology, sociology, anthropology, historiography, political science, and general systems theory (Bailis 1984–85, 18).

The moment sharing of concepts is called for, the possibility of unity appears. The search for unity, which Ulrich Eisel dubs "euphoric interdisciplinarity," potentially renders interdisciplinarity an ideology. Claims to unified knowledge promote a metaphysical model that is rooted ontologically in an interrelated, monistic concept of the world. Ironically, though, holism and interdisciplinarity aggravate the very process of disintegration they aim to stop (Eisel 1992, 246). Holisms are contradictory both within and among themselves. Their broad capacity also tends to be splintered in day-to-day practice. Operations research, for instance, has become identified with specific techniques, mathematical models, and algorithms, not a general ability to deal with management problems. In the sciences and many of the social sciences, holistic thinking is also considered philosophical, hence insufficiently analytical and rigorous.

Postmodernism produces a critique of another kind. Both holism and interdisciplinary activities forged in critique are conceived as philosophical problems. That puts them at the epistemological end of the spectrum of claims. Holism and critical interdisciplinarities share a common interest in questioning the boundaries of genre, discourse, discipline, practice, and theory. Most critical interdisciplinarities, though, are skeptical of concepts and theories that systematize knowledge, culture, or society. They run the risk of becoming totalizing master narratives: whether it is the reduction of all phenomena to the metaphor of a system or a structure, the naive reduction theory of the unity of science, or the dominance of materialist dialectics in Marxist-Leninist philosophy. Even as they critique totalizing, though, critical interdisciplinarities perform their own boundary work of totalizing by asserting greater explanatory power, whether it is semiotics, deconstruction, or categories of language, gender, race, or class. Frederic Jameson, for example, argues that Marxism is an interdisciplinary metanarrative grounded in the priority of the political as "the absolute horizon of all reading and all interpretation," not an optional auxiliary to other interpretive methods (1981, 17).

The role of the critical function is a crucial factor in distinguishing claims. All interdisciplinary work is critical in that it exposes the inadequacies of the existing organization of knowledge to accomplish given tasks. Instrumentalism, though, minimizes critical reflection. It retards or altogether ignores analysis of ends and means, even when impediments to efficient problem solving are acknowledged. Critical perspective is limited in two ways. From a disciplinary standpoint, disciplines lose control over research. Loss of the disciplinary critical function propels an "epistemic drift" away from strictly internist criteria and reputational control to externally driven criteria that are more open to external regulation in the policy arena (Elzinga 1985, 209). As an increasing share of research activities becomes located outside teaching departments and outside universities, a parallel "research drift" is occurring (Clark 1995, 12). From an interdisciplinary standpoint, instrumentalism minimizes or negates reflexivity. Public interest in exogenous problems and political intervention to create new facilities to address those problems have propelled a strategic interdisciplinarity in areas of high technology, genetics, space and cancer research. Interdisciplinarity serves the political economy of national needs and marketable trends. In this instance interdisciplinarity is drawn more closely to the problem of knowledge policy (Fuller 1993, 33).

Problems of epistemology, institutional structure, and cultural theory are fronted in interdisciplinarities that locate the question of interdisciplinarity in critique, not efficient problem solving, building better bridges, or achieving unity of knowledge. The authority of disciplines is challenged, not repackaged or enhanced (Kain 1993, 317–18). The primacy of critique in many poststructuralist practices of the humanities and social sciences is so strong that it has fostered an interdisciplinary backlash. Older interdisciplinary activities that combine existing disciplines are disavowed in favor of more radical "cross-disciplinary," "antidisciplinary," or "counterdisciplinary" formulations. Arthur Kroker (1980), writing in the context of Canadian studies, drew a distinction that is implicitly shared in all critical interdisciplinarities. "Vacant interdisciplinarity" mechanically normalizes existing modes of thought. In contrast, an interdisciplinarity rooted in critical thought reinvents scholarly and public discourse by regenerating method and epistemology. When intellectuality is premised on rediscovery and rethinking, resocialization and reintellectualization, interdisciplinarity becomes not just a way of doing things but a new way of knowing.

Conflicting claims expose conflicting beliefs about appropriate actions and institutional structures. Mark Kann depicts the conflicts as forms of political explanation. Conservative elites want a specific kind of explanation that enables them to solve problems and devise practical answers, divorcing questions of politics from questions of knowledge. A liberal explanation emerges among those caught between older positivisms and newer, radical perspectives. Locating themselves in the middle ground of harmonious interaction, they too are bridge builders. Radical dissidents, in contrast, demand that interdisciplinary explanation be useful to oppressed groups seeking greater sociopolitical equality (1979, 197–98). They are restructuralists.

Problem solving, pluralism, and critique create different conditions of knowledge, shaping in turn differing beliefs about appropriate institutional structures, criteria for judging outcomes, and the relation between disciplinarity and interdisciplinarity. These differences arise continuously in debates not only over allocating resources for interdisciplinary activities, but over the more fundamental question of what place they occupy in the academy.

Part 1
Boundary Crossing

One strand of the argument is that what are variously
described as segments, sub-disciplines, specialisms, schools,
sects and the like, form their own counter-cultures which
may press against the overall culture of the discipline of
which they form part, and may thus seem to threaten its
unity. Another is that they may have significant features in
common with component entities in other disciplines, and
accordingly may have the potential to promote greater
interdisciplinary understanding. The central theme, however,
is that the existence of these elementary particles in the world
of academe is deserving of consideration in its own right, and
that their nature and characteristics are too important to be
ignored in any serious study of disciplinary cultures.

Tony Becher, "The Counter-culture of Specialization," 1990

Vacant interdisciplinarity is a direct product of conservative
social economy. It constitutes a disciplining of intellectual
administration which is intended to suppress the free play of
intellectual imagination and to establish critical thought as
the "difference" which marks the outer edges, rather than
the interiority, of the academy. . . . What makes the thematic
of interdisciplinarity substantial in its purposes and critical
in its intentions is precisely the degree to which it engenders
a method, a style of scholarship which is simultaneously
public, discursive and *archaeological.*

Arthur Kroker, "Migration from the Disciplines," 1980

CHAPTER 1

The Interdisciplinary Present/ce

John Higham describes the academy as "a house in which the inhabitants are leaning out of the many open windows gaily chatting with the
neighbors, while the doors between the rooms stayed closed" (*Challenge of
Connecting Learning* 1990, 15). A great deal more, in fact, is going on. Some
are happily chatting. Some are arguing with their neighbors, and others have
fallen out the windows. Many doors remain closed. Yet other doors have been
broken down, and in some cases entirely new buildings have been constructed. Interdisciplinary activities cannot be depicted in a single image. The
metaphors of a web, a network, and a system are often invoked. From an institutional perspective, however, activities resemble scattered and regrouped is-
lands. Guy Berger's metaphor for the diverse dimensions and structures was
an archipelago (1972, 23).

Interdisciplinary activities are located across an expanse of physical sites
and social relations. Because disciplinarity has been the dominant system
over the course of the twentieth century, they have had to establish identity
and place within a "dependent political economy" (Milliken 1990, 318). The
characteristic structures are programs, centers, and projects, not departments, colleges, and freestanding institutions. Freestanding interdisciplinary
institutions exist, but they are rare. Some institutions are noted for an interdisciplinary milieu, but they are not the norm. This does not mean, however,
that interdisciplinary activities do not have significant presence and impact.

The Shift to Complex Structure

When the OECD's Center for Educational Research and Innovation conducted the first international survey of interdisciplinary activities in the late

1960s, it found five major origins: the development of science, student needs, demands for professional training, the original needs of society, and problems of university functioning and administration. The development of science, meaning "knowledge" in the European sense, has produced new hybrid inquiries and fields. Student needs, expressed as a protest against parcelization and artificial divisions of reality, have stimulated innovation in the curriculum. Likewise in professional settings, the concrete conditions of practice promoted reorganization of training. The social and technological problems of the modern world have also fostered new topics, such as environmental and urban studies. And, the economic considerations of managing facilities, instrumentation, and resources have required new contractual arrangements and new kinds of problem-oriented and collaborative work (*Interdisciplinarity* 1972, 44–48).

When Klein and Newell revisited the question of origins recently, they found familiar motivations alongside new ones: general education, liberal studies, and professional training; social, economic, and technological problem solving; social, political, and epistemological critique; holistic, systems, and transdisciplinary approaches; cross-fertilization of borrowing and subdisciplinary interactions; new fields, hybrid communities, and interinstitutional alliances; faculty development and institutional downsizing.

The presence of older claims alongside new and in some cases fundamentally different activities has led to a new complexity of interdisciplinary activity. General systems theory, Klein and Newell propose, provides a metaphor for conceptualizing what is happening. Briefly stated, simple systems operate according to a single set of rules, even if they have multiple levels and connections arranged in a hierarchy. Complicated systems are variations on the themes of simple systems. Complex systems, in contrast, have nonhierarchical structures. They obey multiple conflicting logics, utilize positive and negative feedback, reveal synergistic effects, and may have a chaotic element. The terminology and methods for understanding the system change as those in the system move through it. To understand what is happening, we must replace reductionist thinking by nonlinear thinking, pattern recognition, and analogy. Activities may be interconnected in a shifting matrix, replete with feedback loops and unpredictable synergistic relations in any array of nested contexts (1969).

Complexity is evident in the increased number and kind of activities. Some contend that there are fewer interdisciplinary programs now than in the 1970s (Peterson, 1990, 223). Yet surface appearances are deceiving. A significant amount of activity takes place under other names and in other guises (Hutkins 1994, 3). If the starting point is altered—from what is on existing charts to what the people in the system are actually doing—the answer changes. Interdisciplinary activities are taking up increasing amounts of faculty time, complexifying both institutional structure and knowledge taxonomy. In reviewing the track records of interdisciplinary experiments of the 1960s and 1970s, Keith Clayton concluded that little progress had been made in "overt interdisciplinarity." The "concealed reality of interdisciplinarity," though, suggests that interdisciplinary studies are probably flourishing most where not labeled as such: in, for example, medicine, veterinary science, agriculture, oceanography, and Clayton's former field of geography. Behind the "'subject' facade" interdisciplinarity is flourishing (1984, 1985).

Individual faculty members embody this "concealed reality" and the complexity of the system. A sociologist may be teaching traditional courses in a sociology department while directing dissertations in the sociology of science and coordinating a program in science studies. A member of the history department may be teaching a women's studies course while collaborating with a colleague in art history on representations of women in early American painting and helping to design a new cultural studies program. A political scientist may be teaching a course in an environmental studies program while studying the history of environmental legislation and preparing to offer testimony to Congress on a proposed law affecting local wetlands. An economist may teach courses in classical economics while participating in a cross-institutional, government-funded study of long-term trends in health and living standards. A member of the Spanish department may be conducting research on settlement patterns along the United States–Mexico border while helping to develop a Latin American studies program and holding joint appointment in a research center that is designing interdisciplinary approaches to teaching language and culture. An engineer may be teaching a section of a required general education curriculum while working with members of the business school on reformulating business education and directing a research project in microelectronics. A biologist may be helping to design a new basic science course in the medical school while conducting research in molecular biology and working for a private firm manufacturing genetic material (Klein and Newell 1996).

And so on. . . . The most visible activities take place in self-consciously interdisciplinary universities, colleges, programs, centers, laboratories, and other research facilities such as experiment stations. Some are sufficiently large or prestigious to be regarded as part of the surface structure of a particular college or university. In the curriculum, they include interdisciplinary approaches in general and liberal education, new fields and specialty interests, professional training, the educational functions of research centers, individual courses, and course segments, as well as internships, practicums, and travel-study. (For an overview, see Klein 1990b, 19–54, 119–81; Klein and Doty 1994; Klein and Newell 1996.)

The lesson of complex structure is that a significant amount of activity is occurring in less visible forms that play an important role in knowledge production. They include shared interests, common problem domain, borrowing, networks, faculty learning communities and informal clusters, participation in interdisciplinary fields, team teaching and collaborative research, and new alliances bridging government, industry, and the academy. From the perspective of buildings and equipment, they include shared use of facilities, instrumentation, and databases. The least visible part of the shadow structure is the grassroots presence in disciplines. Activities at this level encompass the interdisciplinary traditions and practices of a discipline, borrowing, problem-focused research, theme-based coursework and connection making in the curriculum, and national and international projects. They are an important part of the unofficial, concealed reality of interdisciplinarity.

Although they are remarkably diverse, these activities, the affiliations they create, and the institutional sites where they are located constitute the social worlds of interdisciplinary work. Any group with shared commitment to a common task is a "social world" (Gieryn 1995, 412). A social world is simultaneously an organization of people, an identity, and a location. All social worlds share three properties: segmentation, legitimation, and intersection. Segmentation entails dividing into subworlds. Legitimation involves defining and enforcing standards and boundaries. Intersection is the interactions of social worlds. An intersection, Elihu Gerson explains, consists of a system of negotiating contexts (1983, 360, 363). The interactions that stimulate interdisciplinary social worlds vary greatly, but each marks a commitment to advance certain claims. Their common feature is their hybrid character.

The Hybrid Communities of Interdisciplinary Social Worlds

Hybridization reflects the need to accomplish tasks at the boundaries and in the spaces between systems and subsystems (Gibbons et al. 1994, 37). The idea of interdisciplinary social worlds as hybrid communities combines a number of concepts that originated in different contexts. Peter Galison (1992) proposed that distinct scientific cultures may interact through development of a "trading zone." Ilana Lowy takes the notion of trading zone one step further, suggesting that several patterns of interaction may develop. A loosely structured trading zone may become a stabilized "pidgin zone." In linguistics, a pidgin is an interim form of communication based in partial agreement on the meaning of shared terms. In some instances a "creole zone" may emerge, in the linguistic sense of becoming a main subculture or native language of a group. When a creole emerges, participants develop a new hybrid role and professional identity (1992, 374). (Steve Fuller, elsewhere, critiques two notions of "trading zone," 1993, 44–48.)

Lowy considers the evolution of hybrid professional roles a specific and extreme case within the larger domain of heterogeneous interactions in science. Over the course of the twentieth century, though, the evolution of trading zones, pidgins and creoles, hybrid communities and hybrid professional roles has become more prominent in the knowledge system. There are significant historical examples.

The Biotheoretical Gathering was a social forum composed of about a dozen British men and women. A "scientific Bloomsbury," this transitory forum provided epistemological space for validating alternative, pluralistic, and participatory models of scientific unity. In recasting historical relations between physical and biological sciences, the group opened the way for future programs that developed a dual structure capable of resolving once contradictory meanings, such as "biological" and "molecular," into a new post-classical synthesis of molecular biology (Abir-Am 1987). The Social Science Research Council (SSRC) was a deliberate organizational attempt to foster interdisciplinary work. Created in 1923, the SSRC brought together representatives of anthropology, sociology, political science, economics, psychology, statistics, and history. One of the central justifying elements was breaking down boundaries by creating an integrated science of society, though ultimately, over a twenty-year period, individuals retreated behind the tightening cognitive boundaries of individual disciplines (Fisher 1990, 1993).

Matrix structure is another older form of hybrid community. "Matrix" is both structure and metaphor. The word denotes something that gives form or origin. In organizational theory, the term designates a program structure superimposed on an existing hierarchy (Pearson, Payne, and Gunz 1979, 114). In business and in universities, matrix structures facilitate problem-focused projects, such as the design of new pharmaceutical projects, engineering tasks, and social and technological problem solving (Klein 1990b, 121–39). In science policy circles, "hybrid community" has a technical definition akin to matrix structure on an interinstitutional scale. The Starnberger group developed the name to designate a group of researchers, politicians, bureaucrats, and representatives of different groups who come together to formulate a research program. New social organizations such as the Work Research Institute, a state institute established in Norway in 1965, are sites for hybrid, problem-solving communities (Mathiesen 1990, 411–13). Newly allied scholars and policy makers constitute a transformative alliance. This alliance encompasses the organizational frameworks of policy making and social research as well as the discourse in which problems are defined, investigated, and handled. The new hybrid discourse coalition promotes interaction among individuals who might not otherwise work together (Hagendijk 1990, 58–59).

A more informal form of matrixing is also occurring in business and industry. Intraorganizational projects have been appearing more frequently under the name "project" and "venture," "team" and "working group," "ad hoc committee" and "task force" (Dermer 1988). Increasing reliance on temporary groups documents a widely noted gap between the growing scale and complexity of industrial processes and the present capabilities of industrial, government, and academic structures (Dahlberg 1986, 14). This phenomenon, coupled with other developments in science and research, led Michael Gibbons and five colleagues from Britain and Sweden to define a new form of knowledge production (Gibbons et al. 1994). The practices characteristic of this new mode are still at an early point of development, yet they have already weakened disciplinary and institutional boundaries while broadening criteria of quality control.

Mode 1 is the traditional form of knowledge production. It is primarily academic, homogeneous, and hierarchical. Comprising ideas, methods, values, and norms that are embodied in the Newtonian model of science, mode 1 emphasizes disciplinary boundary work and certification. Mode 2 is framed by the context of application and use and characterized by closer interaction among scientific, technological, and industrial modes of knowledge production. It is nonhierarchical and transdisciplinary, and it is distinguished by heterogeneously organized forms. Research problems are not set within a disciplinary framework. Human resources are more mobile, and the organization of research is more open and flexible. As a result, sites of knowledge production have increased in number and in kind. Knowledge is now being produced not only in universities but also in industry, government laboratories, think tanks, research institutions, consultancies, and an array of collaborative arrangements and relationships that include transient clusters of experts grouped around large projects. Collapse of monopoly power accompanies diversification. As the organizational boundaries of control blur, the underlying notion of competence is redefined.

In contrast to the simple sharing of resources in mode 1, mode 2 entails ceaseless reconfiguration of resources, knowledge, and skills. Burton Clark speaks similarly of "restless research" that moves out in many directions from traditional university settings (1995, 195). Each new configuration becomes a potential source of knowledge production that is transformed in turn into the site of further possible configurations. A complex set of actors form hybrid forums that stimulate the supply and demand of specialized knowledge. Both theoretical and practical knowledge are generated in these forums. Since exploitation of knowledge requires participation in its generation, discovery and application are more closely integrated than in the past. In a dynamic and socially distributed system with feedback loops, markets set new problems more or less continually. Sites of knowledge production and their networks of communication move on, creating a web that reaches across the globe in growing density and connectivity.

Gibbons and colleagues (1994) contend that mode 2 knowledge production is also occurring in the humanities and social sciences. The social sciences, however, receive short shrift. They focus at greater length on the humanities, highlighting a general increase in boundary blurring, the genre mixing characteristic of postmodernism, heightened reflexivity, social contextualizations of knowledge, and the exemplars of textualism and the *Annales* school of history. In the end, though, they reduce the humanities to, alternatively, "quizzical commentators who offer doom-laden prophecies or playful critiques" or "performers who provide pastiche entertainment or heritage culture." The theory of mode 2 knowledge production is valuable because it gives a name to significant trends. By privileging application and use, though, it sketches only a partial picture of knowledge. The elemental traits of mode 2—hybrid forms, complexity, boundary crossing, and heterogeneous growth of knowledge through differentiation and diffusion—derive from a wider range of forces than application and use.

Understanding the full range of forces requires examining the current balance of shadow and surface structures. Across all knowledge domains, an enormous amount of interchange, or interdisciplinary traffic, is occurring in shared problem domains, common interests, and other forms of cross-fertilization. Faculty learning communities exemplify interactions at this level. During the 1980s many private study groups formed on U.S. campuses to examine how other disciplines interpret language, knowledge, and culture. The Committee on Interpretation, formed at Bryn Mawr College in 1984, was paralleled by other voluntary associations that responded to the intellectual ferment of poststructuralism sweeping across the humanities and social sciences. Their members typically studied Marxism, feminism, deconstruction, postanalytic philosophy, semiotics, psychoanalysis, and textual interpretation.

Outcomes varied, from informal conversations to the formation of new programs. A number of these hybrid communities became influential sites of interdisciplinary knowledge production. At the University of California at Berkeley members of a study group founded the journal *Representations,* a forum for converging interests that became known as "new historicism" (Campbell 1986). At Rice University the Center for Cultural Studies evolved from a collaborative discussion group known as the Rice Circle, self-consciously named after the Vienna Circle. The Rice Circle brought together members of the Anthropology Department and several humanities disciplines. The Center subsequently served as a Rockefeller-funded residency site for postdoctoral fellows whose work often crossed disciplinary boundaries (Fischer 1992a, 126). Over the past decade similar groups have formed throughout the United States to encourage research and curriculum development in cultural studies. The agenda of another group, Cornell University's Society for the Humanities, made it an ideal forum for interchange among scholars interested in the disciplining of music. Their conversations led to a local conference, a special session at the American Musicological Society, and a major book on the topic (Bergeron and Bohlman 1992).

Established professional organizations are key sites for developing hybrid interests and launching new coalitions. The Modern Language Association (MLA) and the American Association for the Advancement of Science have long hosted special-interest groups. Relations with disciplinary hosts vary. Some, such as the MLA's special interest group on literature and science, maintain a presence in the parent body even after establishing their own quasi-professional apparatus, usually anchored by an annual meeting, a newsletter, and a journal. The MLA categorizes as "interdisciplinary approaches" interest groups focused on language and literature in women's, ethnic, and gay studies; popular culture; children's literature; literature's relations with other arts and the sciences; and anthropological, linguistic, philosophical, psychological, religious, and sociological approaches to literature ("Divisions and Discussion Groups" 1993, 653–54). The 1993 meeting of the MLA was the site of a forum on "Disciplining Performance." Performance has traditionally been the subject of theater departments and, to a lesser degree, theater interests in English departments and performance-related topics in speech and communications departments. Contemporary inquiry into performative aspects of the arts and social life has extended the study of drama, theater, and performance beyond older modes of literary and theatrical formalism. Performance-related topics now appear in the literatures of ethnography, performance studies, cultural studies, and literary theory.

The mere existence of such a group, William Bechtel cautions, is not a panacea for the chronic isolation experienced by teachers and scholars on individual campuses. They may carry specialized standards for doing research into the interdisciplinary arena. Organizing meetings and editing publications becomes a playing out of interdisciplinary politics on a microscale (1986b, 36). Interdisciplinary journals are a parallel form of hybrid community. The very existence of a widely cited journal that lies along the boundary between two disciplines is an important sign of affinities (Rigney and Barnes 1980, 118). Some, such as *Science* and *Nature,* are large and prestigious. Most, however, are small. They tend to have loyal followings but limited circulation.

Interdisciplinary journals serve several functions. Some bridge traditional disciplines, such as *Comparative Studies in Society and History, Philosophy and Public Affairs, Journal of Law and Economics,* and *Les Annales,* which synthesizes history and geography. Name is not always a clear indication of interests. *International Organization,* for example, bridges traditional studies in international organization and more recent approaches to international political economy. Some cover self-consciously interdisciplinary problem-focused fields, such as the *Journal of Peace Research* and the *Journal of Conflict Resolution.* Others advance hybrid fields, such as the *Journal of Economic History,* the *Journal of Historical Geography,* and the *Journal of Psycholinguistic Research.* Others are based on a particular hybrid methodology, such as the *Journal of Mathematical Sociology* and the *Journal of Optimization Theory and Application* (Dogan and Pahre 1990, 162–63).

As the locus for cross-fertilization, an interdisciplinary journal promotes communication among individuals who are dispersed across disciplinary and professional sites. The journals *Chest* and *Cell Calcium,* for example, provide focal points for needs and interests that are addressed across several medical and medical-technical professions. Interdisciplinary journals also provide outlets for work that may not find a ready niche in traditional disciplines. Generally speaking, they are characterized more by shifts in orientation and interest claims than by sustained lines of synthesis. Facing multiple pressures for definition, they are caught at the epistemological crux of a dichotomy that pits innovation and openness against rigor and legitimacy. Benson and Bonjean's (1970) chronicle of the early history of the *Social Science Quarterly* is a case in point. The journal's focus varied over the years owing to changes in editorship, shifting interests in core disciplines, concerns about disciplinary integrity in related professional associations, patterns of disciplinary dominance, and periods of greater interdisciplinary emphasis.

Of the many hybrid communities on campus, research centers and interdisciplinary studies are the most visible and most commonly associated with the idea of interdisciplinarity. They merit closer attention, because they exhibit the dynamics of the relation between surface and shadow structures.

The Ambiguity of the Center

Centers augment the traditional departmental structure, primarily for the purpose of conducting research (Winsborough 1992, 275; Klein 1990b, 123–26; *Federally Funded Research* 1991, 187). They arise for several reasons: to address problems and topics that require a large pool of physical and human resources; to launch new programs; to facilitate interdisciplinary work; to enhance the social visibility of the university; to respond to the interests of external donors; to attract outside funding; to keep or attract particular faculty and administrative entrepreneurs; and to provide an institutional framework for specialized methods and approaches.

Centers also collect resources that are used directly for research, such as computers, survey-research facilities, small-group laboratories, specialized libraries, and specialized data. Certain kinds of work are more likely to be done in centers. Survey researchers and demographers, for example, tend to find homes in research centers. Historical sociologists, social psychologists, critical sociologists, and organizational scholars do not. The reason has to do with their characteristic "round of life." Demographers tend to require costly technology or unusual administrative arrangements. Historical sociologists do not. They also tend to lead a more solitary research life (Winsborough 1992, 275, 285–89).

Centers are ironically named. The word "center" implies centrality, but most of them are peripheral to the main academic enterprise. Most centers are *at* the university, not *of* the university (Friedman 1978, 63). There are flagship models, most notably the Center for Interdisciplinary Research (ZIF). A central institute at the University of Bielefeld (Germany), ZIF was established before other faculties of the university, primarily as a science center, though its projects have included the humanities and public-sector issues. On most campuses, centers evolve from clusters of scholars who are interested in specific topics, fields, problems, world areas, or institutions such as law and medicine. Typical examples include the School of Pacific Studies and the East/West Center, technical and scientific centers such as the Second Institute of Physical Chemistry at the Free University of Brussels, the research projects of the Max Planck Institutes, and the Beckman Institute for Advanced Science and Technology at the University of Illinois Urbana-Champaign campus.

A remarkable variety of centers exists on U.S. campuses. The following list indicates the breadth of interests, grouped roughly by kind:

women's, ethnic, and cultural studies
period studies, from the ancient world to the late twentieth century
textual and discourse studies, comparative literature

local, regional, national, area studies
policy, international, and peace and conflict studies
legal studies and criminology
family, labor, and urban studies
media and telecommunications
education, employment training, the handicapped, and developmental disabilities

engineering, computers, materials research, and manufacturing
biomedicine and biotechnology, molecular biology and cancer biology
polar research, water resources, transportation, global change, and the environment
cognitive science, information sciences

Centers span a range of organizational models, from informal groups with little more than an office and a letterhead to highly visible, well-funded enterprises. In their classic study, Ikenberry and Friedman (1972) identified three generic types: standard, adaptive, and shadow institutes. *Standard institutes,* such as computer centers and materials research laboratories, have relatively stable goals and resources, a full managerial hierarchy, a permanent professional staff, and the ability to invest in equipment and space. *Adaptive institutes,* such as water resource centers and centers for educational research and school service, are characterized by persistent instability of goals and staff. Only a small nucleus of professionals have continuing ties. *Shadow (paper) institutes* exist part time. They have a designated director but lack staff, budget, a central location, and visible accomplishments (1972, 34–37).

Some units function as departments in all but name. They have independent teaching programs and degrees. Most, however, do not hire their own faculty or have control over decisions regarding tenure and promotion. Because duties, responsibilities, and organization often differ from those in traditional departments, faculty participation and the place centers occupy on organizational charts are not always clear. Center membership also tends to change over time. Many centers, especially in the natural sciences and to some extent the social sciences, host postdoctoral fellows and other research workers as well. Over time these staff members develop an image of the intellectual material of a field that is engendered more by the environment of the center than by the home departments of teaching faculty. Some of them have specialized skills associated with programming, interviewing, running libraries, and drawing samples. They also develop support services connected with specialized typing and document preparation. They keep books on large research grants and remain knowledgeable about changing academic and government rules on grant submission and management (Winsborough 1992, 274–76).

Interdisciplinary claims are common but for the most part are exaggerated (Friedman 1978, 62–63). Most centers either are dominated by a single discipline or bring together a mix of disciplines. In a large center, the portfolio of projects may include discipline-dominated projects, isolated or loosely linked multidisciplinary inputs, and some collaborative activity. Few centers clarify their interdisciplinary nature in mission statements or, like interdisciplinary teaching teams, spend much time clarifying exactly what they mean when they use the term "interdisciplinary." Their inclinations are indicated by the tension between departments and centers. A department is the place where the centripetal pull that centers on disciplinarity is expressed and reinforced (Halliday 1992, 30). It is the place where traditional reward systems operate most strongly (Cabrese 1987, 9). Part of the tension is economic. The financial structure of centers may drive a wedge between rich and poor faculty while heightening divisions between research and education. Their educational function is often limited to graduate students working with faculty in their own departments. Centers also affect collegial relations. Faculty simply do not meet as often in the department over the coffeepot, at the mailbox or photocopy machine, or in the supply room (Bechtel 1986b, 35; Winsborough 1992, 272–73, 293–95). In addition, centers may sacrifice intellectual autonomy for the strictures of contract research or segregate scientific and humanistic branches of the same discipline (Halliday 1992, 28).

Currently, centers are enjoying high social capital in the humanities, though relatively small economic capital compared with science and technology. (Centers in engineering and in science and technology are discussed in chapter 6.) No complete directory of humanities centers exists. The MLA's 1992 list of humanities research centers in the United States numbered seventy, though a 1989 tally by the Humanities Research Institute at the University of California, Irvine, numbered almost three hundred. When members of the Consortium of Humanities Centers and Institutes gathered at Yale University's Whitney Humanities Center in April 1991, no single model emerged. Humanities centers vary in agenda, facilities, funding levels, administration, orientation toward research or education, availability of fellowships and seminars, service functions, and public outreach. Like their counterparts in the social and natural sciences, they also vary in their structural relations with host institutions, from close links with departments to autonomous status. Comparably, approaches to knowledge range from the eclectic to the integrative (Kaplan 1991).

The MLA's 1992 list reveals the range of interests centers serve: humanities (as part of a formal title); Slavic, French, and Japanese studies; Louisiana, Ozark, southern, Appalachian, and western studies; early American, medieval and Renaissance, seventeenth- and eighteenth-century and twentieth-century studies; women and politics, ethics and social policy, the study of values, ideas and society, ethics and American institutions; theory and criticism, literary and cultural change, critical analysis of contemporary culture; culture and communication, arts and humanities, and popular culture; historical studies, oral tradition, immigration history, and the history of business, technology and society; folklife, folklore, and ethnomusicology; philosophy of children; biographical research; and Baudelaire studies ("Humanities Research Centers" 1992, 992).

Humanities centers have emerged for a number of reasons. They enable the work of particular individuals, support new fields, enhance an institution's reputation, and provide hospitable environments for innovation and exchange. The University of Utah's center arose from a desire to go beyond empty rhetoric of support for the humanities to a formal mechanism. One of the major purposes in founding the Whitney Humanities Center at Yale was to provide scholarly support for a new doctoral program in American studies. Like the Humanities Research Institute at the University of California's Irvine campus and the Stanford Humanities Center, the Whitney Center has played an influential role in new research that bridges the humanities and social sciences. At Yale, Irvine, Stanford, and elsewhere, new interests are advanced by targeting specific topics, funding visiting posts for prominent scholars, and hosting national meetings and international symposia. Like many of its counterparts, the University of Iowa's Center for Advanced Studies supports leading-edge scholarship on campus. The choice of name is significant. The adjective "advanced" has become a new keyword in the humanities signifying groundbreaking work and interdisciplinary connections.

When leading directors of humanities centers issued a document on the state of the humanities in 1989, they emphasized the need for contexts that allow moving beyond the constraints of specialization. The humanities also need to be protected from further marginalization by the better-funded sciences and criticism stemming from national debates on multiculturalism and poststructuralism. The most intense debate at the Yale meeting concerned whether centers should target specific issues and play a prominent political role in the national debate on multiculturalism. Center directors are highly conscious of managing a "space in between," an "other" or shadow structure that is the site of flexibility and ferment. Most centers are considered places to be experimental or trendy, not routine. There is a difference, though, between an experimental posture and an oppositional posture, between providing a hospitable environment and overtly working against the grain. Most directors regard their centers not as places to develop a new interdisciplinary order but as places and contexts that allow the best contemporary thinking to be brought to bear on both classical material and new questions (Levine et al. 1989, 31).

By and large, disciplinary boundaries on local campuses remain firm, and departments retain their power. Yet dialogue on campus has changed. Center directors are ambivalent. They lament obstacles while touting successes. Existing curricula have been enriched and reformulated, interdisciplinary dialogue has been heightened, and the humanities and interdisciplinary issues have been rendered more visible. Influential conferences and publications are signposts of broader success. Thad Tate (1991) of the College of William and Mary's Commonwealth Center for the Study of American Culture suggests that the growth of humanities centers may reflect the larger growth of interdisciplinary objectives in higher education. Economic retrenchment will probably lead to some "shaking out" of weaker and newer centers and centers in institutions with weak financial standing. By their own efforts, centers are not changing disciplinary maps, yet they are often in the forefront of that process. That posture, Tate speculates, may well be their greatest weapon for survival.

Historical perspective sheds light on whether centers represent a fundamental structural change. When an extensive system of independent centers existed primarily on a private basis and in fields of applied research, they were not regarded as serious threats to traditional institutions of higher education. Over the past four decades, they have become more visible and numerous while attracting greater public interest. The accretion of problem-related topics and the problem-driven organization of research has been the strongest reason for their proliferation (Halliday 1992, 23). This trend is international, though it is strongest in the United States, France, Germany, and

Japan (Hanisch and Vollman 1983, 13). Differences of national style persist. The tradition of independent research institutes is stronger in Europe than in the United States, where research has been concentrated more fully within universities (Klein and Porter 1990, 12; Clark 1995, 226). In Germany the separation of research into extrauniversity institutes is common. In the former Soviet Union and Eastern European countries the key institutions of intellectual power have been the academies of science and their research institutes. Even in Europe, though, the prominence of modern institutes such as the Centre des Recherches Nationales Scientifiques and the Ecole des Hautes Etudes is read as proof that French universities have lost their elite status and knowledge functions to other institutions (Scott 1984, 22).

The image of knowledge in any one center varies by local focus and resources, yet their collective presence reinforces the view that official partitions of knowledge are too rigid. Demands for task, mission, and problem orientation, coupled with the need for forums hospitable to all types of interdisciplinary research, will continue to reinforce the view that centers are not peripheral to the system of knowledge production but a necessary part of it. The same claim is made about interdisciplinary studies.

Interdisciplinary Studies as Categories of Knowledge

The label "interdisciplinary studies" (IDS) is applied to an immense variety of educational programs. Historical precedents date from the classical era, in the model of Plato's Academy, to the nineteenth century, in the integrative theory of education promoted by Wilhelm von Humboldt in the founding of the University of Berlin. In the United States, the earliest programs in higher education are linked with the general education movement in the opening decades of the twentieth century. During the 1930s and 1940s, the core curriculum movement promoted integrative approaches in schools, and two fields conceived as interdisciplinary undertakings emerged—area studies and American studies. The late 1960s and early 1970s constituted a watershed era. New knowledge fields emerged alongside new programs, cluster colleges, and universities founded on interdisciplinary principles. Most new programs were small and involved a limited membership of faculty and students. Consequently many were relegated to the periphery of their host institutions. Although educationally powerful they were often politically weak, and many were eliminated or curtailed during economic retrenchments of the late 1970s and 1980s (Gaff 1989, 5). By 1978 the euphoria had passed. Yet even as the death knell of IDS was being sounded, a rebirth was under way in general education, women's studies, honors programs, and new hybrid fields of knowledge (Klein and Newell 1996).

The contemporary college and university register this history, making IDS a familiar part of the academic landscape. IDS is so familiar, in fact, that Ludwig Huber recently dubbed the United States "the eldorado of interdisciplinary studies" (Huber 1992a, 197). Programs span fields of hybrid specialization (the Social Ecology Program at the University of California at Irvine and the Consciousness and Culture Program at the College of the Atlantic), cluster colleges in the liberal arts tradition (Eugene Lang College at the New School for Social Research, the State University of New York's College at Old Westbury, the Hutchins School of Liberal Studies at Sonoma State University, and Watauga College at Appalachian State University), general education in the great books and great ideas tradition (St. John's College and Shimer College), and the clustering of disciplinary courses around a common integrative seminar (the Federated Learning Communities at SUNY Stony Brook and the "loop" sequence of traditional and bridging courses at California Lutheran College). (For program models, see Newell 1986. For course models, see Davis 1995.)

The label "interdisciplinary studies" is applied to two kinds of programs: multi- and interdisciplinary approaches to general and liberal education, ranging from a single course to a four-year degree and masters of liberal studies; and multi- and interdisciplinary programs connected with a specific field of knowledge. The distinction between the first and second kinds is not absolute. Components of field-based studies are sometimes taken as part of general education, as minors, or as electives. Some cluster colleges and degree programs also allow students to pursue disciplinary or hybrid specialization.

Over the past decade and a half, a resurgence has been occurring in both the first and the second kinds. In Europe renewed calls for coherence and connectedness are being heard in the professions and across university subjects. The contexts include the environment and ecology, energy, health, Third World and development policies, information technology, media studies, European unification, and intercultural communication (Huber 1992b, 297). In the United States, the greatest growth in subject-matter areas of general education today encourages interdisciplinary approaches in areas such as international studies, American multicultural and gender studies, and the inherently synoptic areas of historical consciousness and ethical understanding (Casey 1994, 56). Interdisciplinary studies are also being mainstreamed in general education and disciplinary settings in the form of topical first-year seminars, required core courses, advanced courses on problems or intellectual themes, and senior "capstone" seminars and projects involving research or artistic production (Stember 1991, 3).

The present climate of general education reform has a different dynamic than reforms of the 1960s and 1970s. Even with expansion of the canon to include once-excluded texts and voices, many of today's reforms tend to be "renovative rather than radical." They are linked with a strongly felt need to revitalize the core of liberal arts by fostering coherence and excellence in higher-order skills of integration and synthesis (Newell 1988, 8; Gaff 1989, 5). In a fragmented world, the integrative skills needed for problem solving and dealing with complexity are stronger warrants for interdisciplinarity than is unity of knowledge. These tendencies are strongest in general education, though they have become a leitmotif of educational reform in the disciplines and professions as well. Studies of the second kind also exhibit these traits, but they differ in an important respect: they are engaged in producing new knowledge.

Studies of the second kind include two of the seven categories of inter-disciplinary approaches that Raymond Miller (1982) has identified: *topical focus,* professional preparation, *life experience perspective,* shared compo-nents, crosscutting organizing principles, hybrids, and grand synthesis. Pro-fessional preparation is an important site of interdisciplinary study, but it differs from topical focus in being more self-contained programmatically, vo-cationally oriented, and influenced by accreditation standards. Interdiscipli-nary topics frequently emerge from perceived social problem areas. Crime, for example, is a social concern addressed by every social science discipline. Interdisciplinary research is conducted on the subject, and interdisciplinary programs have been organized in criminology and criminal justice. Area is another topical focus, and in response to labor-management conflicts, re-search institutes and academic programs in industrial relations were founded. Later, responding to other needs, urban studies, gerontology, and environ-mental studies emerged. Miller's third classification, life-experience perspec-tive, became prominent in the 1960s and 1970s with the advent of programs in ethnic and minority studies (1982, 12–20). More recently, peace and con-flict, computers and information sciences, cognitive science and artificial in-telligence, science and technology, and global studies have been expanding.

The programmatic face of interdisciplinary fields varies greatly, from in-dividual courses and cross-departmental programs to freestanding depart-ments. The tendencies that Daniel Rich and Robert Warren (1980) observed in the field of urban affairs occur across all studies of the second kind. More programs carry the name than grant the degree, and few offer all baccalau-reate and graduate degrees. Programs on individual campuses also exist on dissimilar time scales and respond to local interests. Significant variations derive from preexisting patterns of campus power, local community pres-sure, and external economic incentives. There are, moreover, significant differences in administrative fit, political components, and the importance placed on education, research, and service. Reflecting conflicting stances on the proper balance of scholarship and problem solving, academic and activist or vocational values are represented differently. Cognitive, social, and political pluralism are valued in the rhetoric of interdisciplinary studies, but their relative weight is disputed. One of the most tenacious challenges has been the lack or minimal level of formal integration among specialists who have shared interests but are located in different disciplinary and professional units of the same campus (Rich and Warren 1980, 56).

Seven types of structures and identities have emerged, either in practice or in discussion. With hybridizing across types and the obvious exception of professional identity, they appear in all studies of the second kind (composite of Rich and Warren 1980, 56, 59 and Caldwell 1983, 255): an augmented specialization within an existing department; coordinated multidisciplinary studies, usually consisting of courses taught in traditional departments and linked by a core course and a faculty coordinator; a component of a larger multi- or interdisciplinary program combining elements of other related areas; a freestanding department, center, or school with or without degree-granting authority; a new interdisciplinary field aimed at synthesizing category related material produced in other disciplines; a new autonomous discipline; and a new field of professional and technical preparation.

Categories of knowledge are institutions not in the conventional sense of buildings and organizations but as a set of marks constructed and maintained in cultural space. These marks enable collectivities to tell their members where they are, where they may or may not go, and how to conduct themselves. New categories of knowledge do not attain influence unless they are institutionalized (after Shapin 1992, 355). The concepts of "critical mass" and "capital" aid in understanding how interdisciplinary fields make marks in cultural space. The concept of critical mass derives from physics, where it means the minimum quantity of nuclear fuel required to start a chain reaction. The elements of critical mass in interdisciplinary fields are grouped roughly by kind:

> an adequate number of individuals sharing common interests
> an adequate number and scale of programs in terms of faculty, students,
>   and researchers
>
> an adequate infrastructure for communication
> adequate economic and symbolic capital
>
> formal conducting and contracting of research
> formation of hybrid communities and mediating structures
>
> autonomy in budget matters
> control over degree requirements
> the power to appoint, to promote, to grant tenure, and to control salary
> a secure location in the organizational hierarchy of a campus

the rise of a scholarly body of knowledge
the capacity for interdisciplinary synthesis and generation of new
    knowledge

Gaining and maintaining leverage is quantitative to the extent that a viable field requires enough personnel, infrastructure, and intellectual development to sustain itself. Getting to that point entails four forms of capital that Bourdieu (1993) identified in reconstructing the field of cultural production. The first, *economic capital,* is indicated by wealth (financial resources) or possession of the means of production. The second, *social capital,* consists of social relations and influence that are revealed in networks and institutionalized in status, professions, and hierarchies. The third, *cultural capital,* is knowledge in the broadest sense of general education and special qualifications, plus the production of books and works of art that are institutionalized by the educational system in titles and qualifications. The fourth, *symbolic capital,* is brought about by higher levels of the three previous kinds, though especially economic capital and personal characteristics such as charisma. Symbolic capital is not easily distinguishable from social capital, but the term does identify certain aspects of authority and credibility. A scientific reputation, for example, is a form of symbolic capital that can be used to gain greater access to research funds, technology, graduate students, and publication outlets (Posner 1988, 173). Symbolic capital is thereby retransformed into economic and social capital. (For a model of how the four forms operate in disciplines, see Huber 1990.)

Economic and social capital are crucial to building an infrastructure of support for new knowledge fields. Shortfalls of either form of capital can inhibit or undermine the buildup of critical mass. The track record of interdisciplinary studies is mixed. They have stimulated new patterns of knowledge production. Their overall effect, though, has been more additive than transformative. The additive strategy has obvious advantages of economy, flexibility, and political appeal, but it falls short of the promise of transformation enshrined in the rhetoric of many fields. Interdisciplinary studies, like centers, wind up caught in the balancing act of being institutional and extrainstitutional at the same time. They have tended to reside in the shadow structure of institutions, but they are the vital surface structure of their underlying fields of knowledge.

The boundary work of interdisciplinary studies is threefold. They detach a category as subject and object from existing disciplinary frameworks, thereby loosening boundaries and stimulating trading zones. They fill gaps in knowledge from lack of attention to the category, thereby developing new pidgins and creoles in hybrid communities. And if they attain sufficient critical mass and have adequate forms of capital, they redraw boundaries by constituting new knowledge space and new professional roles. If their infrastructures are shallow, however, they are vulnerable to retrenchment in times of financial exigency. They are, in effect, contained.

Six major examples—urban studies, environmental studies, borderlands studies, area studies, women's studies, and cultural studies—are the sustained focus of chapter 4. Before turning to case studies, though, we need to better understand the reasons for boundary crossing.

CHAPTER 2

The Permeation of Boundaries

Boundaries are divisive barriers, but they are also permeable membranes. There are six major and sometimes overlapping reasons for permeation: the epistemological structure and cognitive orientation of a discipline; the borrowing of tools, methods, concepts, and theories; the pull of intellectual, social, and technological problems away from strictly disciplinary focus; the current complexity of disciplinary research; relations with neighboring disciplines; redefinitions of what is considered intrinsic and extrinsic to a discipline (Klein 1993, 187). Boundaries are permeable because disciplines are not isolated units. Permeation is part of their character. The evidence appears at three levels: discipline, specialty, and the criteria of demarcation that distinguish one discipline from another.

Permeation and Disciplinarity

One of the commonly held beliefs about disciplines is that some are more permeable than others. This belief is reinforced by the value-laden terminology that authors of handbooks, textbooks, and knowledge histories use. They describe some disciplines, especially the sciences, as hard, tight, restrictive, neat, narrow, compact, homogeneous, and mature. They distinguish other disciplines, especially the humanities and some of the social sciences, by the rhetorical foils of softness and breadth. The latter are said to have high degrees of differentiation and to be in a state of preparadigmatic development (Becher 1989, 13). Assumptions about boundaries follow suit.

Impermeable boundaries are associated with tightly knit, convergent communities. These communities presumably have clear boundaries, circumscribed domains, and "neat" problems that are controlled through cognitive restriction and social consensus. Pantin's (1968) notion of "restricted" disciplines stipulates that most physical sciences, especially physics and chemistry, will exhibit strong linkage between research areas but lesser ties with other disciplines. In contrast, the humanities and social sciences are associated with greater permeability. They are considered more holistic, personal, value laden, and less codified. Loosely knit, divergent groups are thought to have a more fragmented, less stable, less theoretically specific, and more open-ended epistemological structure. Their boundaries are likely to be more open, their cognitive border zones more ragged and ill defined. Pantin's notion of "unrestricted" disciplines stipulates that most social sciences, with the exception of economics, will exhibit diffuse links among research areas both within and outside the discipline.

These traits are widely recognized, but they are not absolute. Hard, soft, pure, and applied characteristics are not neatly contained within particular domains, and they are distributed unevenly. A presumably pure discipline may have clearly applied elements—such as the current development of optics and materials in academic physics—or the reverse—jurisprudence as a specialty in law. A field regarded as hard and quantitative may contain relatively soft, qualitative elements, such as the study of political economics in economics. In physics the specialty of solid state physics exhibits hard-knowledge elements, while the subspecialty of meteorology exhibits soft-knowledge elements. Comparably, soft, qualitative areas may host hard, quantitative components, such as aspects of philology or linguistics in literary studies. Psychology spans a range of practices, from behaviorism and psychometric research to psychoanalysis. Product-oriented branches of knowledge also vary. Some of the theoretical branches of mechanical engineering move into the pure, hard territory of mathematical physics. In contrast, the study of highly complex phenomena in metallurgy is better characterized as pure soft knowledge (Becher 1990, 334–35).

Two kinds of disciplines, the applied and the synoptic, are associated with such high permeability that they are often described as "inherently interdisciplinary." Disciplines emphasizing application and having well-established vocational fields tend to be more eclectic than purist in their epistemological conception of themselves (Heckhausen 1972, 86). Many degree programs in medicine, engineering, architecture, management, public administration, social work, education, and law involve courses or course elements focused on integration or complex issues. Management studies are appearing in engineering, social studies in medicine, and foreign languages and computing in other professional fields. "The addition of the word 'studies,'" Geoffrey Squires found, "often implies a shift away from a conventional disciplinary approach." These developments and the problems of interrelating constituent elements are usually discussed in terms not of interdisciplinarity but of "integration," "coordination," or the role of "service" courses taught by other departments. The problem tends to be perceived as pragmatic or organizational, not theoretical. In newer professions that respond to changing problem awareness in society, such as food science or transport studies, use of the term "interdisciplinary" points toward some uncertainty about identity and status (Squires 1992, 205–7; Huber 1992a, 197).

The complexity of problems that professionals face in practice creates a sense of interdisciplinary necessity. Complex problems pull research away from classically framed disciplinary problems. By their very nature they are open ended, multidimensional, ambiguous, and unstable. Considered "wicked" and "messy," the problems at the heart of many professional fields cannot be bounded and managed by classical approaches to the underlying phenomena (Mason and Mitroff 1981; Rittle and Webber 1973). The field of planning illustrates the conflict. Modern planning theory was formed when the special model of rational behavior adopted by neoclassical economics developed into a general theory of rational decision making. Despite its scope and wide applicability, the theory was framed by the paradigm of economic rationality. The gap between technical rationality and the day-to-day problems of practice has stirred challenges to the paradigm. These challenges, which are often cast as signs of disciplinary crisis, include interdisciplinary approaches, ecological concepts, systems theory, and contingency models that advocate contextually determined decision making (Klein 1990–91). In the curriculum, the older hierarchical model of moving from basic science to applied science to professional attitudes is also being rethought. Alternative models intermingle tracks around a problem focus (Davis 1995, 40–41).

"Synoptic" or "synthetic" identity is rooted in the belief that some disciplines have a looser aggregation of interests, implying greater openness to ideas from other disciplines. This identity is strong in literary studies, history, philosophy, anthropology, and geography. Synoptic identity will not be the only source of interdisciplinary activity. Sociology is a case in point. The diversity of the discipline was apparent from its inception. Early approaches spanned conflict perspectives, functionalism, social Darwinism, microsociology, and interpretative sociology (R. Turner 1991, 59). The synthetic identity derived from this variety persists, but holistic and generalist claims contradict actual divisions of disciplinary labor (Calhoun 1992, 138). Sociology winds up with a dual interdisciplinary identity: in principle it is "synthetic," but in practice it tends to be "interstitial," filling in gaps with other social sciences and working along their borders (Rigney and Barnes 1980, 116).

Geography offers an extended illustration of why boundary crossings differ even in the same general domain. The discipline encompasses a hard physical geography on one side and a soft human geography on the other. It also exhibits a pure historical geography at one end and an applied field of climatology at the other. Boundaries are defined in part by a discipline's cultural history. In the United States, geography developed within certain departments, especially geology and in some cases history and anthropology. In Germany it developed from earth science, in France from history, and in Britain from the interests of managing an empire (Mikesell 1969, 228). The first generation of geography professors were trained in other fields, usually the natural sciences and, less often, the social sciences. Over the course of the twentieth century, geography gradually moved away from the natural sciences and humanities. As the discipline bridged older dichotomies of nature and culture, moving from physical to social factors, its focus expanded to include human-environment relations, area studies, spatial structure (or location theory), and physical geography as a component of earth sciences. Its methods expanded from cognitive description and cause-and-effect analysis to include functional, ecological, and systems analysis (Doornkamp and Warren 1980; Bulick 1982; Soja 1989, 10–42).

As a result of this history, geographers often use the word "interrelation" to describe the problems they address (Bulick 1982, 46). The discipline has been labeled a "multivariate discipline" (Minshull 1973, 269), and a "crossroads science" at the confluence of natural and human sciences (Claval 1988, 1). It now encompasses subfields of human, cultural, economic, political, urban, and regional geography as well as biogeography, geomorphology, climatology, environmental science, and cartography. Each subfield in turn relates to specialties outside the discipline. The current links with sociology, for example, include human ecology, environmental sociology, rural sociology, and urban studies (Dogan and Pahre 1990, 94). Correspondingly, geographers have assumed hybrid identities, adopting the compound names of cultural, social, behavioral, regional, physical, historical, Marxist, and economic geographer as well as geomorphologist, climatologist, and human ecologist (Warrick and Reibsame 1981, 422–23).

Patterns of boundary crossing also shift. During the late 1970s, applications of physical geography to engineering, planning, and problems of land and resource management led to an explosion of interdisciplinary publications (Doornkamp and Warren 1980, 102). The trend today is away from questions focused primarily on pattern, form, and structure toward observations of behavior and analysis of the processes that underlie structures (Bulick 1982, 44–45). In its historical movement from being a physical science to becoming a social science, the discipline has expanded to include a human geography that incorporates a wide range of interests, from plant and animal distribution to the interactions of societies (Bahm 1980, 31). Postmodern approaches, which reconstitute the field as a critical human geography, have further weakened the grip of older categories. The formerly central is being pushed to the margins, and once "tactful fringes" are asserting a new centrality. Given its plurality, Edward Soja suggests, "geographies" is a more appropriate label than "geography" (1989, 60).

The examples so far have been standard ones. Many knowledge fields, however, are of more recent origin. A significant number of them evolved from cross-fertilization of hierarchically unrelated fields, mission-oriented fields, and interdisciplinary subject fields (Dahlberg 1994, 60). In order to study new subjects that do not fit into the domains of established subjects, or even take on the classical characteristics of a discipline, new scholarly domains have been created (Davis 1995, 133) and boundaries redrawn through "ontological gerrymandering" (Woolgar and Pawluch 1984, 216; Fuller 1988, 197). Correspondingly, the number and variety of institutions devoted to knowledge production have increased since 1945 (Gibbons et al. 1994, 141). Specialization is a major factor in this development.

Permeation and Specialization

Most boundary crossing occurs at the level of specialties, not entire disciplines. A discipline is composed of clusters of specialties that form the micro-environments where research and communication take place (Chubin 1976, 455). Specialized knowledge is both partial and synecdochic. Specialties are concerned with and even confined to the significance of selected factors. Yet they are given to portraying the whole category of nature, behavior, or experience as if it resembled the part each one studies in a parochial manner (Bailis 1993, 4–6). By emphasizing their differences from other specialties, practitioners justify claims to departmental status and resources. Identifiable communities do not always emerge, but certain subfields bear such hallmarks of disciplinary organization as professional associations, journals, and programs of graduate study (Whitley 1976, 472–73; 1984, 17).

Specialization is self-amplifying (Clark 1995, 245). From a quantitative perspective, the results are staggering. By the year 1987, there were 8,530 definable knowledge fields (Crane and Small 1992, 197). By 1990, roughly 8,000 research topics in science alone were being sustained by specialized networks (Clark 1995, 193). The claim of disciplinary primacy rests on the continued fissioning of knowledge into greater numbers of specialties. Specialization, though, is also a major cause of increased boundary crossing and interdisciplinary activity.

One explanation, specialty migration, is a familiar subject in science studies. The rank-and-file researcher typically works within a closely related set of specialties. Yet the population of migrants who move beyond single specialties or narrow clusters of specialties is not trivial. The "occupational nomadism" (Becher 1990, 344) of specialty migration occurs because any population of active researchers is heterogeneous in training, ability, and style (Chubin 1976, 471). They do not necessarily work within a single collectivity, nor do they always remain within the same social group. Migration is closely tied to innovation, pathbreaking ideas, and new lines of research. A simplistic view of knowledge space, however, arises from the tendency to portray specialty migrants in the rhetoric of the frontier.

The analogues of the specialty migrant are the trailblazer and the pioneer. Cutting-edge research, like the opening, staking out, and settling of new territory, is often depicted at a distant outpost. The place specialty migrants work, though, is not always remote from the disciplinary mainstream, just as certain "frontier" conditions exist in settled regions and inner cities. Sometimes disciplines meet in unexplored territories of experimental work, sometimes at the inner core of prominent methods and approaches. Depending on the particular case, interdisciplinary activity may be peripheral to or part of the current mainstream. As new goals develop and interests change, the core of practices may also shift (Whitley 1976, 483). At this point in the history of specialization, both frontier and core are spreading. This situation is especially strong in molecular biology, biotechnology, new material, nanotechnology, liquid crystal and solid state physics, nuclear fusion, infomatics, and superconductivity (Gibbons et al. 1994, 160).

Migration implies the boundedness of specialties. Boundaries, though, shift and overlap because ideas and techniques do not exist in a fixed place. Researchers carry them along as they participate in multiple groups. Specialties possess no inherent boundaries. They are defined in terms of relative concentration of interests (Becher 1990, 344; Chubin 1976, 464 n. 35). Migration occurs on different levels and time scales. The move may be permanent or temporary. A member of a French department who was educated in traditional modes of reading literary texts may migrate to a new specialism such as interpretive theory or contribute to an established hybrid field such as women's studies or move to a new hybrid field such as cultural studies. A member of a chemical engineering department may temporarily join a team designing a new urban transportation system or develop a new line of research on new chemical properties in manufacturing design or completely relocate to a materials science program.

Migration is not random. Scientists who move into new fields, for instance, tend to come from areas with specific characteristics, including a pronounced decline in the significance of current results, insufficient avenues of research, the presence of members with special competence in or knowledge of techniques with wider application, and disruptive events that originate outside the research community. Migrants move into areas offering special opportunities for productive research, utilization of their skills, and promising career developments (Lemaine et al. 1976, 5). Studies of borrowing in the social sciences reveal an added tendency, toward upward modeling in the direction of a more prestigious discipline (Sherif and Sherif 1969b, xii). One measure of a discipline's status is to what extent other disciplines are attracted to it. This form of social capital is evident in the current elevated status of literary theory and art history. Differences in disciplinary structure also affect migration. Economists, for example, tend to move in more organized fashion than sociologists, who move in a wider and more random manner. Economics as a discipline exhibits greater consensus than sociology (Dogan and Pahre 1990, 112–13).

Radio astronomy and molecular biology are classic examples of migration that led to the production of interdisciplinary knowledge. These fields began when some researchers concluded that a new line of inquiry looked scientifically more interesting than existing avenues (Chubin 1976, 457). Both resulted not from the movement of an entire research community or a particular discipline or specialty but from the activities of individuals. In the case of molecular biology, physicists migrated to a discipline with lesser status because biology had the greatest number of unsolved problems appearing open to fruitful investigation at the time. Even the underlying metaphor of migration, Paul Hoch suggests, may in some ways be ill conceived. Most migration occurs because research areas are in a constant process of reformulation around new problems, not because practitioners decide to move (1987a, 493). This process is related to a more profound explanation for increased boundary crossing—historical change.

Over the course of the twentieth century, the fracturing and refracturing of disciplines into new specialties has been the dominant pattern of knowledge growth (Scott 1984, 6). This phenomenon has resulted in both greater fragmentation and greater convergence. A significant number of new specialties have a hybrid character, and their variety is as striking as their number. They range from astrophysics and artificial intelligence to medical anthropology and child development to feminist theory and a host of new queries lumped under the umbrella term "cultural studies." To explain and locate these interests, new terminology has been developed. The term "aggregative approach," for example, labels fields such as gerontology and urban research, which share the focus of different disciplines and exhibit a methodologically and theoretically integrative approach. They constitute a second form of specialization that is focused on areas missed or only partially examined by traditional disciplinary specialties. Even when perceived as interdisciplinary, though, each tends toward specialization through the boundary work of asserting its unique perspective and defining appropriate approaches (Van den Daele and Weingart 1975, 254–55).

Dogan and Pahre (1990) attribute the development of hybrid fields to a process of *specialization-fragmentation-hybridization.* Specialization is the first stage. As specialization reaches a point of density, defined in terms of relative mass of people, disciplines fragment and innovative scholars recombine specialties across disciplinary lines. Density at the core opens up room for innovations at the margins. Hybridization, born of the continuous reintegration of specialties across disciplines, is the second stage. There have been more recombinations and border crossings by innovative scholars over the past three decades than in the previous millennium. Hybridization is both cause and effect. A relatively recent phenomenon, it produces two types of hybrids: formally institutionalized subfields of one or another formal discipline or permanent "cross-disciplinary" committees or programs that regularize exchanges among scholars from different disciplines and informal hybridized topics, such as development, that may never become institutionalized hybrid fields.

Dogan and Pahre's theory has several weaknesses. In focusing primarily on innovators, they overstate the influence of individuals while understating opposition and structural features of change. Even they concede that the core-density relationship is more complicated than their focus on innovators and margins allows. The distance from center to border varies from one discipline to another. Like Geertz, they eschew the term "interdisciplinary," associating it haphazardly with an all-encompassing knowledge of two or more entire disciplines that, realistically, never occurs. Their illustrations, though, are the familiar stock of interdisciplinary claims. More important, the term "hybridization" provides a name for a process at work in all domains. Like Gibbons et al.'s theory of mode 2 (1994), hybridization calls attention to new defining conditions of knowledge production.

As older fields have divided into smaller units through fissioning, they have confronted the fragments of other disciplines. The deeper specialization goes, the greater the number of specialties, and the greater inevitability of specialists meeting at the boundaries of other disciplines. The first force driving interdisciplinarity identified by the OECD, recall, was the development of science through specialization. Specialization produces narrower and narrower fields, nearly all of which correspond to the intersection of two disciplines. This interaction limits the object of examination, but it also necessitates a manifold approach. Depending on the case, "interdisciplinarity" may be used as a symbol of crisis, the means of exploding an overrigid discipline, or the foundation for a new discipline. Technical progress may also produce a conjunction between a discipline and a particular application of that discipline. Teaching and research in space medicine in the United States, for example, stem from development of the biological sciences and the need to respond to particular problems raised by space flights. A different variant of diversification occurs in using common elements, such as mathematics, the concept of a structure, or specific models (*Interdisciplinarity* 1972, 44–45).

Hybrids, moreover, beget other hybrids. This is especially true in the natural sciences, where greater fragmentation and hybridization are present. Neuroendocrinology, an alliance within physiology between endocrinology and neurophysiology, is a second-generation hybrid. Mapping migrations of prehistoric peoples through analysis of mitochondrial DNA, which is transmitted solely by females, involves genetic biologists and biological anthropologists (Dogan and Pahre 1990, 72). The extent of boundary crossing at this level suggests that subspecialty interactions may now be more reliable indicators of interdisciplinary activity than the emergence of new hybrid disciplines, perhaps even knowledge production in general (Lepenies 1976, 302; Dogan and Pahre 1990, 64). Internal divisions can create barriers to cooperation, but specialties are vital sites of cross-fertilization. This aspect of specialty relations is confirmed at the smallest level of detail, the criteria that differentiate one discipline from another.

Permeation and Criteria of (Re)marcation

Textbooks, knowledge histories, and studies of knowledge practices mark distinctions between disciplines by pointing to the different objects that are examined and the subjects that are studied. Within distinct material fields of focus, different methods, tools, and concepts are also used and different theories and laws are developed. These criteria are well-established points of demarcation, but they are also nodal points of connection. Ironically, criteria of demarcation are also criteria for cross-fertilization and interrelation.

Material field comprises a set of objects that presumably reside within a discrete domain. Physicists and chemists study material objects, botanists study plants, anthropologists study humans, and so on. Because material fields overlap, though, the notion of a field of objects must be supplemented by recourse to how objects are defined and treated. In some fields, moreover, domains not only overlap but are identical, as in certain practices of physics and chemistry and of linguistics and literature (Posner 1988, 168, 176). *Subject matter* seems the simplest distinction. Yet in day-to-day practice, subjects are rarely separated as neatly as they are in taxonomies. The practice of one discipline may also be treated as the subject matter of another. This meta-theoretical role occurs in history of sociology, sociology of history, and anthropology of medicine (Paxson 1996).

Generally speaking, boundaries are determined more by method, theory, and conceptual framework than by subject matter. When studying the same topic, scholars may fragment their disciplines along specialist lines that connect more across disciplinary boundaries than down the hall of the same department. A Marxian economist, for instance, may share more concepts, approaches, and methods with a Marxian literary theorist than with a neo-classical economic theorist (Amariglio, Resnick, and Wolff 1993, 151). Likewise, three scholars working on French politics may differ greatly in approach. One may use game theory, the second may use statistical methods, and the third may present empirical analysis expressed in the vernacular. They do not speak the same language, they are not interested in the same topics, and their discourse patterns differ. The first may talk with other game theorists in economics or with applied game theorists in international relations. The second is more likely to communicate with statisticians and social psychologists, the third with historians and sociologists. They perceive different neighbors, work in different networks, borrow from different contexts, and use different methods (Dogan and Pahre 1990, 54, 84).

Theory and *law* are no more straightforward. Not all units called disciplines are clearly identified with laws, and few if any have a unified theory that defines boundaries without dispute (Bechtel 1986b, 11; Posner 1988, 176). Theory-based groupings—such as functionalism, structuralism, semiotics, and Marxism—bridge disciplinary divisions and display similarities that generate independent ideologies (Becher 1990, 337). The theories of one discipline may also be substantially revised in light of criteria for theory assessment imported from another. Philosophy of mind, for example, has been reshaped by contact with other disciplines in the area of cognitive science. It has begun using criteria characteristic of cognitive psychology, computer science, and to an extent neurophysiology (Paxson 1996). In the humanities and social sciences, the importation of postmodern theories from Europe stimulated cross-fertilization and interaction. And in a reversal of cross-Atlantic influence, the international appeal of Talcott Parsons was due in part to his propensity toward general theoretical discussion and his resistance to disciplinary limits, far more than other postwar American theorists in sociology (Calhoun 1992, 140 n. 3).

Comparably, *methods* and *analytical tools* are sites of both difference and connection. Forms of observation are common in astronomy, geology, and botany, less so in mathematics and logic. Laboratory experiments are common in physics and chemistry, biology and psychology, less so in sociology, literature and the arts, or mathematics and logic. Questionnaires and polls are common in sociology, psychology, and economics, less so in literature, the arts, and jurisprudence. Nonetheless, a variety of methods may be present in the same discipline, and method-based groupings, such as crystallography, transcend subject matter boundaries (Posner 1988, 168–69, 176; Becher 1990, 337). Methods and analytic tools have been highly generalizable across subject matter. Experimentation, statistics, computer modeling and simulation, cybernetics, and information policy have functioned as "diagonal sciences," stimulating cross-fertilization of analytical tools (Heckhausen 1972, 84–85). Computer simulation cuts across fields as diverse as political science, sports medicine, and architecture. In the social sciences, symbolic languages are often borrowed in the form of mathematical fads, such as factor analysis, game theory, nonlinear dynamics, operations research, catastrophe theory, and chaos theory (Pahre 1994, 21).

Problem is the least clear-cut distinction. It is no longer controversial to suggest that research problems fall between the cracks of established disciplines (Chubin 1976, 466). All problems are not of the same kind. George

Reynolds suggests that scientists address three different kinds of problems. Reynolds's formulation is valid across knowledge fields, not just the sciences.

> Problems of the first kind: intellectual problems within a traditional discipline.
> Problems of the second kind: multidisciplinary problems that are basically intellectual rather than policy-action in nature, but that cannot be successfully undertaken within the boundaries of a single discipline.
> Problems of the third kind: distinctly multidisciplinary problems generated increasingly by society and distinguished by relatively short-time courses calling in some cases for a policy-action result and in other cases for a technological quick-fix.
>
> (Sigma Xi 1988, 21)

For problems of the first kind, traditionally the mainstay of disciplinary practice, disciplining is at its strongest. One of the major effects of interdisciplinary work, though, has been to redefine problems of the first kind as problems of the second kind. This reformulation occurred when textuality, traditionally constructed as a literary problem, became a problem in anthropology and sociology. Reformulation exerts centrifugal pressure on disciplines and departmental structures (Halliday 1992, 26). The development of science has also posed ever broader tasks that lead to growing interconnections among natural, social, and technical sciences (Fedoseyev 1984, 13). The multi- and interdisciplinary nature of problems is often highlighted when research is located in centers: when, for instance, a polar research center addresses problems of ice core research, polar ecology, Antarctic tectonics, and glaciology (OSU 1991, 18).

The pressing weight of exogenous problems has fostered a widespread belief that problems of the third kind are the major reason for increasing interdisciplinarity and boundary blurring. Because their impetus lies beyond the boundaries of the academy, "practical" problems are outside the scope of classical problems of the first kind or intellectual problems of the second kind. The urgency of modern social and technological problems has increased the share of problem- and mission-oriented research in the university to the point that a significant portion of basic research now includes the adjective "mission oriented" (Ruscio 1985, 16). To accommodate this type of research, the number of problem-focused structures and work modes has increased. Disciplines involved in mission-oriented research are also exhibiting fuzziness at their boundaries. In some areas knowledge production is no longer occurring strictly within disciplinary boundaries. The leading examples are the Human Genome Project and the fields of biotechnology, molecular biology, risk assessment, and technology assessment (Gibbons et al. 1994, 138, 147).

The pull of problems is so strong that researchers are often depicted as following problems wherever they may lead. Problems, though, are not anthropomorphic. Problem definition is the result of human action. Setting a problem establishes boundaries by naming the things that will be attended to and framing the context in which this occurs (Schön 1983, 40). The same problem may be treated as à problem of the first, second, or third kind. As a result, disputes about interdisciplinary programs are often based on disputes about problem definition. The problem of political behavior, for example, has been central to the definition of contemporary political science. The question whether "political behavior" and its underlying aspects are treated in a strictly disciplinary manner depends, in significant part, on how the problem is framed and whether its interdisciplinary formulation is perceived as duplicating disciplinary research and education or offering a shallow substitute (Elder 1992).

The simultaneity of boundary maintenance and boundary crossing is underscored by the multiple ways that problems are defined and objects are treated. A problem such as "poverty" appears at the same time in economics, policy studies, sociology, and women's studies. Likewise, the problem of "disease" appears simultaneously in social medicine, anatomy, gerontology, and a host of medical specialties. The problems are constructed differently in each domain, but trading zones of common interest emerge, and hybrid communities form to develop those interests. Comparably, depending on the questions asked about it, any object may fall within the domains of several different fields. Stephen Toulmin's classic example bears repeating: "The behavior of a muscle fiber, for instance, can fall within the domains of biochemistry, electrophysiology, pathology, and thermodynamics, since questions can be asked about it from all four points of view: and, in principle, the same fiber could be brought within the scope of still other sciences, by making it a topic for (say) quantum-mechanical or psychological questions" (1972, 149).

Like the problems of poverty and disease, the object of a muscle fiber is constructed differently. In one domain subcellular chemicals constitute the object. In another it is an injured tissue, in another domain a dynamic entity (Ellen Messer-Davidow, pers. comm., 12 May 1995). Yet the relational characteristics of *objects*—their proximity, causality, analogy, and organic interdependence—are sources of disciplinary contact (Stone 1969, 18). One of the prominent themes in knowledge description today is the reconsideration of relations between disciplines that constitute the same object differently. As new aggregate levels of organization are being revealed, "multidisciplinary" is becoming a common description of research objects. The current differentiation of biology, for instance, means that many biologists are working at the borders of neighboring fields. "In effect," Hedi Bel Habib explains, "the same object—an organism—is at one and the same time a physical (atomic), chemical (molecular), biological (macromolecular), physiological, mental, social, and cultural object" (1990, 6). Biology, as a result, increasingly is characterized by its ties to "ancillary sciences," especially chemistry and physics (Pilet 1981, 635).

Concepts are powerful sources of cross-fertilization. Certain highly charged concepts, Katherine Hayles points out (1990), appear in various combinations throughout a culture, not just in the authorized versions that crystallize around new paradigms. Chaos is a timely example. Traditionally turbulence was viewed from the perspective of fluid flows. Today it is a general phenomenon. General connection, though, does not mean commensurability. Literary theorists value chaos because they are concerned with exposing the ideological underpinning of traditional ideas of order. Chaos theorists, in contrast, value chaos as the engine that drives a system toward a more complex kind of order, not subverting it. Even when the same problem is formulated on isomorphic assumptions, the arrows in each field do not all point in the same direction. When concepts circulate within a cultural field they stimulate cross-fertilization, but they also bear the traces of local disciplinary economies. Consequently the universe of discourse is both fragmented and unified. Cultural fields bespeak interconnectedness, but local differences bespeak the power of specialization within contemporary organizations of knowledge. The only truly interdisciplinary theory possible, Hayles rightly concludes, is a theory about the impossibility of creating a theory that is not implicated in disciplinary practice (1990, xiv, 4, 37, 116).

Put in terms of boundary work, concepts facilitate general connection because of their hybridity, but they still exhibit the specificities of disciplinary location. Interrelated propositions appear concurrently in separate discourses because they are compatible with cultural environments, making structuralism and general systems appealing to one generation, textualism and chaos appealing to another. They function, in effect, as "boundary concepts." The idea of boundary concept emanates from the sociological tradition of symbolic interactionism. Star and Griesmer (1988) proposed the notions of "boundary object" and "boundary concept" to explain something that lies at the heart of interdisciplinary work—heterogeneous interactions.

Star and Griesmer distinguished four kinds of boundary objects: repositories (such as a library or a museum), ideal types (the concept of species in biology), coincident boundaries (a geographic unit such as a state), and standardized forms (indexes). A *repository,* such as a library or a museum, can function as a common site for work involving members of different fields. Their primary example, the Berkeley Museum of Vertebrate Zoology, resulted from the cooperation of a hybrid community composed of professional biologists, amateur naturalists, trappers, administrators at the University of California's Berkeley campus, the general public, philanthropists, conservationists, and taxidermists. By using common procedures and forms, they were able to bridge boundaries separating them through cooperative work that served the goals of the museum. Professional and amateur status remained distinct, but *standardized forms* and procedures for recording information were boundary objects that linked individuals from different social worlds.

Ideal types and *coincident boundaries* also link social worlds. Concrete and conceptual objects are robust enough to maintain unity across fields but plastic enough to be manipulated. Weakly structured in common use, they are strongly structured at individual sites. Like the boundary stones from which they take their name, they are negotiable entities that simultaneously delimit and link particular territories. In cognitive terms, they facilitate hybrid intellectual work. In social terms, they facilitate intergroup alliance. Although the concepts of "boundary concept" and "trading zone" originated in different contexts, they are, Ilana Lowy suggests, complementary. By facilitating heterogeneous interactions between different professional groups, boundary concepts stimulate trading zones and, if they more develop fully, the interlanguages of pidgins and creoles emerge (1992, 374–75). Many concepts operate in this manner, from Star and Griesmer's example of species in biology and Lowy's example of the self in immunology to status and role in the social sciences, organism and ecosystem in the sciences, and the concepts of urban, environment, border, area, women, and culture examined in chapter 4.

The effort to bring a wider range of explanation to bear on disciplinary objects is a major instance in the humanities. Historical, sociological, psychological, and political explanation were traditionally treated as background information. Whether the object was a painting, a poem, or a musical composition, it was constructed as a discrete entity. Contextual circumstances were kept in the background. In current scholarship, the boundary separating foreground and background has been crossed, in some cases even dissolved, by rendering context subject to the same difficulties of interpretation as a text. An artistic work or body of works becomes a cultural text that transcends older divisions of high and popular culture. The boundary between, say, a painting attributed to Rembrandt as a "thing" and its reception as an "event" becomes a plural site. It is the locus of reflection on cultural discourse and visual practices in history (Bal 1991, 6, 11). When an object is contextualized in this manner, other disciplines become indispensable. This move, which forces boundary changes (Stember 1991, 2), is signified in the humanities by the metaphor of "circulation" of forces within a cultural field.

The metaphor of circulation is not unique to the humanities. Cooperation between the military and physicists during World War II illustrates how technique is an actor that circulates across boundaries. The conventional account of efforts to devise an atomic bomb and radar systems, Andrew Pickering explains (1993), usually depicts each of the two sides surrendering part of its autonomy in return for benefits the other could provide. Physicists provided the know-how and the hardware for radar systems and a bomb. The military provided funding on an unprecedented scale. The relationship, though, was not a simple matter of adding onto, allying with, or incorporating an existing, stable institution. Instead, despite resistance, the military essentially *re-formed* around physics. Physical technique was placed at the heart of a changed military machine that optimized itself around exploitation of that technique. The military in effect *enfolded* physicists, changing shape and wrapping itself around them. In the process of enfolding, physics moved to the center and the military became dependent on it. The topological metaphor of enfolding connotes intimacy, reconfiguration, and irreversibility. Physical technique was produced by one actor, physics, then a component of it was siphoned off and consumed by another, the military-industrial complex (Pickering 1993, 105, 109–10, 114).

The Implications of Permeation

The implications of boundary permeation are apparent in both individual identity and disciplinary classification. Naming is an important index. Names and the classifications they signify represent attempts to stabilize the flux of social life. They even, to an extent, create the realities they purport to represent. Mapping and naming natural or cultural things are important intellectual parts of their institutionalization (Douglas 1986, 45, 108). The act of naming entails a concurrent process of gathering, sorting, comparing, and contrasting within an evolving view of reality. Naming a field or a practice lays claim to the nature of an object as it expresses methodological and theoretical commitments (Armstrong and Fontaine 1989; Olson and Gale 1991, 200). The classifications embodied in institutions, structures, and maps are neither static nor permanent, since people challenge and sometimes change even the most hardened designations (Gieryn 1995, 30).

Trevor Pinch (1990) relates a personal anecdote that illustrates the rhetorical boundary work of classification. Pinch admits he may call himself a sociologist. In his research on the rhetoric of science, however, he has more in common with linguists at other universities than with the person in the next office who is writing a book about sociological theory. In 1987 the University Grants Committee of Great Britain participated in a national effort to evaluate research output in universities that used teaching subject areas— such as physics, chemistry, or sociology—as residual categories. The committee categorized Pinch's work and that of two colleagues at York University as "history of science." When informed by the committee of the results, the vice-chancellor of the university congratulated the History Department on its ranking, only to be told the department neither taught nor conducted research in the history of science. Ambiguity over labeling continued in 1989 when their work was reclassified as "sociology." Such events are not mere residual boundary problems arising from attempts to apply a classificatory scheme. They are fundamental to disciplinary definition. For purposes of government evaluation of research, some labels are appropriate for constructing common identity. In other contexts, different labels are appropriate. Labels are neither meaningless nor arbitrary, but they are malleable (Pinch 1990, 298–300).

Biology again comes to mind. The boundaries of its subfields are not always easy to discriminate, and some individuals prefer titles such as "immunologist," "biochemist," or "ecologist." One researcher Kenneth Ruscio interviewed admitted he might be called a "biologist," but he can no longer do so in good conscience. When asked about his discipline, another usually replies "immunology." That is his research area. Yet he coordinates a cell biology course and declares, "I am really a cell biologist," even though in studying how cells function he is involved in problems that go beyond immunology into genetics (Ruscio 1985, 14–15). These days an embryologist and a geneticist may be more alike in knowledge, techniques, and interests than two chemists. In this circumstance, is it proper to call collaboration between the geneticist and the embryologist "interdisciplinary" while classifying the joint work of two chemists who labor to understand each other as "disciplinary" research (Wolfle 1981, 6)? Is it proper to call the scientist who investigates certain molecular structures of DNA a molecular biologist, a geneticist, a biochemist, or a quantum mechanic (Swoboda 1979, 53)?

Complications of individual identity are related to disciplinary complexity. The degree of specialization and volume of information in any given discipline are now larger than any individual can master (Campbell 1969, 330–31). Disciplines conventionally include a number of subfields located at a distance from each other—conceptually, methodologically, and normatively. As a result, meetings of large professional organizations that represent a single discipline—such as the Modern Language Association, the American Anthropological Association, and the American Historical Association—are actually congeries of specialties in varying degrees of proximity. This development means that the term "discipline" can no longer be used without critical reflection on its meaning. To put the matter succinctly, is atomic physics a subdiscipline of physics? Or is atomic physics the discipline and physics a supradiscipline? Is the recipient of a Ph.D. in Arctic biology from the University of Alaska really practicing the same discipline as someone receiving a degree in mathematical biology from the University of Chicago or a degree in radiation biology from the University of Rochester (Swoboda 1979, 53)?

Disciplinary complexity is further apparent in departmental organization. The concept of an academic "department" dates back to the organization of the University of Paris in 1213. In 1815 Harvard College reorganized into six "departments," though modern departmental structure dates from the 1890s. Influenced by changes at Harvard, Yale, Princeton, Columbia, and the University of Chicago, the term took on connotations of specialization and administrative autonomy. The shift to departments as elemental administrative units heightened the sense of competition with other departments while transferring the power to judge the suitability of courses and programs and to recommend appointments, promotions, salary increases, and other rewards (Davis 1995, 29; Dressel 1970; Winsborough 1992, 272; Graff 1987, 58). For the first half of the twentieth century, disciplines were contained and controlled within department units. The proliferation of specialties, new hybrid fields, new structures of knowledge production, and new educational formats has strained the premise of containment.

As disciplines have differentiated into increasing numbers of specialties, they have become decentralized into smaller units that exert day-to-day social control over what is studied and how it is studied. These units neither certainly nor inevitably lie within conventionally defined boundaries. Alternative sites of research—programs, centers, institutes, and laboratories—have further weakened disciplinary control over subject definition, conceptual approaches, cognitive structures, goals, and norms. From the standpoint of institutionalization, any one college or university is a representation of selected disciplinary parts. In many sciences today, the strict identification of intellectual disciplines with undergraduate departments is no longer a social reality. Only a few departments now claim or can afford to represent the entire range of specialties categorized under the same label. Universities specialize in particular parts of physics or chemistry, even if the hierarchy of specialties ensures that the ones at the top will be represented in most departments. The discipline as a set of research activities has also outgrown the departmental basis of employment and careers (Whitley 1984, 12, 18–20).

New specialties put added pressure on departmental organization. Mergers created by new hybrid fields are handled differently. Biochemistry, for example, is sometimes structured as an independent department, sometimes linked to biophysics, sometimes joined with physiology, and at other times organized by an interdisciplinary committee composed of members of departments of biology and chemistry. At the level of individuals, teaching assignments do not always correspond to the kind of research faculty members do or how they identify themselves. A taxonomist and an evolutionary theorist may be located in an anatomy department, while a theorist of evolutionary and developmental biology is in a department of biochemistry and biophysics. Their closest teaching colleagues may differ from their closest research colleagues (Bechtel 1986b, 16).

New specialties also lead to reorganizing traditional departments. In the late 1980s, the University of Chicago Medical Center merged many of its departments of biological sciences and eliminated others. From one standpoint, the arrangement was a matter of administrative and economic convenience, but it also recognized current overlaps in the knowledge being taught in different departments (Winkler 1987, A14). Anthropology illustrates another type of reorganization. At present, many lines of research are thriving in the discipline. Some speculate that archaeology and physical anthropology—with their current ties to ecology, evolutionary biology, and anatomy—may divide from the rest of the field. Echoing these developments, Duke University recently reassigned physical anthropologists from the arts and sciences to the medical campus while distributing archaeologists to various departments and reconstituting anthropology as a department of cultural anthropology (Calhoun 1992, 148 n. 14).

The view of disciplinarity that emerges from an analysis of boundary permeation does not deny the value of specialization, the inevitability of differentiation given the current scale of knowledge, or the inertial strength of institutionalized disciplinary formation (Calhoun 1992, 184; Stocking and Leary 1986, 57). It does, though, challenge misconceptions that arise from standard models. Standard models stress stability, predictability, and autonomy. Discipline, however, is not a neat category (Becher 1990, 335). Disciplines differ in the ways they structure themselves, establish identities, maintain boundaries, regulate and reward practitioners, manage consensus and dissent, and communicate internally and externally. "Far from there being a single, standard theoretical or conceptual structure," Geoffrey Squires observes, "one finds all sorts of internal 'maps': a tight theoretical core, with applied offshoots; a number of parallel 'spines'; a set of Venn-like overlapping fields; a matrix of intersecting problems and methods; a loosely related set of sub-fields" (1992, 203).

On closer inspection, disciplines are actually fissured sites comprising multiple strata and influenced by other disciplines (Easton 1991a, 13). As disciplinary activity evolves and adapts to changing environments, it produces reformulations of the present body of knowledge (Heckhausen 1972, 83). A discipline, like an individual, is a "shifting and fragile homeostatic system." Research tracks and specialties grow, split, join, adapt, and die (Bateson 1972, 35–46, 62–79; Abbott 1988, xi, 33). A major aspect of their ongoing growth is the set of activities that derives from boundary crossing. Locating the discussion at the level of specialties also highlights another aspect of knowledge production that is often overlooked.

Tony Becher invokes the analogy of an active biological culture viewed under a microscope. At close range a discipline is a constantly changing "kaleidoscope of smaller components," varied in form but still related through a general process of specialization. One of the salient features of subdisciplinary groupings is their relative lack of stability compared with parent disciplines. Individual cells are in a "state of constant flux." They subdivide and recombine, changing shape and disposition in a constant process. Some subunits exhibit an "anarchic tendency" to appear more closely allied with counterparts in the heartlands of other disciplines than to subunits of their own disciplines. These groupings create "countercultures" that in some respects conflict with and may even undermine the cultures of disciplines they derive from (Becher 1990, 333, 336, 343–44). Many faculty members, as a result, are conscious of behaving counterculturally when they engage in interdisciplinary research and teaching (Alberta 1990, 5).

The final realization is that boundary crossing has become part of the process of knowledge production, not a peripheral event. Teaching and learning, research and scholarship, and service work are no longer simply inside or outside the disciplines. Interdisciplinary work is *in* the disciplines as much as it is *outside* them. Disciplines now routinely experience the push of prolific fields and the pull of strong new concepts and paradigms (Jantsch 1980, 306). As specialization has expanded into new problem areas, the scope of knowledge has extended into new areas of experience and phenomena (Blume 1985, 145–46). Intensification of interests in new areas has produced new domains that fall between older disciplines, such as sociobiology and biochemistry and, at the extremes of prior capability, particle physics and cosmology. Extensification of interests has produced new areas that draw together existing disciplines to model more complex phenomena, such as concrete economic and public health problems (Fuller 1988, 285).

The rhetoric of interdisciplinarity calls for lowering disciplinary walls, opening gates between fiefdoms, and lessening tariff mentality. Even as new interests challenge and reconstruct boundaries, however, they are enmeshed in boundary work.

CHAPTER 3

Boundary Work in Inter/Disciplinary Relations

B oundary work is ongoing, from the point of making claims to legitimating practices and judging outcomes. It occurs in all interdisciplinary activities, from borrowing tools and methods to forming new hybrid disciplines. The nature of any one activity lies in the relation between bounding and hybridity.

The Bounding of Interdisciplinary Practices

Any interdisciplinary field encompasses a range of existing and potential affiliations. This hybridity theoretically creates an ever-expanding obligation to learn the techniques and concepts of many disciplines. In practice, though, selected cuts are made. Even interdisciplinary knowledge is partial knowledge. Cognitive science and Chicano urban history illustrate the strains that hybridity creates.

Cognitive science has a professional association, an identifiable set of journals, degree programs, and a special library classification. These and other trappings of disciplinary communities make it possible to develop an approach to the subjects of psychology, logic, linguistics, artificial intelligence, and neuroscience that renders them integral parts of an interdisciplinary inquiry into the nature of mind. The field continues to grow as it incorporates advances in neighboring fields, especially computer sciences, linguistics, and mathematics. Technological advances in noninvasive brain imaging, for example, enable researchers to study process in action. As the field enlarges, though, differences in definition and methodology create conflicting claims (Becher 1994, 30).

As researchers have attempted to fill gaps in knowledge of Chicano urban history, they too have encountered problems. Reform emphasis, social science methodology, interdisciplinarity, and topical diversification have advanced understanding, but they have also lengthened the list of relevant social sciences, multiplied the topical agenda, and introduced more intricate methodologies. Advancement comes at a price. Appropriate methods have proved most applicable to narrow case studies and topical problems. As Roger Lotchin put it in an overview of the field, "We cannot lengthen the agenda of urban history, narrow its geographical and topical foci, master new methodologies, and simultaneously answer or even address the big questions about the process of urbanization or national history. We have learned to our sorrow that all the world is neither Philadelphia nor Newburyport" (1983, 232–33).

The hybridity of interdisciplinary fields is at once their strength and a continuing source of difficulty. Part of the difficulty is the impossibility of doing everything. Interdisciplinary fields also experience greater traffic in and out of pertinent disciplines and the fields themselves. Multidimensionality is a vital stimulus, but it is also a constant source of jurisdictional disputes. The taken-for-granted assumptions common in established disciplines are often lacking, leaving the foundation in contention (Messer-Davidow, Shumway, and Sylvan 1993a, 19). Multidimensionality also conflicts with one of the most powerful agents of boundary work—peer review.

The national park system of the United States illustrates the conflict. In 1968 the system was divided into three zones—natural, historical, and recreational. National Park Service money for research in the parks as "natural zones" was restricted to projects that fell within the physical and life sciences, even though the parks are valuable laboratories for broader ecological research. This is not an isolated example. On many occasions outsiders such as chemists and physicists have found themselves excluded when they apply for medical-oriented research funds from medical agencies (Sigma Xi 1988, 44, 48). Plate tectonics is a major example.

Plate tectonics is a comprehensive theory that explains mountain building, earthquakes, and volcanism. The new theory was unexpected; it emerged quickly over a period spanning roughly 1957–70. Paleomagnetists, seismologists, and oceanographers, geologists and geophysicists whose specialties had been diverging over time came together through new information, producing a chain of scientific papers and voluminous collaborative research. The results fundamentally altered understanding of the earth's crust. The underlying idea was not new. Since the pioneering work of Arthur Wegener in the 1920s, a small minority of earth scientists had been making qualitative arguments for continental drift (*Scientific Interfaces* 1986, 93). The year 1960 was a watershed. Henry Hess provided the basis for the modern theory of sea-floor spreading in a speculative text titled *History of Ocean Basins.* That same year, the British Royal Meteorological Society awarded its Napier Shaw Prize to an essay on polar wandering and continental drift that indicated the integrated character of the coming revolution (Sigma Xi 1988, 1–4).

The results were profound. In the words of one marine geologist, people who squeezed rocks, people who identified deep-ocean nannofossils, and people were mapped faults in Montana suddenly all cared about each other's work (McPhee 1981, 201–2). The impact of the new theory was rapid, comparable to the speed with which Shannon's information theory and chaos theory moved into other disciplines. Its rapid emergence, though, raises a fundamental question. How sudden was plate tectonics? The authors of Sigma Xi's 1988 report on boundary crossing in science frame the question: "Was the plate tectonics revolution the result of interdisciplinary cooperation at the margins of the disciplines concerned? Or could it be interpreted as a recognition of the impact of principles, theories and data that were all central elements of the different disciplines? If the latter was the case, does this have significant implications for the policies governing the support of these disciplines and science as a whole?" (3–4).

Was plate tectonics at the core or at the periphery of the affected disciplines? If it emerged unexpectedly, what justification would there have been for any major funding agency or other science policy–oriented body to identify tectonics as ripe for interdisciplinary activity before the revolution was well under way (40–52)? If it was there all along, its rapid emergence calls into question the logic of the boundaries maintained by funding categories. The "vocabularies of justification" that operate in peer review are not necessarily consonant with research practice, but they act as strong inhibitors of interdisciplinary research (Chubin 1990, 148). The emergent quality of much interdisciplinary research means that loss of innovation occurs. The importance of a piece of research to an allied field can be assessed only retrospectively, *after* an unexpected finding has been published, slowly recognized as legitimate, and placed at the center of the theories or paradigms of existing fields (Perper 1989, 29).

Reductionism and dominance are also forms of boundary work. The axiomatics of one discipline were imposed at a hierarchical level when the fields of planning and management and organization were reformulated around empirical and reductionist concepts of applied behavioral sciences. This form of disciplinary influence also occurred when purely economic criteria and linear methods were applied to education and to scientific research and development (Jantsch 1980). In a hybrid field, one discipline may also have greater voice.

A cursory view of criminology, for instance, suggests the field is "solidly interdisciplinary," judging by the breadth of book titles, the flagship publication, the variety of journals in which research is published, and the array of participants. Patterns of disciplinary ethnocentrism, though, are evident in the history of the field and its attitudinal structures. Segmentation was apparent in the earliest textbooks and has been reinforced in the structure of graduate education. Psychology and psychiatry initially assumed dominance through the intelligence testing movement and the initiation of a separate court system for juvenile offenders in 1899. With the revival of sociological criminology, sociology's influence grew. Some sociologists actively promote interdisciplinarity. They also draw on other disciplinary perspectives, use multifactor approaches, and argue for greater recognition of individual differences. Sociological criminology, nonetheless, has greater status and influence in the field and in the American Society of Criminology (Binder 1987).

The parceling of wholes into their disciplinary parts is a common form of reductionism. The concept of an ecosystem, recall, implies a hybridity of approaches and perspectives. The concept appears in social and geographical sciences, resource management, environmental impact assessment, planning and decision making, and social science research. Yet the dominant academic tendency has been to represent it partially. When energy flow is at issue, ecosystem ecologists tend to reason about ecosystems from the perspective of physics. When nutrient cycling is of interest, chemistry is the primary focus. When control and stability are considered, systems analysis plays a more influential role (Golley 1986, 290–92).

Parceling also occurs in projects. Because they do not fit conventional categories, projects often rely on multiple grants to fund discrete portions of research. The Philadelphia Social History Project (PSHP) was a large-scale, collaborative, and multidisciplinary investigation of the industrial development of Philadelphia and its diverse ethnic groups. The PSHP was funded by grants from the Center for Studies of Metropolitan Problems of the National Institute of Mental Health, the Division of Research Grants of the National Endowment for the Humanities, the Sociology Program of the National Science Foundation, and the Center for Population Research of the National Institute for Child Health and Human Development (Hershberg 1981, xiii–xiv). Achieving integrated knowledge in large projects is often dependent on participants' goodwill and the director's ability to sustain uneven commitments. In order to establish disciplinary credentials, individuals publish discrete portions of the total output. Even journal issues and books devoted to interdisciplinary topics tend to consist of juxtaposed voices speaking separate tongues, linked by their encyclopedic alignment, the editor's prefatory remarks, and authors' introductory and concluding paragraphs.

Parceling also occurs in a social form of reductionism—uneven influence. Status dynamics create a disproportionate influence that relegates some participants to peripheral roles (Klein 1990b, 127–28). Geographers often complain of being limited to the role of "outside" expert or data supplier on archaeological and historical projects. Similarly, the social sciences often become a kind of "service industry" in many scientific research projects (Eisel

1992, 243). In a telling example, Simon and Goode chronicled the problems they encountered as anthropologists involved in policy research. The project focused on the efforts of newly laid-off employees and union leaders to save jobs in the supermarket industry.

Minus the specificities of anthropology, the four models of collaboration Simon and Goode identified are potential levels of interaction in all interdisciplinary projects: *background or context information,* an additive step that can be supplied separately from contributions of other researchers and may appear as an appendix or separate case study; *elaboration or explanation of findings* from quantitative components, still an additive, not integrative role that typically produces a concluding chapter valued as descriptive detail, not as "findings"; *definition of important variables or categories* for quantitative study, a step that sometimes occurs at the outset or before finalization of research design, structured instruments, or analytic approaches; *creative combination of ethnographic and multivariate approaches in research, analysis, and interpretation,* a rare instance in which fundamental questions are refined using mutually illuminating ethnographic approaches (1989, 220–21).

Simon and Goode's experience highlights many of the specificities of interdisciplinary boundary work. Divisions of disciplinary labor and the restrictions set by funding agencies create an a priori bounding. Collaborative work is impeded by territoriality and turf battles, disciplinary pecking orders and status dynamics, the differing status of quantitative and qualitative inputs, resistance to innovation, insecurity and mistrust, and lack of integrative skills. Interdisciplinary development is limited by constraints of time and budget, avoidance of complexity, lack of systems thinking, reductionism, and shortfalls of integration. Program development is stalled by inadequate incentives, rigid budgetary and administrative categories, inadequate forums for exchange, the "dangerous courtesies" of accommodation, inertia, and marginality. These factors are all present in three generic contexts of disciplinary interaction: borrowing, relations with disciplinary neighbors, and the formation of interdisciplines.

The Cross-fertilizations of Borrowing

The perception that knowledge is increasingly interdisciplinary derives in large part from the daily cross-fertilizations of borrowing from other disciplines. The better-known examples span tools and instruments, methods and techniques, data and information, concepts and theories: computers, lasers, the electron microscope, and techniques of gene splicing; statistical methods, formal mathematical models, data sets, and systems engineering; game theory, organizational theory, and factor analysis; survey and interview techniques, participant observation, thick description, and explication de texte; evolutionary theory, information theory, systems theory, and structuralism; the concepts of role, status, decision making, information, and communication; and feminist and Marxist analysis.

Disciplinary relations are affected differently by borrowing. Tom Paxson (1996) classifies interactions in terms of strength and closeness. Levels 1 and 2 involve increasing impact. Levels 3 and 4 involve increasing connectedness.

Instrumental borrowing exemplifies level 1. Disciplines often use the tools, instruments, or techniques of other disciplines. Chemists, for example, use mass-spectroscopy techniques that were originally developed by physicists. Disciplines also use the data produced and interpreted by other disciplines. In normative ethics, philosophers use anthropological evidence on diverse cultural patterns of ethical judgments. The simple use of data and method does not tend to transform boundaries or fields. For instance, any concept or method from statistics—such as description of a Gaussian distribution, sampling rules, Bayesian inferences—is substantively "empty." It matters little what is being counted—gold-mine production, deaths in war, or quasar emission (Pahre 1995, 249). Neither borrowing nor lending discipline is modified, and their epistemic natures and cognitive structures are not challenged.

Borrowing a symbolic language or concept differs from borrowing a language or concept along with its operationalization. The chaos community is an interdisciplinary social world based on the exchange of symbolic language. The political economy community, in contrast, exchanges both symbolic languages and operationalizations (Pahre 1994). In literary studies both occur. Scholars often borrow concepts without their operationalizations. They borrow the metaphor of "chaos," for example, then engage in a thematic search for images of chaos in literary texts. In borrowing Marxian analysis, literary scholars have operationalized it by looking at systems of literary production in terms of the material production of texts and relations of production that are instantiated (Ellen Messer-Davidow, pers. comm., 12 May 1995).

Generally speaking, borrowing methods does not enrich the parent discipline. The use of mathematics by social scientists has not contributed significantly to mathematics as a discipline. Likewise, widespread borrowing of economic models has not altered economic method. Economists have expanded into the traditional domains of sociology, political science, anthropology, law, and social biology in a limited but powerful form of imperialism based on applying economic methodology to the subject matter of bordering disciplines (Dogan and Pahre 1990, 111–13, 138). At level 2 interactions are deeper and more fruitful, although disciplines do not grow toward each other. Sometimes identifiable borrowing communities form. A relationship between part of economics and part of political science has persisted for decades. Economics both exports theory to and imports data from political science. Political economy is an example driven by the theoretical imperialism of economics. There is a sizable economic literature on economic regulation, a topic relevant to political science. Economic policies have also become part of the explanandum of economics, and there are economic fields, such as economics of regulation or endogenous tariff theory, that explain politics in economic terms (Pahre 1995, 246).

Sometimes a borrowing is assimilated so completely that it is no longer regarded as a foreign product and may not even be considered an interdisciplinary event. In the history of science a number of laws borrowed from one domain have been successfully applied and adapted in a process Marcel Boisot named "linear interdisciplinarity." This form of borrowing occurred when d'Alembert's vibrating strings equation, originally claimed by acoustics, appeared in the same form in electromagnetism. Later, modified by Broglie's fundamental relation, it appeared in wave mechanics under the name of Schrödinger's equation. Similarly, Coulomb's law was applied to gravitation, electrostatics, magnetism, and the principle of economic flow between cities (Boisot 1972, 93). As "linear interdisciplinarity" suggests, borrowings may circulate in complex ways. The concepts of one level may permeate subsequent levels in a process B. Kedrov (1974) calls "pivoting" and Michael Intriligator (1985) names "whirlpool effects." The methods of mathematics, statistics, and systemology are used in mechanics, physics, and chemistry. The methods used in the latter three disciplines are in turn used in astronomy, geosciences, and biosciences (Dahlberg 1994, 68).

Similar events occur in the social sciences. An idea developed in one behavioral science, for example, may be applied to or extended into another. The extension may then be used or further developed in the original science. This circulation of influence occurred with game theory and organizational theory in economics and political science and with the concepts of anomie and cognitive dissonance in psychology and sociology. It also occurred when the concept of "values" was borrowed. When the term appeared in economics, it had a narrow, technical meaning. During the 1920s it took on psychological overtones in the notions of preferences and motives and in the sociological idea of interest. This development, in turn, opened the concept of values up to related meanings such as attitudes, needs, sentiments, dispositions, cathexes, valences, ethics, ideologies, mores, norms, aspirations, obligations, rights, and sanctions. From there the concept was borrowed and adapted in anthropology and political science (Dogan and Pahre 1990, 129, 165).

Many difficulties arise in borrowing. One derives from the nature of the borrowing. It is generally easier, for example, for the mathematical lender field to assimilate new evidence than for the nonmathematical borrower to assimilate mathematics. Borrowing obsolete theories creates tensions between two disciplines. Even when nonobsolete theories are used, they may be used in a way that breaks the logical connection to the lender. The logical standing of one discipline's theory may also differ in the subject matter of another discipline. The Coase theorem, for instance, is an important part of neoclassical economics. It holds that economically efficient outcomes will occur whenever people have well-defined property rights, freedom of contract, complete information, and costless transactions. Economists usually interpret this to mean that markets are efficient and government intervention is unnecessary. Political scientists usually interpret it to mean that government intervention is necessary, both to establish property rights and to remedy market imperfections in a world of incomplete information and costly transactions (Pahre 1995, 247).

Two major examples, the computer and mathematics, illustrate how the same entity may be borrowed in different ways. The impact of the computer ranges from word processing and number crunching to assimilating methods of quantification and generating new theoretical discoveries. Its initial effect was primarily vertical, producing deepened understanding of existing problems. Economics, sociology, and political science quickly adapted new technologies of the computer to processing data (Cohn 1980, 213). Later the computer's horizontal effects became evident. Because of their capacity to manage enormous amounts of information, computers are now being used to tackle complex problems that could not be handled previously. Computer modeling of evolutionary phenomena, for instance, suggests that evolution functions as a pattern-recognition system that promotes some species while extinguishing others. This realization has important implications for learning behavior and economic behavior (Pagels 1988, 41–42).

Science and technology are not the only contexts. In serving scholars in the humanities and social sciences, the computer is potentially as powerful as the microscope was in the biological sciences (Hershberg 1981, xiii). Statistical techniques, other quantitative methods, and computer technology were influential in the rise of cliometrics as a distinct branch of the discipline. Since World War II, some American historians had been utilizing quantitative evidence. During the mid-1950s this tendency became more visible among economic and political historians. The development of machine-readable data libraries was a major innovation in research methods. By the 1960s and 1970s computers had spread to other branches of the discipline, including the new political history and archival work. Bodies of data about aggregates facilitate analysis of groups and individuals. Yet quantification also raises fears among traditional historians that the borrowed tool has become an end in itself, a narrow instrument that fails to capture the dynamic movement of history and threatens disciplinary integrity (Bogue 1990, 89, 99; Burke 1991, 14–15).

Mathematics plays a significant role in all of the natural and social sciences. Interdisciplinary communication in science often assumes a mathematical form. Among specialized fields, mathematics also produces the most extensive generalizations (Fedoseyev 1984, 24). Borrowings often exhibit traces of original disciplinary training and worldview. At the interface of mathematics and physics, the mathematics used by physicists is often considered invalid until it is embedded in the arts of physical description. On the other side of the disciplinary fence, physicists are not considered to be doing mathematics proper, because their argumentation is not guided by the requirements of mathematical theorem proving (Livingston 1993, 369, 390). At certain levels, however, the limits of one discipline become the limits of the other. In the field of mathematical physics, new theory is being generated through computer analysis. Many new discoveries require deep understanding of both physics and mathematics. As new mathematics is introduced by physicists and new physics is introduced by mathematicians, role switching is occurring. In some quarters computational physics is even regarded as an interface subject.

At this level of interaction, technical advances are not "mere" tools and instruments. They exemplify levels 3 and 4. At level 3, disciplines grow toward each other in the sense of forming an interface of theories and subject matters. Through dialectic conversation among disciplines, a new picture or mutual understanding of subject matter may develop. Linguistics, archaeology, history, and the study of myth to decipher elements of oral history all contribute knowledge of prehistoric and early historical population shifts in the western Mediterranean region. Each depends at many steps on the evidence contributed by the others. Even the instrumentality of problem-focused work may lead to a more substantive relation. Collaborative work sometimes requires developing one or more of the participating disciplines. The Manhattan Project, for instance, required major developments in theoretical and applied physics as well as chemistry. Advances in each area had implications for the research needed in the other areas in order to achieve the project goal (Paxson 1996).

At the highest level of interaction, an interdiscipline is recognized. The biology-physics interface is a major example. The mathematical theory of nonlinear dynamics has advanced understanding of the complex hierarchy and partial disorder of biological systems and their critical processes. Many physical techniques have also become so fully integrated into biological research that their origin is often forgotten until an underlying physical advance in a particular method provides a reminder. Electron microscopy, X-ray crystallography, and spectroscopies are notable examples. Advances in the physics of lasers have increased the time resolution of pulsed laser spectroscopy by an added factor of ten. This development, which provides access to faster biomolecular processes, is not simply additive or supplementary: it has transformed a significant part of the relation between physics and biology (*Scientific Interfaces* 1986, 10–11, 27–29, 36–38, 47–49, 109, 114, 131–32).

One of the most visible examples in recent decades has functioned variously as a borrowed method, a boundary concept, a trading zone, and a hybrid community. It has spawned a pidgin, a creole, and hybrid professional roles. Commonly referred to as the rhetorical turn in scholarship, this extended example of borrowing demonstrates that cross-fertilization may be as implicated in disciplinary history as in interdisciplinary history.

The Rhetorical Turn

Rhetoric is an ancient discipline traditionally associated with artifice, elocution, ornament, civic oratory, and the writing of history, poetry, and literary criticism. Because of this history, the modern fields of rhetoric, composition studies, and literary studies share common roots. Their separation was institutionalized in the nineteenth-century university. In Britain instruction was segmented into two areas, rhetoric and belles lettres. In the United States composition became a branch of rhetoric. During the early twentieth century, the traditional concerns of rhetoric were addressed in English departments, where writing was taught and the service dimensions of instruction in composition were accentuated. Newly formed speech departments assumed responsibility for history, methods, and theories of rhetoric. During the 1960s and 1970s, several developments created a different space for composition and rhetoric (McQuade 1992, 486–89, 491–92, 498).

New interests promoted the possibility of a new field. They included the movement known as "theory," several forms of critical analysis, redefinition of the literary canon, and the rise of women's studies and gender studies. Scholars also challenged prior emphasis on models and correctness in composition pedagogy. In addition, new research on writing process stimulated a reintegration of linguistics into the curriculum as an essential discipline offering insight into basic questions of orality and literacy. At the same time, the discipline of linguistics was moving outward from an emphasis on phonological theory, syntactic theory, and idealized forms of language to broader concern for language acquisition, second-language teaching, and the study of language in its social setting. At yet another site, in speech and communication departments, rhetorical analysis was expanding deeper into media and public affairs.

As a result of these changes, rhetoric came to be regarded as a terrain of choice (Culler 1992, 217). By the end of the 1960s composition studies had a new name, an emerging specialist language, an expanding research agenda, greater visibility, and a growing scholarly apparatus. At that point claims for disciplinary integrity and independence arose. The professional identity of composition studies had changed from being merely subject *to* literary studies to becoming a subject *for* scholarly inquiry and speculation in its own right (McQuade 1992, 504). In a characteristic genealogical move, scholars traced prior interconnections of literary and linguistic inquiry in the discipline of philology (Baron 1992, 28). The interplay of general connection and specificity is apparent in the tension between invoking breadth and naming practices. In introducing a collection of essays on the state of the field, Charles Bazerman described it as a "loosely defined area" whose plurality is reflected in its many names: "composition," "teaching of writing," "rhetoric," "the study of written language," and "literacy studies" (1989, 223).

The claim for interdisciplinarity is often made on methodological grounds. Methodological influences span historical, social, linguistic, semiotic, socio-cognitive, and cognitive approaches as well as survey techniques, rhetorical analysis, case studies, ethnographies, psychometric and statistical sampling, and statistical inference (Hillocks 1989, 261). During the early 1970s terminology from cognitive psychology and psycholinguistics began appearing as researchers changed the language used to describe composition from *writing* process, already a move beyond writing *product,* to *composing* process. This shift accentuated cognitive activities (Bizzell and Herzberg 1990). Empirical work and theoretical influences are closely linked, and most empirical scholars have been willing to shift perspective and methods as needed. Cognitive approaches, for example, are rooted in an empirical tradition rich in theory. They draw on work on reading, memory, language processing and acquisition, human development, perception, and creativity (Schriver 1989, 276, 282–83).

As usual, assessments differ, from a mere fad to arrival in the disciplinary groves of academe to dismantling of disciplinary boundaries. Beyond the intellectual constructs, rhetoric and composition studies also constitute a labor issue. Historically, few members of English departments were trained to teach composition; being freed of the task is still a status symbol in many departments. In contrast to the more contemplative, aesthetic domain of literature, hierarchical metaphors characterize teaching composition as service, lower-division, basic skills, and required course. Composition studies remains a contested territory along the borders of literature, literary criticism, and rhetoric—in the words of one scholar, an "academic borderland with a fractured history" (McQuade 1992, 484, 487). Scholarship has elevated respect for the field, yet the profession is anchored by a growing fleet of part-timers and nontenure-track instructors who teach writing at lesser pay with little or no prospect of employment security. Prognostications of a new discipline and revitalizing the humanities are of cold comfort to these laborers in the undergroves of academe.

Beyond English departments, rhetoric, discourse, and text function as boundary concepts in a general trend that is cutting across sociology, psychology, anthropology, law, and many traditional disciplines of the humanities. This wider interest stems from the idea that language is the very condition of thought, not its one-to-one representation. Consequently, the movement is sometimes labeled a linguistic or an interpretive turn. Attention to the ways language constructs reality has opened up behavior, culture, and historical epochs to reading as texts. No longer are texts the province of English departments, metaphor the business of literary critics, and narrative the stuff of fiction. Mathematical proofs and statistical analyses, novels and ethnographic records, works of art and paintings, tools and rituals, social actions and public policies are read as texts (Klein 1992, 10). Scientific data are viewed as symbolic constructions, scientific descriptions and theories are treated as narratives, mathematical proofs are analyzed as rhetorical tropes, and the ongoing activities of scientific communities are read as conversations (Simons 1989, 5).

The space of the rhetorical turn is decidedly plural. It is constituted by shared problematics, a pidgin shaped by widely used metalanguage, a creole among particular clusters of scholars who have assumed new hybrid identities, new models of scholarship, seminal texts, and shared concerns about how the authority of canon, gender, and discipline constructs knowledge. The shared problematics of representation and interpretation have fueled debate on the adequacy of disciplinary representation and the validity of claims about the world. In the social sciences, to take a domain beyond rhetoric's institutional home, rhetorical analysis has been a significant means by which social science disciplines, especially anthropology and sociology, have established common ground with humanistic disciplines, especially literature and philosophy (Gusfield 1992, 117). One of the most productive zones of interaction has been the convergence of literary theory, interpretative anthropology, and new forms of ethnography.

Exhibiting a common tendency in interdisciplinary practices, social scientists use the term "rhetoric" in different ways. For many, rhetoric is a borrowed method, a tool for understanding how texts employ devices of tone and style, metaphor and imagery, authority and persuasion. For others, methodology and conceptual purpose cannot be easily separated. In their work, rhetorical analysis overlaps with critical interpretative approaches, especially poststructuralism, deconstruction, hermeneutics, critical pluralism, Habermasian critical theory, and archetypal and genre criticism. Each in turn carries its own attendant assumptions about language, culture, and knowledge. For others it overlaps with an expanding sociology of knowledge and rhetoric of inquiry that is focused on the language and argument of communities of inquiry. Consequently there is no single rhetoric of social science. The term is used synonymously with the terms literary, critical, linguistic, reflexive, social constructivist, and deconstructionist, as well as the language of feminist, neo-Marxist, neo-Freudian, and Lacanian critique.

This variety is evident in concrete practices:

> the reading of culture and society as texts
> analysis of the rhetoric of individual disciplines and fields

reflection on problems of authority and representation in ethnography
recognition of the role of language and meaning in psychology and
    psychoanalysis
readings of the tone, style, inflection, and grammar of cultural history
new poetics for sociology, history, and law
new methods and approaches such as thick description, cognitive aesthet-
    ics and symbolic realism, and experimental forms of ethnography
studies of the language of efficiency in making public policy
studies of public opinion and political ideology through interpretation of
    texts
studies of the persuasive nature of data, sampling, regression analysis, for-
    mal language, experimental tests, thought experiments, metaphor and
    analogy, models, and appeals to authority in economics

(Klein 1992, 13)

Practices are located differently. Sometimes rhetorical interests coalesce into identifiable trading zones, usually distinct schools of thought and networks of practitioners. They have also attained material institutionalization in the form of conferences, publications, research projects, joint appointments, job listings, changes in the editorial policies of journals, and new curricula. Some practices have been naturalized into mainstream disciplinary discourse. Others have been enclaved as alternative approaches. Some proponents forecast a new unity. James White's (1985) vision of rhetoric as a new "central discipline," though, is less likely to occur than Nelson, Megill, and McCloskey's (1987) prediction of a general increase of self-reflection in every field of inquiry and strengthened connections across particular domains.

Dilip Gaonkar (1990) theorizes the operations of the rhetorical turn as a double move. An explicit rhetorical turn occurs in works that recognize the relevance of rhetoric as a critical interpretative method, especially among the new rhetoricians. They include Chaim Perelman, Kenneth Burke, Richard McKeon, Paul de Man, Walter Ong, and Tzvetan Todorov. An implicit turn occurs in a more widespread theoretical and epistemological enterprise that uncovers traces of rhetoric everywhere, including the tropological and persuasive aspects of disciplinary practice. These topics were previously located outside mainstream disciplinary discussion. The authors of the implicit turn are more numerous. They include Kuhn, Feyerabend, Lacan, Gadamer, Habermas, Foucault, and others whose work has a rhetorical orientation, among them sociologists of knowledge and symbolic interactionists. "The contemporary intellectual landscape," Gaonkar emphasizes, "is replete with signs of an implicit rhetoric turn" (1990, 352–55).

Rhetoric thus exemplifies the complex boundary work of interdisciplinary fields. It does disciplinary work as it cross-fertilizes. The discourse structures that formed in the trading zone of the rhetorical turn are both loosely affiliated and tightly woven. They exhibit the traces of general connection as well as local disciplinary economies. This double function is no less apparent in the second generic context, the interactions of disciplinary neighbors.

Neighbors

The idea of overlapping territory appears at several levels of interaction. Overlaps are apparent in three forms of boundary work. The first, conflicting interpretations of the same phenomena, leads to boundary disputes. The second, tacit or overt divisions of intellectual labor, leads to boundary maintenance. The third, a closer sense of identification with inhabitants of neighboring territory, leads to boundary blurring (Becher 1990, 334–36). The idea of a border zone marks the place where two disciplines meet. Huerkamp et al.'s (1981) "border interdisciplinarity" and "interdisciplinarity of neighboring disciplines," Talcott Parsons's (1970) "zone of interdependence," and S. N. Smirnov's (1984) "borderland interdisciplinarity" are different names for this idea.

Overlaps are implicit in the mental maps that knowers have of their disciplinary neighbors. Becher's interviews with 220 academics, spanning twelve disciplines and eighteen institutions in Britain and the United States, reveal several common perceptions: "Economics was said to have one common frontier with mathematics and another with political science; some trade relations with history and sociology; and a lesser measure of shared ground with psychology, philosophy and law. Biology was portrayed as being bounded on the one side by mathematics and the physical sciences (especially physics, chemistry and physical geography) and on the other by the human sciences (in particular by psychology, anthropology, and human geography)" (1989, 36).

The concept of a "neighbor" is both temporal and spatial. For historical reasons alone, the idea of affinity makes sense. Taking the metaphor of relations at face value, anthropology and sociology are relatives because they grew up in the same household. Not surprisingly, Wittgenstein's notion of "family resemblances" is a popular metaphor for disciplinary relations. New developments create another set of affinities. Many elements of biochemistry, for instance, are based on new developments, even though the name "biochemistry" stems from a prior organization of knowledge (Perper 1989, 49). The current discipline-specialty relation is a major reason. Commonalty at the specialty level often derives from methods, concepts, and problems that did not exist previously or were not highlighted historically.

Because disciplinary neighbors derive from both historical and modern sources, genealogical claims are anchored in precedent as well as change. Current mutual interest in the problem of interpretation in law, literary theory, and art history is an excellent example. Connections are justified based on both long-standing hermeneutical interests and recent poststructuralist work on the problem of meaning. The nature of a relationship, though, may remain a matter of disagreement. Some scientists believe the subject matter of biophysics, for example, consists of biological phenomena studied by physical methods. Others insist its subject matter consists of physical processes existing in a special biological form (Smirnov 1984, 68–70).

Relations also shift over time. Citation analysis provides an empirical measure of change. Patterns of publication citation reveal that sociology's closest neighbors, for instance, have shifted from anthropology in the 1940s to psychology and psychiatry in the 1950s, political science in the 1960s, economics in the 1970s, and history in the 1980s. In the 1990s, closer ties to anthropology became apparent (Winsborough 1992, 270 n. 1). From the 1960s forward, an additional pattern became visible. Citations to interdisciplinary journals, economics, and the fields of organizational, administrative, management, and labor studies became more numerous. Interdisciplinary social and behavioral science publications were also cited more frequently, and the field of political economy moved from a minor relation to a significant source, propelled by the rise of interdisciplinary Marxist journals and development studies. In recent years sociologists have been central participants in political economy and development studies, not just borrowers from or supplementers of economics (Calhoun 1992, 143–45, 180–83).

The discipline of history offers an extended example of what happens in the trading zones of interdisciplinary neighborhoods.

The Neighborhoods of History

The concept of interdisciplinary history antedates use of the actual term. Its meaning depends very much on what is being counted and on the choice of origin. American-trained historians have used the term since the early 1950s. During the 1960s the term became fashionable, and in 1970 it gained further legitimacy with the founding of the *Journal of Interdisciplinary History* (Horn and Ritter 1986, 429). Interdisciplinary claims have several bases: from synoptic identity and older cultural synthesis to borrowed methods, quantification and computers, psychoanalysis, several movements labeled "new history," the rise of hybrid specialties, and recurring demands for rapprochement with neighboring anthropology, sociology, and economics. Traces of this genealogy appear in bulletins of the Social Science Research Council (SSRC), which document campaigns to teach historians to be, alternatively, social scientists or humanists.

History has never been isolated, Over time, though, it became more closely tied to other branches of knowledge, to the point that it was recently dubbed "one of the busiest areas of cross-disciplinary combinations" (Flenley 1953, 324, 326; Dogan and Pahre 1990, 87). When history separated from the social sciences in the early twentieth century, it was relatively insular (Ross 1991, 474). As the community and synthetic capacity of late nineteenth-century scholarship eroded, the notion that any single group could control the entire territory of "history" began losing ground. Broadening involvement with the whole range of human activity has encouraged historians to be more interdisciplinary, in the sense of learning from and collaborating with others. Intellectual innovations today are linked strongly with the willingness to draw on other disciplines for theoretical and methodological insights. These developments have led in turn to expanding and redefining the political orientation of traditional historiography (See especially, Burke 1991).

Today's history tends to be more analytic and thematic than narrative and chronological. The focus has shifted in several ways: from studying politics to considering virtually every human activity; from narrating events to analyzing structure and trends; from viewing history from above, through documents and events, to viewing it from below, using a greater variety of evidence; from the "objective" stance of determining what "actually happened" to accepting the limits of cultural relativism and heteroglossia (Burke 1991, 2–6). As a result of these shifts, researchers rely more on statistical tables, oral interviews, sociological models, and psychoanalytic theories than on constitutions, treaties, parliamentary debates, political writings, or party manifestos. They are also more interested in classes and ethnic groups, social problems and institutions, cities and communities, work and play, family and sex, birth and death, childhood and old age, crime and insanity than in regimes and administrations, legislation and politics, diplomacy and foreign policy, wars and revolutions (Himmelfarb 1987, 14).

Change has not occurred without controversy. Furthermore, heightened interactions have not solved the problem of synthesis implied by synoptic identity. History is more fragmented than ever before. Reflecting the current prominence of interactions at the level of specialties, evidence of rapprochement tends to exist at local and regional sites, in subdisciplinary sectors, and in new work on the interrelation of events and structures, narrative and analysis (Burke 1991, 6, 18–19). A pluralistic view of discipline does not rule out common assumptions. It does, though, resist totalizing definition by one dominant part. It also recognizes, not sidesteps, the problem of boundaries and struggles for professional control (Rabb 1981). Relations with individual neighbors are defined against this general backdrop and the particularities of the neighbors in question. Like the rhetorical turn, they are weighed differently. They are promoted as vestiges of ancient union, a promising pathway, an identifiable subfield, an alternative practice, a new hybrid discipline, and proof of impending (re)convergence.

History's "natural overlap" with archaeology is strong in studies of the ancient world, where historians must rely on information that archaeologists uncover. Historians have also turned to anthropology, sociology, psychology, botany, and mineralogy to make up for deficiencies in written documentation and to gain new perspectives. The relationship with archaeology has shifted over time in what C. J. Arnold calls "shades of confrontation and cooperation" (1986, 32). The reasons are both historical and cultural. Archaeology has served different disciplinary masters. In Europe, they were primarily history, philosophy, and humanistic learning; in the United States, anthropology and other social sciences (Kubler 1975, 766). During the sixteenth century through the eighteenth, European archaeology in its nascent form developed as an "adjunct" for history (Bintliff 1986, 5). It was considered a "natural tool." In the United States, archaeology and history developed largely in isolation from each other. Archaeology remained for the most part within the larger domain of anthropology (Wilderson 1975, 115–16, 129).

The relationship between history and anthropology likewise varies. Anthropology has been described as everything from "undertapped" to a "codiscipline." Degrees of convergence are visible in particular fields—historical anthropology, *histoire de mentalités,* and historical demography—and in particular projects—interest in norms, value systems, and rituals; the expressive functions of forms of riot and disturbance; symbolic expressions of authority, control, and hegemony; and use of material from cultures that Western historians traditionally did not study (Lepenies 1976; Davis 1981, 267). A formal debate, held at the tenth anniversary meeting of the Social Science History Association (Kertzer, Rutman, Silverman, and Plakans 1986) is an index of the relationship and differing assessments. Three themes cut across the voices joined by the debate: the richness of interactions, their disputed status, and impediments to a more comprehensive relationship.

"Interdisciplinary forays" between history and anthropology, David Kertzer reports, have ramified in a variety of directions over the past decade. The premise of a relationship is not disputed so much as the way it is conducted. Individual historians align themselves differently. Some identify with the anthropology of social organization and social structures exemplified by British social anthropology. Others identify with the symbolism and construction of reality exemplified by part of American cultural anthropology, especially the work of Clifford Geertz. Reacting to "Clio's dalliances," Darrett Rutman questions the quick succession of "wild but not very deep relationships" with several social sciences. "Infatuation" with statistics seems the most serious. Yet in all her dalliances, Clio has displayed more a split personality than fidelity to one suitor and little interest in a genuine melding or collapsing of boundaries.

Speaking in turn, Sydel Silverman suggests that differences hinge on the question whether historians should move beyond current collaborations to creating a new discipline, whether it be anthropological history, historical anthropology, or another designation that grants each component equal status. Collaborations are well in place. Anthropologists have gone beyond the ethnographic present of fieldwork to greater historical perspective. Historians, for their part, have incorporated anthropological interests and ideas into their work. Yet the ultimate objective, Silverman and many others insist, is to make "better anthropology and better history, not a hybrid creature." Understanding the nature of the boundary better is likely to produce more informed collaboration, not a wide-scale breakdown of boundaries.

Andrejs Plakans weighs the evidence. Some activities have attained legitimacy in the form of key prizes. Interactions are especially strong at the subspecialty level and in the work of individuals. Some historians are dissatisfied with the colonization of history by anthropology, yet an organized backlash seems unlikely. The number of practitioners is increasing but remains small, and full-scale disciplinary technologies of funding and graduate training are not in place. Furthermore, current interactions do not appear to threaten the core methodologies of either discipline. A historian using interview evidence and an anthropologist using documentary evidence do not necessarily change professional identity or sever connections with prevailing bodies of theory. Even with these limitations, prospects for continuing interaction are favorable. The proof lies in grant support, a growing network of conferences and publications, an even distribution of scholars across age cohorts, and tangible signs of interest among graduate students. Two developments hold particular promise. The reorientation of social historians during the 1960s toward research on microstructures and microprocesses is part of a larger shift toward structural analysis that is especially strong in family history. Discourse analysis built on the work of Clifford Geertz has also become a viable model for historical interpretation.

The possibility of increased interaction is suggested by growing validation of anthropologists' interest in historical dimensions and, on the other side of the traditional boundary, greater exposure to social science research, including new topics. When specialized methodologies are unmasked, a number of major problems appear similar. They include questions of time, contextualization, satisfactory ways of dealing with the involvement of individuals in multiple systems of social roles, shared interest in demography, and the place of theory. Their impact, nonetheless, remains limited. They have not effected a global merger; they entail work at the junctures formed by common problems and limited puzzles. Despite Lévi-Strauss's contention that the two disciplines are at bottom the same endeavor, Plakans concludes, they are likely to remain separate, both operationally and institutionally.

History's relationship with another neighbor, sociology, yields a parallel picture. Both are broad in scope, and they often examine the same phenomena (Dogan and Pahre 1900, 187). A generation ago sociologists were inclined to portray the difference in terms of scientific analysis versus description. This depiction perpetuated a view of sociology as nomothetic and history as idiographic. Two major developments, social history and historical sociology, indicate the possibilities and the limits of interdisciplinary practice. They have similar origins in post–World War II transitions in society, the impact of the 1960s, and the academic rehabilitation of Marxism. Historical and comparative sociology expanded in the United States in part as a result of an internal struggle against technically oriented research. Opposition to the ethnocentrism of 1950s-era American functionalism, attempts to counter the neglect of struggle as a factor in social life, and efforts to consider the possibility of radical change were added stimuli (Calhoun 1992, 156–60).

Both fields were quickly deemed interdisciplinary. Of the two, social history was initially more staid. It was characterized primarily by borrowing analytic techniques from nonhistorical social science for application to historical research problems. Ultimately, social history became the more radical of the two. It was not just a new specialty but a new way of defining boundaries in time and in place, with deeper epistemological and theoretical contrasts. Traditional historians initially attempted to solidify the internal boundary and isolate the new specialty from the mainstream (Roy, in "Comment and Debate" 1987, 59). Both movements, though, became, in the words of one major scholar, "robust, maturing tendencies" (Skocpol, in "Comment and Debate" 1987, 21).

By the mid-1980s nearly a quarter of the articles in main sociological journals were dealing with historical topics and using historical data. A historical section of the American Sociological Association had also formed (Knapp 1984, 51). The most significant indicator was the appearance of historical sociology as a specialty in the *Employment Bulletin* of the American Sociological Association (Cornell 1987, 51). In a customary act of interdisciplinary genealogy, renewed searches for legitimation through progenitors are now under way in American sociology and history. As in the history-anthropology relation, interactions have not produced a comprehensive synthesis of the two disciplines. They remain distinct along several dimensions. Each dimension opens an avenue for developing hybrid historical sociologies in particular subfields, but not in all dimensions simultaneously. This diversity inhibits development of a single hybrid (Dogan and Pahre 1990, 187–88).

A debate on historical sociology and social history, which appeared in *Social Science History,* provides another ear to the ground of boundary work in interdisciplinary neighborhoods (Schwartz 1987; Skocpol, Zunz, Cornell, and Roy in "Comment and Debate" 1987). The themes of the debate are familiar.

Mildred Schwartz rejects the idea that historical sociology constitutes a full-fledged specialty. Refusing to revitalize the name, she argues instead for a general incorporation of time into research and explanation. William Roy contends that social history is moving back toward narrative history while comparative historical sociology is becoming an established part of the mainstream. Its continuity with conventional historiography is being articulated, once marginal figures are being canonized, and institutionalization is under way through inclusion in graduate training. Theda Skocpol predicts both movements will nonetheless continue to be somewhat different, making convergence unlikely. Even so, prospects for greater overlap and cumulative achievement are strong.

Significant reorientations of particular sectors have occurred. Over the past fifteen years, Roy reports, historical sociologists have rebelled against the twin orthodoxies of grand theory and abstracted empiricism that dominated sociology until the late 1960s. They have fundamentally reworked understanding of the causes and forms of collective action and revolutions. They have also developed new historically grounded and sensitive analyses of subjects such as working-class formation, ethnic relations, and the development of modern welfare states. Social historians, for their part, have exploited new sources of evidence and borrowed explanatory approaches and new research methods. The roster of influence spans Durkheimian ideas about social modernization, Marxian ideas about modes of production and class conflict, application of computers and linear statistical techniques, and data about aggregates of individuals. In rebelling against narrative political history, proponents have "gained leverage" by using sociological concepts and methods, such as modernization theories and aggregate statistical techniques.

In contrast to the 1950s, major sectors of the two disciplines now show a greater inclination toward each other. The connection between hypothesis and evidence is sufficiently tight in historical sociology, Robert Pahre noted elsewhere, that common disciplinary stereotypes are rendered inaccurate. Both participating disciplines produce results that are useful to each other. This interaction contradicts the stereotype of sociology exporting theory to history and history exporting facts to sociology (Pahre 1994, 25–26). Despite overlapping tendencies and concerns, though, many activities have occurred primarily on disciplinary turf. Both movements exhibit traces of the disciplinary orthodoxies their practitioners rebelled against. Historians and sociologists relate the particular to the general in different ways. Even in the midst of a book arguing for common purposes and methods, the historian still tends to use a rhetoric of close presentation, seeking to persuade through dense detail. The sociologist tends to use a rhetoric of perspective, seeking to persuade through elegant patterning of connections seen from a distance. Social historians will likely continue to have more to say about lived experiences and historical sociologists more to say about structural transformations (Abrams 1980).

Olivier Zunz defines the bottom line: "Context does matter in interdisciplinary discourse" (1985, 38). Boundaries of time, place, and person constitute subdisciplinary interests that structure the academic communities where scholars communicate. They shape the logic by which separate disciplines approach evidence, comparison, and causation (Roy in "Comment and Debate" 1987, 27). This institutional framework, L. L. Cornell points out ("Comment and Debate" 1987), is visible in the seminal works that define the field. Theda Skocpol's *Vision and Method in Historical Sociology* (1984) is organized by important individuals. Consequently history modifies sociology. Olivier Zunz's *Reliving the Past: The Worlds of Social History* (1985) is organized by geographic region and conventional historical distinctions based on time and place. Consequently social science modifies history.

Analytic orientations derive from divisions of labor in parent disciplines. While appearing to loosen boundaries by articulating zones of interdependence, Cornell cautions, ultimately new work can contribute to the social construction and reproduction of boundaries within parent disciplines by returning to the time-place specialties of history and the methodological-institutional-theoretical specialties of sociology. These tendencies do not minimize the impact or the importance of interactions. Social history continues to challenge conventional divisions of labor and internal boundaries. It raises basic questions about the relation between theory, method, and evidence. Nevertheless, as long as the disciplines remain socially segmented, more extensive comparison will be deterred and generalization will remain limited.

The relationship between history and social theory is a parallel example. Philip Abrams once suggested that sociology as a theoretical discipline and history as an empirical discipline have been "happily drifting towards one another for several years" (1980, 4). Their border, though, is often jealously guarded by arguments that brand analysis on the other side of the fence, in Peter Knapp's spirited characterization (1984), as "pernicious, fraudulent, or merely irrelevant." The belief that scientific explanation of the general is separate from humanistic understanding of the particular acts as a kind of moat, despite observed regularities in social theory that are based on historical context and milieu. In the debate over the covering law of history, one side pictures the social sciences as producers of theory while the other side portrays history as the supplier of examples. Theories, like power tools, presumably sit on a shelf until a historian or a social theorist needs a hole drilled or a board sawed. At that point application of theory is no longer problematic. Meanwhile, the other side depicts the gap as even bigger, with historians constructing and employing a kind of theory entirely different from and incompatible with the theories being used in social science (Knapp 1984, 34).

In recent years many scholars consider the relationship between sociology and history to be receding. Social history, once a radical alternative, has become institutionalized as one part of the mainstream. It is no longer regarded as idiosyncratic and has even become the object of attacks by poststructuralists. Current practices suggest that social history is likely to continue in this direction, contained and compartmentalized, not challenging the limits of conventional sociology and the myopia implicit in historical understanding of sociological topics. Historical sociologists appear to have settled for acceptance as another special area. Comparative historical sociology remains a minority orientation within the discipline, despite the prominence of individual practitioners and awards for distinguished scholarship. The relationship is not a general one but a set of affiliations. These affiliations are based on part of a subset of sociologists who specialize in historical topics and often draw data or authoritative descriptions from published historical works in order to construct relatively conventional sociological analyses. The ultimate test of whether sociology overcomes its self-distancing will lie in whether sociologists begin to "think historically," to recognize the historical context of their work, to use historical data, and to make historical structuration and change a basic part of the way the social world is conceptualized (Calhoun 1992, 156–59, 168–69).

At present, anthropology and literary theory have moved into the ascendancy of interdisciplinary influences on history. Some of the most influential work emanates from efforts to recast intellectual history as cultural history. The long-standing taboo against self-conscious theorizing among historians has also been broken by social history borrowings from the social sciences and intellectual history borrowings from literary theory and philosophy. An emerging body of theoretically self-conscious historical work refutes earlier depictions of history as disengaged from the social sciences. Dissenting voices, nonetheless, have little use for sociological history. A telling number of sociologists are skeptical of the turn toward historical work, especially when it means moving away from sophisticated quantitative methods (Calhoun 1992, 153, 164–69). The current emphasis on history and literary interpretation in anthropology has little in common with the anthropology that looks to archaeology or physical anatomy (Clifford in Winkler 1987, A15).

The boundary work revealed by the rhetorical turn and history's relations with its neighbors is no less evident at the very point where interdisciplinary development is often portrayed as reaching its highest point—the formation of a new hybrid discipline.

Interdisciplines

In summarizing the sense of the pioneer seminar on interdisciplinarity, held by the OECD at Nice in 1970, J. R. Gass proclaimed, "The 'inter-discipline' of today is the 'discipline' of tomorrow" (*Interdisciplinarity* 1972, 9). In 1984, at the OECD's second international meeting on interdisciplinarity, Keith Clayton branded the idea the "Nice nonsense." The popular version of the Nice nonsense is the belief that a successful interdisciplinary field becomes "just another discipline." The assumption is widespread, but it is an oversimplification. Interdisciplines differ in origin, character, status, and level of development.

Interactions at this level correspond to Paxson's level 4. They address internal imperatives, not the external imperatives of instrumental problem solving. They arise for a number of reasons. An interrelationship may be postulated between entities examined in one discipline and those examined in another. In biology, reconceptualization of genes as part of chromosomes tied genetics to molecular biology. Or two disciplines may become conceptually connected while retaining different but overlapping foci, principles, or theories. Physics and chemistry, for example, were linked through the "bridge laws" of thermodynamics. Or one discipline may be absorbed into another, as astronomy was absorbed into physics. Or two disciplines may join into a more general single discipline through the translatability of their fundamental principles, as the geometric and arithmetic sciences became unified into one mathematical science (Paxon 1996).

When disciplines come together, a process of horizontal integration is theoretically under way (Pagels 1988, 41–42). Horizontal integration alters the architectonics of knowledge by strengthening connections outside what is regarded as the discipline proper. Wolf Lepenies used the term "run-through categories" to name categories of knowledge that structure problem areas in comparable ways within different disciplines. Normalcy, for example, ran through varied regions of the human and social sciences, physiology, and medicine from the tenth century forward. Likewise, the model of the organism runs through medicine and politics (1978, 58). Run-through categories are akin to boundary concepts. They have the capacity to characterize several disciplines or parts of them, thereby weakening other divisions of labor, exposing gaps between them, and stimulating cross-fertilization. Transmutation of categories renders definition of a field a theoretical problem, not a matter of conventional agreement. It fixes a new field of focus, implying a new division of labor, redistribution of resources, realignment of institutional structures, and redefinition of epistemological and ontological premises (Landau, Proshansky, and Ittelson 1962, 14–15).

When a new field of focus forms, it does not escape boundary work (Dogan and Pahre 1990, 100). Comparison of three frequently cited exemplars— social psychology, molecular biology, and biochemistry—shows why an interdiscipline is not "just another discipline."

Represented initially by the work of Allport, Sherif, Chapman, Volkmann, and others, social psychology deals with problems that lie between sociology and psychology. A visible separation from its parent disciplines was apparent in 1908 when two textbooks with the words "social psychology" in their titles were published, one by the psychologist William McDougall, the other by the sociologist E. A. Ross. This point of origin marks the shared, interstitial character of the new hybrid discipline, though it minimizes its complex pattern of embeddedness in philosophy, *Völkerpsychologie,* social history, and psychiatry. The golden age of social psychology occurred over a twenty-five-year period that spanned World War II and the postwar years. It was characterized by a great wave of enthusiasm for an "interdisciplinary" social psychology and establishment of training programs and research centers in several major U.S. universities (House 1977).

By the mid-1960s the golden age had vanished. By the 1970s social psychology was segmented along three lines: *psychological social psychology,* focused on individual psychological processes as they related to social stimuli and emphasizing the use of laboratory experimental methods; *symbolic interactionism,* concentrated on face-to-face social interaction processes and using participant observation and informal interviewing in natural settings; and *psychological sociology,* centered on the reciprocal relationship between social structure and individual social psychological behavior and relying mainly on survey methods (also labeled "social structure and personality") (House 1977; Sewell 1989, 88). By the time this trifurcation was apparent, William Sewell recalls, social psychology had attained a strong presence in psychology departments but was on the decline in sociology.

As the trappings of an interstitial discipline emerged—programs and departments at major universities, new research centers, graduate student interest, and training grants—prospects for institutionalizing social psychology seemed strong. The field had access to funds from the National Institute of Mental Health (NIMH), though it received less than other branches of psychology and sociology. Funding needed to be justified based on relevance to mental health. It was more readily available for research and training in medical sociology, social problems, urban problems, juvenile delinquency, substance abuse, and aging. These areas involved social psychological research, but they competed with social psychology programs. In addition, national survey research centers at Michigan and Chicago were underused as sites for training, and no unified body of social psychological theory emerged. The explanatory power of social psychology theories and models remained relatively modest, providing small but statistically significant results. Improvements in theory were usually made in relatively isolated bodies of special social psychological theories, such as small-group processes and interpersonal relations.

Over the past twenty years, the proportionate role of psychology in the joint field has increased, especially with the declining prominence of attitude-survey methods. A considerable number of sociologists still consider themselves social psychologists and relate their work closely to that of colleagues in psychology. This link is strong in topical interdisciplinary fields such as human development, life course studies, and family studies. In other fields, such as small-group research, sociologists have all but disappeared. In the curriculum, social psychology is now a catchall category that lumps symbolic interaction, studies of groups and interpersonal relations, much of cultural sociology, studies of the life course, and the work of Erving Goffman and ethnomethodologists. The most important change in the relationship may well lie outside the joint subfield of social psychology, in the declining concern of general (or macro) sociological theorists for establishing a psychological grounding for their theories or a complement to them (Calhoun 1992, 170–71).

A significant amount of what is regarded as the best social psychological research is now being conducted by sociologists who do not identify with social psychology per se. They identify with specialties such as sociology of education, sociology of the family, medical sociology, sociology of the life course, sociology of gender roles, and sociology of the emotions. In many cases sociologists working on similar problems are unaware of each other's research and use different names to describe the same phenomena (R. Turner 1991, 70). The reasons social psychology failed to achieve its initial promise, Sewell concluded, are linked to a complex set of conditions. Some conditions are specific to social psychology, especially its theory and method. Two are more generic: the traditional institutional structure of American universities and the place social sciences hold in that structure; and the system of funding science that has become institutionalized in the United States and the unfavorable position of the social sciences in that system.

In contrast to social psychology, Sewell explains, interdisciplinary programs in the natural sciences fared better. Molecular biology was spurred by significant theoretical breakthroughs stemming from discovery of the structure of DNA, powerful new instruments, and complex research problems. The problems were solved by bringing together the skills and knowledge of physicists, chemists, geneticists, bacteriologists, zoologists, and botanists. In the early years most scientists who were involved maintained their departmental connections, performing research in teams. The level of cooperation between parent departments and new programs of molecular biology was never uniformly high, yet these programs did not face the level of resistance that social psychology encountered from parent departments. Adequate funding was available for researchers, graduate students, and the vital infrastructure of research, composed of new buildings, laboratories, and equipment. In some cases molecular biology was even able to attain full departmental status (Sewell 1989, 95–96).

The field of biochemistry evolved from development of a clear conception of what was thought to be involved in intermediate chemical processes of metabolism. As biochemistry evolved, it might have continued at the crossroads between the two general disciplines of physiology and chemistry. It might even have become an applied area of organic chemistry and a foundational part of physiology. By the 1930s, however, the field had coalesced into a well-defined discipline with its own domain at its own level of inquiry (chemical reactions involving macromolecules that perform physiological functions), its own theoretical schemes (most notably the citric acid cycle), and its own research problems and techniques (Abdelal 1986, 55; Bechtel 1986a, 101).

The researchers who developed biochemistry came from a variety of backgrounds. They had a shared cognitive interest in enzymes as key agents in life processes. The early members came from pharmacology, physiological and pathological chemistry, organic chemistry, experimental zoology, bacteriology and immunology, and immunology and hygiene. In the late 1930s biochemistry was not a homogeneous consensual community. It was a heterogeneous collection of programs adapted to diverse institutional niches. The common core was a specific theory of life or a research agenda. The core was constituted by a growing collection of techniques and problem solutions explored as strategies for program building in particular institutions. Techniques and their instrumentalities were more stable than the differing and often conflicting theories they supported. Three strategies emerged for constructing the new discipline: the first was broadly biological, the second physiological and biophysical in orientation, and the third oriented toward clinical medicine (Lenoir 1993, 81–82).

Today biochemistry is a recognized name for academic departments. It has its own professional organization, subsocieties, and journals. It is not, however, a homologous entity. The name "biochemistry" often occurs in conjunction with other disciplinary names, and conflict continues between those who adopt the name "molecular biology" and those who claim molecular biology is simply a subarea of biochemistry (Bechtel 1986a, 77). Conventionally defined, biochemistry and molecular biology differ in an important respect. Both biochemistry and biophysics extended chemical and physical approaches, respectively, into biological territory without questioning the positivistic scientific order that is based on colonization of some disciplines by more "basic" ones. In contrast, molecular biology contested the prevailing reductionist scientific order by searching for parity between physics and biology as a new basis for scientific unity. The basis for modern studies in molecular biology lies in the premise that all biological phenomena can be explained in physicochemical terms (Abir-Am 1987, 33; Abdelal 1986, 57).

The simple branching of knowledge and the simple confrontation of specialist branches are common explanatory models of interdisciplinary activity. The formation of molecular biology, though, was not a simple matter of one branch of research proliferating into a new field. Its development entailed a complex series of syntheses across physics, biology, genetics, and biochemistry. The problem of deciphering the DNA code was solved only after extensive migrations of physicists and chemists to the field (Bechtel 1986b, 33; Mullins 1973). In the process multiple boundaries were crossed. A series of reformulations and recrystallizations of ideas occurred across social groups and parts of those groups; across research areas and parts of those areas; across knowledges originating in different milieus and specialties; and across national, cultural, or local institutional orientations within what, broadly speaking, could be counted as the same specialty (Hoch 1987a, 483).

Molecular biology relocated the essence or very basis of life to the physical-chemical structure of one component of the cell—the gene. In the process, the concept of "life" was redefined and the goals of biological science were recast. Biology was transformed from a discipline that described organisms to a discipline that experimented with genetic materials. Molecular biology also illustrates the link between cognitive development and social control of institutional mechanisms and assets. The rise of molecular biology in the 1960s was predicated on a range of preceding and succeeding policy actions that enabled ongoing contacts between biological and physical scientists, especially bacterial geneticists and X-ray crystallographers of proteins and nucleic acids. The key discoveries were made in research institutes supported by government initiatives in science policy during the postwar period and in the late 1950s (Abir-Am 1985, 110; 1987, 27, 44).

Molecular biology, Evelyn Fox-Keller adds, illustrates the relation between social and material forms of power. Physics and physicists provided a resource of greater importance than particular skills. Their social authority played an influential role in reframing the character and goals of biological science:

> This borrowing proceeded in a variety of ways: first, by borrowing an agenda which was seen as looking like that of physics; second, by borrowing the very names of physicists. Indeed, even the borrowing of purely technical expertise, ostensibly in the name of making biology "better," was instrumental in reframing biology, in making it different. And in all of this borrowing—of agenda, language, attitude, names, technique—the material underpinning of the social power of twentieth-century physics and physicists lay in close view, evoking in some at least the hope that the technological prowess of physics was perhaps also borrowed. (1993, 57)

Molecular biology was not only a set of concepts but a sociopolitical restructuring and dislocation of the traditional scientific order. An empirically grounded disciplinary pattern of scientific authority gave way to increasingly "transdisciplinary" patterns that were based more in theory than in empirical phenomenology. Social control shifted from boundary obstacles and strict identification with a discipline of original training toward a looser feedback mechanism among skills, people, problems, technologies, and concepts from differing disciplines. Shifts in social control were enabled by a science policy that relaxed tight control of academic disciplines, encouraging the flow of large numbers of people across disciplinary boundaries and stimulating alternative modes of research funding (Abir-Am 1985, 74, 108–11).

An important lesson emerges from the analysis of boundary work across levels of interaction. Disruption and difference play important, productive roles in interdisciplinary work. There are, Roland Barthes once observed, few genuine breaks. "Interdisciplinarity is not the calm of an easy security." It begins *effectively,* in contrast to a mere declaration or wish, when the solidarity of existing disciplines breaks down. This breakdown may occur suddenly, even "violently," through disruptions of fashion and the interests of new objects or new languages that lack a place in the fields being brought together. The starting point is an "unease in classification." From there a "certain mutation" may be detected. This mutation must not be overestimated: "it is more in the nature of an epistemological slide than a break" (1977, 155).

The metaphors of mutation and slide parallel a third metaphor—noise. William Paulson (1991) likens interdisciplinarity to the concept of self-organization from noise. The idea comes from information theory. When there is noise in an electronic channel during transmission, the information received is diminished by a function known as ambiguity of the message. The message received is neither pure nor simple. Importing terms and concepts from other disciplines creates a kind of noise in the knowledge system. Perceived as unwanted noise in one context, variety and interference can become information in a new or reorganized context. Paulson illustrates with a typical intellectual problem in the humanities, the relation between a reader and a literary text. In becoming aware of a new relation, the reader creates a new context in which a previously disruptive event or variety is reread. New meaning is constructed out of what first appeared to be noise as the exchange of codes and information across boundaries was occurring.

Put another way, noise becomes a signal. Noise, Gregory Bateson suggested in *Steps to an Ecology of Mind,* is the only source of new patterns. "What appears to be a perturbation in a given system," Paulson adds, "turns out to be the intersection of a new system with the first." This view of interdisciplinarity underscores the roles of disequilibrium, complexity, and emergence. Whatever is extrasystemic at one level may be taken as an index of another level, another system with a new kind of coding. Interdisciplinary cognition is located in the attempt to construct meaning out of what initially seems to be noise (Paulson 1991, 44, 49; Bateson 1972, 410; Atlan 1983, 123). Noise occurs in the introduction of a borrowing, in addressing technical problems by drawing on competing perspectives, in developing hybrid interests, and in disrupting and restructuring of traditional practices.

The unsettling of existing assumptions is much in evidence in the case studies that follow. They provide models of boundary studies at three different levels: interdisciplinary fields, individual disciplines, and national research systems.

Part 2
Boundary Studies

CHAPTER 4

Interdisciplinary Studies

Most of the interdisciplinary programs were responses—of a very limited sort—to the demands of praxis: immediate service to interested sponsors and clients able to pay for them. They did not arise out of the inner necessity of the evolution of thought. . . . The immediate nature of these interdisciplinary responses, in institutions not otherwise sensitive to the demands of their times, suggests that there has been something superficial, even contrived, about them. In fact, all of these groupings have had little intellectual effect on the universities; they have left the disciplinary structure intact. Moreover, they have produced an administrative sort of expertise in their own fields, rather than original thought or scholarship. They have not, in other words, extended our view of the world, but rather have constituted routinized responses to changes in that view which were determined elsewhere—in the society's centers of decision and power.

Norman Birnbaum, "The Arbitrary Disciplines," 1969

There is, however, no possibility for the return of traditional classifications within which knowledge can be contained. But it is not a question of interdisciplinary studies replacing traditional departments. More likely is the persistence of departmental boundaries within which a permanent crisis exists, a crisis that has already produced efforts to co-opt the new cultural studies. This is accomplished by declaring, even when there is little or no comprehension, that the given discipline is prepared to accommodate the new without surrendering an inch of ground except under extreme duress.

Stanley Aronowitz, "The Punishment of Disciplines," 1991

A place on the map is also a place in history.

Adrienne Rich, "Notes toward a Politics of Location," 1986

M apping interdisciplinary studies of the second kind is not an easy task. The hybridity of their underlying categories of knowledge, the heterogeneity of practices that advance those categories, and their variegated institutional topography complicate description. Their history and description, moreover, are scattered across a wide array of forums, from the literatures of disciplinary, professional, and interdisciplinary fields to educational theory, institutional histories, and new studies of knowledge practices. Scattered though they are, accounts of interdisciplinary studies have a striking feature in common. They have a strong narrative component. By telling personal and institutional stories, scholars and teachers situate themselves in a collective "lifeworld." Lifeworld, in the Habermasian sense, means the totality of socio-cultural facts, events, and objects that constitute a field of knowledge. Inter-disciplinary stories occur not only in texts but also in the ongoing work of contesting a disputed past and constructing an alternative future.

Any selection of examples is necessarily an arbitrary choice from a multi-tude of possibilities. The following paired examples of "urban" and "envi-ronment," "border" and "area," "women" and "culture" allow comparative analysis of how social space and cognitive space are reconfigured. Another major example, American studies, is discussed in the next chapter, since it is so closely tied to the history of literary studies.

Urban and Environment

"Urban" and "environmental" studies are leading examples of interdiscipli-nary studies that arose during the era of the 1960s and 1970s. Their parallel trajectories also shed light on the entwined intellectual and institutional dy-namics of interdisciplinary categories of knowledge.

Urban

Study of urban phenomena predates the emergence of urban programs in universities. The urban focus of many disciplines expanded after World War II, but no single discipline had organized inquiry or modes of applying knowledge in a way that made it a logical vehicle for responding to urban crises during the 1960s. Daniel Rich and Robert Warren, who have written a genealogical account of the field, view the emergence of a set of self-defined and self-contained programs as a comprehensive market response—in eco-nomic, social, and academic terms. The economic signals were clear and strong. Between 1959 and 1974 the Ford Foundation allotted $36 million in hopes of applying academic skills directly to urban problems. During the middle and late 1960s, the United States government supplied even larger amounts for solution-oriented training, research, and services. It also allotted payments for advice and consulting services for setting up, operating, and evaluating federally initiated urban projects (Rich and Warren 1980, 53–54). Norman Birnbaum's charge of opportunism in the opening epigraph is cor-rect, to the extent that one of the motives for establishing an urban-related program was, in many cases, ensuring that a local campus got its share of available funding.

Economic capital was not the only factor. The necessary social capital was also in place, in the form of widening public concern about poverty, racism, and environmental deterioration. Faith in the capacity for problem solving was reinforced by two precedents: accelerated production of engineers after the 1957 launching of the Soviet spaceship *Sputnik,* and accelerated production of degrees in special education in the 1970s. The transfer of technology and skills to the problem of space flight is a striking parallel, though targeted calls for certification of graduates to perform designated tasks differed from a general demand for solutions to complex social problems. Initial hopes ran high. Universities, especially those with interdisciplinary urban programs, were regarded as "ready-made Cape Canaverals" capable of channeling new technologies into cities through applied research and expert advice. A second form of social capital derived from militant demands and popular support for greater social and economic equity (Rich and Warren 1980, 54–55).

The rise of urban studies occurred at a significant point in interdisciplinary history. In the 1960s and 1970s interdisciplinary studies enjoyed unprecedented support. One of the arguments legitimated by the institutionalization of new programs was that disciplinary boundaries made it difficult, if not impossible, to address urban issues and the social problems that cities were experiencing. The emergence of urban affairs is linked to social and political upheavals that sparked not only government social programs but also new academic journals, a handful of new programs, new curricula, and research and degree-granting centers (Schmandt and Wendel 1988, 3–4). The organizational possibilities of interdisciplinary fields were enhanced by demands for reducing barriers between the university and its communities. Interdisciplinarity was not the primary motivation. It rarely if ever is. In newly forming urban programs, educational innovation, greater equity and upward mobility for students were primary goals, along with crossing the boundary between university and community. Nonetheless, these goals enhanced the prospect of interdisciplinary approaches (Rich and Warren 1980, 55).

Other developments created a favorable climate. Alongside the rapid emergence of undergraduate and graduate programs in urban affairs and urban studies, urban and regional planning programs were expanding beyond their traditional focus on design and land use. Urban and regional economics also emerged as an identifiable field. The birth of new scholarly journals over a relatively brief period documented the self-reinforcing growth of societal interests, university programs, and research dollars. The journal *Urban Studies* appeared in 1964, *Urban Affairs Quarterly* in 1965, *Regional [Science] and Urban Economics* in 1971, the *Journal of Urban Economics* in 1974, and the *International Journal of Urban and Regional Research* in 1977. Three decades later the mood had changed ("Introduction" 1993, 229–30). The reasons are both specific to the category "urban" and generic to the prospects of interdisciplinary studies.

The first decades in urban affairs were marked by creation of new units, experiments with innovative teaching methods, applications of academic skills to community problems, and political activism. These activities took priority over establishing an appropriate niche in university bureaucracies, achieving consensus on the content and boundaries of the intellectual field, and building effective communication among dispersed networks and individuals. By the early 1970s, consolidating the institutional status of more than two hundred programs was becoming a matter of concern. Across local programs, there was no uniform balance of teaching, research, and service components. The vagaries of local projects, lack of sufficient incentives for community service, nonpublishable research, and failure to establish a system of university extension agents were major reasons. A similar diversity characterized research and service units arrayed across renamed bureaus of government service that provided technical assistance to local governments and extension programs. These units dealt directly with minority groups and the poor. A similar diversity was evident in interdisciplinary theoretical and applied research centers that were, by and large, unevenly integrated with teaching programs. This diversity reflected the richness of the field and the multiple needs it served. Yet isolated components have a heightened vulnerability (Rich and Warren 1980, 55–56).

Diversity was not the only challenge. During the 1970s the economic and social capital that enabled urban programs eroded significantly. The United States economy declined at the same time as public support and academic values began shifting. Diminishing support for educational experimentation meant that all but the healthiest programs suffered. As a result, the field fell short on the critical mass scale. It was further affected by a process of *re*professionalization. Market signals moved in new directions, away from normative commitments, and the powerful social movements that had earlier turned to academe for problem solving weakened. As this occurred, demands mounted for research on productivity and the training of urban administrators in fiscal management skills. As a result of these shifts, visibility and support lessened. The distinguishing points of founding programs—interdisciplinary experimentation, innovative teaching, and extension services—declined as budget priorities in many universities. Some programs were strong enough to survive; others repositioned themselves in response to new market signals. Local political economy, though, was a greater factor in program survival than coalescence of a mature intellectual field (Rich and Warren 1980, 56–59).

Intellectual identity was caught up in these changes. Periodic identity crises in interdisciplinary studies are related to low degrees of conceptual coherence in their related fields of knowledge (Miller 1982, 13). Debate usually centers on whether the field in question constitutes a discipline, an interdisciplinary field, or in pertinent cases, a profession. Urban affairs lacks the necessary resources and commitment to become a discipline, in the sense of having developed a deductive theoretical and empirical base for a distinctive body of knowledge. It tends to be an importer rather than an exporter or an autonomous generator of knowledge. Its concepts, theories, and much of its data are borrowed from other fields and disciplines (Rich and Warren 1980, 59).

The research published in *Urban Affairs Quarterly* from 1965 to 1987 reveals a broad range of subjects, from local politics in Gary, Indiana, to urban social movements in Third World countries. This diversity, though, masks the fact that urban research is dominated by political scientists, sociologists, and to a lesser extent economists. In recent years the economic concept of city as marketplace has gained prominence, but in research the city has been conceptualized primarily as a legal-political unit. Of 722 contributing authors, of whom 680 could be identified with a specific discipline, 37 percent were political scientists, 28 percent sociologists, and 11 percent economists. The rest came from other disciplines, including geography, anthropology, history, planning, education, and business management (Schmandt and Wendel 1988, 5–6, 24–25).

Institutional critical mass is an added factor. The limited scale of individual and collective programs, coupled with a limited number of faculty and staff at the graduate level, may be below the threshold needed for sustained theoretical and empirical research. After three decades, few campuses have enough faculty to do graduate teaching, conduct research, and perform extension services. When a critical number of faculty has been reached, the urban unit has usually been part of a larger public affairs program. This institutional condition limits the possibilities of autonomy (Rich and Warren 1980, 58–59). There are also insufficient opportunities for collective work. In 1993 Rich and Warren reaffirmed the conclusion they reached in their earlier genealogy: "The combined absence of a collective commitment to the generation of new knowledge, a critical mass of advanced research and graduate programs, and a well-developed communication network among faculty and staff all act against disciplinary growth. Yet, if this particular model were abandoned as a formal option for urban affairs, a certain minimal conceptual growth and clarity would still be necessary to fulfill virtually any other option for collective development" (1980, 60; 1993 telephone interview).

Any option—disciplinary, professional, or interdisciplinary—requires a level of coherence and critical mass. Professional and paraprofessional models imply standards of appropriate behavior, agreed-on values, a specified collective orientation, and an intended clientele. In urban programs the most visible academic success has been master's level training of students who find employment in nonacademic jobs, typically in the public sector. Public service careers will likely continue to be the arenas where external funding is applied. Special claims for urban focus, though, must still be distinguished from other aspiring public service professions that are present in overlapping domains, especially public administration, policy science, city management, and urban planning (Rich and Warren 1980, 59–61). These overlaps are apparent in the varied naming of the field as "urban affairs," "urban studies," "regional planning," "metropolitan studies," "city planning," and "urban planning" (Collin 1989, 1).

The boundary separating university and society is also implicated. The integrative rhetoric of fields with normative components implies that academic and applied activities are mutually supportive. Scant evidence exists, though, to prove this occurs naturally. Rich and Warren's findings apply across all interdisciplinary studies with strong normative components. Local research and service projects have frequently been "amorphous, sporadic, and of variable durations," thus difficult to integrate with academic programs. For their part, universities have rarely provided sufficient incentives to overcome the chronic imbalance in rewards for faculty production of publications versus nonpublishable research and community service. The original concept of university-based urban extension agents proved less viable than anticipated and in most cases has been abandoned (1980, 56–57).

The question of interdisciplinary identity is just as complicated. Early expectations were based on an all-encompassing definition of the field that included anything related to the city or region where a campus was located. More recent versions have expanded to include anything "public," a diffuse and encompassing view at odds with the notion of a discrete academic program defined by specific teaching, research, and service functions. Efforts to achieve synthesis have usually aimed at finding appropriate mixes of disciplinary inputs and providing additive value to participating disciplines, not interdisciplinary coherence. Shortfalls of integration are apparent in two ways: in the naive assumption that an interdisciplinary product will emerge spontaneously from mixing different disciplinarians in classrooms; and in overhead umbrella structures that shelter an immense variety of esoteric or traditional interests (Rich and Warren 1980, 60).

The commitment to interdisciplinary research continues to be affirmed in editorial policy statements of journals with an urban focus. Whether the claim is valid or not depends on how the term is defined. Schmandt and Wendel (1988) identified three operative definitions in the research results published in *Urban Affairs Quarterly (UAQ)*. In the first instance, investigators draw on theoretical constructs and methods from other disciplines. This is a common practice in contemporary social science research and much of the work being done in the urban field. In the second, the efforts of specialists from various disciplines are brought to bear on particular urban phenomena. This is a frequent occurrence in *UAQ*, since many authors focus on the same problems or issues. The third operative definition entails close and active collaboration of two or more specialists from different disciplines on a shared research project. The last form occurs less frequently. Judging by publications, most teamwork in urban research appears to have taken place between scholars from the same discipline.

Absence is as important as presence. Despite interest in the interplay between public and private sectors, Schmandt and Wendel found, urban scholars still pay less attention to the role of nongovernment institutions as urban policymakers. Topics that do not lend themselves to mathematical treatment are also underrepresented, and seldom are philosophical and ethical questions addressed. Among contemporary urban researchers, grand theory in the style of classical sociology has lost much of its appeal. They tend to relate theory more directly to policy issues and problems. The exceptions are neo-Marxist work and the theoretical approaches of models of global dimension in public choice.

The current mixture of subjects, topics, and interests underscores the sense that an "interdisciplinary pluralism" prevails. Since the 1960s, conventional subjects such as electoral behavior, racial segregation, citizen attitudes, neighborhood roles, demographic trends, lifestyles, administrative management, and intergovernment relations have remained standard. Changes have occurred primarily in methodology and degree of quantification. The appearance of older topics in new guises indicates new or altered approaches to recognized problems and issues. The most obvious example is city revitalization. The shift to economic or market perspective, away from prior social-oriented views of urban problems, parallels deemphasis in national policy on large-scale social programs and increases in private-sector involvement. New and previously visible topics are also being investigated. They include service delivery, voluntarism, and coproduction, black suburbanization, structural shifts in the economy, fiscal austerity, and social networks. Some of these topics reflect the current trend toward privatization and the market concept. New developments have also stimulated topics or issues that previously failed to hold or to recapture interest. They include collapse of the metropolitan government movement as well as older research fads and topics that fell out of fashion, such as community power structure, advocacy planning and community control. Many of these interests also exhibit the reformist orientation characteristic of the 1960s (Schmandt and Wendel 1988, 5–9, 22–27).

Notable parallels appear in urban research interests within the disciplines of sociology (Gottdiener and Feagin 1988, Hutchison 1993), anthropology (Kemper 1991a, 1991b), and history. In history, for example, calls for innovation and responses to the "urban crisis" in history during the 1950s yielded the usual efforts—interdisciplinary conferences, individual efforts to absorb relevant literatures in ancillary disciplines, and mounting interdisciplinary programs and panprofessional associations. Interdisciplinary conferences and publications are vital forums for gathering scholarship that is dispersed across a variety of disciplines. Without these hybrid discourse structures, pertinent knowledge and information may not make their way into other disciplines until after approaches have been discredited or discarded in the disciplines where they originated. Yet individuals still wind up accused of dilettantism, of being "Jack of all trades, Master of none." Their graduate students, in turn, find little room in already crowded programs. Interdisciplinary programs offer courses, but they are not always able to promote and sustain active research across disciplinary lines. Consequently they continue to be consumers of interdisciplinary knowledge more than producers. Interdisciplinary associations often lack sufficient mechanisms for integrating the disparate research they encourage. As Theodore Hershberg put it, "They sustain interdisciplinary communication, but not interdisciplinary process" (1981, 26).

Where is urban studies now?

The varied names and program structures mark the nagging problem of identity. When Bingham, Henry, and Blair (1981) attempted to rank urban affairs graduate programs, they had trouble finding them. Of the fifty-six programs identified through a sourcebook and the Council of University Institutes for Urban Affairs, even the clear-cut cases presented complications. The director of a unit explicitly named Urban Studies and Planning Programs defined it as a professional program in urban and regional planning, not an urban studies program. One institution was eliminated from the survey because its designation—"Urban Life Faculty"—was considered too general. It encompassed 212 dispersed individuals. Other possibilities were eliminated because they had no core faculty or department in the traditional sense, even though they offered a degree in urban affairs or urban studies. With the final list culled to thirty-one "bona fide" units, the survey began. One of the excluded types, though, was programs that had a director and offered a graduate degree in urban affairs without a resident faculty. They drew on a group of courses in traditional academic departments. These structures are not uncommon in interdisciplinary studies. It is legitimate to exclude them from a formal survey of interdisciplinary programs when the criteria of selection stipulate integrating seminars and a coherent integrative philosophy. Yet cataloging programs and inventorying activity produce different pictures of a field (William H. Newell, pers. comm., 22 November 1994). The lesson of complex structure is that activities are more numerous than overtly named programs.

For several decades now "urban" has been a visible point of reference. Yet its viability as an interdisciplinary category continues to be threatened by intellectual drift. Urban projects and programs encompass descriptive, pragmatic, theoretical, and normative dimensions that are neither clearly nor fully integrated. Individual scholars and local programs have tended to focus on one dimension or another, not on their interdependencies and complementarities. Fields with strong normative components invest heavily in descriptive and pragmatic dimensions. However successful normative emphasis is in promoting problem solving, though, it limits theoretical development because of the short time horizons and rapid turnover endemic to project cycles. An added foreshortening of theory occurs in the pull of local needs and interests. Local needs, while vital to program identity and survival, tend to focus attention away from problems of urban systems in general. Even normative concerns, which played a major role in early development of urban programs, have not been elaborated, formalized, or focused. They have emerged, instead, as general claims of social relevance or stated commitments to the goals of equity and social justice. Theoretical and normative developments are interdependent, but their interdependency has not been adequately clarified (Rich and Warren 1980, 60).

Developing a "functional interdisciplinary orientation" in urban studies, Rich and Warren concluded, will likely depend less on particular teaching and research formats than on the evolution of a "state of mind and integrative capacity." Capstone core courses are one solution, but even the soundest curriculum does not substitute for long-term investment in conceptual growth or sustained communication among colleagues, students, and practitioners. Defining relations among component parts must be an ongoing activity, considering not just relations among pertinent disciplines but also related fields that are themselves loose umbrella structures for competing interests. Establishing a "center for gravity" is one solution. Centering, though, can impede interdisciplinary synthesis by fixing definition prematurely. In American studies this form of dominance occurred in the early influence of the myth-and-symbol and the consensus schools of thought.

In 1965, in the inaugural issue of *Urban Affairs Quarterly,* sociologist David Popenoe asked, "What is the focus of the field of urban studies and what are its boundaries?" Early supporters envisioned the field as predominantly problem oriented, normative, and prescriptive, open to the collaborations of academicians and practitioners. Over time the field became less normative and reformist, less inclined to build research-related bridges between academics and public functionaries, less confident that scholars can design effective social programs, and closer to the conventional social sciences most researchers come from. Nonetheless, despite erosion in the number of sponsored research opportunities, urban affairs persists as a distinct field of study and research. The emergence of an identifiable field has revitalized a neglected area of social science research. Through its research centers, academic programs, and scholarly journals, the field continues to play a vital role in focusing attention on urban phenomena and in providing common identity to a body of research that continues to grow (Schmandt and Wendel 1988, 4, 25–26).

Urban and regional studies are no longer growth industries ("Introduction" 1993, 230). Yet, the current editor of *Urban Studies* suggests, from the standpoint of research the field has grown significantly over the past few decades, despite the underlying Balkanization of territory that is driven by disciplinary boundaries and the diverse nature of problems posed by the category "urban." Significantly, the boundaries of the field are not strictly disciplinary. Over the past decade a global turn has been under way, heightening contextualized awareness of interconnections across urban spheres and the global economy (Andranovich and Riposa 1993, 15; "Editor's Introduction" 1992, 341).

The parallels in environmental studies are striking.

Environment

Environmental studies promised to do for the environment what urban programs promised to do for the city. Before the 1960s and 1970s environmental consciousness and concern were not prominent in the university or in government. During the late 1960s the advent of ecology and the rapid rise of environmental awareness generated popular support for the cause of saving the earth. Spurred by media coverage, a flurry of conferences, and some corrective legislation, the mounting of environmental programs followed. Like its urban counterpart, environmental studies entered universities on waves of social capital and interdisciplinary rhetoric.

A similar diversity of programs and courses emerged. Although they were significant in number, their structural identity was not always clear. Many existing programs simply added "environmental" to their titles. "Sanitary engineering," for example, became "environmental engineering," and "environment" replaced "conservation" in many course descriptions. Some departments contributed entire courses to an environmental studies program, such as environmental geology, environmental psychology, and environmental law. But this "syncretic assemblage" rarely resulted in synthesis. Instead of coalescing into a discrete field, Lynton Caldwell recalled in a genealogy of the field, environment-related aspects of the disciplines and professions were brought together into a curriculum that was and still is, "essentially eclectic" (1983, 249–51).

Like urban studies, environmental studies also suffered disengagements of economic and social capital during the late 1970s and early 1980s. Opinion polls documented continuing public support for environmental quality and protective measures, but moderate arguments for "balance," "common sense," and "reason" gained favor over radical action. This stance was reinforced in formulations of public policy. Except where mandated by statute, federal assistance ended for the most part with the Reagan administration. The Office of Environmental Education was discontinued, and many political supporters either left Congress or shifted their attention to other priorities. Environmental protection measures remain in place, but policy reversals in the form of budget cuts and eased regulatory measures have continued to undermine the environmental movement. In addition, several large private foundations dropped or significantly reduced their interests in environmental research and education (Caldwell 1983, 251–53).

Political shifts had analogues in academic structure and values. During the late 1960s new titles, courses, and programs conveyed the hope that academic institutions would cultivate good environmental citizenship and respect for nature. Prospects for achieving critical mass dimmed with economic cutbacks and competition from social programs focused on people-oriented issues such as poverty, racism, and war. By the early 1980s several universities were reviewing their environmental and natural resource–related programs, considering elimination. At roughly the same time, a shift in professional values occurred. Confidence in specialization, reductionist methods, statistical rationalization, and the primacy of economic considerations was reasserted (Caldwell 1983, 252). The parallel to urban studies is not a mere coincidence. The limits of traditional academic values were widely conceded, but these values were heavily relied on in formulating public policy. In a meeting with one hundred leaders of environmental studies programs in fifty-six universities, Russell Peterson found most of them felt they were treated as second-class citizens on their campuses. They have lost ground in budgets, degree approval, and faculty tenure cases (1990, 221).

The question of identity also yields parallel answers. Environmental studies encompasses the subject matter of many fields of knowledge, thereby straining the disciplinary concept. Like "urban," certain aspects of the "environment" have also become objects of professional and technical training and practice. This means relations need to be clarified with pertinent fields of practice, such as architecture, agriculture, engineering, law, and medicine, and the practical concerns of human society, such as pollution control, urban design, resource management, public health, and economic growth (Caldwell 1983, 248). In practical settings or in professional schools, one set of academic disciplines relates broadly to natural resources. This commitment is evident in schools of agriculture and natural resources. Another set, evident in schools of engineering and technology, relates to industry. Other areas, which may be classed as service sectors, relate to medicine, law, business, and finance. These multiple affiliations reflect divisions of rural/agricultural and urban/industrial sectors (Dahlberg 1986, 13). A secondary set of interests creates added conflict across divisions of the environmental issue. They take the form of segmented social and political commitments to air and water pollution, eutrophication of lakes and streams, degradation of landscapes, and decimation of wildlife (Caldwell 1983, 248).

In the related field of natural resources, two patterns of specialization have emerged. One is based in intellectual separation of natural resource systems from urban/industrial areas and problems. The other is based in disciplinary specialization. These patterns generate a number of intellectual and practical problems in universities. Tensions arise between practically oriented and theoretically oriented approaches and departments. Often couched in terms of "applied" versus "basic" research, these tensions reflect differences in approach and underlying rationale. Academic work on natural resources has tended to be strongly based on the natural sciences, although organizational separations are made between aspects related to resource exploitation and aspects related to conservation. These divisions manifest themselves organizationally in separate departments of soil science, plant physiology, forest management, and so on. Within the social sciences, separate subdisciplines or departments have tended to develop in agricultural economics, rural sociology, and economic geography. Until recently, little attempt was made to involve the humanities (Dahlberg 1986, 13).

The most common educational format has been a topical focus on "environment" in a coordinated multidisciplinary program. This is the least disruptive arrangement, but it still depends on cooperation from disciplines. It does not readily lead to new insights into environmental relationships or reveal gaps in scientific knowledge that handicap formulation of sound environmental policies. An applied problem focus may be adopted, but it will not automatically integrate disciplinary inputs unless a concerted effort is made to establish a hybrid interlanguage. The problem of synthesis is further implicated in the differing status accorded to holism, reductivism, and pluralism. Ecology emerged early as a lead framework, yet the idea of a holistic strategy for ecosystem development has been controversial. Theorists have erected complex systems, but general statements are criticized because they are not based on observation and testing. Pressure continues to jettison "multidisciplinary mish-mash" in favor of "real" science, defined in terms of reductionist approaches, observation, and testing (Caldwell 1983, 254).

Despite these difficulties, ecology remains an important locus for integration. A broad discipline, ecology is composed of linked subdisciplines that Likens (1992) depicts along a gradient extending from strictly biological concerns to strictly physical phenomena. Meteorology, geology, and hydrology exhibit an abiotic focus. Systematics, genetics, and physiology exhibit a biotic focus. In most subdisciplines, though, a mix of abiotic and biotic focus is necessary. Hence subdisciplines such as biogeochemistry, chemical ecology, and population ecology appear at points between abiotic and biotic ends of the gradient.

The number and diversity of journals, publications, and scientific societies that address ecological topics have also increased. New data, creative tests, and novel generalizations have been produced. New or neglected questions are being addressed, and use of ecological information has increased in such key areas as environmental policy and management, conservation biology, restoration ecology, watershed management, and global environmental change. This growth marks the hybridity of the underlying category of knowledge, but it also exacerbates fragmentation. As subdisciplines become more dense, they develop their own viewpoints and assumptions, definitions, lexicons, and methods. This divergence is apparent in the different meanings given to the same terms. "Regulation," "development," and "evolution" have different meanings in studies of population, community, and ecosystem ecology. Over time, as the conceptual frameworks of areas continue to diverge, interrelating subdisciplinary viewpoints becomes more difficult. Physiological ecology and biogeography, for instance, have common roots, but at present they barely intersect (Pickett, Kolasa, and Jones 1994, 3–5).

What might constitute a workable synthesis? Several answers have emerged all across interdisciplinary fields: a multidisciplinary matrix of disciplinary parts, a broad field with a particular disciplinary dominance, a metadiscipline that overrides special interests at a global level, or an open critique that permanently resists fixing identity. The parallel field of science, technology, and society (STS) offers an illuminating analogy. Like urban and environmental studies, STS arose from social upheavals of the 1960s and 1970s. Alongside emerging critiques of the idea of progress, cognate changes in a number of disciplines beckoned a shift away from internalist-oriented subdisciplines interested in history and philosophy of science and technology to more externalist and sociologically oriented interpretations of academic disciplines. STS programs now number approximately a hundred. Hundreds more courses, groups of courses, professional organizations, and assessment groups are concerned with STS issues. In an account of the field, Stephen Cutcliffe suggested that interdisciplinarity can be achieved from more than one perspective. Relations among multiple commitments and constituencies must be clarified, though, in a general way, at the level of theory (Cutcliffe 1989). This task is complicated by conflicting constructions of the field, ranging from business as usual and a strong science program to differing degrees of contingency (Fuller 1993, 11).

Ecology again provides a parallel, with generic points of importance to interdisciplinary fields highlighted. Whether *combining separate areas* into a new composite understanding or *extracting components of different areas* in order to produce a new understanding, the mechanics of integration and synthesis require a strong community. Strengthening the community may entail *progressive sharing of empirical and theoretical contents* or *focusing on a spe-*

cific linking relationship. Integration can occur at *any scale or breadth of scope,* from a finer scale that combines models relatively close in focus and approach to a grander scale that links disparate approaches to ecology. Components of prior theories may be excluded, but *contradictions between theories* may require developing deeper theories that expose unity among phenomena. This step has occurred in current theories of the four fundamental forces in modern physics. Perhaps the important general lesson is that integration is not necessarily a matter of reductionism or grand unity. It may involve *nested hierarchies* of several broad theories that might yield a novel integration (Pickett, Kolasa, and Jones 1994, 129–34).

The category "urban" provides a parallel on another count, Realistically, Rich and Warren concluded, synthesis is more likely to emerge from "a tentative and shifting coalescence of concepts" (1980, 60, 65). After three decades, there is no precise or commonly used definition of "urban," though most definitions include the interrelation between people and space. The literature reflects the continuing diversity of topics, backgrounds, and methodologies. Multiple paradigms mark conflicts over basic assumptions, choice of methods, and the relation between basic research and application. Some convergence has occurred in shared theories and methodologies. Convergence is also suggested by the general agreement that urban research should include the characteristics of urban space, the organization of institutions and processes underlying urban political, social, and economic relations, and links between urban centers and their relations with the larger political system, society, and the economy. Often a single topic functions as a matrix of underlying processes and outcomes. Research on urban economic development, for instance, involves examining issues such as local political institutions and processes, intergovernmental policies and policymaking, regional labor markets and transportation systems, and educational and cultural institutions. Each component, in turn, may fuel further research projects. The curriculum echoes this diversity, encompassing courses such as anthropology, architecture, economics, geography, history, political science, planning, and sociology in addition to explicitly interdisciplinary programs (Andranovich and Riposa 1993, 3–5).

The shared conceptual problem at stake in all interdisciplinary studies is how best to move beyond narrow sectoral interests that make environment, urban, and other hybrid categories one more competing special interest, not a representation of general interests. Interdisciplinary categories are organizational and intellectual principles that focus attention on the importance of clarifying and bridging the ways that different approaches and overlapping fields of interest order knowledge (after Caldwell 1983, 254). Evaluation is complicated by their relative youth. Questions of scope and content are still unanswered, and for most fields academic status remains unsettled. The lessons of critical mass underscore the importance of a collective commitment to generation and synthesis of new knowledge, an adequate number of advanced research and graduate programs, and a stable infrastructure of communication networks, meetings, publications, and flow of students into programs. The key element in stimulating an infrastructure of community is dialogue. Dialogue opens up lines of communication within which there may be—indeed should be—competing answers (Rich and Warren 1980, 65).

Ultimately the problem of interdisciplinary studies is the problem of fit. The metaphor of fit, Caldwell concluded from the experience of environmental studies, prejudges the epistemological problem at stake. Interdisciplinary categories arise because of a perceived misfit among need, experience, information, and the prevailing structure of knowledge embodied in disciplinary organization. If the structure must be changed to accommodate the new field, perhaps the structure itself is part of the problem. Environmental and urban studies, like all studies of the second kind, represent "a latent and fundamental restructuring of knowledge and formal education" (Caldwell 1983, 247–49). They mark the broader move into complex structure, and they operate as boundary concepts. The boundary work of advancing interdisciplinary claims pulls them centripetally toward specific investments. At the same time, they respond to and stimulate centrifugal movement toward hybrid constructs. As a result they wind up caught between their shadow location and pressure to fit into the surface structure by establishing legitimacy in a political economy that forces them into competition for resources with more strongly positioned disciplines. Legitimacy, though, may come at a high price—the loss of openness that gave rise to interdisciplinary claims in the first place.

Border and Area

"Border" and "area" name fields of geographic location. They are also powerful metaphors of interdisciplinary study. They offer a comparison at strikingly different levels of scale. Border studies refers here to a particular area, the United States–Mexico region. Area studies is border studies writ large, on the map of the world. Even at different levels, they confront common issues of critical mass, identity, and synthesis.

Border

Interest in border regions is not new. During the nineteenth century, European conquest and the archival material generated by conquest produced a sizable body of published work about border zones. This knowledge consisted largely of descriptions of indigenous peoples, diaries, personal narratives, commentaries, and testimonies. Opinion differs on the origin of a distinct field of interest concentrated on the United States–Mexico borderland. At least a half dozen phases have been identified, each characterized by pioneering efforts that were in turn dependent on accomplishments in prior phases (Stoddard 1982, 211). The earliest studies tended to reflect the outlook of a single discipline or a blend of closely associated disciplines. Together they fleshed out a historical and ethnographic picture of the United States–Mexico border region. This picture was not without the same lingering strains of romanticism that also characterized forerunners of area studies.

In several genealogical accounts, Ellwyn Stoddard (1982, 1986, 1992) has traced the history of the field and its professional organization, the Association of Borderlands Studies. During the 1950s and 1960s, informal networks of scholars began building an infrastructure capable of sustaining mutual interests. In 1954 an important event occurred far from the actual border, at Michigan State University. Charles Loomis, a leading rural sociologist, assembled a team of scholars for a five-year Carnegie-funded project. Members of the team came from history, anthropology, sociology/demography, political science, and economics, with added assistance from medical personnel. The most comprehensive parts of the project were assembling a bibliography of pertinent historical materials and making a demographic comparison of border-state characteristics. Smaller studies dealt with selective issues such as politics, education, health, disaster relief, and other border-related subjects.

Exchanges between team members were fruitful, resulting in broadening the project beyond the original focus on technological change. When the project was not renewed for another five-year cycle, however, most of the well-known scholars who directed the initial grant dispersed, along with their graduate students. The concept of multidisciplinary study survived among scholars spread across several locations, including San Diego State University, the University of Arizona, Notre Dame, and the University of Texas at El Paso. Their work was largely unfunded or based on local funds. Circulation of unpublished work stimulated the growing network but did little to advance individual careers. In addition to exchanging information and resources, the group shared frustrations in personal stories of problems in selecting dissertation topics and finding publication outlets. Marginality is not uncommon in interdisciplinary fields. It is a social condition in which individuals experience conflict over the systems of values, symbols, and power relations that define two or more groups. One undermines the other's claims to exclusivity or monopoly over truth, thereby generating a crisis for individuals (Abir-Am 1987, 35).

Growing demands on the information network began to overtax the fragile structure of overlapping interests. In the spring of 1976 the Association of Borderlands Studies (ABS) formed. It began as an experimental section of the Western Social Science Association (WSSA). The ABS lent vital organizational support to several projects, including an encyclopedic inventory of border-related source materials. In attempting to secure funds for a borderlands sourcebook, researchers confronted what Stoddard aptly calls the catch-22s of interdisciplinary funding. Disciplinary categories and better-established interdisciplinary fields tend to be favored over new, risky, and large-scale multidisciplinary projects. Of the fifteen major agencies that were approached, all previously involved in funding border research, even agencies expressing initial interest tended to retreat. When the possibility of coordinating the project across separate program categories was raised, enthusiasm waned. One program officer even made a site visit to the University of Texas at El Paso. Yet when referees from sociology evaluated the application, they were critical of including "nonessential material" such as climate, soils, and archaeology. The foundation eventually considered the proposal at a higher level, using discretionary funds. They were still reluctant, though, to fund the entire spectrum of material, offering to reconsider the project only if chapters dealing with socioeconomics, demography, and social institutions were excluded.

During the 1980s some funding became available for projects aligned with popular issues such as transportation. The red-flagging of hot issues is a form of parceling that privileges some aspects, especially issues of public and political interest, while minimizing others or excluding them altogether. In the case of the United States–Mexico border region, they have tended to be immigration, water resources, pollution, drugs, and trade. Competition for resources exacerbates parceling. The rhetoric of interdisciplinary commitment in the brochures and applications of funding agencies exhorts scholars to go beyond the boundaries of traditional categories. Yet funding patterns belie the promise. Prior sanctions operate beneath surface rhetoric in the form of peer review and interdisciplinary targeting. Interactions with the Department of Housing and Urban Development yielded similar results, with recommendations to divide the social science material from "the rest." This pressure resurfaced in contacts with various government agencies whose operations touched on the border.

Parceling continued in the area of publication. Multidisciplinary proposals that lack provisions for breaking up data into smaller, more discrete pieces are undercut by the selling of component parts to separate disciplinary and multidisciplinary journals. This pressure is acute in new fields and in geographically regional work, which is more likely to be published by university presses. Confronted by strained budgets, escalating costs, and heightened pressure to limit book length while making market-oriented decisions, university presses are being forced into bottom-line policies that treat less established interdisciplinary fields as optional in times of financial exigency. When university presses were approached about the borderlands sourcebook, they suggested someone else publish the early history, archaeology, and geography-geology portions. They also advised authors to extract chapters dealing with controversial issues.

In recalling the sourcebook example, Stoddard confronted the problem of fit: "Neither the publisher's more stringent mode nor the newly imposed journal requirement fit the complex nature of multidisciplinary research results. Therefore, multidisciplinary proposals which do not contain internal provisions for publishing the results are forced to breakup the data into smaller, more discrete pieces to be 'sold' to separate disciplinary journals—an anathema to multidisciplinary scholarship" (1982, 214). Eventually, in 1983, The *Borderlands Sourcebook* was published by the University of Oklahoma Press.

The move into professionalism is a complicated step. Professionalism propels the separation of knowledge fields (Ross 1991, 158–63) by creating a form of monopoly over recruitment, certification of skills, graduate training, and entry into the academic labor market. A profession has five major attributes: a systematic body of theory and extensive training; professional authority and monopoly of judgment; sanction of a community; a regulative code of ethics; and a professional culture and lay stereotypes (Greenwood 1982, 207–18). The central activity of professionalism is coalescence into a group, creating a feeling of solidarity and a sense of place. The "culture of professionalism" also encompasses a set of learned values and habitual responses (Bledstein 1976, x), comparable to Bourdieu's concept of habitus. A "habitus" is an assumed system of principles that generates schemata for perceiving, thinking, valuing, and acting. A disciplinary habitus can be a powerful form of resistance to interdisciplinary affiliations, but an interdisciplinary habitus may also develop.

In the most recent professional history of ABS, Stoddard characterized the early days of the organization in a manner that will ring true for members of many interdisciplinary fields: as "a constant struggle to provide the services and image of a full-fledged professional organization on the budget of a Brownie troop" (1992, 29). Over the years, member affiliations supplied vital support for administrative and publication projects, especially the geography departments at California State University, Northridge, and the University of California, Riverside. By 1990 ABS had grown to nearly three hundred members, and a permanent secretariat was located at New Mexico State University. In quantity alone members represented nearly one-third of all sessions at the WSSA meeting. Local institutions play a crucial role in attaining critical mass. When local budgets are pressed, however, overall position may erode. Interdisciplinary fields often lack sufficient "economies of scale." A broad-based infrastructure is crucial to organizational resilience.

Organizational strength may also be more tenuous than assumed. ABS membership grew during the 1970s, and a core of members continues, but many early political officials and marginally interested individuals disappeared. Even after establishment of the journal and timely dues collection, membership slipped again. Members are not always diligent in paying dues, and they fail to share their border expertise in the mundane yet essential work of submitting manuscripts and book reviews. Although increasingly cited in other fields and disciplines, the journal is still limited by lack of material and reviewers with adequate breadth of knowledge. Interdisciplinary journals also experience a foreshortening of interdisciplinary development in the loss of manuscripts to more prestigious journals that advance individual, and often disciplinary, career prospects.

In its brief history, ABS has also experienced the possibility of being taken over by expanding border programs and institutes throughout California and the Southwest. In order to survive, interdisciplinary organizations are sometimes subsumed into disciplinary and multidisciplinary "parent" organizations, comparable to the collapsing of interdisciplinary programs into the disciplinary homes of participating faculty and cross-departmental structures. By strict definition, ABS has had an uneven history of professionalism. Lack of internal review and certification precludes claims of judgment over border-related issues. During the organization's critical years of struggle, ABS control of the field has been further eroded by a profusion of "instant border experts" backed by financially motivated consultant firms and, more recently, border-related agencies. Border interests are also located in other fields, such as Latin American or Chicano studies. Those fields have their own identities, agendas, and marginalities. Much of the field's standing is based on the professionalization process in members' original disciplines and their individual accomplishments in the multidisciplinary context of borderlands research. Tallying outcomes, Stoddard characterizes ABS as a "spare parts" professional field.

The multidimensionality of the field is further apparent in the ambiguity of individual identity. Every scholar, Stoddard reflected, has at one time walked the delicate line between mainstream demands of his or her discipline and multidisciplinary collaboration. Legitimacy, for the most part, occurs on the terrain of individual disciplinary identity. The academic standing, doctoral training, and professional appointments of individuals enable ABS to claim the authority of a profession. When border experts have been highly visible as top-level decision makers the field's legitimacy has been disproportionately greater. This pattern appears across world areas: in the work of Nigeria's border commissioner, A. I. Asiwaju; in geographer Michel Foucher's advice on contemporary European issues of geopolitical dimensions; in Jorge Bustamente's influence on Mexican border policies and reactions to United States programs; in Gerhard Sandner's efforts to clarify maritime boundaries in transition; and in Hans Briner's activities as secretary general of the Regio Basilenses on multinational regional planning in the Rhineland and increased cooperation on issues such as border commerce and nuclear energy resources (Stoddard 1992).

Correspondingly, the body of theory for United States–Mexico borderlands research was derived initially from the "conceptual reservoirs or disciplinary accumulations" of the field's early members. Some of these tools and methods have remained intact. Others have been modified and adapted to fit the unique milieu of borderlands. In their desire to contribute meaningfully to borderlands research, scholars have moved across material, employing amorphous terms to characterize vague theoretical frameworks. Within its professional organization and its journal, borderlands studies is primarily multidisciplinary. At the level of individual work, partially integrative levels have been achieved (Stoddard 1991; 1992, 2). The difference between "association/coordination" and synthesis is evident in all interdisciplinary fields. In an associative relationship, individuals trade data but do not integrate it into their own experience and perception. Synthesis requires a higher level of task organization. An interdisciplinary field, Stoddard suggests, is like a system of transparent overlays in which the scope and content of each discipline are superimposed on a common phenomenon. Individual scholars integrate ideas and concepts, not the contributing disciplines (1991).

Borderlands is not a mature field in either a disciplinary or an interdisciplinary sense. It lacks agreement on a reliable lexicon, conceptual tools, and assumptions. ABS does hold the promise of being a reputable indicator of scholarly expertise and professional acumen. Recently, in fact, a strong sentiment has been voiced for greater organizational autonomy. Current member dues are high enough to finance the added expenses of autonomy. ABS attained this level, however, because of tremendous personal and institutional subsidies. The trope of progress lionizes individuals, flagship models, and notable accomplishments, but it minimizes persistent strains and impediments. In 1992 fewer than a dozen scholars in ABS had sufficient breadth to carry forward the task of synthesis, including the vital "switchboarding" role of individuals who promote exchange of information and knowledge. The growth of any professional culture produces a basic set of fictions or myths about origin and progress that need to be examined periodically for veracity (Stoddard 1991, 1992, 5–6, 17).

Even the constitution of border studies, Michael Kearney (1991) warns, is a matter for concern. The project of border theory tests boundaries not only between nations but also between cultural productions, identities, sexualities, and disciplines (Welchman 1996). Yet, institutionalizing border studies risks developing new disciplines that control territorial and epistemological boundaries. At present a blurring of cultural and political spaces and identities is occurring in the border area as Mixtec alien migrants construct new identities out the bricolage of their transnational existence. In the liminal area of the border, spatial, categorical, and political distinctions of self and other are increasingly blurred. Like the disciplines that study it, the border is riddled with holes and contradictions. It is a zone of contested space, capital, and meanings. Classical constructions of anthropology and history have been challenged and replaced by new studies of the border area and its cultural politics. Many of these studies are antidisciplinary in the sense that they transcend the domains of standard disciplines and have formed outside the official institutional body of the state. Like the *Annales* project, they displace the vantage point outside national history while transcending formulations of historiography.

The dangers of institutionalization are real. Yet border studies underscores the importance of building a viable infrastructure for hybrid research, teaching, and problem solving. It also documents the double function of interdisciplinary work. Members of borderlands studies are members of other professional groups, disciplines, and local institutions. At those sites, they are changing the material and intellectual space that constitute discipline. This double presence is equally apparent in area studies.

Area

Sustained scholarly interest in distant parts of the modern world dates from the nineteenth century (Lambert et al. 1984, 2–4). The rise of area programs in the United States, though, was due to a specific historical event—World War II. Designed to produce knowledge about the contemporary foreign cultures of "enemy peoples," area studies programs were a "minor enterprise in the war effort" (Schwartz 1980, 15). A partial institutional base was already in place. Before the war the Rockefeller Foundation had funded the first generalized institutions of international relations, including the well-known Yale Institute of International Studies. Even with this base, only a few area specialists in universities and other personnel had extensive expertise on areas outside Western Europe. War was the chief enabling condition, but the creation and maintenance of a substantial cadre of experts on other parts of the world did not occur without deliberate government commitment to a targeted mission. Some disciplines might have become more cosmopolitan over time, but it took a powerful combination of economic, political, and military capital to give area studies an institutional presence in the United States and abroad (Lambert 1991, 172–73).

The location of area studies in centers staffed with civilian professors resulted from an "almost accidental" organizational decision that had significant structural and intellectual consequences. The professors and other personnel being trained were in enclaves away from the rest of the campus. It might have made as much sense, Richard Lambert suggested in a recent genealogy of the field, to have made area centers freestanding, government-supported units outside the university system. Had this happened, army specialized training units might have become prototypes for the academy style of organization typical in other countries. Elsewhere, area studies is often conducted within a government agency or a separate academy that is both responsive and responsible to government needs. In the United States, the bulk of basic research and writing on other countries occurs in universities. This location reinforces the teaching function, often absent in other countries. Additionally, in other countries academic debates on area versus disciplinary focus, research technology versus content, and applied versus pure research have not been prominent. Topical and disciplinary focus is often determined by interests of public policy, especially the need to devise effective political or economic strategies (Lambert 1991, 172–73).

Viewed from the standpoint of interdisciplinary history, area studies was to the social sciences and humanities what the Manhattan Project and operations research were to science and technology. An unprecedented level of demand for trained interpreters, analysts, and administrators capable of dealing with the conquest and occupation of Germany and Japan sanctioned boundary crossing. Changes in the scale and form of social organizations were visible throughout American life (Pye 1975, 5). There is a striking parallel between the wartime fluidity of gender boundaries separating kitchen from factory and disciplinary divisions in universities. Both boundaries were allowed to loosen during time of national need but were expected to rebound "naturally" when soldiers returned to their former jobs and the exigencies of wartime research ended. Nonetheless, just as the Manhattan Project and operations research marked the growing shadow structure of interdisciplinary research in science and technology, just as Rosie the Riveter symbolized expanding roles for women, the challenge of area studies lingered.

The lesson of World War II was clear. The problem of understanding distant nations exposed the limits of conventional ways of organizing knowledge and the need for new approaches to learning about foreign societies. Changes in the external world, Lucian Pye reflected, raised powerful questions about how responsive universities should be to public problems, how readily the academy should follow the path paved with foundation funds, and in a rapidly changing world, what could guide those seeking integrity in the cause of knowledge (1975, 4–5). Put another way, problems of the second and third kinds were put squarely on the academic desk. The structural implications were as significant as the advent of new interdisciplinary programs during the 1960s and 1970s and the increased variety of hybrid knowledge forms today. After the war, when the military need that fostered the rapid rise of area studies disappeared, many programs were dismantled. With financial help from several private foundations, fourteen campus-based programs remained. Many were expanded versions of the small nuclei that survived from prewar days (Lambert 1991, 173).

From that point forward, area studies began to diversify. Shortly after the war, the Carnegie Corporation funded Russian Research Centers at Harvard, and in a parallel effort to advance study of Communist China, the Universities Service Center was established in Hong Kong. Area studies further expanded from the Asia-Pacific theater of war and the former Soviet Union to cover the whole of the non-Western world and even marginal parts of the West, though in Latin American studies the Spanish and Portuguese were emphasized over indigenous peoples. Subsequently, area programs developed in some British and continental European universities, and in Canada, Australia, and New Zealand. Europeans had an apparent edge in the amount of knowledge about areas they once ruled, yet it was often slanted in favor of official policies and circumscribed by colonialist pigeonholes. In recent decades the Western monopoly on studies of the non-Western world has been broken by work being done in Japan, India, Singapore, Ghana, and other Asian and African countries (C. A. Fisher 1973, 185–86).

Of the organizations that supplied funding, the Ford Foundation had the greatest impact. From 1950 through 1973, it gave $278 million for international studies. Of the $176.6 million classified as grants for international training and research, a considerable proportion went to work now classified as area studies (Pye 1975, 11). The availability of fellowships for overseas fieldwork conferred greater legitimacy. Funded by the Ford Foundation, the Foreign Area Fellowship Program was established in 1952. This prestigious program recognized excellence in both disciplinary and area work. An important part of the expanding American system of graduate education, the program is credited as probably the single most influential formal institution in helping reduce the confrontation between area studies and disciplines; the program promoted the image of a new kind of scholar capable of being an innovator in a discipline while commanding esoteric knowledge and the language of a non-Western country. Area studies gained added visibility with the National Defense Education Act (NDEA). Between 1958 and 1973, NDEA Title VI provided roughly $206 million. Of that amount, $68.5 million went directly to language and area centers that totaled 107 for many years. NDEA-funded centers produced 35,000 bachelor's degrees, 14,700 master's degrees and over 5,000 Ph.D's (Pye 1975, 12).

Quantitative critical mass alone indicates that a threshold level has been achieved. By 1988 there were about six hundred self-declared area studies programs on American campuses, ranging from a handful of faculty and students to several hundred. A survey of the field in 1984 revealed that eighty or so programs at the top of the range, in terms of number and quality, annually receive support from the United States government. Between 1959 and 1981, these programs produced 88,000 students with academic degrees in language and area studies. Since then, rapid expansion has come to an end, with the notable exception of Japanese studies. At present a stable corps of about 7,000 academic area specialists is scattered throughout higher education, both within and outside organized centers (Lambert 1991, 175).

The degree of area specialization, Lambert found, varies along a continuum that ranges from an individual conducting a single piece of research to a scholar whose entire professional life is centered on area work. The latter is clearly the minority. Most area specialists identify with a broad country label. The long-term trend has been toward narrower geographic specialization, moving from world region to country to a particular section of a particular country. Within organized programs a substantial portion of faculty do not spend most of their professional time in areal specialization. Even among faculty in federally funded language and area studies centers, which educate most of the country's area specialists, only 77 percent of the inner core spend 25 percent or more of their professional time devoted to an area (Lambert 1991, 171, 177). Individual identity is compounded by geographical distance, the need for mastery of a second language, and an ethnographic tradition that may require years in the field. Needing disciplinary, linguistic, cultural, and interdisciplinary skills, area specialists face the demands of dual, triple, even quadruple competence.

The question of field identity is complicated. China studies is an instructive example. A review of the field by a joint committee of the American Council of Learned Societies (ACLS) and the Social Science Research Council illustrates the issues at stake ("Review of Joint Committee" 1990). The committee presides over a vast and complex field that stretches over more than two millennia of Chinese history and more than a dozen disciplines. The field's coherence derives not from common methods or assumptions but two major characteristics common to scholars: a commitment to in-depth study of some aspect of Chinese civilization, and recognition of the relevance and importance of Chinese experience to common problems studied by different scholars. At a minimum, these commitments are marked by an ability to conduct original research in the Chinese language and a willingness "to blend" questions about Chinese civilization with the particular questions and approaches of an individual discipline or intellectual tradition. The growing size of the field, though, makes it impossible for any one specialist to have more than passing familiarity with a significant proportion of the knowledge being produced.

That was not the case thirty years ago, when a China specialist would likely have been familiar with literary developments, economic trends, leadership changes, the thoughts of Chairman Mao, and other subjects pertaining to post-1949 China. The older contemporary field no longer exists. Today a China specialist is not just a student of China but also a student of economic development strategy, microeconomic incentive structures, political clientelism, urban social structure, region, or kinship. The questions inspiring specialists today often come from disciplines, and some of the best research on contemporary China is published in forums such as the *Journal of Comparative Economics, World Politics, American Sociological Review, Signs,* and the *New England Journal of Medicine.* As a result, China studies is experiencing a compounded fragmentation—by period, by research specialty, and by intellectual trends within particular disciplines. Ten years ago historians might be distinguished by the extent to which they used approaches from the social sciences and the new social history. Today they differ, at a finer level, by the social sciences they draw on. In addition, new interpretive or multidisciplinary approaches are being adopted alongside traditional work in literature, religion, and philosophy that derives from the older disciplines of sinology.

The ACLS committee consequently winds up in a delicate balancing act: juggling standards of scholarship that define a general commitment to Chinese studies while attempting to "tie together" work performed in disparate disciplines and specialties. Some members of the field complain that the committee plays too active a role in shaping the field, especially in late imperial and modern social history. Others charge that humanistic scholarship has been slighted in conferences and workshops, though others complain about neglect of certain social sciences, especially political science. If any tilting has occurred, the review committee concluded, it has been in the direction of the humanities, though some imbalance in favor of social sciences appears in conference themes and subject matter. Social history has often co-opted study of literary texts at the expense of more traditional approaches to the humanities and certain social sciences. As the earlier study of disciplinary neighbors revealed, individual perceptions and preferences play a strong role in judgments about whether disciplinary relations are beneficial and fruitful or instead resemble what the committee called a "shotgun marriage" of incompatible partners.

From a macroscopic perspective, certain patterns common to interdisciplinary studies appear. At times the U.S. government has attempted to shape area studies, primarily through special financial support of underrepresented disciplines and understudied countries and through targeted efforts to raise levels of language competency. For the most part, though, the growth of the field at large is tied to many separate institutional and individual decisions unrelated to government support. Area studies is, in Lambert's words, a "highly variegated, fragmented phenomenon, not a relatively homogeneous intellectual tradition." In U.S. universities, distribution of scholars by level of specialization, world area, and discipline results from a "laissez-faire model." The implied singularity of "area" and other interdisciplinary categories of knowledge masks important differences across institutional practices. The first task in studying the field is to "unreify," to realize that the *it* in question is not a singular phenomenon. Some features are shared by people who dedicate all or part of their careers to the category in question. Yet the features that characterize scholars in one set of disciplines may not apply to those in others (after Lambert 1991, 176). The categories that anchor interdisciplinary studies are general rubrics, not precise specifications.

Patterns of disciplinary distribution are illuminating. The immediacy of war skewed initial distribution of the knowledge produced. Paralleling the beginnings of border studies, the bulk of existing American expertise on many countries tended to come from missionaries, former foreign service officers, and to a lesser extent itinerant businesspeople or immigrant nationals. A skewed picture of the world emerged. The area specialists already in place tended to be in particular disciplines: history, classical literature, and occasionally linguistics. Language, history, and anthropology were already organized in a manner conducive to useful categorization of a contemporary orientation. Between 1952 and 1972, the Foreign Area Fellowship Program awarded 2,050 fellowships to students in forty different disciplines. The largest number, 605, went to historians; the second largest, 439, to political scientists. If international relations is included in the classification "political science," the count rises to 498 (Lambert 1991, 173, 188).

Generally speaking, the more a discipline is focused on what are presumably universal principles, not substantive particularities, the less hospitable it has been to area work. Anthropology and political science, where elegant description-oriented analyses are valued, are better represented than psychology, which has been moving toward a biology-based science, or economics, whose center of gravity is in econometrics and macroeconomic theory, or to a lesser extent, sociology. Most social sciences involved in area studies tend to be at the "soft" end of conventional taxonomy. Substantial numbers of humanists work within several areal groupings, and many topics have a humanistic thrust. This presents an unusual opportunity for cross-fertilization among scholars who might normally have little contact, yet it reinforces the perception among "hard" social scientists that area studies are nonscientific and "nondisciplinary." Longitudinal survey data indicate that the heart of area studies now lies in four disciplines: language and literature, history, political science, and anthropology. A significant portion of conferences, symposia, book collaborations, and jointly taught courses fall within the range of these disciplines. Across world area groups, roughly two-thirds of specialists are in these disciplines, except for Southeast Asian studies. On close inspection, distribution varies further. Inner Asian studies has emphasized history, language studies, and "nondisciplinary" concentration on the area. History is well represented in East Asian and East European studies. Economics is strongly represented in African, Latin American, and Southeast Asian studies, though never more than 15 percent. Anthropology is prominent in developed societies, and sociology is underrepresented everywhere (Lambert 1991, 186–88, 192).

Another form of boundary work occurs in the formation of distinct "tribes" of scholars. Study of Japan is considered the province of Japanologists, study of China the turf of sinologists, and so on. Some bridging occurs in the metaphor of the Pacific Rim, which links some Latin Americanists and East Asians, and in merging scholarly interests in the Muslim world. For the most part, though, area tribes tend to inhabit "relatively watertight intellectual domains." The notable exception occurs among U.S. scholars who study formerly Western European countries. They tend to see themselves as disciplinarians. "Ologizing" stems from the need to draw boundaries separating legitimate experts from dilettantes. The ologist tradition is especially strong in areas where mastery of regional languages is time consuming for Westerners. Ologizing has pushed the disciplinary balance of area specialists away from the social sciences toward the humanities. Language competency and substantive knowledge of other countries have been more likely to occur in the humanities, where a certain "fungibility of interest from one topic to another" has been greater. Ologizing has also tended to exclude the hard end of the social sciences, such as econometrics, demography, and political modeling. The supremacy of analytic technique over substantive content finds its greatest adherents in these realms (Lambert 1991, 182–83).

The answer to the question of interdisciplinarity depends, as it does in all studies of the second kind, on exactly what is being described: the field at large, individual practices, the epistemological ground of inquiry, or particular clusters of practices, methods, conceptual and theoretical frameworks. It is a mistake, Lambert cautions, to think of area studies as predominantly an "interdisciplinary" enterprise (1991, 189–91). Much of what would be defined as "genuinely interdisciplinary" work has occurred at the juncture of the four disciplines that currently provide the bulk of area specialists. At that hybrid intellectual space, a kind of historically informed political anthropology has developed using material in local languages. History has operated as a swing discipline. Blending of disciplinary perspectives occurs most frequently in two sets of activities: conferences, symposia, and thematic sessions at professional meetings and research by individual specialists. In the first instance, broadly defined themes have been the dominant pattern in scholarly papers, creating a collective "multidisciplinary" perspective. The topic of any particular conference, symposium, or session "drives the disciplinary mix." In the second case, topics regarded as substantively important to understanding a particular country frequently "do not respect disciplinary boundaries." The anthropomorphic notion of topics not respecting knowledge boundaries only reaffirms their constructed nature.

Area studies and other interdisciplinary studies are "transdisciplinary" in several respects. The U.S. tradition of area studies has been a "nonenclaved endeavor" characterized by a loose definition of expertise. Programs often resemble a cafeteria of courses in many disciplines. Blending is often left to the students, and the overwhelming proportion of their courses lies within their major disciplines. Professional organizations serving area interests are "transdisciplinary" in the sense that they draw members from a large number of disciplines, even though the work of individuals tends to lie within their own disciplines. Area studies programs have been "nondisciplinary" in the sense that research topics are usually chosen because of their importance for understanding a particular society. These topics often fall within domains where the conceptual and methodological apparatuses of Western-oriented disciplines have not been completely helpful or do not pertain. This limitation echoes the realization in Native American and African American studies that the underlying holistic basis of thought and action is not fully served by Western epistemologies and indeed sometimes falls outside their scope.

Lambert's final distinction is the most insightful and the most under-realized aspect of interdisciplinary work. It also provides further evidence of the importance of interactions at the specialty level. Area studies are "subdisciplinary" in the sense that research by individual specialists, especially in the social sciences, has tended to concentrate on particular subdomains. Most economists in area studies work in three subfields: agricultural, development, and planning economics. In peace and security studies, which often crosses the hybrid domain of area studies, several disciplines have subfields that are concerned with relevant components of core problems in the field. The components for security policy include attitude formation and change at individual, group, institutional, or national levels; the development, appeal, and functioning of mass protest movements; bureaucratic and organizational behavior, especially receptivity and resistance to change; as well as the role of public opinion, Congress, and the executive branch in formulating security policy. The challenge of interdisciplinary research, Richard Lebow suggests in an apt metaphor, is coaxing them "to climb out of their disciplinary trenches in order to survey the entire battlefield" (1988, 523–24).

Citation analysis suggests that the tendency for area studies, when it has prospered, has been consolidation into a quasi-disciplinary field separate from practitioners' original disciplines, with less influence on those disciplines that often hoped or publicly expressed (Calhoun 1992, 141). The full impact of area studies cannot be weighed without factoring in a broader shift. As political tensions rose in many developed areas and problems of scholarly access grew, the relation between discipline and area studies changed. In the field of political development, for example, the status of area specialists changed as political scientists recognized their expertise. Area specialists initially sought to gain skills and concepts from the disciplines. As they gained confidence as social scientists, they shifted direction and began questioning the utility of concepts developed in disciplines in Western societies and, more particularly, in U.S. politics. As the division of labor between general theorists and area specialists eroded, normative questions and larger conceptual questions became more important (Pye 1975, 19–21).

Ultimately, the question of interdisciplinary studies and their underlying categories of knowledge can be answered only within overlapping contexts of laissez-faire patterns of growth, disciplinary distributions, and historical change in disciplinary practice.

Women and Culture

Arthur Kroker's vision of critical interdisciplinarity is being enacted in women's and cultural studies. The two categories offer an intriguing comparison. One—women—is often treated as an enabling part of the reformulation of the other—culture.

Women

Once again, the underlying category is not new. Historically, knowledge about women was largely a by-product of work done in disciplinary contexts. In coeducational and all-female institutions, some women offered courses and conducted research pertaining to women, especially sex and gender issues. Until the women's studies movement of the late 1960s and 1970s, though, their experiments were largely ignored or even abandoned. Over the course of two decades, the growth of a feminist presence on campus resulted in women's studies becoming, for many, an exemplary model of a successful interdisciplinary field. Women's studies was enabled by a combination of historical events and social capital. They included a new push for general education reform, demands for social justice and racial equality, concerns about dissipation of the talents of educated women, the entrance of women of all races and classes into the public labor force, and new technologies of reproduction that helped to redefine women's sexuality (Stimpson 1992, 254–56).

Like urban and environmental studies, women's studies is "the academic arm" of a larger social and political movement (Coyner 1991, 349). The first program in the United States was formally approved in 1970 at San Diego State University, though the first "political" women's studies course was reportedly taught at the Free University of Seattle in 1965 (Boxer 1982, 663 n. 6). In 1969 roughly 16 courses in the country were devoted to the subject of women and gender (Stimpson 1992, 257). By 1973, approximately 5,000 courses on women were being offered in American institutions of higher education (DuBois et al. 1987, 4 n. 4). In 1977, when the National Women's Studies Association (NWSA) was founded, 276 programs were in place nationwide. By 1982 there were more than 300 programs and more than 30,000 courses in colleges and universities (Boxer 1982, 662). By 1990 there were

520 programs, 235 of them undergraduate majors and 404 minors. A recent survey by the American Council on Education found courses at 68 percent of all United States universities, 48.9 percent of all four-year colleges, and 26.5 percent of two-year colleges. Across this curricular array, more students take courses in women's studies than major in it, and double majors are the norm ("Women's Studies" 1990, 214).

The intellectual history of the field is as revealing as its institutional history. What began as "compensatory education" became nothing less than "a comprehensive intellectual and social critique" that addressed hegemonic issues ("Women's Studies" 1990, 209). Reflecting the field's origin in a larger social movement, the syllabi of early courses were dominated by popular writings, such as Simone de Beauvoir's *The Second Sex,* Caroline Bird's *Born Female,* Betty Friedan's *The Feminine Mystique,* and Kate Millet's *Sexual Politics.* These courses aimed to promote greater reflection on female experience and feminist goals. Usually taken as electives, they were not firmly anchored in their host institutions (Boxer 1982, 663 n. 7, 681). They were taught mostly by women, many of them political activists. Few had status as resident faculty in women's studies programs.

The field grew rapidly for two reasons. It met urgent political and intellectual needs. Its founders also took advantage of existing frameworks and structures employed by other interdisciplinary fields, especially Black, ethnic, and American studies ("Women's Studies" 1990, 210; Gerstenberger and Allen 1977). In the early 1970s, Sandra Coyner recalls, "women's studies" was a restricted choice from limited alternatives that were not of women's own design. A pattern for name and structure already existed, permitting women's studies to become established relatively quickly and obviating the need to fight more general battles about innovation and crossing disciplinary boundaries. Seldom, though, was there debate on whether that structure was the most appropriate one, let alone what the ideal structure might be (1991, 350).

By the late 1980s a formidable scholarly apparatus was in place in the form of specialist journals, newsletters, professional networks, and a viable presence in universities and on some commercial press lists. Production of knowledge about women followed a common pattern in interdisciplinary fields. Initial gains are greater in the accumulation of data and information. Early feminist criticism appeared to be "an empirical orphan in the theoretical storm" (Showalter 1981, 180). The data/theory split, though, is not a strict dichotomy or a simple diptych, an observation Chalmers Johnson made in area studies. Data gatherers are not arrayed on one panel, with theory builders on the opposite panel (1975, 81). New empirical work challenged and reinvigorated existing theory, exposing the partiality of conventional axioms, received truths, and the premise that facts were neutral. The archaeological mission of ciphering and translating silent sediments of the historical past (Kroker 1980, 9) raised substantive questions: Why did gaps and voids exist in the first place? Why were they treated as "in-between" spaces, not as primary spaces?

Mere accretion of woman-centered topics—the augmenting strategy Charlotte Bunch dubbed "Add women and stir" (Shumway and Messer-Davidow 1991, 215)—would not be adequate. Only radical reconstruction of knowledge and consciousness would effect genuine change, moving the field beyond "mainstreaming" knowledge about women as a subset or component of knowledge about men to a genuine "transformation" capable of "breaking the disciplines" (Minnich 1990, 12; Howe 1978). The goal of challenging dominant intellectual traditions and institutional structures, enshrined in the founding rhetoric of the NWSA, has been accomplished in a number of ways. The scholarly practices that define and advance the field span older and newer traditions of liberal humanism, challenges to established disciplinary canons, strategies of reading that emphasize differences within language, and specific methods and theories linked with structuralism and poststructuralism, cultural studies, neo-Marxist theory of ideology, and women's perspectives on African American and postcolonial experience and identity (Stimpson 1992).

No single description adequately accounts for this diversity, though several stages of feminist scholarship have been identified. Early deconstructions of error and bias led to reconstruction of philosophical and scientific reality and, in turn, to the construction of general theories (Stimpson 1978, 14–26). The first generation of scholars addressed primarily omissions and distortions in the form and content of traditional disciplines (Hoagland 1978, 17). This initial phase was characterized by identification of male bias and discovery of how it led to omission or distortion of the study of women. The second phase was characterized by development of original feminist perspectives on the methods and assumptions of disciplines (DuBois et al. 1987, 15–18, 40). Stages of development have not been neat or consecutive. Three major activities have supplemented, corrected, and sometimes overlapped one another: defiance of difference; celebration of difference; and recognition of differences among women (Stimpson 1992, 259–67). The recent turn into gender studies encompasses interests that were formerly identified as feminist along with studies of masculinity, sexuality, and lesbian and gay studies (Schor 1992, 262, 275).

Inevitably, as feminist scholarship developed within and across disciplines, the question arose whether women's studies was a discipline. The emergence of specialized terminology suggested the possibility. In distinguishing two modes of feminist literary criticism, for example, Elaine Showalter (1981) coined the terms "gynocritics" and "gynocriticism" to distinguish intellectual work that focused on the woman writer and a genuinely women-centered ground of inquiry. Later Alice Jardine (1985) used the term "gynesis" to label expansion into cultural representations of gender and patterns of masculinity and femininity. Taking women's writing as the primary subject forced the leap to a new conceptual vantage point, away from the ideological dilemma of reconciling revisionary pluralism into an epistemology grounded in difference. Research, teaching, and service premised on difference often begin by redressing grievances and building on existing models.

Diane Elam (1990) defines the space of women's studies as a "discipline of difference," a construction that calls into question the autonomy of discipline by appealing to disciplinarity as "cross-disciplinarity." Disciplinary borders are crossed through continuous inter- and intradisciplinary cross-fertilization. Reconstituting disciplinarity as cross-disciplinarity does not elevate feminism to the status of a theoretical metalanguage or a totalizing master narrative. Like argument 3, embodied in Jeffrey Peck's vision of a critical interdisciplinarity in German studies, this move asserts that borders are neither stable nor impenetrable. The premise of difference is comprehensive. Older critiques of disciplinary structure are joined by new demands for self-definition, reflexivity, and alternative forms of knowledge production (Boxer 1982, 686). Epistemological concerns are also realigned with their political implications.

Despite their differences, ethnic, minority, and women's studies exhibit an implicitly shared epistemology that dismantles the boundary separating knowledge from action, discipline from politics. In a notable parallel, Russell Thornton (1977) argued that Native American studies should be allowed to define and build its own intellectual traditions, based not on the differentiated social and political systems of Anglo culture but on the holistic "undifferentiated systems" of Native American cultures. That means focusing on oral traditions, treaties and treaty rights, tribal government, forms of organization, group persistence, Native American epistemology, and the practical needs of community. Similarly, Ronald Walters argued that African American studies is "disciplined" by the centrality of racism in American life. Curriculum and research are based on the "unity and the order of Blackness." They are defined by praxis, not grand theory (1970, 144). Analysis is not objective in the traditional sense but is interested work—corrective, descriptive, and prescriptive work. Theory building and problem solving have an integral relation grounded in the needs of community (Semmes 1981, 15).

The fusion of critique and problem solving theoretically places political and intellectual work on the same level. Yet they are not valued that way in the academic reward structures, or among members of the same field. In women's studies, some of the most extensive debates have focused on the relation between activist and academic goals. This tension requires a balancing act in the NWSA among individuals who came to women's studies at different periods, through different routes, with differing conceptualizations of the field (Boxer 1982, 674–75). Furthermore, despite a handful of feminist public policy centers and organizations composed of friends of women's studies, few structures span academic and other communities. Despite courses that treat social change historically, theoretically, or practically, knowledge of discourse has not been of significant use to child incest victims whose stories are discredited in court because they are inconsistent with standard judicial criteria for valid discourse. Models exist, among them a Mankato State University course called "Collective Action/Analysis" and an internship in feminist organizations at the University of Massachusetts, Boston. They are still few in number, however (Messer-Davidow 1991, 301). Moreover, despite other manifestations of feminism on campus—centers that address sexual assault and harassment, advocacy and action groups, affirmative action offices, activities by and for minority women, and special programs for women in math, engineering, and the sciences—women's studies scholarship has rarely acted directly to produce change (Coyner 1991, 351).

Women's studies has also had to confront its own exclusions and distortions. "Women" is not a category unto itself. It is part of a matrix of interrelations with gender, race, class, and national culture. The founding generation of academic feminists found themselves charged with being an elite corps holding good jobs and privileged positions but removed from the social circumstances of many of the women they purported to represent. In the past, heterosexual, white, and even upper-class female perspectives dominated feminist inquiry, fostering what Micaela di Leonardo called the "feminist metonymic fallacy" of universalizing women's experiences without regard for power differentials (Addelson and Potter 1991, 260). Mainstream feminist scholarship has been critiqued in the work of African American, Chicana, Native American, and lesbian scholars who are engaged in their own projects of rediscovery and reevaluation (DuBois et al. 1987, 63). The emergence of Black women's studies during the 1980s and a clearly defined community of African American women writers created new institutional locations where Black women intellectuals are producing new specialized knowledge. Black women's history and feminist literary criticism have been important sites in this renaissance (Collins 1991).

Women's studies also confronts the dilemma of professionalism. The notion of a "both-and" strategy emerged early, in the vision of a core of faculty trained in more than one discipline to become "interdisciplinary women" capable of working with interested teachers in their diverse locations. This strategy, on the surface, implies a professional paradox of being "both in the disciplines and in opposition to them" (Messer-Davidow 1991, 281–82). Progress in all of the studies, though, has been bidirectional. Scholars and teachers work across the grain and against it, operating both inside and outside discipline. One coordinator of a women's studies program argued early on that "in order to change or add to the traditional perspectives of disciplines, women's studies has to be of them, in them, and about them" (Boxer 1982, 671 n. 34, 693). Being located within institutions while wielding their forms of power and authority for interested purposes amounts to a dismantling from within a professional class position (Addelson and Potter 1991, 271).

The question of interdisciplinarity is complicated by the plurality of disciplinary and ideological perspectives. From the beginning, women's studies was conceived as interdisciplinary in the sense of providing programs where disciplinary boundaries could be broken down and a broader, more complete approach to understanding women developed. This conception often embodies implicit criticism of the entire structure of higher education. Gloria Bowles speculated early on that one day the Renaissance man might be replaced by "the interdisciplinary woman" (cited in Boxer 1982, 687). Her exact identity has been debated ever since. In the 1975 inaugural issue of *Signs,* the founding editors suggested several patterns of work. They ranged from one person skilled in several disciplines but focused on one subject *to* several persons skilled in single disciplines yet focused collaboratively on a subject together *to* a group of disciplinarians who publish in random conjunction within the same journal. Two years later, Catherine Stimpson acknowledged that the interdisciplinary promise had proved more difficult than envisioned. Resistance to moving outside one's field of expertise was as strong in women's studies as in other interdisciplinary fields. Stimpson called for translators able to "interpret the languages of one discipline to persons in another" (Boxer 1982, 685–87).

In the ensuing years the term "interdisciplinary" appeared in conjunction with a number of strategies: developing alternative curricular structures and pedagogies, borrowing disciplinary methodologies, engaging in community service and political work through activism, and forging a new body of knowledge through self-defined epistemology. Reflecting a widely shared belief that women's studies is a prototype of academic organization in the twenty-first century, the metaphors of a matrix, a network, connection, and dialogue have been prominent in descriptions of the field ("Women's Studies" 1990, 212). In the curriculum, the familiar umbrella structure loosely relates a variety of practices that are mostly multidisciplinary and interdepartmental (Boxer 1982, 683). Programs typically mix courses from single disciplines and courses with a topical approach. Women's studies journals typically publish research from both disciplinary and interdisciplinary perspectives (DuBois et al. 1987, 1, 4).

Over the past decade a number of collections have weighed the impact of feminist scholarship on the disciplines, foremost among them *A Feminist Perspective in the Academy: The Difference It Makes* (1983), *Feminist Scholarship: Kindling in the Groves of Academe* (1987), and *(En)Gendering Knowledge: Feminists in Academe* (1991). The journal *Signs* also continues to provide reports on the latest research emerging from the disciplines. The collaborative team that wrote *Feminist Scholarship* found that feminist scholarship simultaneously challenges and is shaped by disciplinary inquiry. Patterns of journal publication from 1966 through 1980 in five disciplines (history, literature, education, anthropology, and philosophy) revealed uneven influence. Measuring impact is complicated by the multiple ways feminist scholarship develops at different sites. The general trend has been toward increasing receptivity. Distribution, however, varies. The diversity of topics that may be counted as "on women" complicates measurement. A significant portion of scholarship appears in interdisciplinary journals devoted to women's studies. Special issues echo the problem of fit. They heighten awareness, but they have an ambiguous status. They raise awareness, but they do not substitute for sustained consideration in the mainstream. Building distinct subfields and assigning special rubrics are effective ways of mounting a feminist presence, but this strategy may ultimately reinforce marginalization (DuBois et al. 1987, 155–202).

The authors of *Feminist Scholarship* concluded that research frameworks and standard analytic concepts such as family, class, race, community, socialization, social control, and social conflict must be reformulated in order to take into account relations between men and women and to encompass research on women (DuBois et al. 1987). Sociology is an example. Citation analysis shows that feminist work has been slow to enter mainstream journals of the discipline. The journal *Signs,* edited in part by sociologists, was cited only a handful of times in a sampling conducted by Craig Calhoun, and interdisciplinary periodicals on women's and gender studies accounted for an almost "negligible" part of overall citation patterns. Feminist work in sociology has centered on studies of the social circumstances and problems of women in a fairly conventional sociological manner. It has not been a sustained occasion for more fundamental reconsideration or reconstruction of mainstream disciplinary orientation (1992, 163 n. 35).

The early assumption that research on women would coalesce into a single interdisciplinary field has been limited by the complexities of doing interdisciplinary work and differences of disciplinary location. Analytic concepts such as gender, oppression, and agency have been powerful unifying themes. In addition, most of the women interviewed in Aisenberg and Harrington's *Women of Academe* reported preferring "cross-disciplinary" to discipline-bound inquiry. They have been more likely to study unformulated subjects at the edges of disciplines rather than sharply defined subjects at their centers (Hartman 1991, 18, 30). Nevertheless, some boundaries have been more permeable than others. Citation data indicate that much of feminist scholarship retains a strongly disciplinary character. The deepest differences are methodological. Even when focused on the same topic, research results may be disparate and incommensurable. This tendency underscores another duality of interdisciplinary scholarship. An overall commonalty exists, but the work produced just as often bears the stamp of a particular field (DuBois et al. 1987, 38–39, 198–202).

From their locations within the disciplines feminists have dispersed centripetally into specializations. Within the shared space of women's studies, they have moved centrifugally to "cross-disciplinary" research and teaching (Hartman and Messer-Davidow 1991, 5). The broader field offers intellectual community and an institutional site for feminists who are still doing most of their work within disciplines, further legitimating courses, journals, conferences, research, and projects that use gender as a category of analysis (Addelson and Potter 1991, 271). In developing gender as a category of analysis, they have used the practices of disciplines to change focus and even the practices themselves. Feminist scholarship, as a result, is less a single map than "a portfolio of maps." In establishing the unreliability of other knowledge maps, scholars and teachers have charted new knowledge territory and heightened reflexivity on all mapmaking (after Stimpson 1992, 251).

Defining women's studies by patrolling its borders or specifying its center is less reliable a descriptive strategy than reading efforts to understand the relation of disciplinary parts to an interdisciplinary whole, including links with the feminist movement that fostered a new academic field (DuBois et al. 1987, 196). The whole in question is not a totalizing unity. It is a complex critical holism anchored by a hybrid category of knowledge—gender. The term "feminist" has many meanings: political, professional, theoretical, and practical (Addelson and Potter 1991, 259). Correspondingly, the label "women's studies" rarely specifies a single identity. Most people working in the field also identify with another academic community, as feminist historian, literary critic, psychologist, or social worker. Naming tends to designate a position in a program—as women's studies faculty, student, or director—rather than the work performed. Women's studies is a location—institutional, political, and sometimes physical. The kinds of work done in these locations can be inferred from practice more than name. They span teaching and curriculum, miscellaneous advocacy, organizing speeches and events, research, publishing, and scholarship. More than anything else women's studies attempts to identify and actualize a space shared by two important institutions and establish a place within each of them. These moves brought feminism into the academy while adding applied teaching and scholarship to the goals of the women's movement. Depending on which home is most salient, definition shifts (Coyner 1991, 349–51).

Echoing the ambivalence in other interdisciplinary studies, feminists sometimes proclaim that new scholarship has changed the very nature of academic work. At other times they despair that research on women is ignored and shunted to the margins of disciplines (DuBois et al. 1987, 158). Feminism, like Marxism, contains political dimensions that threaten the very foundations of disciplines. Yet individual disciplines, Ben Agger (1989) found in a parallel examination of textbooks for introductory sociology courses, flatten their critical nature and agenda. Descriptions of the field vary according to perceived containment. By and large, feminist scholarship has not transformed the academy. Assessing the current state of the field, authors of the report on the field for the Association of American Colleges and Universities' study-in-depth project, concluded that women's studies remains in the shadow structure. Yet conditions of marginality are at the same time conditions of strength: "By insisting on interdisciplinary flexibility and reflexivity, by refusing conventional categories and labels, and by asserting obligations to a self-conscious critique of the politics of knowledge, we resist absorption into an 'acceptable' (and safe) liberal pluralism at the expense of our radical critique." The epistemological power of women's studies depends on its location in spaces where conventional intellectual boundaries are blurred ("Women Studies" 1990, 210–11).

The categories of knowledge at stake in all interdisciplinary studies are caught in a seized conjunction, in the hedged grammar of "Yes . . . but." Gerda Lerner (1979) framed the issue for women's studies in terms of "contribution history." The danger is being reduced to a contributing role in a framework whose analytic categories are not of one's own making. Carol Berkin (1991) framed the issue in terms of "dangerous courtesies" that plague women's history and other disciplines of the humanities. Three of the seven courtesies plague other interdisciplinary fields as well. The "roll call" adds women to lists but does not change underlying categories or measures of achievement. The "intermezzo" includes vignettes, biographical sketches, or dramatic moments of history but treats them as self-contained, not part of the central text. "Waiting in the wings" charts progress but still consigns women to backstage as understudies.

Most of the dangerous courtesies are common to interdisciplinary categories. They take the generic form of inclusion in texts but exclusion from interpretation and additive stances that hold interdisciplinary studies in abeyance. The newest and final example, cultural studies, is the ultimate testing ground for a critical interdisciplinarity that moves beyond accommodation to reconceptualization.

Culture

"Cultural studies" is the umbrella label for a profusion of academic, social, and political interests that signal wider alternatives across national contexts. Many practices were already introduced through other interdisciplinary fields and new approaches to the study of culture in disciplinary domains. The label is also affiliated with a number of revitalized interests, including neo-Marxism, social history, ethnomethodology, and textualism. The field's current momentum derives from overlapping structural, pedagogical, and ideological changes that have occurred in universities since the 1960s (Bathrick 1992, 321). The theory and canon wars of the 1960s and 1970s occurred when most current practitioners were cutting their intellectual and political teeth. They emerged into middle age in a time of bad job markets, postcolonial political movements, the growing influence of mass and popular culture, and a widespread sense of disciplinary "crisis" (Brantlinger 1990, ix).

The "culture" of cultural studies is not a single entity but a cumulative reformulation of the concept of culture. Three interrelated problems are being explored: the production of cultural meanings, textual analysis of those meanings, and the study of lived cultures and experiences (Denzen 1992, 34). One of the major purposes and effects of these investigations has been to breach the traditional boundaries separating elite and formal culture from popular, mass, working-class, everyday culture. A "double articulation of culture" is occurring. Culture is simultaneously the object of study and the site of critique and intervention (Grossberg, Nelson, and Treichler 1992, 5). Like other interdisciplinary fields, cultural studies exhibits both generality and specificity. It is located within disciplines, on their margins, and in the newly cleared space of interdisciplinary studies (Wolff 1992, 716). Disciplinary economies register in concrete practices, but those practices also have a relational character borne of shared interests (Nelson, Treichler, and Grossberg 1992, 17).

The field is currently experiencing "an unprecedented international boom" (cited Nelson, Treichler, and Grossberg, 1992, 1). Hence there is a prodigious amount of scholarship from which to map a field described as a "loosely coherent group of tendencies, issues, and questions" that are not congruent in theory, practice, political orientation, or institutional structure (Brantlinger 1990, ix; J. H. Miller 1992, 13). No one subject metonymically represents the field. It is defined by complex interrelations of institutional, historical, political, and intellectual development. Scholarship spans studies of the home and the workplace, media and technology, popular fiction and pornography, AIDS and the body, and ethnic, gender, and postcolonial identities. The suggested groupings of a recent anthology of essays, which stemmed from a major international conference in 1990, indicate the most prominent subjects and topics (1992, 18–22).

history of cultural studies	rereading history
gender and sexuality	pedagogy
nationhood and national identity	politics of aesthetics
colonialism and postcolonialism	culture and its institutions
race and ethnicity	ethnography and cultural studies
popular culture and its audiences	the politics of disciplinarity

discourse and textuality   identity politics
science, culture, and the ecosystem   global culture in a postmodern age

Correspondingly, no single method or theory characterizes the diversity of practices. The most common methods are Marxism, feminism, deconstruction, psychoanalysis, ethnography, race and gender theory, semiotics, and textual analysis. Sometimes methods are combined, meshing survey research with ethnography, information from modern marketing research with more utopian conceptions of empowered consumers, and textual or ethnographic analysis with social, political, and cultural commentary. Methods typically reflect original disciplinary training, amplified by situational borrowings. The choice of practice depends on the question being asked. The question, in turn, depends on the context (Nelson, Treichler, and Grossberg 1992, 2–3).

Individuals use different labels to identify themselves and their work. Most self-identified members of the field are working at disciplinary sites and in the trading zone of cultural studies. In addition to using the label "cultural studies," they name themselves historians, literary critics, anthropologists, sociologists, and art historians as well as feminists, African Americanists, and members of Australian and other national groups. The units that house cultural studies vary from isolated components of curriculum and research to cross-departmental programs, new departments, and research centers. Names bespeak commitments. Some use older rubrics of critical theory, history of consciousness, or multidisciplinary tags such as "Philosophy, Literature, and Social Theory." Older programs, such as the older History of Consciousness Program at the University of Santa Cruz, exist alongside new programs located in Pittsburgh, Syracuse, Illinois, and Wisconsin–Milwaukee. The latter espouse the names "culture," "cultural," and "theory" in their titles (Aronowitz 1991, 139–40; Brantlinger 1990, ix–x).

The word "plural" is both an adjective and a problematic. It is a common description for the immense variety of subjects, topics, and methods, yet pluralism is also indicted as an inclusive politics comparable to "contribution history" and the "dangerous courtesies." The current publishing boom and the field's rapid institutionalization, especially in the United States, have made cultural studies an accelerated microcosm of other interdisciplinary studies. Because it is a "hot" field at the moment, economic and social capital have quickly coalesced, though at the lesser economic scale of the humanities. Cultural studies topics enjoy a growing presence in conference programs, journal pages, and press lists; in courses and in programs; and in dissertations, jobs, and professional organizations. A familiar climbing on the interdisciplinary bandwagon is also occurring. Echoing the pattern in environmental studies, a number of existing units have been renamed "cultural studies," "cultural theory," and variations on the field's thematics. "Too many people," Nelson, Treichler, and Grossberg lament, "simply rename what they were already doing to take advantage of the cultural studies boom" (1992, 10–11).

Young though it may be, cultural studies is already producing its own ge-nealogy. Archaeological recovery of once subordinated subjects is under way, and the history of the movement is being rewritten in light of new discoveries, agendas, and appraisals. History is constructed on several grounds: a "generational intellectual tendency" (Aronowitz 1991, 139), key institutional movements, pioneer works, the Frankfurt School and the Birmingham Center, new international developments in contemporary Marxism, a cultural, pragmatic approach to community studies, feminist cultural studies, deconstruction of cultural texts following Derrida, and critical readings of postmodern society in the manner of Baudrillard, Lyotard, and Jameson (Denzen 1992, 74–75). The biographical ground of the British cultural studies movement figures large in the history of the field.

The attribution is understandable. The seminal texts of the field include the works of Raymond Williams (*Culture and Society* in 1958 and *The Long Revolution* in 1961), Richard Hoggart (*The Uses of Literacy* in 1957), and E. P. Thompson (*Making of the English Working Class* in 1962). For Hoggart and Williams, the major site was literary criticism; for Thompson, orthodox political and economic history; and for all three, Marxism. Their work propelled a shift in the definition of culture away from narrow disciplinary practices and an inert sense of period and texts toward a more broadly anthropological definition. In the process, "culture" was transformed into a dynamic, heterogeneous field that encompasses a way of life, social practices and forms, and historical processes (Brantlinger 1990, 36–37, 64; Fiske 1992). Significantly, Hoggart and Williams were also from working-class families, and most of the first generation taught in adult education programs outside the university. They were among the first to gain access to elite institutions of higher education and to make their heritage part of the concept of culture that was studied in universities (Nelson, Treichler, and Grossberg 1992, 12).

Because of the British tradition, the Center for Contemporary Cultural Studies at the University of Birmingham is often treated as a point of institutional origin. Stuart Hall, director of the Center from 1969 to 1979, called the Center "the locus to which we *retreated*." Founded by Hoggart in 1964 and developed out of the Sociology Department, Birmingham was the place where the name "cultural studies" was adopted, constructed, and formalized for a set of projects. Birmingham was a place, an event, a strategy, and a prototype for collaborative, contextual cultural analysis (Nelson, Treichler, and Grossberg 1992, 9). Hall expressed discomfort at the way the Center's work has become entrenched in a "grand narrative" that appears more linear than it actually was (1992, 277). The Center's history was, more accurately, a series of negotiations and ruptures. Inspired by Hoggart's work, researchers created a physical site and an intellectual context for analysis of the forms, practices, and institutions of contemporary culture and society.

The initial production of knowledge retained literary inclinations. That tendency changed as concrete historical modes of work emerged alongside ethnography and a series of interventions. As researchers began grappling with material, social, and historical conditions, a break into a Marxism occurred. This move restored to the debate about culture a set of theorizations around the problem of ideology. Two subsequent interruptions, around feminism and questions of race, further reorganized the field by opening the question of the personal as political. In later years cultural studies at Birmingham ceased being "a dependent intellectual colony." It became a collaborative set of projects with its own direction, object of study, set of themes and issues, and distinctive problematic. In the course of these developments, the meaning of "culture" shifted from older discipline-specific notions of text and artifact into a broader anthropological definition centered on cultural practices, then into a more historical definition that questioned anthropological meaning and interrogated its presumed universality through concepts of social formation, cultural power, domination and regulation, resistance and struggle (Hall 1979, 1992).

In terms of work patterns, the Center was a microcosm of interdisciplinary fields. In day-to-day activities, Hall recalled, different methodological emphases emerged. Some projects relied on ethnographic fieldwork and interviewing, some on analysis of texts and discursive practices, some on historical methods of research on archival, documentary, and other sources. Methods were not kept separate, however; they were combined and recombined across projects. A certain "regionalism" thus emerged, each region maintaining intellectual responsibility for its particular area. At the same time each was open to other projects, thereby developing cultural studies as a whole. One of the central, strategic tasks was collectively combining regional and general emphases. Even with collaboration, the result was not a homogeneous body of work. The knowledge produced was characterized by disagreements, divergencies, and outright conflicts (Nelson, Treichler, and Grossberg 1992, 10). Projects and fields, Hall adds, are discursive formations in Foucault's sense. They have no simple origins. They comprise multiple discourses with different histories, trajectories, methodologies, and theoretical positions. The Center was a site where new disciplinary combinations were applied, criticized, and remodeled. New interventions reflect events outside a discipline, but they also have effects within it. They work to reorganize a set of problems or field of inquiry and to reconstitute existing knowledge under the sign of new questions.

Classifying the many turns, breaks, and movements is not easy. Initially, Hall reflected, they were defined as "sociological" in a loose sense. The break into a complex Marxism fostered new kinds of questions about the politics of culture. Some part of the subject matter of sociology fell within their scope. However, because they could not conceptualize relationships within the dominant structural-functionalist paradigm, researchers began appropriating sociology from within. At the same time they were becoming familiar with other traditions that attempted to deal with social action and institutions as objectivated structures of meaning. As concrete historical work developed, the dichotomy of literature versus sociology dissolved into a new emphasis on lived practices, belief systems, and institutions. Both sociologists and humanists reacted. The sociology being used was not "'proper' sociology" in the sense of Parsonian theorizing or structural-functionalist methodology. Traditional humanists, for their part, reasserted the definition of "culture" inscribed in canon and the values of liberal scholarship.

The break into a complex Marxism was made possible, but not necessarily easier, by changes within mainstream sociology. These developments included a phenomenological reprise associated with Berger and Luckmann's social construction of reality and ethnomethodology's focus on language and conversational analysis as a kind of paradigm for social action. The rehabilitation of social interactionism was indicated by interests in narrative, textuality, and communication and use of qualitative methodology. It was further evident in new studies of youth culture, the cultures of school and work, and women's work and experience. The ethnographic tradition linked cultural studies at Birmingham with at least two other related developments: descriptive emphases of some kinds of social anthropology and the "history from below" promoted by new social history (Denzen 1992).

Knowledge cartography is cultural as well as epistemological. After the closing of the Birmingham Center, cultural studies in the United Kingdom continued in other forms, including the curriculum of the Open University; journals such as *New Formations, Cultural Studies,* and *Screen;* and the work of the Center's former members. In the United States, cultural studies experienced a parallel founding during the 1950s, but the field was more rapidly institutionalized (Hall 1992, 285–86). In both countries cultural studies was shaped by debates over mass culture and the mass media's place in contemporary cultural life (Denzen 1992, 75). In Britain the question of ideology emerged sooner and more sharply than in the United States, where Marxism has a different status in the larger social and political culture. The concept of "popular" also occupies a different place within the dominant culture of the United States. In addition, discussions of countercultural movements in the 1960s tended to be identified with middle-class, mostly white, male college students, in contrast to an orientation toward working-class subcultures at the Birmingham Center. In the United States, the more developed institutional site for study of the working class was labor history (Brantlinger 1990,

117, 119). Opposition to traditional practices of American studies has been another major site.

In Australia cultural studies had to find space within existing disciplinary boundaries. This meant working within a strong tradition of left-conservative history, within critical and nationalist movements in literary studies, and new interests in film and media studies that were reinforced by revival of the Australian film industry. It also meant seeking a home within the eclectic field of Australian studies. The tendency in Australian cultural studies has been to concentrate on local texts, institutions, and constitutive discourses. Major theoretical categories and protocols have been derived from Europe, especially Britain. Emphasis on national identity, though, has meant that Australian cultural studies was compartmentalized in the past from feminist criticism and its intersection with a range of debates surrounding Aboriginal and Pacific studies and multicultural issues (Turner 1992, 640, 643, 653; Morris 1992, 651, 653).

New knowledge claims lead to disputes over territory. Cultural studies is a sheltering space, a catalyst, a subfield, an alternative practice, a network of overlapping projects and comparative theory, and a general problematizing force. Scholars in departments of English, sociology, communication, and anthropology have historically studied the same topics now being claimed as the province of cultural studies. Their control over the domains of mass communications, social problems, the family, and cultural texts is increasingly challenged. At the same time new areas—the popular film, popular music, pornography, and pulp literature—are appearing at different sites across disciplinary and institutional terrain (Denzen 1992, 75). A "terminological mutant" (Bathrick 1992, 321), the label cultural studies, as Hall put it, is an "uneasy marker" for a diverse and contentious set of competing but related discourses that legitimate new moves through the hybrid category of culture.

A critical interdisciplinarity conceived in opposition to both disciplinarity and past interdisciplinary practices is counterdisciplinary in stance, usually multidisciplinary in form, sometimes collaborative in its work patterns, and transdisciplinary in its creation of a broadly shared category of culture. The rhetoric of interdisciplinarity is both old and new. The familiar call to "prod" the disciplines becomes a strategy of transgression that faults disciplines for their "blindness' (Brantlinger 1990, 11, 148). Interdisciplinary keywords are entwined with keywords of disciplinary redescription—"negotiation," "intervention," and "transgression." Epithets of restructuring signify an interdisciplinarity that irritates and disturbs, disrupts and destabilizes. "Bricolage," the ultimate postmodern cross-court word, is not just a trendy way of stating an old idea. Loosely translated as "odds and ends" (Schor 1992, 272), bricolage signifies the character of critical interdisciplinarities. The older interdisciplinary move from part to whole becomes a recursive movement from part to whole and back again as new interests arise and rearticulations are made.

In the United States, three areas have provided direction for developing a programmatic understanding of what cultural studies might mean within the framework of existing disciplines: critique of ethnocentrism of scholarship and curriculum within ethnic studies, African American, Third World, and Latin American programs; critique of essentialism and universalism in feminism; and questioning of separations of culture, race, and gender in popular and mass culture (Bathrick 1992, 328–29).

The label "cultural studies" will continue to have a characteristic "elasticity." It is not so much a specific discipline or theoretical and political tradition as a "gravitational field" in which a number of traditions and forces are finding a "provisional rendez-vous" (Bennett 1992, 33). It is "a sort of magnet" that gathers coalescing practices into a problematic, perhaps even impossible synthesis. The holism of culture emerging in new work is not *unified* in a totalizing sense but *unifying* in the sense of shared values and objectives across multiple sites. Whether the effort can be integrative without sacrificing reflexivity and critique will depend on sustained dialogue across multiple sites. In constituting a new cultural criticism, cultural studies is also forging new patterns of intellectual work and a new cultural politics that bridges academic and public spheres. It strives to overcome the continuing fragmentation of knowledge within both the disciplinary structure of the university and the larger society the academic structure mirrors (Brantlinger 1990, 10, 16). By challenging all systems and structures, it aims to be a "permanent border action," working within while seeking to dissolve the institutional and discursive formations that were necessary to its emergence in the first place (Bathrick 1992, 322).

Using a label is easy. Grappling with the methodological difficulties of actually doing interdisciplinary work is more difficult. In cultural studies, the task is only beginning. Nelson, Treichler, and Grossberg distinguish "brief intellectual excursions into other domains"—culling good quotations, citing theoretical works and positions from outside, and encapsulating requisite background material—from projects and positions grounded in questions of what and how much must be learned from other fields in order to contextualize the object of study in any given project (1992, 15 n. 2). A genuinely integrative contextualizing will require moving beyond the more relational interdisciplinarity of "literature and . . . ," "sociology and . . . ," "anthropology and . . . ," "history and . . ." to a more constitutive relationship.

In art history, for instance, the society being studied must be configured as more than a painted background or a tableau of social groups. Current practices, Janet Wolff (1992) reports, exhibit both an excess of textuality, in literary and art studies, and an inhibition with regard to texts, in sociology.

The sociology brought to bear on texts is often shallow and mechanistic, effecting a crude determinism embodied in the metaphor of "reflection," the "influence" of social process (ideas, events, institutions) on art, and the ways art is "used" in social process. Sociology's continuing inclination toward positivism and its resistance to new developments in theory often preclude discussion of actual paintings. As a result, the relation between representation, ideology, and social process is obscured by a naively realist view of cultural institutions and products. The claim to interdisciplinarity is often made on the ground of intertextuality. A mutually constitutive relationship, however, requires integrating textual analysis with sociological investigation of institutions of cultural production as well as the social and political processes and relations in which production occurs.

Patrick Brantlinger calls the tracks that cultural studies is making in the disciplines "multiplying footprints in the sand" (1990, 11). The much-heralded transformation into a postdisciplinary academy has not occurred. Some structural transformation is occurring in institutions where new units are possible. The University of Birmingham has a newly constituted Department of Cultural Studies, led by a sociologist. Even in a time of tightening budgets, new curricula, projects, networks, and journals are appearing across the United States and the United Kingdom. Many activities, though, remain in the shadow structure. Holding an endowed chair at an elite research university or working in an autonomous unit is a rarer circumstance than struggling for minimal space in the curriculum of a state university or community college and having work discounted in the tenure and promotion process. The bold new frontier at one institution is a rebel camp or an isolated plea at another. Claims about the field need to be cognizant of both institutional realities.

Unease about institutionalization is understandably a recurring concern. In cultural studies, it often has the force of polemic. Claiming that marginality and critique cannot be institutionalized, though, underestimates the difficulty of creating new departments. It also sidesteps the issue of critical mass. The question of becoming a department, Wolff submits, is less important than the best strategy for institutional survival. Setting up centers and departments is not in and of itself counterproductive if the critical spirit is protected and cultural studies is not ghettoized. Even when attained, departmental status does not end the struggle for legitimacy. Control over hiring, tenure, promotion, and the curriculum may exist only at a lower level of institutional hierarchy (1992, 713–14). The fatal compromise of institutionalization that Giroux, Shumway, and Sosnoski (1984) warned about is real. Yet to claim, as is often done in cultural studies, that the authority of disciplines is gone and boundaries have dissolved is naive, even dangerous. The comparative history of interdisciplinary studies makes it emphatically clear that the only constancy in the knowledge system is boundary work. Advancing interdisciplinary claims depends on sustained dialogue on the kinds of inter-disciplinarity that are practiced, core boundary concepts, critical mass and integrative process, and the double movement of general connection and dis-ciplinary specificity.

CHAPTER 5

Interdisciplinary Genealogy in Literary Studies

> It is not criticism but psychology when we treat poems or novels as case books and attempt to discover in them not the art but the personality of their authors. It is not criticism but history or sociology when we read imaginative writings for what they may tell us about the manners or thought or "spirit" of the age which produced them. It is not criticism but ethical culture when we use them primarily as means of enlarging and enriching our experience of life or of inculcating moral ideas. It is not criticism but autobiography when we content ourselves with stating our personal preferences with regard to them.
> **John Crowe Ransom, "Criticism, Inc.," 1938**

> If you are anything like me, you may feel yourself unsure of what, as a critic these days, you ought to be talking about—whether literature qua literature, literature as rhetoric, literature as politics or as history, whether about the persistence of romanticism or the waxing of postmodernism, the decline of Yale or the rise of Duke.
> **Jerome Christensen, "From Rhetoric to Corporate Populism," 1990**

From Philology to the New Critical Embrace

The current heightened rhetoric of boundary crossing in literary studies provides an occasion for interdisciplinary genealogy in a synoptic discipline. Interdisciplinarity is neither singular nor static. Over the course of the twentieth century, multiple interdisciplinarities have emerged from the interplay of mainstream and alternative practices. These developments are allied with changes in the enabling conditions of literary study, the relational balance of "text" and "context," and the ways the keywords "general," "historical," "critical," "political" and "cultural" have demarcated the boundaries of the discipline. The traces of this history appear in patterns of practices and their representation in a series of handbooks and guides published by the leading professional organization of the discipline, the Modern Language Association.

The Disciplining of Literature

The concept of "literature" in the sense of imaginative writing emerged during the late eighteenth century. Previously the term had encompassed a broad range of meanings, from the older notion of polite letters and poetry to anything written, though especially serious writing (Kernan 1990, 13). Literature has been a vehicle for education since ancient times. It was considered part of the cultural heritage of a people, a humanistic repository that did not merit separate study or require special method. The study of literature was ancillary to study of other subjects: Greek and Latin languages; rhetoric, oratory, and forensics; theology and Renaissance humanism (Graff 1987, 19; Gunn 1992a, 240). As an academic subject, literature first appeared in the English academies of the late seventeenth century. As a university subject, it appeared in Scottish universities during the middle of the eighteenth century, though departments of vernacular languages were not formed until the final quarter of the nineteenth century (Graff 1987, 1).

In the United States the discipline had a threefold origin: as an outgrowth of training students in composition, oratory, and forensic rhetoric; as the study of vernacular literature in the tradition of scientific philology; and as a development of humanism, especially the version of humanism associated with Matthew Arnold (Miller 1991, 119–20). The contradictions of these origins are still apparent in the multiple practices housed within English departments.

From approximately 1860 to 1915, philology and literary history played dominant roles in the disciplining of literary studies. Philology, traditionally, was a discipline of wide scope, an *Altertumwissenschaft* that encompassed language and literature (Culler 1982, 5). It aspired to a total view of civilization, with a command of its languages and a method capable of integrating the humane disciplines. This broad, humanistic generality conflicted with the narrow, positive science (Graff 1987, 67–69) that developed in newly forming English departments. Based in its main forms on biblical scholarship and classical philology, the new version promised rigor for the profession of language teaching.

New procedures and rationale for studying vernacular literature embodied the principle of universal accounting, manifested in tasks of editing, annotating, collating, and establishing texts; compiling bibliographies, dictionaries, and concordances; conducting source studies and etymological research; discovering and verifying historical and linguistic facts; and writing biographies and literary and intellectual history (Miller 1991, 120–23).

Between 1925 and 1930, literary history gained prominence over linguistic philology. This development heightened emphasis on biography and literary types, the social backgrounds of literary periods, establishing texts and bibliography, lexicography and sanctioned methods of historical inquiry (Leitch 1988, 62).

Fortified by philological research and literary history, literary studies qualified for departmental status in the research university. Its legitimacy was enhanced by growing numbers of graduate students, substantially improved library collections, and the equating of "department" with disciplinary specialization and administrative authority. Harvard was the first place where one of the major results was institutionalized: the split between literary scholarship and teaching English composition. This split has remained typical of English departments in the United States (Graff 1987, 56, 67). Powerful though they were, philologists' right to define the terms of professionalism did not go undisputed. Competing conceptions of literary study were based in traditions of rhetorical analysis; popular, nonacademic criticism; oratory; a reaction against narrower Germanic methods that opened up curricular space for literary history as literature, not philological pedantry; and the ideal of general culture.

During the late nineteenth and early twentieth centuries, the ideal of general culture was upheld in departments of English and modern languages by a dissenting tradition of generalists (Applebee 1974, 28; Graff 1987, 55–56, 67, 101–2). The rise of literature as a professionalized subject occurred alongside the erosion of the idea of a communal literary culture and the close connection of literature with genteel models of liberal and general culture. Literature's affiliation with the "culture camp" of the humanities perpetuated the Renaissance ideal of a *litterae humaniores*. The culture camp consisted of classicists, some philosophical idealists, and individuals from English literature and history of art. They resisted specialization and scientific imagery by emphasizing knowledge as cultural process, not scientific product (Scott 1984, 50). Their conception of the humanities was rooted in older dogmas of spiritual idealism and culture, not technical procedures. The culture camp was in one sense a rearguard action (Graff 1987, 55–56). Disciplining was already altering the identity of the humanities. Older and more unified fields of inquiry were decomposing under the centrifugal forces of differentiation. This development hastened the decentralization and fragmentation of education where traces of traditional synthesis survived, foreshortening unifying hypotheses and eroding the older unitary principles of the university (Stone 1969, 15; Kluver and Schmidt 1990, 305).

The tradition of generalist culture had a further presence in the new general education programs that emerged in the early twentieth century in response to the proliferation of specialization and vocationalism (Boyer 1981,

4). Many of these programs reinscribed the broader, predisciplinary notion of literature. The collective ideals of a culture were presumed to lie in texts that included both literary and nonliterary classics. The most influential models of the time had a strong literary orientation: in Meiklejohn's belief that books form the basis of intelligence, in Eliot's five-foot shelf of classics, and in Erskine and Hutchins's great books curriculum at the University of Chicago. Their legacy remains strong in the undergraduate curriculum of the United States, from the great books curriculum of St. John's College to general education programs based on great texts and important ideas.

Both generalists and the new literary scholars experienced tensions between the older synoptic claims of humanism and the new disciplinary claims of professionalism. Professional research was theoretically a vehicle for general humanistic culture, but few individuals and departments successfully integrated the two. Philologists experienced tension between expectations that they act as specialists and that they also fulfill responsibilities for general education that lie outside the purview of professional training. Ironically, the form of humanistic scholarship now considered traditional was regarded by traditionalists of an earlier era as an unwanted innovation. Opposing members of English departments faulted new research procedures much the same way later traditionalists indicted the orthodoxy of New Criticism and today's traditionalists attack literary theory—for elevating esoteric, technocratic jargon over ethical, humanistic values and for turning literature into an elitist pastime for specialists and the quantifiable production of knowledge (Graff 1987, 3–4, 79, 81–82, 173).

Transmitting humanism remained a stated goal of English departments, but the professional capital of discipline was moving in an opposite direction. The heightening of philology and literary history marginalized the generalist, relocating general knowledge outside the discipline proper. Increasingly, the idea of academic seriousness also excluded reflection on the relations of one field to another and critical analysis of the historical process by which individual disciplines established boundaries. The historical dimension became extrinsic to the business of literary scholarship, and history was just one more discipline (Weber 1987, 32). Literary texts tended to be abstracted from history, bypassing the problem of historical and cultural change while keeping the disciplines of sociology and history at a distance (Graff 1987, 136). When Irving Babbitt and Paul Elmer promoted new humanism in the 1920s, one of their objectives in invoking the universal truths embodied in literature was to guard against intrusions of historical scholarship into the literary domain (Wilson 1988, 723).

The dominance of philology, literary history, and later the movement known as "criticism" has fostered a tendency to depict the first half of the twentieth century as a time when extrinsic approaches were held in check.

Yet, Gerald Graff contends, "The direction of postwar academic literary studies was interdisciplinary as much as it was intrinsic" (1987, 121, 209). Although not organized, the activities were numerous. At the time, the concept of interdisciplinarity had a double life. Synoptic identity implied an inherent "centrifugal heterogeneity" of multiple elements (Bate 1982, 50; Bergonzi 1990, 26) that has remained a persistent strain of disciplinary identity. In 1950 Leslie Fiedler proclaimed that "literary criticism is always becoming 'something else,' for the simple reason that literature is always 'something else.'" In 1992, at a very different time in the history of the discipline, Jonathan Culler declared that the "very comprehensiveness of literature draws theoretical discourses from other fields into theory."

Synoptic identity, William Paulson proposes, posits a view that literary studies is less a discipline than a residue of the broad, prescientific, and predisciplinary form of knowledge associated with the idea of "literature" in the seventeenth and eighteenth centuries. Modern theoretical efforts have fostered narrower disciplinary formations by privileging particular levels of phenomena and by establishing particular methodological principles for investigating them. Each effort attempts to promote disciplinary rigor. In contrast, literature conceived in terms of an "interdisciplinarity from within" recognizes multiple levels of phenomena. The literary text cannot be described at a single level, whether it is linguistic phenomena, rhetorical figures, global structures of poetic or narrative form, psychological or ideological categories. The reductionism of accounting for the whole in terms of a single set, part of a set, or a single procedure for organizing parts will always be incomplete. Paulson's metaphor of "noise" reappears. The goal is not to produce grand synthesis but to disturb, to enrich, even perhaps to displace by injecting information that is sufficiently foreign to function initially as noise. From interference arise new forms of explanation and new articulations between levels of phenomena (1988, 8–29; 1991, 46–49).

Over the next several decades, interdisciplinary interference would become more noticeable than the older synoptic tradition. In 1948 Stanley Edgar Hyman described modern criticism as "*the organized use of non-literary techniques and bodies of knowledge to obtain insights into literature*" (1955, 3). Hyman's model critics borrowed from linguistics and psychology (I. A. Richards), anthropology (Maud Bodkin), sociology and rhetoric (Kenneth Burke), Marxism (Christopher Caudwell), and linguistics and psychology (I. A. Richards and William Empson) (Graff 1987, 210). In Europe interdisciplinary research was promoted as the model for a regenerated study of literature opposed to strict formalism and open to historical awareness. By the mid-1950s similar voices were heard in the United States in the name of "multiple interpretation," "multiple parallelism," and "multiple causation." Some prominent scholars attempted to counteract narrow interpretations of individual works by combining several methods. One of the most influential, Kenneth Burke, sought to integrate sociological, psychoanalytical, and linguistic explanations (Hermand and Beck 1968, 150).

By the late 1940s, interdisciplinary trends were sufficiently strong that the counteraction was under way.

The New Critical Integration

As early as the 1890s, polemics on behalf of criticism began appearing in the professional literature. By the mid-1930s a two-pronged campaign became visible in the United States. One strain leaned toward aesthetic formalism, the other toward a humanist moralism that concentrated on the qualities literature shared with philosophy, ethics, and general ideas (Graff 1987, 121–22, 126–28, 145). These differences became opposing strains in the work of two groups of scholars who attempted to install criticism as the prevailing form of academic professionalism (Bergonzi 1990, 70). Their agendas differed. The New Critics emphasized close reading of poems treated as organically unified objects. The "Chicago critics" emphasized theory. Despite their differences, both groups believed disciplinary integrity was threatened.

R. S. Crane, founder of the Chicago critics, warned against treating literature as psychology, history, sociology, ethics, or autobiography. New Critic Allen Tate chided literary critics for being "obsessed by politics." He faulted the historical approach for undermining the unique nature of literature. Fellow New Critic John Crowe Ransom charged that the English department might as well proclaim itself a branch of the history department and, occasionally, ethics (Graff 1987, 147–49). The shoring up of disciplinary integrity through intrinsic criticism posted strong taboos against going outside the literary text for clues to interpretation (Patterson 1992, 185). By embracing the idea of timeless universality that Aristotle attributed to literature, New Criticism rejected historical knowledge. The stance was not strictly academic. Criticism emerged at a time of tremendous change, and formalist protocols offered a bulwark against threats to an older order. In insisting on the special status of poetry, advocates of criticism also legitimized professionalization and authority through special vocabulary and methods (Tompkins 1980, 223). Theoretically the universal qualities inherent in works of literature were accessible to everyone, and this premise justified making literature a required course for every student. The claim for universality, however, was made on the grounds of disciplinary autonomy.

The difference between the New Criticism and the "new history" of the time is instructive. At another site in the academy, James Harvey Robinson promoted a new history aimed at combating fragmentation of knowledge by constructing a new synthesis. Robinson exhorted historians to shift their gaze toward the social sciences. New history's account of the past was intended to include economic, psychological, social, and political life. The New Critics, in contrast, excluded other disciplines (Thomas 1991, 89–90, 93, 96, 153–54). The disciplinary specificity of literary language protected against encroachment by the social sciences, which are intellectual rivals for the study of human culture and behavior (Wilson 1988, 712.)

The logic of intrinsic criticism is conspicuous throughout the first full-length study of disciplinary relations published by the Modern Language Association (MLA), the 1967 *Relations of Literary Study* (Thorpe). The timing of the volume is significant. By 1967 the influence of New Criticism was waning, a trend signaled by repeated skepticism about its extremes. In introducing the volume, editor James Thorpe heralds a series of new vantage points that promise a more "stereoscopic view." Yet in announcing that the ultimate purpose of scholarship is a deeper, more complex, "truer" understanding of literature, Thorpe signals the intrinsic thrust of the volume. The governing metaphor of relations is kinship. History is "everybody's sister." As "the ancilla of her more artistic sisters," Rosalie Cole explains, Clio is a pluralistic muse who offers differing kinds of "assistance." Intellectual history and history of ideas, though, are privileged over other approaches. Low art, the focus of so much attention these days, is excluded in favor of the high art of a cultural elite.

Sociology is one of literature's "first cousins," though some relatives are favored over others. The major forms for literary purposes are sociology of literature and literary uses of sociological knowledge. At the time, sociological investigations of literature were more advanced in Europe. Marxist explanation had a different status in the United States, and work in sociology of literature was scarce. "Tentative communication" was occurring in studies of modern mass culture and media. But, Leo Lowenthal reports, sociologists tended to use "bits and pieces" of literary work without much concern for interpretation. The potential of Raymond Williams's work, which stimulated the later movement into cultural studies, is acknowledged. Some bridge building was also occurring in conceptualization of literature as a manifestation of social history. The promised "rapprochement" of social sciences and humanities, however, was still more promise than reality.

One after another, the seven "extraliterary" disciplines are brought *into* literature as tools to be exploited. Social history is treated as "somehow part of all literature, and all literature is part of it." In accounting for literature and religion, J. Hillis Miller warns about the danger of a self-enclosed integration that cuts poetry off from "its mesh of defining circumstances." Studies of literature's contexts ran the risk of moving so far beyond the poem that it becomes something else. The goal of literary study remains elucidation of intrinsic meanings of poems, plays, and novels that "show themselves forth as they are." The psychoanalytic critics that Frederick Crews applauds have absorbed Freudianism "into their literary sense." Leon Edel depicts the sister discipline of biography as a "department of literature." It is not extrinsic but "integral" and "intrinsic."

The major interdisciplinary event of the era, in many minds, was Northrop Frye's system of archetypal criticism. Frye's theory blurred disciplinary distinctions by conceiving of a mythopoeic structure that extended into literature, religion, philosophy, political theory, and many aspects of history. Myth criticism utilized substantive categories of interpretation from psychology and anthropology. The approach was widely influential, because it served both pioneering and traditional critics. It accommodated allegorical and genealogical modes of inquiry as well as sociological, religious, historical, and formalist approaches. It also proved compatible with the developing interdisciplinary fields of American studies and comparative literature. Ultimately, though, myth criticism was more profoundly disciplinary than interdisciplinary. In declaring the study of myth an essential activity, Frye shifted the work of civilization to the inside of literature. Literature properly understood, Frye explained in the 1967 *Relations,* was myth. Ten years earlier, in the *Anatomy of Criticism,* he had cautioned against using theoretical frameworks and categories from other disciplines, lest literary works be reduced to manifestations of the nonliterary. Myth, properly understood, was "not the study of literature in terms of something else" (Leitch 1988, 124–42; Davis 1978, 66).

In the end, the interdisciplinarity of the 1967 *Relations* is an intrinsic integration. Oscar Kenshur (1991) calls the book a "selective New Critical embrace of other disciplines" that dissolves their otherness. One of the Chicago critics, Richard McKeon, recalled the way rhetorical, dialectical, and grammatical criticism were restated in terms of art objects. The formalist critic could talk about the poet, the audience, and the cosmos by reconceiving extrinsic concerns in terms of a poetic text. Intrinsic criticism played a pivotal role in both disciplinary and interdisciplinary history, defining and legitimating the allowable terms of extraliterary influence. Moral and social significance were not purged: they were made a function of the formal properties of the text "itself."

The dominance of intrinsic criticism did not eliminate other approaches. Intrinsic criticism was just that—dominant. New Criticism never established complete hegemony in the profession (Greenblatt and Gunn 1992a, 8). Nevertheless, while intrinsic approaches held sway, interdisciplinary approaches were in "a state of noticeable arrest" or, where not completely arrested, were "seriously eclipsed" by formalistic, intrinsic methodologies (Gunn 1992a, 252). From the late nineteenth century through the mid-twentieth, they remained confined to the shadow structure of scattered practices, isolated subspecialties, and alternative approaches. Many younger critics with generalist inclinations moved toward literary journalism, making a living through book reviewing, translating, and occasional editorial work. Others adapted generalist interests to the methodological mold of New Criticism. Others yet dissociated themselves from generalists' moral and social interests (Graff 1987, 147).

One group in particular, known as the New York intellectuals, conceived of literature as a cultural phenomenon open to other critical approaches. Marxist and sociological analysis fueled an expanding cultural criticism. In the United States, though, continuing bias against Marxist explanation impeded fuller development of sociopolitical analysis (Leitch 1988, 86–87, 131). In the 1930s Marxist cultural and literary criticism arose in response to and as part of a mass working-class movement. In the 1950s, it continued to exhibit disinclination toward aesthetic questions. Not until a new upsurge of radicalism in the 1960s did the status of Marxist criticism change significantly, bolstered by growing methodological sophistication, success in theoretical and cultural studies, and the emergence of an American Marxist intelligentsia that crossed generational and national lines (Cohen 1992, 330–33). At midcentury, however, Marxism and other interdisciplinary approaches were still subject to charges of dilettantism, superficiality, and—the most disabling charge of all—lack of professionalism.

Loose Interdisciplinarity and Liminal Criticism

From the late 1960s through the early 1980s the most prominent interdisciplinary influences were hermeneutics, phenomenology, structuralism, semiotics, and social history. During the late 1970s and early 1980s, feminism, the language-based psychoanalysis of Lacan, and semiotics opened new lines of investigation. Deeper into the 1980s a set of practices grouped, however inexactly, under the umbrella label "poststructuralism" gained wider attention. In addition to the expanding influence of feminism and Lacanian analysis, they included the movements known as theory and deconstruction, new kinds of Marxist criticism that emerged out of the New Left, new historicist and Foucauldian scholarship, and postcolonial critique. New ways of reading also extended beyond New Critical explication de texte to a variety of critical, rhetorical, and sociological approaches (Miller 1991, 129–30).

Structuralism and Theory

In the early part of the period, structuralism was the most prominent interdisciplinarity. Structuralism overrode existing disciplinary categories by positing the idea of an underlying system of forms whose relations were articulated in terms of synchronic description. Its methodological patterns derived from disciplines, such as linguistics and anthropology, where the poetic text was treated as part of a common domain of discourse. The reformulation of the older disciplinary concept of "text," defined as a problem of the first kind, into the boundary concept of "textuality," defined as a problem of the second kind, was a clear challenge to the autonomy of New Criticism (Harth 1981, 8). Structuralism was not without its own exclusions. The synchronic studies of Jakobson and Lévi-Strauss disregarded biography, literary and cultural history, and readers' responses to texts. As a result, structuralism tended to remain separate from contexts of production and reception that fueled different interdisciplinary practices focused on readers' responses to texts (Leitch 1988, 345).

Structuralism operated as a "loose interdisciplinarity," a phrase Jonathan Culler used to describe the chameleonlike shapes of theory. The loose interdisciplinarity of both structuralism and theory indicates the modern terms of the "general." The approach to language in structuralism, and even in poststructuralism, was intended in a sense to generate a unified field theory by subsuming research in a variety of fields into general theory. Consequently both have been likened to physicists' efforts to encompass the phenomena of small-particle physics and cosmological physics into a unified field theory capable of integrating quantum physics with theories of astrophysics (Berman 1988, 291). A general theory never emerged, but structuralism did expand into a more global discipline with commitments to linguistic modeling and sign theory.

During the 1970s various American art historians, historiographers, musicologists, philosophers, theologians, and other specialists began exploring possible applications of structuralist and semiotic methods and models. Semiotics focuses on the use of signs and their interrelationships. In the United States, literary structuralism and semiotics moved through four phases: during the 1960s, linguistic and stylistic analysis of a formalist/poststructuralist kind; during the early 1970s, French structuralism; during the late 1970s, a looser broadening of boundaries as structuralism moved into semiotics; during the early 1980s, a softening of scientific claims and increased methodological skepticism as structuralism encountered the full challenge of poststructuralism (Leitch 1988, 260–63).

"Theory" is the common label for a variety of frameworks stimulated by new approaches from Europe. The loose interdisciplinarity of theory encompassed methods and approaches from anthropology, art history, gender studies, linguistics, philosophy, political theory, psychoanalysis, social and intellectual history, and sociology (Culler 1992, 203–5). As the importation of approaches from Europe began, many saw theory as the best hope for revitalizing the exhausted methods of New Criticism. The American critics, historians, and theorists who responded earliest and most eagerly to new developments were primarily in departments of English, modern languages, and comparative literature (Buttigieg 1987a, 18). Even when later accommodated in the mainstream, the new "liminal" criticism proved more compelling in some parts of the university than in others. It attained greater influence in literary criticism, Continental philosophy, interpretive social theory, and intellectual history than in literary history, analytic philosophy, positivistic social science, and conventional historiography (LaCapra 1987, 236).

Despite uneven influence, theory moved beyond the vanguard toward the core of literary research. It became institutionalized in three ways: the proliferation of courses, programs, textbooks, dissertation topics, and changes in degree requirements; a growing presence in mainstream conferences, journals, and press lists; and formation of new interdisciplinary centers, institutes, and flagship departments. Its primary development occurred in new specialized journals (such as *Diacritics, New Literary History, Critical Inquiry*), new institutions (the School of Criticism and Theory and the International Summer Institute for Semiotic and Structural Studies), new theory groups (the MLA's Division on Literary Criticism and the Society for Critical Exchange), new books and translations of important theoretical works from prestigious presses, the growing social status of leading theoreticians, expanding use of new terminology, and attention to new issues and questions (Leitch 1988, 383–84).

Theory turned a critical lens on the entire boundary complex of social and political, institutional and epistemological formations (Culler 1992, 207, 209). Yet as theory became located in the very institutional structures that had authorized and legitimated older claims of humanism and culture (Dhareshwar 1990, 234–35), it became caught in the dilemma of critical interdisciplinarities. Institutionalization connotes academic respectability, but inclusion as one more specialty in an increasingly crowded field is ultimately a form of marginalization. The larger field remained intact (Miller 1991, 132). Liminal criticism embodies the problematic of critical interdisciplinarities in several ways. It refuses to seek a quarantined place in the margins of established discourses or disciplines and demands, instead, their generalized displacement and rearticulation. In raising doubts about internal criteria of purity or autonomy and in unsettling the boundaries and protocols of fields, new practices operate as discursive agitations running through a variety of disciplines. As a result, they have an uneasy relation to their own institutionalization. They seek out threshold positions but cannot securely locate their own theoretical grounds and may cultivate the risks of hybridized discourses (LaCapra 1987, 236–37).

Given its plurality, theory has been an interactive, reflexive set of theoretical vocabularies that fix attention on problems that bear in turn a multitude of personal, disciplinary, and institutional inflections. Methodologically, theory performs double duty. Kreiswirth and Cheetham distinguish theory with a long view from theory with a close view. Theory with a long view takes an expansive problem, usually one with metatheoretical implications, and surveys it panoramically from a variety of critical and self-critical perspectives. By moving above and between texts and disciplinary formations, it foregrounds horizontal and synchronic citations and alliances. Theory with a close view lets a critique develop from intensive textual plodding. Problems of legitimation and authority occur at several levels. They are inherent in the theoretical turn itself, in its pragmatic consequences, and in the claims made for doing theory (1990a, 5–8).

Not surprisingly, even as it was being institutionalized theory remained a fluid, heterogeneous, and contentious site. New and established practices met and sometimes competed with a vigor, Vincent Leitch recalls, that made earlier struggles of the thirties, forties, and fifties among Marxists, New Critics, Chicago critics, New York intellectuals, myth critics, and existential critics seem in retrospect only "modest skirmishes" (1988, 383). Theory, Vivek Dhareshwar adds, illustrates what Bourdieu meant by a magnetic field made up of a system of power lines. Relations among constituting agents or systems of agents are forces that determine the structure of a field at any given time. The institutional space of theory was a field of social representation where intellectuals coming from different historical and cultural positions as well as political and epistemological stances met. They did not simply coexist. Neither were their differences resolved into a neat synthesis or a new discipline. They remained in active tension (1990, 234–35).

Like structuralism, theory went through several phases: from an initial linguistic turn into a widening rhetorical turn and, more recently, into a historical or ideological turn (Kreiswirth and Cheetham 1990a, 3). Over the course of two decades, theory changed the character of literary studies in three major ways: wide-ranging reflection on language, representation, and the categories of critical thought that were themselves undertaken by deconstruction; analyses of the role of gender and sexuality in every aspect of literature and criticism by feminism and gender studies; and development of historically oriented cultural criticisms that study a variety of discursive practices involving many objects (the body, the family, race, the medical gaze) not previously considered as having a history (Culler 1992, 201).

Other practices affirmed the character of the era. The study of readers' responses to texts was, in Susan Suleiman's often-quoted description, "not a single widely trodden path but a multiplicity of criss-crossing, often divergent tracks that cover a vast area of the critical landscape." Suleiman identified six major and sometimes combined approaches: rhetorical, semiotic and structuralist, phenomenological, subjective and psychological, historical and sociological, and hermeneutic (1980, 6–7). Reader-response theory evolved in the late 1960s from social, intellectual, and literary developments in Germany. These developments provided a new way of examining both the established canon and once-excluded works of mass media and popular literature. As audience-oriented criticism evolved, it moved beyond the specifics of German reception theory into a general interweaving of categories and procedures from linguistics with literary theory. It further incorporated social and political histories of readership. In its role as a cross-fertilizing agent, reader-response criticism operated as a loose interdisciplinarity and simultaneously bore traces of local disciplinary economies. As it took root in literary studies, art history, and sociology, it was often folded back into the disciplinary primacy of word, image, and behavior. Reader-response critics in language and literature departments usually continued to emphasize analysis and interpretation of texts (Leitch 1988, 377; Tompkins 1980).

Representing Heterogeneity

New practices exacerbate old fears even as they are changing the very nature of discipline. Delivering the 1980 MLA presidential address, Helen Vendler warned against "a general interdisciplinary Polonius-like religious-historical-philosophical-cultural overview." She admonished scholars to maintain "our own separateness from other disciplines" (Graff 1987, 254). Six years later, delivering the 1986 MLA presidential address, J. Hillis Miller depicted a vastly different profession. It had undergone "a sudden, almost universal turn" away from theory toward history, politics, culture, and society (Montrose 1989, 15). Some of the reasons are depicted in two books, one focused on the curriculum, the other on research.

Prospects for the 70's (Finestone and Shugrue 1973) emanated from a two-year series of seminars sponsored by the Association of Departments of English (ADE). Graduate students, teachers, and English-department chairs joined specialists from other disciplines in investigating relations between English and other fields. The concept of interdisciplinary study in *Prospects* emanates from a desire to "enhance and regenerate" the teaching and learning of language and literature, not to threaten, supplant, or overturn the discipline. Participants were responding to new pressures and interests: the declining role of the humanities and dropping enrollments in English departments, the growing role of community colleges in postsecondary education, worldwide demands for educational reform, heightened concerns about literacy, expanding awareness of other cultures, growing interest in mass media and popular culture, a sense that the most pressing questions and problems are interdisciplinary, and the need for better connections with new research in the social and natural sciences.

Seminar participants shared an implicit sense of what constitutes the right and the wrong kinds of interdisciplinarity. The right kind is grounded in the identity and integrity of individual disciplines. Voicing a common belief, Daniel Bernd proclaims, "We must begin with the premise that there is nothing wrong with the disciplines as disciplines." Departments, Theodore Gross adds, should remain intact. They are convenient political arrangements that perpetuate a cultural tradition worth offering to students. They would also, he projected, be crucial anchors in an education he foresaw becoming increasingly interdisciplinary. Warnings against dilettantism abound in repeated rejection of "eclectic," "encyclopedic," "generalist," and "Leonard-esque" programs. "Anti-" and "nondisciplinary" foci, which would become prominent in the 1980s, are also rejected. So is producing a new kind of specialist. The disciplines need not be sacrificed to make room for interdisciplinary skills.

The theoretical leanings of the volume are another index of the era. Caroline Shrodes proposes an organic approach that draws on theories from philosophy, cultural anthropology, depth psychology, and studies of archetype and myth. Her dynamic, holistic conception emphasizes the reader's role. Irving Deer crafts a holistic approach from new developments in science, most notably the theory of complementarity and its compatibility with systems thinking. In proposing a theory of convergence, illustrated by a course that blends literature and social science around the problem of alienation, Henry Winthrop goes furthest in grappling with the problems of actually doing interdisciplinary work. Winthrop addresses disciplinary relationships and methods of using information. He also offers the only detailed typology, classifying curricular approaches in the five categories of survey, problem orientation, subject matter, field theory, and general systems theory.

Exemplary practices are equally revealing. The interdisciplinary curricula of the time were primarily enhanced disciplinary courses and interdepartmental courses and programs that concentrated on popular culture, ethnic studies, and contemporary issues and problems such as alienation, poverty, social class, the future, the city, and the community. A new theme-based organization of the curriculum is also promoted, whether installed over or alongside traditional historical periods. Signs of readiness for greater cooperation with the social sciences were visible, but the first reason for becoming interdisciplinary, Alan Hollingsworth reports, is "self-preservation." The 1973 *Prospects* is a declaration of interest and intent, written in a cautious tone. Disciplinary relations are conceived in terms of complementarity, convergence, nonfictional information, and historical and philosophical background. The case for a critically conceived interdisciplinarity was present in the discipline but not at the center. It was being developed elsewhere, in the shadow structures where poststructuralist practices were gaining critical mass.

Almost a decade later, *Interrelations of Literature* appeared (Barricelli and Gibaldi 1982). Registering the proliferation of interests that followed its predecessor, the 1967 *Relations,* the book contains almost double the number of entries and has expanded from 151 to 329 pages. History and biography do not appear, because they are covered in a separate volume. Myth, psychology, sociology, religion, and music reappear. The new entrants are linguistics, philosophy, folklore, politics, law, science, the visual arts, and film. Given the editors' admission that developing successful pedagogical approaches and structures remain a serious challenge, the 1973 *Prospects* is surprisingly ignored, reinscribing a dichotomy of teaching and research.

The interdisciplinary rhetoric of the era abounds, with talk of "interplay," "inherent" ties, "reciprocal process," "interpenetration," "interaction," "symmetries," "symbiotic" and "complementary" relationships. Nevertheless, the "extraliterary" relations of literature are brought into a world in which *literature,* the editors announce, is "the hub of the wheel of knowledge," a center that provides the "logical locus" for integration of knowledge. Like the profession, the book stands on shifting ground: pointing forward to the complexity of Giles Gunn's depiction of "Interdisciplinary Studies" in 1992 while harking back to the disciplinary primacy of the 1967 *Relations.* Centripetal approaches, such as the study of literature as an isolated aesthetic or national entity, theoretically deny the centrifugal movement of literature across international borders and its intersections with other forms of art and knowledge. Yet, the editors assert, the interdisciplinary thrust of comparative literature has restored literature to its "pristine position as a central cognitive resource in society, as its most faithful and comprehensive interpreter."

The definition of practices depends on many factors, from the project at hand and the discipline in question to individual perceptions. There are, as Gerald Mast says of the literature-film relation, lumpers and splitters, resulting in different perceptions of contiguity and use. Most relations are portrayed as long-standing, a common genealogical tact. Jonathan Culler invokes the close classical association of language and literature in the discipline of rhetoric, Giles Gunn traces the literature-religion relationship "to the very origins of literature," and Steven Scher roots the music-literature relation in a notion "as old as the first stirrings of aesthetic consciousness." The most consistent theoretical premise is the distinction between influence and constitutive relation. In the former, literature appears *in* the work of another discipline, another discipline appears *in* literature, or one makes *use* of the other. In the latter, relations move beyond analogy, allusion, and simple influence to homology and identity. Even the latter distinction, though, is subject to an added factor—time. Literature and philosophy, Thomas McFarland reports, sometimes come together in mutual fecundation, sometimes occlude one another, and at other times move wide apart. The account of literature and religion also highlights the shifts that take place over time.

From classical antiquity to the Renaissance, Giles Gunn explains, literature exhibited a complementary and often supportive link with inherited religious traditions. Toward the end of the Renaissance the relation became more adversarial. By the end of the eighteenth century, literature was viewed as an alternative to religion or a substitute for it. Modern studies have not produced a self-conscious or systematic field; the relationship has also tended to be misunderstood or discounted in contemporary forums. Description was also dominated for a long time by Anglo-American scholars who drew on the theoretical legacy of European existentialism. When critically self-aware, studies had developed in overlapping stages characterized by distinctive forms and methods. The first, dating from the late 1920s to the dawn of World War II, was pastoral or therapeutic in orientation. The second, dating from after World War II to the mid-1960s, was either broadly apologetic and correlative or essentially historicist. The third, beginning in the middle or later 1960s, focused on issues that were either generic or anthropological in orientation. More recently, new methodologies of structuralism, phenomenology, hermeneutics, and poststructuralism have challenged traditional constructions.

Jonathan Culler's account of linguistics reveals another characteristic of disciplinary relations. Despite a strong historical record of contacts, including new developments born of poststructuralist approaches, interactions have occurred within the broader context of a "fundamental and continuing separation." In the early 1980s, allegiance to the philological ideal of a comprehensive discipline remained alive in classical and medieval studies. Yet when *Interrelations* appeared, the most emphatic calls for linguistic analysis were coming from advocates of the new linguistics of discourse, not defenders of contemporary linguistics per se. In the subdomain of stylistics, opposing tendencies reflect the tension between literary effects and "true" understanding of literary significance. Linguistics, Culler concluded in 1982, might be considered primarily a body of knowledge to draw on in developing a systematic account of the functioning of *literary* language, not as a general tool for interpretation or a method of objective interpretation.

The historical balance point of the era is indicated most clearly, once more, by the account of myth and literature. Four definitional aspects were prominent at the time, not as clearly defined methodologies or schools so much as differing influences and personal predilections: formal traits of narrative character, image, and theme; causal connections linked with temporal or logical priority or coincidence; historical and specific sources, influences, and models; psychological dynamics. Echoing Northrop Frye's earlier account of the relationship, John Vickery acknowledges that myth criticism had stimulated connections, especially with anthropology and psychology. This stimulus reversed the intrinsic directionality of New Criticism. Yet even when "espousing the necessity of extraliterary knowledge," myth criticism reserved the right to legitimately extend or alter its sense in accordance with the needs of literary study.

"Literature itself" also remained the unifying point of view in the relationship between literature and sociology. The relationship, Priscilla Clark concludes, comes down to a choice of which category—literature or society—is the explicans and which the explicandum. The core concepts of "writer," "public," "genre," and "literature" are redefined by the contexts in which they occur. Yet sociological analysis does not supplant the primacy of literary inquiry. Individual practices vary along a continuum of commitments to social factors and literary meaning. Ultimately, the task of any sociology of literature is to clarify the *literary* significance of social contexts of literature and the complexity of those social relations. Sociology of literature *extends* understanding of literature and is concerned with the production and effect of *meaning.* The social relations of literature are "not extraliterary but are literature itself."

Radical Interdisciplinarity and the New Cross-disciplinary Consciousness

Over the latter half of the twentieth century, the MLA published a series of guides and handbooks to professional practice. *Aims and Methods of Scholarship in Modern Languages and Literatures* appeared in 1963 and in 1970. Its successor, *Introduction to Scholarship in Modern Languages and Literatures,* appeared in 1981 and was revised in 1992. An additional volume of description came out in 1992 under the title *Redrawing the Boundaries: The Transformation of English and American Literary Studies.* The guides were intended primarily for graduate students and younger scholars. By the early 1990s, however, even veteran members of the profession needed a map through the maze of new developments and reorientations. Once organized primarily around close reading of a stable set of masterworks, literary studies is now being reorganized at many sites around diverse historical projects and new critical idioms (Greenblatt and Gunn 1992a, 3, 8–9).

The Changing Profession

Changing practices register in changing classifications. Both the 1963 and 1970 editions of *Aims and Methods* depicted a fourfold division of the discipline into linguistics, textual criticism, literary history, and literary criticism. The 1981 *Introduction* retained familiar categories but substituted "Historical Scholarship" for "Literary History," while adding "Literary Theory" and "The Scholar in Society." Their addition, the editors explained, signaled two diverging trends in scholarship. One was moving toward the speculative and abstruse, the other toward the complex relation between scholarship and the "real" world.

The results are visible in the organizing principles of the 1992 *Introduction.* There are three major sections, with "The Scholar in Society" serving as epilogue. The subheadings illustrate the current diversity of the discipline:

Language and Composition
  Linguistics
  Language, Culture, and Society
  Language Acquisition and Language Learning
  Rhetoric and Composition
Literary Studies: Text, Interpretation, History, Theory
  Textual Scholarship
  Canonicity and Textuality
  Literary Interpretation
  Historical Scholarship
  Literary Theory
Cross-disciplinary and Cultural Studies
  Interdisciplinary Studies
  Feminist and Gender Studies
  "Ethnic and Minority" Studies
  "Border" Studies: The Intersection of Gender and Color
  Cultural Studies

These changes were tied in no small part to the changing faces of the profession. Between the 1950s and 1980s, English departments expanded and diversified. In the post–World War II era, a new generation of faculty from a broader base of class and ethnic backgrounds moved uneasily into the high modernist formalism of literary education. In the 1960s and 1970s they moved into a university marked by social and political movements (Levine 1992, 135). Their presence, along with renewed demands for academic reform, widespread critique of mimetic representation, and growing interest in the politics of institutionalized knowledge, began to affect what was studied and how it was analyzed. Official description was not always quick to register the changes. The 1981 edition of the MLA *Introduction* contained no essay on feminist criticism, even though feminist theory and practice were gaining visibility and influence by the close of the 1970s.

The current claim that literary studies has evolved into cultural studies, Michael Ryan suggests, results from the combined effect of three sets of influences: *feminist, ethnic, and leftist criticism,* forcing recognition that literary texts are fundamentally documents and social texts with sociohistorical referents; *the projects of structuralism and semiotics,* demonstrating that texts are shaped by social codes, conventions, and representations, thereby rendering defunct the idea of literary autonomy; *the rising importance of mass media and popular culture* over the centrality of literary classics, compelling critics to admit the crucial formative and educational roles played by these new discourses (cited Leitch 1988, 404).

The object "itself" had also changed. The shift from the discrete disciplinary object of text to the boundary concepts of textuality and discourse widened the field of interest. Literary experimentation also bred new forms of fiction characterized by multigeneric, multidisciplinary tendencies. The multidisciplinary interest of much of the current work in humanities has at least one origin in transgressing the generic boundaries that traditionally separated prose from poetry and scholarship from imaginative exposition, philosophy, and cultural critique. The most influential poststructuralists—Derrida, Lacan, and Foucault—wrote in literary styles. In the work of Jacques Derrida, deconstruction engaged texts as discursive contents and institutional structures. The intertextuality of deconstruction and other new practices placed literature in a wider conversation with philosophy, history, linguistics, psychoanalysis, and intellectual history. This move reframed literary topics in ways that had significance for a wide range of professionals (Esch 1992; Rowe 1992, 184, 186, 192–97).

One of the strongest indicators is the relationship of literature and history.

The Neighborhood of Literature and History

In the 1963 and the 1970 *Aims and Methods* (Thorpe), literary history was conducted in a literary idiom. Developing a secondary specialization was encouraged at an amateur level, but scholars were admonished not to let "subinterests" became primary. The "true literary historian," Robert Spiller cautioned, "however far he may wander, is always on his way, by a circuitous route, back to the literary work as his primary object." By the 1981 *Introduction* (Gibaldi), Barbara Kiefer Lewalski judged the "high walls thrown up in the 1930's to safeguard the purity of literary criticism and literary interpretation from the supposed encroachments of literary history, and vice versa, have been large demolished." The territory Spiller mapped in 1963 and 1970 had become more extensive and less clearly demarcated. Nonetheless, contextual investigations still occurred primarily in the interests of interpretation and criticism. Lewalski warned against imposing contemporary political perspectives on historical materials, lest literature become merely a document or be transformed into sociology. Comparably, scholars in the history of ideas and social and cultural history were cautioned to "honor the uniqueness of the literary work."

In depicting the relationship for the 1992 *Introduction* (Gibaldi), Annabel Patterson reflected on the dominant categories and activities of preceding decades. Primarily literary in conception, they encompassed biography, sources and influences, background contexts, the history of literary elements, forms and genres, literary history proper, and social and cultural history. In contrast, recent changes might eventually be located in the traditional domains of social and cultural history. Scholarship has expanded to incorporate subjects previously classified as external "contexts," especially contemporary politics and social milieu. Once autonomous literary texts are now being placed within the historical, social, political, and economic conditions that produced them. Correspondingly, new topics have emerged, such as suicide, amnesia, war memorials, economic status, women's education, gynecology, the role of police, incarceration and hospitalization, literacy and the history of reading, the history of the literary marketplace, dress as a social code, and the relation between forms of recreation and class consciousness.

The "road back to history," Patterson recalled, began with structuralism, the rise of social history, and the cultural archaeology of Michel Foucault. In blending philosophy with social history, Foucault cut across disciplinary boundaries, emphasizing disjuncture and dispersion rather than unity and coherence. The earliest notable impact was in studies of the English Renaissance, generating the movement known as new historicism. Before the rise of new historicism, scholars typically combined formalist techniques of close rhetorical analysis with elaboration of relatively self-contained histories of ideas, literary genres, topics abstracted from their social matrices, commentaries on political commonplaces, and erudite ciphering of meaning. By and large, the past was a reductive history limited to decorative or pigeonholed background. History, applied "with positivistic force" on literary interpretation, produced a wealth of detailed factual information about textual and biographical history.

New historicism is, in part, one more sign of dissatisfaction with past and present practices, whether in New Critical or in deconstructive guise. More profoundly, Patterson emphasizes, it reflects a larger shift in the *épistème*. Today's new history has the "force of a polemic." It is propelled by the conviction that literary texts are products of historical, social, political, and economic environments once deemed "outside" the text and must be resituated within them. Literary history has undergone extensive reconceptualization. New historicism also moved beyond American and British literary studies to literary and cultural studies of other nations as well as other disciplines of the humanities, especially art history. Like other interdisciplinarities, new historicism is both a specific practice and a general trend. Most anthologies of scholarly work contain a mixture of affiliations and positionings that mark relations with the older historicism, theory and deconstruction, the periods and the isms that traditionally structured the discipline, definitions of disciplinarity and interdisciplinarity, and the agendas of individual practitioners.

The most powerful result is reconfiguration of the relation between the categories of "history" and "culture." Culture is a partial, fragmentary, and conflictual terrain, not a single, coherent, or totalizing system. Reflecting this shift, older metaphors of linearity and reflection have been replaced by metaphors of network and interplay, circulation and negotiation. Older organic models, Brook Thomas explains, were dominated by the rhetorical figure of synecdoche. New historicism replaces synecdoche with chiasmus, a rhetorical figure that reconfigures the part-whole relation, extending literary analysis to cultural analysis. Literature no longer speaks for or represents culture as a whole. Chiasmus places literature in relation to other cultural practices. This move is evident in the proliferation of course titles such as "The Literature of Psychology and the Psychology of Literature" or "The Law of Literature and the Literature of the Law."

Since one of the objectives is to produce a new cultural poetics, Thomas adds, an older Aristotelian problem resurfaces. Can details serve as concrete universals? Scholars speculate about connections between parts, but they resist granting any one part the power to speak for the whole. Critical perspective is heightened when the parts being related are not only social practices but ethnic and national cultures as well. Both the site and the classification of analysis have been reconfigured. The social and the aesthetic circulate through the entire network of practices, beliefs, and institutions that constitute culture as a whole. In keeping with critical interdisciplinarity, culture is not a totalizing whole. By placing literature in relation to other disciplines, chiasmus creates networks of relations that resist totalizing. When established categories are defamiliarized, discussion of character, language, and theme are not apportioned solely to literary scholars, "primitive" customs are not strictly the concern of anthropologists, and demographic patterns are not matters for social historians alone (Thomas 1991, 9–12).

Circulation does not occur without the traces of disciplinary economies. The organic model, Thomas adds, retains firm roots in social and intellectual cultures. Individual practices tend to transform the chiasmatic relation from difference to identity. When this occurs, disciplinary imperialism masquerades as interdisciplinary work. Most literary specialists tend to begin with and emphasize a work of literature or to assume the starting point is somehow connected with other literary works of a period. Shifting history from background to a "shared code" has not made historians out of literary scholars. The methodologies of new historicism have tended to produce a thick description that brackets literary and ethnographic analysis (Montrose 1989, 19).

Mapping Interdisciplinarity

The most striking representational change in the 1992 *Introduction* is the addition of an entire section devoted to "Cross-disciplinary and Cultural Studies." Being accorded a separate section, though, is only the most obvious measure. Interdisciplinarity is pervasive. No longer confined to a special volume, subsection, or essay, it has become part of the rhetoric of disciplinary practice. Multiple interdisciplinarities are present, from simple borrowings and methodological thickening to theoretical enrichment, converging sites, and a general shift away from older interdisciplinary studies to new "cross-" "counter-" and "antidisciplinary" positions that front the problem of how meaning is produced, maintained, and deconstructed. The foregrounding of representation has been a central move of almost every major critical practice—feminist, Marxist, deconstructive, new historicist, Foucauldian, and Lacanian (Levine 1992, 150).

In tackling the formidable task of describing "interdisciplinary studies" in the 1992 *Introduction,* Giles Gunn winds up reflecting equally on the problem of mapping. One cannot be separated from the other. The first and simplest approach to mapping, Gunn explains, is on disciplinary terms, in this case the familiar literary critical coordinates of author, reader, material or linguistic components of a text, and the world the text refers to. When the four coordinates are compared, interdisciplinary work has clearly placed more emphasis on the reader and the work. If a single coordinate forms the cartographic axis, the picture changes. Recent criticism centered on the reader, for example, highlights the reader's experience in terms of (1) feminist, ethnic, and class-oriented ideological motives; (2) psychoanalytic, structuralist, feminist, deconstructionist, or semiotic interests; and (3) combinations of the foregoing categories.

This is a simpler, more coherent, and more conventional way of mapping. The primary tactic of the 1967 *Relations* and the 1982 *Interrelations,* this approach produces accessible taxonomy based on the associate relations of literature *and* other disciplines. Gunn tallies notable developments: *literature and philosophy:* phenomenological criticism, hermeneutics, deconstruction, neopragmaticism, ethical criticism, the new rhetorical criticism; *literature and anthropology:* structuralism, ethnography, or "thick description," folklore and folklife studies, myth criticism; *literature and psychology:* psychoanalytic criticism, reader-response criticism, anxiety-of-influence criticism, cultural psychology; *literature and politics:* sociological criticism, cultural studies, ideological criticism, materialist studies; *literature and religion:* theological apologetics, recuperative hermeneutics, generic and historical criticism, rhetoric studies; *literature and linguistics:* Russian formalism, stylistics, narratology, semiotics (249).

However illuminating it is, this strategy too is problematic. The relational logic of "Literature and . . ." places the question of interdisciplinarity on literary ground. In asking what literature has to do with other material or fields, relational mapping conserves existing categories, comparable to the first interdisciplinary movement in the social sciences. Put another way, it builds bridges but does not restructure. In contrast, "genuine interdisciplinarity," in the view of Gunn and many critical interdisciplinarians, requires altering the question. Relational study is single-sided. Interdisciplinarity forged in critique is double-sided, raising other questions. How might insights or methods of other fields or structures remodel understanding of the nature of literature and the literary? Conversely, how might literary conceptions and approaches remodel conception of allied fields and their subject material?

Mapping may occur in yet another way. What new subjects have emerged? This approach highlights a diverse array of inquiries, ranging from the history of the book and materialism of the body to the semiotics of signification and ideologies of gender, race, and class. Simply identifying new topics is not sufficient. Each topic in turn attracts and projects further lines of interdisciplinary investigation:

> Studies like *The Body in Pain* by Elaine Scarry, for example, have woven psychoanalytic, cultural, materialistic, neo-Marxist, and new-historicist strands of disciplinary interrogation; studies of representation such as Stephen Greenblatt's *Shakespearean Negotiations* have drawn into new combinations historicist, reader-response, cultural materialist, hermeneutic, semiotic, and often deconstructionist inter- and cross-disciplinary modes. But in much of the new interdisciplinary scholarship, studies of the body become studies of representation. Thus the threading of disciplinary principles and procedures is frequently doubled, tripled, and quadrupled in ways that are not only mixed but, from a conventional disciplinary perspective, somewhat off center. (248–49)

The last approach to mapping is rarely acknowledged. Over the past quarter century, correlate fields have changed. One of the most significant reasons is initiatives that other disciplines either stimulated or helped sustain. Like new subjects that emerge and do not stay put, disciplinary inquiry has not stayed put. Literature's relations with other fields and structured forms have not followed an orderly pattern. Neither is one set of associations fully descriptive of all other conceptual and methodological filiations. Interdisciplinary cartography is not a straightforward task. The moves it tracks, Gunn correctly notes, are "overlapping, underlayered, interlaced, crosshatched affiliations, coalitions, and alliances." Very often they are as much a part of disciplinary history as of interdisciplinary history.

From Practice to Theory

Two prominent characteristics emerge in disciplinary practices today: a new momentum of interdisciplinary identity and the continuing claims of older approaches and conceptualizations. These themes and their implications for theorizing interdisciplinarity are evident in three major areas—period studies, disciplinary relations, and the interdisciplinary field of American studies.

Period Studies

Period studies has long been the chronological scaffolding of disciplinary structure. Changes are apparent in all periods, though they are neither identical nor even. The changes were depicted in *Redrawing the Boundaries*. Surveying Victorian studies over the past twenty-five years, George Levine (1992) finds an "almost total transformation of the landscape," a "fundamental generational break" marked by textual and ideological changes. Victorian literature was previously taught as a roughly agreed upon set of characteristics, problems, and preoccupations. Earlier practices invoked a world of isomorphic relations cast in a seamless unity. Inquiry was structured by notions of cause and effect, genre, organic forms, centrality of the human subject, and the mimetic fit of discourse and social reality. Social and historical emphasis, textualism, culture, Foucauldian analysis, and feminism created different commitments. At present Victorian scholarship cannot be adequately represented by maintaining strict separations in the older binary categories of textualism, historicism, contextualism, and formalism.

Medieval studies, in comparison, is more steeped in tradition. Semiotics, deconstruction, and anthropological paradigms have had relatively little impact. Describing current trends, Anne Middleton (1992) draws a striking parallel. Both medieval studies and area studies were distinctive institutional products and thought structures of the Cold War era. The invention of medieval chronological terrain, like the geographical terrain of area studies, rendered the Middle Ages an institutionalized object of minute analysis. This standpoint minimized intersubjective and historical relations. During the mid-1960s borders became more permeable, and the idea of a new "superdisciplinary field" arose. Since then, groups, journals, and venues for regular exchange with medievalists in other disciplines have grown rapidly. As a result, traditional demarcations have blurred.

No single type of interdisciplinary practice dominates. Some specialized work on medieval artifacts—such as paleography, codicology, and liturgy—does not have a single disciplinary home. In new literary historical work on the period, social history is cited more frequently than interpretive discussion, and historical narratives are less likely to be treated as mere documents. In studies of medieval literacy, the older boundary separating oral and written discourse has been redefined. In another area of interest, religion is being reformulated as practice, not doctrine. Renewed attention is also being paid to the material and institutional base of medieval studies. Reconstructing literary study as both a site and a contested form of action has moved scholars outward from a relatively small number of canonized texts and authors toward questions no longer regarded as the strict province of social and cultural historians. The retreat from older vocabularies and concepts suggests that a "rapprochement" is occurring between historical and literary practices. A new philology has also been proposed as a model of critical practice. The new philology is rooted in a manuscript matrix of texts that are conceived as a cultural place of "radical contingencies," not the rationalized, codified forms of earlier humanist philology.

In another chronological realm, eighteenth-century studies, new practices have been greeted with celebration and scorn. For some, especially older traditionalists, they threaten to contaminate literary study. For others they beckon transformation into a wider field where the older dichotomies of text/context, intrinsic/extrinsic, and disciplinary/interdisciplinary are dissolved. The American Society for Eighteenth Century Studies was founded in 1969 to foster communication and cooperation among scholars studying eighteenth-century culture. The four Enlightenment categories of older scholarship, John Bender recalls, were aesthetic autonomy, authorship, disinterestedness, and gendered sexuality. The Enlightenment aesthetic was a complex geometry of divisions of knowledge that separated individual arts from each other and from historical, scientific, and argumentative discourses. During the 1970s boundary crossing escalated in studies of poetry. In scholarship on Alexander Pope, for instance, emphasis began shifting from an intrinsic focus unconcerned with time, place, and nonliterary relations to new antiformalist investigations that attempted to reconstruct the worlds of the poet and the reader.

What began in 1969 as a "movement" escalated to a "stampede" (Harth 1981, 4). The spring 1979 issue of *Eighteenth-Century Life* registered the reactions. David Sheehan distinguished two kinds of practices. A "soft" interdisciplinary approach entails finding material in another discipline to illustrate something already in the text. A "hard" interdisciplinary approach requires turning to materials and methods of another discipline to solve a problem raised in the text. The distinction centers on a crucial difference: between providing context and solving a problem. The problem, though, is still constructed as a "literary problem." In contrast, the radical step of interdisciplinary textuality sees no choice but to go outside the text (Marshall 1992, 174).

Going "outside" the text may be fraught with danger. Richard Schwartz warns about the gap between the promise of interdisciplinary research and the reality of generalists attempting to span the curriculum. "True" interdisciplinary work, he advises, involves highly specialized learning and skills, not universal knowledge; otherwise errors arise from shallow disciplinary depth. Schwartz endorses "contextual" approaches that affirm the primacy of text over political, sociological, and philosophical approaches that render texts "tools for literary ideologues." Arthur Scouten, in turn, warns against overemphasis on interdisciplinary approaches, against going off on tangents of sociology, psychology, and history of science. "Let us," he exhorts, "stop whoring after strange gods and return to the practice of teaching and publishing our best insights on the masterpieces of eighteenth-century literature."

Over the next decade, new historicism, cultural materialism, feminist literary history, and to a lesser extent deconstruction continued to challenge the rubrics of the Enlightenment framework. New work reconstituted the notion of disciplinary work by reaching across the customary boundaries separating literary study, visual arts, history, anthropology, sociology, and the law. It is one thing, Bender explains, to compare literature with other arts, quite another to treat novels, paintings, buildings, logical treatises, legislation, and institutional regulations as texts that participate in complex and contestatory processes. The new approaches, Bender adds, might even be labeled "transdisciplinary," because they work to erode the presumptions on which existing disciplines are founded within schools, museums, universities, and other educational institutions.

Updates on relations with psychology, the law, the arts, and science reveal parallel shifts, though again not without differences across sectors and not without the traces of both generality and specificity.

Disciplinary Relations

No discipline is engaged with the entirety of another discipline. Literary critics have tended to associate psychology with the psychoanalysis of Freud and, more recently, Lacan. In earlier practices unconscious meanings were often assigned ahistorically and impersonally to literary works. By the 1982 *Interrelations* (Barricelli and Gibaldi), psychoanalytic interpretations of literature were exhibiting greater awareness of language and the role that transference and countertransference play. Current construction of the relationship posits a sameness of the two disciplines, though a split between followers of Freud and of Lacan, Meredith Skura reports (Gibaldi 1992), has produced different mappings.

The "psyche" group—composed primarily of Freudians, Kleinians, object relations theorists, and Winnicottian interpreters—emphasizes reading as evidence of individual mind. The "analysis" group—primarily Lacanians—directs attention away from individual mind and an author's unconscious to the text and the larger intersubjective process of language and culture. Critics charge that interdisciplinary psychoanalytic thinking has become simply another branch of postmodernist literary thinking. Answering the charge, Skura contends the boundary between literature and psychoanalysis has disappeared: "Literature may sound like psychoanalysis, but in its Lacanian guise, psychoanalysis has become a form of literary criticism." At first glance literary primacy seems to be reinscribed. Skura describes psychoanalysis as "within literary study itself." Lacan himself proposed the new science of language as an interrogation of all discourse. However, the conflation of disciplines in Lacanian analysis is premised on a radical critique of the essentialism of the intrinsic move that brought psychology *into* literature. The ground is not intrinsic but dual.

Reconfiguration of the literature-law relation reflects a parallel history and the impact of new views of language on disciplinary relations. Since the early nineteenth century, studies of law, literature, and religion have shared an interest in problems of language, meaning, and textual interpretation. Recently, interpretation has also become a recognized problematic in anthropology, sociology, and history (Marshall 1992, 160). The questions raised by the "interpretive turn" in philosophy, science, and culture have redrawn the boundaries of knowledge and methods of a number of disciplines (see, for example, Hiley, Bohman, and Shusterman 1991). Both partners in the law-literary studies relationship depend on abstract formulations and patterns of associative thinking. Since their expressive and conceptual processes resemble one another, a "natural and mutually sustaining partnership" is perceived. In the 1982 *Interrelations,* Weisberg and Barricelli traced the duality of the relation as law *in* literature and law *as* literature. At the time, law *in* literature was the better-established tradition. Law *as* literature was relatively neglected in literary consciousness.

Over the past decade, the rhetorical turn in scholarship and the critical legal studies movement in law schools have forged closer connections on different ground. In conceiving of law as a social and cultural activity, James Boyd White extended understanding of law beyond traditionally configured rules, institutions, and structures or in terms of political science, sociology, and economics. Law, he proposed, is a kind of rhetorical and literary activity. This move shifts law away from the social sciences toward the humanities, making theorists of both lawyers and literary critics (1985, x–xii). Its impact is apparent in the curriculum of law schools, in professional journals, and in tenure cases. Interdisciplinary traffic, however, is never an even flow. The legal partner has done far more borrowing and appropriating than the literary partner (Fish 1989b, 302–8).

The "interarts borderland" has long been recognized as a site of interactions. It bears various names: the "comparative arts," "interdisciplinary arts," "interart studies" or "analogies," "interrelationships," and "mutual illumination." Responding to the growth of interest groups, scholarship, and courses, the MLA helped to define the "discipline" in the 1990 *Teaching Literature and Other Arts* (Barricelli, Gibaldi, and Lauter). This book is a linear descendent of the 1967 *Relations* and the 1982 *Interrelations.* The core problematic of interart comparison is whether disciplinary relations go beyond analogy and similarity to homology, identity, and transformation of disciplinary categories. Among literary scholars, Jon Green found, the relation has been structured in three major ways: the classical *ut pictura poesis* (comparing literature and the visual arts); the romantic *ut musica poesis* (comparing literature and music), and the modern *ut musica pictura* (comparing music and painting). Three major approaches have emerged in scholarship and teaching: investigation of common origins, which searches for an ancient unity from which individual arts branched off; experiential-psychological approaches, which depict the arts as extensions of the senses in time and space;

and structural-semiotic approaches, which view the arts as alternative language systems.

Echoing earlier debates on history and its neighbors, the recurring theme in analyses of the interarts borderland is limited development. In the 1967 *Relations,* Bertrand Bronson traced a variety of collaborations, analogies, conjoined forms, shared motifs, and uses of music *in* literature. Despite this abundance of work, music had developed few techniques that might be "serviceable or suggestive" to literature or literary analysis. While "mutually contingent," the relation retained a characteristic underdeveloped and "pioneering" quality. In updating description for the 1982 *Interrelations,* Steven Scher found that juxtapositions of music and poetry, word and tone, sound and poetry arose with "formulaic frequency." Yet they were rarely substantiated by precise definition. Commonplace juxtapositions had created a "deceptively axiomatic aura of legitimacy." Claims of mutual dependency, though, were belied by separations and correlations that were often illusory, at best metaphorical. The lack of organization of work and workers in the field also meant that scholarship tended to be "individual and unorganized," not the systematic production that derives from groups or coteries, schools of thought, points of view, and standard methodology. Promising comparisons were limited by lack of sophistication in musical matters among literary scholars. This limitation is evident in indiscriminate borrowings of vocabulary and terminological confusion.

In the trading zone of literature and the visual arts, courses are usually organized around historical periods, artistic movements, or shared sensibilities and styles (Mitchell 1990). Historically both fields were mimetic arts, and both were studied in the context of history of ideas. The field of comparative literature has also shown a clear-cut bias in favor of visual arts over architecture and sculpture. Intermedial linkages, Ulrich Weisstein explained in the 1982 *Interrelations,* span a range of "cohabitation and interpenetration": from literature that describes or interprets a piece of art to works whose outward appearance depends on design or graphic elements to borrowed techniques, shared themes and motifs, common styles and symbiotic genres such as the masque or emblem. Traditional practices have tended to identify similarities or differences, to demonstrate the superiority of one art over the other, to polemicize against fusion or separation, and to reduce all arts to the same, usually mimetic, principle. One of the persistent problems exposed by interart comparison is failure to recognize that a feature literally present in one art may be only figuratively present in another.

Contemporary practices, Wendy Steiner reports in the 1990 guide, exhibit greater contextual approaches that replace, or at least extend, the earlier preoccupation with formal properties, loose analogies, and themes. Contextualizing occurs through problem orientation around issues of representation and in reconfiguration of the older relational domain to a common cultural infrastructure. The meaning of interart comparison has been enriched and complicated by a growing body of theoretical scholarship and constant violation of borders between the visual and the verbal. Even with these developments, limits persist. In mapping interdisciplinary studies, Gunn identified continuing differences of practice: "If art historians routinely eschew criticism for cataloguing, evaluation for description, literary historians and critics have typically treated all the fine arts as mere complements, adjuncts, illustrations of the verbal arts." Poststructural textualities, social history, and feminist critique imply incipient transformation. Yet, systematic and institutionalized modes of interdisciplinary inquiry are necessary if reconstitution of materials and methods is to occur on a firmer, wider basis (Gibaldi 1992, 250–51).

Interactions between literature and science have grown tremendously in recent years. Science-related topics have increased in the curriculum, academic conferences and publications have proliferated, and an identifiable group of specialists has emerged. The relationship spans ancient questions about art and nature, the rise of modern science in the seventeenth century, and modern debate on science, technology, and society. Early research and teaching tended to promote the idea that literature borrowed from and popularized science. Influence tended to be considered a one-way street. Scientific ideas and terminology were traced from literature back into scientific sources. This approach produced glosses of scientific meanings in the work of literary artists, privileged the scientific worldview, and valorized great thinkers, ideas, events, and authors. In the 1982 *Interrelations,* the relationship was depicted in terms of science *and* literature and science *in* literature. By the 1990s the subfield had become a major growth industry, stimulated by new developments in the history of ideas, postwar demystifications of science, the expanding field of cultural study, and investigations of writing as social production.

Science and literature, George Levine explains, have three major relations. The first is rooted in the influence of science on literature. The second is based in the rhetoric of science that is shaped by central social, religious, and cultural ideas and attitudes of a time. The third is mutual kinship. Science and literature draw on the same sources in a culture, working out the same project in different languages. Treated in terms of the second and third conceptions, scientific texts have become the subject of literary and rhetorical analysis. The literariness of science has also become a common topic, and texts are being read contextually as responses to internal disciplinary processes and external forces. In the third instance, science, technology, and literature are reconceptualized as permeable discourses within a shared cultural field. Glosses of meaning remain prominent, but the premise of inquiry is constitutive, interactive, and conjunctive (1987, 7).

Anthologies, once again, provide an index of practices. Recent collections encompass intellectual biography, history of ideas, sociology of science, thematic analysis of science in literature, literary and rhetorical analysis of texts and practices, feminist reconsiderations of scientific discourse, and contextual cultural studies. Attitudes toward science vary. Science bashers and science junkies, literary apologists and literary imperialists alike populate the intellectual space of literature and science. The very ordering of the name—*literature* and science or *science* and literature—creates unconscious predilections about which partner has priority and which is the dependent variable (Paul Hoch, pers. comm., 4 August 1991). Given the general lack of scientists, the heavier weight is on the literary side of the copula (Levine 1987, 341). The disciplinary identification of most specialists tends to be literary critic, historian, or historian of science. Most organized programs in the United States are located in English departments of technological universities. In the scholarship of literary critics, social context still tends to be literary or rhetorical, and a textual primacy occurs in reconfiguring science and technology as discourse (Hoch 1991).

By and large, the interdisciplinarity of the movement lies in common vocabulary and conceptual categories of discourse analysis. The rhetoric and literary resonance of science is of little interest to the average bench scientist, though they have played significant roles in history and sociology of science. Yet the discourse analysis of sociologists of science is still oriented toward socioeconomic, political, and institutional contexts. Historians of science devote limited space in their journals to literary and rhetorical issues. Rhetorical analysis of policy statements and practices is expanding, but separations continue to reinforce differences. Literary constructivists might forge closer links with social-constructivist sociologists, but the question of which sociocultural elements are to be considered must be clarified. Potential allies are sometimes viewed as intruders. Meanwhile, historians of technology are polarized into hard and soft wings. They place different values on industrial archaeologies and economic determinants versus general cultural causations, including popular and literary discourse. Soft and hard tendencies are bridged by discourse communities. Reviews of new anthologies and scholarship, though, often castigate authors for failing to do more of one kind of analysis than another (Hoch 1991).

Practices that go beyond relational to interactive terms reconfigure the knowledge field. In a notable example, Katherine Hayles has theorized interdisciplinarity on the shift from discrete entities to Gregory Bateson's notion of an "ecology of ideas." An ecology of ideas neither demands unity nor overrides disciplinary differences. Interest in disorder and unpredictability, to recall the earlier example of chaos, occurs across the domains of literature and the sciences. Yet differences are as real as similarities. Commonalties and differences create a dual emphasis on cultural fields and disciplinary sites. Consequently the universe of discourse is at once fragmented and unified. An ecological approach alone is not adequate to explain differences; an economic model is also required. Disciplinary traditions impute different values to isomorphic paradigms. In seeing chaos as the source of order, the scientific response appears fundamentally conservative. In appropriating chaos to subvert order, poststructuralist literary studies appears radical. When institutional practices are factored in, both responses appear equally conservative. They both perpetuate, not challenge, the existing "economic infrastructures" of their disciplines (Hayles 1990, 4, 176).

The tendencies observed in period studies and in disciplinary relations also occur in one of the oldest interdisciplinary fields, American studies.

American Studies

The institutional roots of American studies lie in the 1920s and 1930s, when the first American civilization courses were offered at Yale, George Washington, Harvard, Pennsylvania, and Smith (Kerber 1989, 415). Like comparative literature, American studies established an alternative to older approaches and New Criticism (Graff 1987, 160). During and after World War II, the field grew in a climate of nationalism, patriotism, and commitment to the study of American values. In the postwar years, intellectual history, history of ideas, and literary criticism dominated research and teaching. With the waning of the intellectual history synthesis, a movement known as the myth-and-symbol school assumed priority.

The myth-and-symbol school fostered a historically contextualized view of literature and culture. By the late 1950s, support for a cultural anthropological view was apparent in history (Brantlinger 1990, 28). The framing concepts of the myth-and-symbol school guided thinking along nationalist, consensus lines and a "holistic rhetoric of the interdisciplinary" (Wise 1978, 517). Both marked an implicit commitment to unifying the plural and harmonizing differences (Brantlinger 1990, 27–38). The sociological mode of myth criticism spawned detailed studies of archetypal American characters, themes, plots, images, genres, and settings. Yet efforts to link text and context stopped short of constructing adequate theories of the relation between, on the one hand, values, beliefs, attitudes, and imaginative constructs and, on the other hand, social structure and forms (Sklar 1975, 258).

During the 1960s and 1970s, new social and political movements, the rise of theory and its offshoots, and reactions to the accelerated disciplining of higher education promoted reconceptualization of the field (Brantlinger 1990, 31). The effort resembled a series of lurches more than a steady, concentrated flow of effort. In 1968 Robert Meredith announced that American studies had come of age. It had moved beyond initial "stirrings of discontent" in English and history departments to an extensive body of inquiry (xi). Five years later, joined by Jay Mechling and David Wilson, Meredith characterized the field as a "parcel of noble strivings tied loosely together by individual will and efforts" (Mechling, Meredith, and Wilson 1973, 367). New developments were propelled by a variety of interests in popular culture, urban affairs, ethnicity, and women, and in science, technology, and ecology. They energized the field, but they lacked methodological coherence at all three levels—theory, method, and technique.

When the new influences began appearing, American studies was anchored institutionally by major graduate programs and an expanding scholarly literature. Its undergraduate presence was characterized more by cross-departmental programs than by departments or autonomous units. Most programs tended to mix existing approaches and subject matters rather than creating a new holism or an interdisciplinary synthesis. Increasingly the words "innovation," "experiment," and "radicalism" were coupled with the term "interdisciplinary" (Shumway 1988, 14). The move toward critical interdisciplinarity was signaled in 1977 when David Marcell called for a "critical interdisciplinarity." He faulted "mere interdisciplinary" attempts at synthesizing disciplinary perspectives. They fell short on two counts: they did not do justice to the pluralism of American culture, and they had not effected a synthesis of the humanities and sciences.

Seven years later Giroux, Shumway, and Sosnoski (1984) called for a full-fledged "counter-disciplinary praxis" of cultural studies. Their indictment of prior interdisciplinary efforts in women's, Black, Canadian, and American studies undervalued the oppositional and counterdisciplinary tendencies of those practices and their limited successes. Their proclamation nonetheless marked the widening turn toward critical interdisciplinarity. At present American studies is on "shifting ground," moving away from literary criticism and traditional cultural history toward determining the role of oppositional criticisms (Brantlinger 1990, 27, 31–33). Conventional historical and literary methods are beginning to give way to cultural anthropology, ethnography, oral history, the study of material culture, reader-response criticism, and sociology of literature (Fox-Genovese 1990, 8). In 1992 Philip Fisher (Greenblatt and Gunn 1992b) assessed the implications for American identity, once the cornerstone of consensus politics. The context is current literary and cultural studies covering the post–Civil War period.

In the 1960s and 1970s, departments and programs of American studies established in the 1930s, 1940s, and 1950s found themselves regionalized into departments of Black or African American, Jewish, women's, Native American, Chicano, and Asian American studies, and in some cases gay studies. New identity claims have bred a new fundamentalism of unmasking hegemony, essentialism, and the operations of power in culture. The characterizing traits of the new regionalism that has developed over the past two decades are gender, race, and ethnicity. Identity has tended to be formed in oppositional terms of Black/White, male/female, Native American/settler, and gay/heterosexual. Alongside this trend, a new American studies has emerged as an alternative or aftermath that attempts to locate a set of underlying but permanently open cultural questions. These questions engage the rhetorics of American culture.

A more comprehensive move into a critical American cultural studies is limited by continuing impediments. Repeating earlier patterns, programs have been added to existing departments and fields in a process of assimilation that falls short of full-scale reorganization of knowledge and the university (Graff 1987, 225). In the 1990 presidential address to the American Studies Association (ASA), Martha Banta reported that interdisciplinarity too often consists of topic-oriented sessions attended by segmented audiences. Most of the energy in ASA still tends to come from two majorities, history and literature. Tempers still flare over conflicting modes of knowledge within and among disciplines (1991, 379–81). Scholars continue to reenact the assumptions of their home disciplines and fail to clarify how they use "culture" as a shared object (Shumway 1988, 16).

Clearly the search for a final comprehensive, true theory, in the older sense of an "'inter- and supradisciplinary' *Einheitswissenschaft,*" has been given up. This effort enacted the hope of devising an all-inclusive synthetic method, a harmonious unity of knowledge, and a totalizing science of culture. The "new rhetoric of the interdisciplinary" that Gene Wise forecast in 1978 is strongly implicit in current theory and practice. Wise's proposal for "cultural field studies" was based on a set of cultural axioms that emphasize density of cultural facts and interconnecting experiences. They cross not only disciplinary boundaries but also the dividing line between the academic and the nonacademic. The core metaphor of knowledge shifts, in turn, from building blocks in a pyramid to a series of dialogues that are inherently unfinishable. The scope of the field is further enlarged by incorporating metareflection on the terms of knowledge practice (Lenz 1982, 60, 71, 81–82).

The possibilities and limits of interdisciplinary study are indicated most clearly in configuration of the relation between text and context. The earliest form of "context," historian Robert Berkhofer (1989) explained in an assessment of American studies, was a vague but polysemic definition of culture among scholars in disciplines as varied as music, art, literature, and intellectual history. In exposing the patterns underlying American culture, they constituted a common framework for moving beyond special interests and methods. Today the cultural and political premises behind their attempts are largely repudiated. Interest in myths, symbols, and images has given way to interest in class, ethnicity, race, and gender. Marking this shift, older keywords of "paradox," "ambiguity," and "irony" have been replaced by "domination," "hegemony," and "empowerment." The underlying definition of culture has shifted from belief in an eclectic unity to division and opposition. Exemplary works have moved from stressing homogeneity to emphasizing diversity and divisiveness. Differing interests, though, continue to yield differing definitions of "context."

The presupposition of a basic or simple contextualism lies at one pole. The quest for one meaning, which Berkhofer dubs "contextual fundamentalism," is strong. Documents, artifacts, and texts are considered self-interpreting. Facts are discovered, not created or constituted, by the frameworks that enable their existence. Documentary and artifactual analysis assumes that historical narrative is verified in an essential structure by parallels in a past reality. That reality is represented in a single (hi)story told by a single voice from a single viewpoint. Classic American studies questioned the simple link between texts and social reality, thereby transmuting what historians and other scholars considered reality into myths and images. Currently, though, a more fundamental challenge to context as social reality is under way. Documentary and artifactual fundamentalism are denied as the premise of one Great Story of history is rejected. In dissolving scholarly and aesthetic boundaries, new work also calls into question the criteria sustaining canons, rendering Culture with a capital *C* just another part of culture with a small *c*. Much of the new historical work in humanities disciplines, especially in the name of "cultural studies," is devoted to demystifying abstract terms, subjects, and categories once considered basic to culture.

Over time, the text-context relation has been reformulated in three major patterns of definition. *Context 1* holds that contextual understanding is derived solely from a text by a reader, whether inscribed by an author, as the intentional model of communication asserts, or constructed by a reader. *Context 2* holds that context derives from other texts in an intertextuality that remains, like context 1, rooted in a closed conceptual realm. Both contexts 1 and 2 are textualist in their problematics and methodology. Social reality is constituted and understood through broadly conceived forms of signifying practices. This approach transforms the human sciences into rhetoric or poetics. *Context 3* is premised on an extratextual world that breaks out of the circularity of textualist definitions, whether linguistic or hermeneutic in origin. Individual methods vary, but the underlying premise is a form of realism that is usually construed in terms of social construction of reality.

Competing views of the proper framework for teaching and research, poetics and politics, rest on contradictory approaches not only to "context" but to American studies itself. Changing vocabularies and perspectives may represent a new phase in American studies, or they may constitute a new American studies rooted in postmodern engagement of poststructuralist, post-Marxist, postfeminist, and posthistoricist theory and practice. Opposing methodologies form the focus and the medium of contests over control of meaning within, between, and beyond disciplines. Despite conflict, the overall direction of change is clear and strong. Older shortcomings of New Criticism and the naive old historicism of "background" and "context" are being overcome in the new interdisciplinary problematics of literary history. As race, class, and gender become formal principles of art, they are rendered integral to textual analysis and the political norms inscribed in aesthetic judgment. They are rendered inherent in the act of interpretation, not the older notion of literature "itself" (Tichi 1992; Bercovitch and Jehlen 1987, viii).

The End of Discipline?

In 1990, in *The Death of Literature,* Alvin Kernan revisited old fears. Literature, he lamented, is being "emptied out in the service of social and political causes" that are considered more important than literary texts. "Deconstructive philosophical terrorist, intellectual revolutionary, and feminist freedom-fighter" may be only fashions of the moment. The assault on meaning, he worries, is more threatening. It may well undermine "the positive authority and even the reality of the subject." If literature becomes an ideological instrument, the accumulated capital of discipline will be dissipated, leaving only a "hodgepodge of institutional odds and ends without a center, a decaying instructional system, a set of professional arrangements, a library category, a high-culture avant-garde art circle, a few publishers and reviews, a few passing political and social causes" (200–201, 211–12).

The distance between such fears and the radical redescription in contemporary guides and histories raises a fundamental question. What constitutes the discipline today? "Literature as it was," John Carlos Rowe wrote in 1992, "can't be saved" (204). "Literature" now encompasses older texts and once "extraliterary" materials such as letters, diaries, films, paintings, and manifestos, as well as philosophical, political, psychological, religious, and medical treatises. "Text," "theory," and "discourse" have become boundary concepts across a range of disciplines, and the current structural trend of the discipline is toward topical and interest-group fragmentation (Middleton 1992, 23). Literary studies, Greenblatt and Gunn recalled in introducing *Redrawing the Boundaries,* was once held together by an uneasy alliance of older historicists and New Critics. They were willing to suspend disagreements for the sake of creating graduate programs that combined historical coverage with training in close reading of principal works in an agreed-upon canon. At present, even where the older consensus is still honored, most members of the profession are situated uncertainly. Few, if any, dispute that transformations have redrawn the parameters of subfields. There is a widely shared commitment to resisting formalism and the extremes of specialism while including new forms of texts and drawing from a vastly expanded repertoire of explanatory tools and frameworks. What individuals are to make of these changes in their own teaching and research is less clear (1992a, 1).

Similar voices are being heard in the other domains of literary study, outside English departments. The study of German literature, for example, is being rejuvenated through historical interests that shape new questions while broadening the textual base, opening up new archival sources, and allowing greater resonance of literary texts and other cultural representations. These moves incorporate new voices and reveal new ways of writing about literature within larger networks of meaning. Attention is also turning to the borders where texts connect with material world, and the classical framing concepts of literary study—representation, authorship, and autonomy of art—are being called into question (Kaes 1989, 211, 213). When Germanists in the United States reflected on new developments in the spring 1989 issue of *German Quarterly,* focused on the topic of interdisciplinary theories and methods, they did not agree. Assessing the multiple claims and depictions, Peter Hohendahl found a "diffuse uneasiness with the present situation" (1989, 227). Some propose an interdisciplinary German studies as the site for pluralistic discourse and reflexive work. Others argue for a clearly defined center in one discipline.

Plurality and tension have resulted in the same duality of description evident in women's studies. William Cain, in a 1985 essay titled "English in America Reconsidered," reported that new theories were breaking disciplinary boundaries. He also noted that the boom in theory had altered the curriculum only in marginal ways, leaving the basic shape of discipline unchanged. An MLA survey of classroom practices in the mid-1980s affirms this perception. A significant percentage of courses are still taught according to the methods and assumptions of New Criticism. The traditional canon still anchors English-department curricula in most U.S. colleges and universities. Changes have occurred slowly, through an additive process that strains the older coverage model. Most English departments still rely on the same structural principles they used twenty-five years ago, though cultural studies is actively practiced among a significant number of younger faculty. Survey data reveal, furthermore, that roughly 70 percent of postsecondary English classes or sections taught in the United States are composition classes (J. H. Miller 1991, 131; Elbow 1990, 138–39, n. 2).

"Canon" is as central a keyword of disciplinary identity as "context." In Lewalski's 1981 account of the literature-history relation, the canon required only a sentence. By 1992, Patterson reported, it had become a "considerable industry." As the influence of new historical practices expanded, the canon of works read in many periods and subfields enlarged. Papers, panels, and publications on canon formation began populating the programs of professional meetings across humanities disciplines. Canon formation controls a discipline by determining what stays in and what stays out, creating an ideal of order and valuing space that is simultaneously material, physical, and visible (Bergeron 1992, 1–2). In American literature at present, exemplary scholarship of a traditional design continues in studies of major authors of the established canon. At the same time, classroom anthologies reveal a decentering from older texts and their chronological ordering that is disguised by continuing use of older taxonomic categories in course catalogs (Tichi 1992).

"Any description," Katherine Hayles advises, "presupposes a frame of reference that limits, even as it creates, what is said." What is known is a function of what is noticed and what is considered important. If the criteria defining center and margin change, the structure of knowledge changes (1990, 135, 144). Literary studies is a field of contest in which subject positions and methodological and theoretical commitments coexist unequally. Across a crowded and disputed terrain, individual practices mark differing relations to both traditional structures and new developments, from more conservative responses to new intersections of gender, color, and postcolonial identity that permanently ride the borders of literature, culture, and ideology (Allen 1992, 305; Bhabha 1992). In such circumstances, Henry Louis Gates suggests, the center-periphery dichotomy may have outlived its usefulness. Most new practices dispute the very premise of center (1992, 310), and tensions within the system of literary study are now considered part of the way the system works (Greenblatt and Gunn 1992a, 7).

The call for return to a model of the literary scholar as cultural critic is a revealing index of the current debate. The model stems from the eighteenth and nineteenth centuries, periods when literary, cultural, and social criticism were more closely related. Opponents of new practices want a version closer to the original. Proponents see the call for return not as a resumption of an older literature-culture relation but as a reconstitution of once discrete disciplinary objects of "literature," "text," and "culture" into boundary concepts. In describing cultural criticism for *Redrawing the Boundaries,* Gerald Graff and Bruce Robbins indicate that "culture" does double work in literary studies today. One meaning emphasizes organic unity and the dualism of organic culture against a technologically false culture. The other meaning rejects unifying claims by emphasizing contradictions and the idea that the poles of any dualism tend to inhabit each other. Cultural criticism of the nineteenth century politicized literature and criticism for purposes of bourgeois idealism. Using the name "cultural studies" rejects that move by reformulating literary studies as an open and plural refusal of the universals of Arnoldian Culture with a capital *C* (1992, 434–35).

At the turn of the twentieth century, the theoretical ground of interdisciplinarity was "general." During the 1930s through 1950s it was New Critical "organicism." During the 1960s and 1970s it was the "loose interdisciplinarity" of structuralism. Then it became theory, the "critical" interdisciplinarities that encompass historical and social borrowings, an omnivorous textualism, and a radical politics. Despite the temptation to believe so, the domain of interdisciplinarity is not entered every time a border is crossed. The desire to see from different sides of the same border is often confused with sustained interactions and reconceptualization of disciplinary relations and subject categories (Greenblatt and Gunn 1992a, 4–5). The intellectual future of interdisciplinary studies, Gunn suggests, depends on avoiding the temptations of disciplinary reductionism—in thinking that methods of one field are sufficient to interpret the materials of many—and the appetite for metaphorical transfer—in treating the materials of one field as mere epiphenomena of the subjects of another. The lesson of critical mass repeats. The institutional and material future depends on adequate economic capital to support development of graduate programs, centers for study, summer institutes, visiting and permanent professorships, outlets for publication, interdepartmental colloquiums and scholarships (Gunn 1992a, 255).

The acid test is always the definition of "true" or "genuine" interdisciplinarity. Over the course of the century, the definition has shifted from a preservationist integration of foreign elements to a form of boundary crossing that displaces or alters boundaries between forms of relational study or constitutes itself in the spaces between those forms (Gunn 1992a, 245). Interdisciplinarity as an agenda, Stanley Fish observed in a widely read polemic, "Being Interdisciplinary Is So Very Hard to Do" (1989a), seems to flow naturally from the imperatives of left culturalist theory. Deconstruction, Marxism, feminism, the radical version of neopragmatism, and new historicism are all critical of two kinds of boundary making: the social structures by means of which lines of political authority are maintained, and the institutional structures by which various academic disciplines establish and extend their territorial claims. New interests have produced different kinds of interdisciplinarity. At one level it is a device for prodding students to cross boundaries. At another level it is an assault on those very boundaries and the entire hierarchy and power they both reflect and sustain. Fish ignores decades of similar claims in other domains, but he recognizes the familiar distinction between merely crossing boundaries and transgressing them in a deconstructive, subversive process. The latter, a *revolution tout court,* is "radical interdisciplinarity."

Herein lies the apparent paradox of interdisciplinarity for postmodernists. Any strategy of knowledge that calls into question the very foundations of all disciplines—proceeding by breakthroughs, leaps, and discontinuities—presumably negates itself if it becomes institutionalized. The multitude of interdisciplinary studies and projects, Fish points out, are not immersed in critique. They center on straightforwardly disciplinary tasks that require information and techniques on loan from other disciplines. Or they move by imperialistic expansion into other disciplinary territories. Or they establish a new discipline composed of people who may represent themselves as "antidisciplinary" but end up constituting a new breed of counterprofessionals and experts. If authentic interdisciplinary critique is negated by routinization and institutionalization, then being interdisciplinary is not just hard, it is impossible.

Although it is a succinct indictment of institutionalization and past failures, Fish's formulation unravels. It is itself a political stance that ignores and discounts what has been achieved. It also reflects a conservative pessimism about interdisciplinarity, and it perpetuates the dualism of disciplinarity and interdisciplinarity (Gunn 1992b, 190). In asserting that interdisciplinarity is impossible because one can "inhabit" only a single disciplinary territory at a time, Fish encounters the limitations of the metaphor of territory or border, reinscribing the notion of static structure and minimizing change as a property of disciplinarity. The metaphor of a river, Arabella Lyon suggests in a formal response to Fish, with its currents and flows, tributaries, eddies, and confluences, highlights the diverse and fluid movements of knowledge practices (1992, 682).

Radical apologists for interdisciplinarity, Giles Gunn adds, get around the poststructuralist trap by realizing that the overlapping and conflicting disciplinary matrices people occupy can be used to check and criticize each other. Scholars can develop awareness of the conditions that authorize and legitimate disciplinary practices even as they practice them. The question of interdisciplinarity is framed not by the stark poles of how to free the mind or how to fix it but by how to "subtitilize" it:

> To subtitilize the mind is neither to suppose that we can dispense with disciplinary boundaries altogether nor to assume that we have to accept those that have already been instituted. It is simply to realize that while no literary study can occur without them, there is nothing about the nature of boundaries themselves, disciplinary or otherwise, that prevents one from seeing from more than one side of them. This alone does not make for a more interdisciplinary environment but it represents one of its most essential preconditions. Without the ability to see from different sides of various boundaries, there is no possibility either of redrawing the boundaries themselves or, more crucially, of changing what can be seen as a result. (Gunn 1992b, 190–91)

The boundary complex that defines literary studies is both general and specific. It encompasses national and geographical, historical and generational, disciplinary and interdisciplinary, racial and ethnic, social and political, ethical and religious demarcations. Less visible, but no less determinative, are the lines differentiating reading and writing, canonical tradition and heretical interests, the elite and the vernacular, print and oral cultures, and high and popular art. "These boundaries," Greenblatt and Gunn conclude, "can be crossed, confused, consolidated, and collapsed; they can also be revised, reconceived, redesigned, and replaced. The one thing they cannot be in literary studies is entirely abolished." Understanding boundaries requires determining a number of factors: what they enclose and exclude; whether the lines are drawn in bold, unbroken strokes or a series of intermittent, irregular dashes; their multiple functions and the stances from which they are accepted or redrawn; the obstacles faced by those who challenge, nullify, or abolish them; definition of the places where boundaries cross, overlap, or converge; and the nature and import of the activities that occur at points of intersection (1992a, 4).

The specific lesson of literary studies is also the general lesson of the humanities. Boundary crossing is occurring across the disciplines of the humanities in the blending of classical and popular styles in architecture, the elision of genres and styles in literature and music, and the erosion of older dividing lines between high, formal, esoteric, official culture and low, popular, mundane culture (Muller and Taylor 1994, 18). In art history (Preziosi 1993; Bal 1991), in music (Bergeron and Bohlman 1992), and in literary studies, differences over canon, object, interpretation, and practice lie at the heart of disputes about the identity of discipline. Reflecting on the interdisciplinary object of text, Roland Barthes asserted that interdisciplinarity arises in disciplinary encounters in relation to an object that traditionally is in the province of none of them (1977, 155). The lesson of literary studies is that interdisciplinarity is defined and located in the acts of naming, legitimating, and theorizing that constitute the practice of discipline.

CHAPTER 6

National Competitiveness and the "Centering" of Interdisciplinary Research

Access to knowledge and expertise, reconfiguring it in novel ways and offering it for sale, are becoming specialized functions and new mediating organizations are being set up to fill this gap.

Michael Gibbons et al., *The New Production of Knowledge*, 1994

Interdisciplinarity is essential to the regeneration of intellectual work, and to its continuing significance within and outside the academic community. It represents the force for change, the challenge to orthodoxy, and the dynamism in the development of scholarship. It is, therefore, inappropriate that interdisciplinarity be regarded as marginal, as an "add on" to conventional academic work. Interdisciplinarity is central to the mission of all universities, regardless of whether they establish interdisciplinary programs.

Liora Salter and Alison Hearn, "On Interdisciplinarity," 1993

Siting Interdisciplinary Research

During the 1980s interdisciplinarity attained heightened visibility in science and technology. The declining economic position of the United States accentuated the need to facilitate the flow of knowledge and inventions across the boundaries of academic disciplines, industry, and government. Economic pressure, coupled with current trends in scientific research, have made interdisciplinarity and competitiveness new keywords in the national debate on science policy. They are endorsed by Congress, executive departments of the federal government, funding agencies, and advisory groups (*Interdisciplinary Research* 1990, 12–13). The case for expanding the academic role in economic development rests on two pillars. First, industry has underinvested in generic research and could profitably utilize research from universities. Second, discoveries of potential commercial value made in universities have not been reaching the marketplace because of inadequate linking mechanisms (Geiger 1986, 147 n. 1).

The issues raised by the debate have been the subject of several major reports. The reports were issued by three groups: the National Research Council (NRC), the Government-University-Industry Research Roundtable, and Sigma Xi (the Scientific Society). Formed in 1916, NRC is the principal operating agency of two private, self-governing organizations that are devoted to furthering knowledge and advising government, scientific and engineering communities, and the public. In 1986 the NRC issued *Scientific Interfaces and Technological Applications,* volume 8 of an extended report on the discipline of physics. In 1990 the NRC published *Interdisciplinary Research: Promoting Collaboration between the Life Sciences and Medicine and the Physical Sciences and Engineering.* The Roundtable is sponsored by the National Academy of Sciences, the National Academy of Engineering, and the Institute of Medicine. It is a forum where scientists, engineers, administrators, and policymakers from government, industry, and the academy develop options for improving the productivity of the nation's research system. In 1987 the Roundtable issued Robert Sproull and Harold Hall's report, *Multidisciplinary Research and Education Programs in Universities: Making Them Work.* Founded in 1886, Sigma Xi is an honor society for scientists dispersed across North American and overseas campuses, governments, and industrial laboratories. In 1988 Sigma Xi published *Removing the Boundaries: Perspectives on Cross-disciplinary Research.*

None of these organizations is an official representative of the United States government. Therefore the reports are not official policy statements. They do, though, have an authoritative force that derives from their authors' stature as influential members of the nation's academic, industrial, and government communities. The issues they address are not strictly economic. Concern about the vitality of the nation's technological and research capacity overlaps with older debates about the proper role of interdisciplinarity and the ideal balance of fundamental and applied research. The reports perform a complex form of boundary work, combining disciplinary redescription and interdisciplinary advocacy, and sanctioning expanded industrial presence in the university. They need to be read historically, within the context of growing legitimation of interdisciplinary research in the academy, and critically, in the context of competing conceptions of science and technology.

Historical Warrants

The history of interdisciplinary research (IDR) is linked with the history of government and industrial support for problem-focused and mission-oriented research. The first research grant from the federal government supported this kind of work. It was awarded in 1930 to the Franklin Institute, for an investigation of the causes of steam boiler explosions by a group of chemists, engineers, physicists, meteorologists, and members of other fields (Wolfle 1981, 5). The tradition of organized interdisciplinary projects and centers dates back to the establishment of large university equipment projects, such as the Berkeley cyclotron (Sproull and Hall 1987, 1–2) and the system of agricultural experimentation stations established in 1887 at state land-grant colleges (Hoch 1990c, 43). In 1942 the earliest reported results of interdisciplinary research in agriculture appeared, involving input-output relations in milk. During the 1950s and 1960s this kind of research continued to be conducted by biologists and agricultural economists (Barker 1982, 101).

The land-grant tradition, the mission orientation of the United States Department of Agriculture (USDA), and its system of state experiment stations provided contexts conducive to collaboration (Russell 1982, 7). The experiment stations gave the nation a readiness level for tackling significant problems, such as the virus and mycoplasma complexes that plagued north-central and southern states during the early 1960s. The important position of corn as a domestic and international commodity meant that corn had been a subject of continuing study in a complex and highly interactive network involving farmers, extension specialists, industrial experts, and federal government and university scientists. Their work proved doubly significant. The immediate problem was solved through development of virus-resistant corn cultivars. In the process, new basic knowledge emerged regarding all aspects of corn virology, genetics, culture and entomology (Barnes 1982, 135).

University faculty and facilities played major roles in military research and development (R&D) (*New Alliances* 1986, 6). During World War I, scientists worked on military problems such as the detection of submarines and artillery sighting. World War II was a major turning point. The most prominent war-related missions were building an atomic bomb, solving problems the British Royal Air Force was experiencing with its new radar systems, and meeting the United States military's demand for a new turbo engine. The Manhattan Project required a rare level of collaborative effort among science, industry, and the United States Army. The radar project was a foundational event in the history of operations research. The collaborative work of physicists and chemists on the turbo engine was a major event in the evolution of solid-state physics. Beyond its immediate practical value, war-related research had the added benefit of sometimes extending the frontiers of knowledge. J. D. Bernal's work on artificial harbors for the invasion of Normandy advanced the physics of beach formation. Alan Turing's effort to design a new decoding machine involved algebraic work that stimulated pure mathematical offshoots (Etzkowitz 1983, 208, 218).

The siting of wartime projects in centers and institutes paralleled the locating of area studies. Scientists were recruited from universities, but much of their work was conducted in alternative structures. Philip Bowden's research on frictional hot spots is a classic example. The problem was important. Hot spots could initiate chemical decomposition, causing detonations and explosions. Bowden's effort to solve the problem was housed in the new interdisciplinary laboratory of the Physical Chemistry Department at Cambridge University. Bowden's research was significant in two respects: it solved the immediate practical problem, and it gave birth to postwar projects in the as yet unnamed area of materials science (Tabor 1990, 9). Royal Air Force projects were conducted in laboratories attached to universities, but they were functionally independent. The most famous example, the Manhattan Project, was located at the newly founded Los Alamos National Laboratory. One of the oldest intramural laboratories of the United States Department of Energy, Los Alamos is still responsible for conducting defense-related research, though it has diversified into additional fields, such as fossil and geothermal energy (*Federally Funded Research* 1991, 119).

Several important changes date from this era. Before World War II, industrial research and academic research usually met only in the form of consultative services. After the war some wartime laboratories continued to operate, especially around the Massachusetts Institute of Technology (MIT). The Lincoln Laboratory at MIT and the Stanford Research Institute stimulated formation of postwar companies that produced commercial devices originally developed in the laboratory. They were mediating institutions between academic science departments and business firms. The facilities were antecedents of today's science-based firms. The personnel who gained engineering and administrative experience in wartime labs were the precursors of today's entrepreneurial academic scientists. After the war, they went in several directions. Some founded high-technology firms near Boston and Stanford University. The ones who returned to university life experienced uneasiness over conflict of interest. This discomfort was only eased, not eliminated, by the exceptionalism of wartime boundary blurring. The traditional ethos of science continued to reinforce the boundary between science and private, profit-seeking businesses. Ambiguities of role and status were sufficiently pronounced that some even attempted to conceal their business ventures, lest they be passed over for academic salary raises and promotion. The gap between the commercial values of industrial culture and the academic values of university culture persisted in the belief that any mercantile was not a "real" academic (Etzkowitz 1983, 198, 214–15).

Despite these value conflicts, locating wartime projects on campuses had accustomed university administrators to large-scale research and collaborative projects in short time cycles. In the immediate postwar era, universities resumed traditional academic activities. Yet they were now perceived as legitimate sites for locating large-scale group research. The prestige of wartime projects also enhanced the status of interdisciplinary research. New laboratories and interdisciplinary institutes were established in the areas of nuclear science (at Chicago and MIT), radiobiology (Chicago), biophysics (Pennsylvania), marine physics (UCLA), and atomic research (Iowa State). By the

1960s and 1970s campuses had changed socially, cognitively, and physically. Declines in government and private funding led to a slackening in the pace of center growth between 1965 and 1968. Many pre-1940 agricultural centers, astronomical observatories, herbaria, and other museums also closed. Alternative structures, however, had become fixtures on the academic landscape (Friedman 1978, 66, 69).

Changes in the structure of research funding further legitimated IDR. During the 1920s and 1930s private foundations were the major external source of university research. Wartime involvement in national defense set in motion a shift from private to public sources that resulted in a systematic relationship between universities and federal mission agencies. In the early 1950s the National Science Foundation (NSF) was founded to support basic as well as applied research. The National Institutes of Health (NIH), founded in 1930, moved dramatically from intramural research to extramural grant making. NSF and NIH would become the main channels of government support of academic basic research. After the launching of Sputnik by the former Soviet Union, federal support increased significantly (Clark 1995, 129–30). The Department of Defense (DOD), the Atomic Energy Commission (AEC), and later, though to a lesser degree, the National Aeronautics and Space Administration (NASA) also provided major R&D support at universities and facilities associated with academic institutions (*New Alliances* 1986, 6). By the end of the 1950s, the Advanced Research Projects Agency of the U.S. Department of Defense had founded the first interdisciplinary materials research laboratories. By the early 1960s, DOD was fostering interdisciplinary science through the Interdisciplinary Research Laboratories (Devon 1990).

The growth of a grants and contracts economy in universities heightened permeability by propelling the bridging of academic and industrial values. The economic capital of research financed an infrastructure of graduate students, postdoctoral fellows, technicians, secretaries, and research associates. "A generation of academics," as Henry Etzkowitz put it, "learned how to raise funds and administer large projects." One of the marks of scientific maturity became the ability to gather the necessary physical, financial, and human resources to conduct science as a collective endeavor. By the 1970s scientists were becoming more amenable to accepting externally set objectives, working in groups, and using highly specialized, complicated equipment. The development of team research also meant that academic groups were exhibiting some of the characteristics of research groups in private business firms. The industrial model of research enhances productivity while allowing more complex research problems to be addressed by large teams with specialized responsibilities, a shared infrastructure, and a principal investigator (PI) who gathers funds (*Federally Funded Research* 1991, 35). A significant number of research groups in universities are now "quasi firms," in the

sense of being continuously operating entities with corresponding administrative arrangements (Etzkowitz 1983, 199, 213–14, 219–20).

Values did not change overnight. Even as structural and role shifts were
under way, funding agencies and the peer review system continued to reinforce the traditional boundaries demarcating the academy from industry. As
late as the 1960s and 1970s, funding patterns still reflected these values. At
NSF and NIH academic researchers played an influential role in allocating
research funds. Nevertheless, parts of that enterprise were now being pulled
into closer contact with business (*New Alliances* 1986, 7). Between 1980 and
1985, at a time when the overall growth in R&D funding at one hundred
leading research universities was relatively slow, industrial funding grew ex-
ponentially—from $179,398,000 to $341,741,000 (Friedman and Friedman
1986, v). Between 1978 and 1988 industry provided most of the increase in
funds for university R&D, at a growth rate averaging 12 percent above infla-
tion per year. During the same decade, the average annual growth above in-
flation was only 5.5 percent (*New Alliances* 1986, 6–7; *Federally Funded Research* 1991, 187).

The Turn into Competitiveness

The current rhetoric of boundary crossing was fueled by several converging
factors. By the 1970s federal support for research was declining at the same
time many scientific fields were requiring more and more money. As biology,
for example, developed new techniques for products and processes, demands
for research funds became acute in fields requiring large-scale, technologically advanced equipment and technical personnel with appropriate skills.
International economic competition created added pressure for a renewed
technology initiative. The perception that the United States was losing
its technological and economic primacy mounted in a number of major high-
technology-based industries, including automobiles and electronics. Japan
and the Pacific-basin countries of Hong Kong, Taiwan, Singapore, and
Korea were expanding their low-cost manufacturing bases into product development and design, setting up new state-run technology and product
engineering centers. At least two areas of cutting-edge technology—computers and biotechnology—were closely tied to academic science (*New Alliances*
1986, 7).

An economic problem was also a knowledge problem. Compared with its
major competitors, especially Europe and Japan, the United States had a conspicuous lack of fundamental research activities in many of the largest industrial areas employing physics-based technology. Counterpart nations were
devoting a higher proportion of their resources to R&D in a better planned
and coordinated fashion. In the field of biochemical engineering, West Germany, Japan, and Great Britain had several government institutes that sup-

ported biotechnology exclusively. These facilities enjoyed substantial operating budgets. They are hybrid communities that bring together academic and industrial investigators around interdisciplinary activities (*Bioengineering Systems Research* 1987, 100, 106). In the United States, the technology corridors of Route 128 in Boston and Silicon Valley in California furnished models for a new academic relationship with industry (*New Alliances* 1986, 7). New avenues of funding arose from additional sources, including the patenting of discoveries by scientists holding academic appointments, the sale of knowledge gained by research performed under contract to commercial firms, and formal partnerships with private business enterprises (Etzkowitz 1983, 198).

Universities and government responded at a vigorous pace. During the late 1970s new mechanisms for IDR multiplied, university patent offices were created or reorganized, new approaches to intellectual property were initiated, and liaison programs were developed. Industry and universities were also drawn increasingly into regional development plans (Gibbons et al. 1994, 87). The most striking enabling condition was the restructuring of law and public policy. The key legislative and executive initiatives are the Patent and Trademarks Amendment Act (1980), the Stevenson-Wydler Technology Innovation Act (1980), the Economic Recovery Tax Act (1981), the National Cooperative Research Act (1984), and the Federal Technology Transfer Act (1986). These acts legitimized, if not outright promoted, academic involvement with industry by rendering the boundary between academy and industry more permeable. The Federal Technology Transfer Act allows government scientists to collaborate with industry in R&D agreements. The Patent and Trademarks Amendment Act permits universities and small businesses to obtain patents on inventions resulting from federally funded research (*New Alliances* 1986, 38).

States and universities positioned themselves in the marketplace of research commodities. A number of states launched economic development programs involving university-industry cooperation in state and regional industries. The Ben Franklin Partnership Program in Pennsylvania and the New Jersey Commission on Science and Technology were prominent examples (*New Alliances 1986*, 7–8; *Federally Funded Research* 1991, 200–201). As senators and representatives sought to grab a piece of the new economic pie, charges of pork barrel politics inevitably surfaced. Universities also positioned themselves legally. Legal staffs that had entered universities during an era of student protests turned to the demands of entrepreneurial science. Correspondingly, the entrepreneurial endeavors of university presidents and their administrative staffs increased (Etzkowitz 1983, 198, 232). The most controversial move involved changes in policies regarding ownership of research results. Universities began setting limits on consulting and entrepreneurial activities. They established policies and procedures to avoid real or perceived conflicts of interest. They also clarified, and in many cases tightened, policies on patenting, licensing, and ownership of intellectual property.

The field of biotechnology illustrates what followed. As new biotechnology firms were established, universities with substantial programs in molecular biology instituted new patent policies to protect their institutional stakes. Stanford University made its patents in genetic technology available to private firms at moderate rates, high enough to generate income but low enough for companies not to attempt doing the research themselves. The profitability of molecular biology was signaled, in October 1980, by enthusiastic responses to an offering of stock in Genentech. Genentech was founded in the mid-1970s to exploit the commercial potential of work initiated at the University of California at San Francisco (UCSF). Following the sale of stock in Genentech, Columbia University changed its patent policy to allow sale of results of research performed in university laboratories. Harvard University reversed its laissez-faire policy and stopped relying on the generosity of its academic staff (Etzkowitz 1983, 199, 201).

Other universities took similar actions. Between 1980 and 1985 invention disclosures more than doubled in most leading research universities maintaining records on disclosures. Patent applications also increased, though at a slower pace (Friedman and Friedman 1986, v). The 1979 agreement between Harvard and Monsanto became a prototype for joint ventures. This pioneer agreement was not without controversy, but it set a pattern for handling complicated issues of patent ownership and licensing, publication rights, and protection of proprietary data. It provided support for selected academic staff members and their students for five to ten years. It allowed Monsanto scientists to participate in and work jointly on ideas and research topics. Harvard retained rights to exploitation of discoveries by its staff. Monsanto gained rights to exclusive licenses for a specified period if patents were being developed commercially (Etzkowitz 1983, 224). By 1990, policies regarding conflict of interests were being reviewed on a wide scale by Congress, the National Institutes of Health, state governments, other academic institutions, and professional organizations such as the Association of American Medical Colleges (*Interdisciplinary Research* 1990, 23).

The National Science Foundation was a strong legitimating agent. In the late 1970s NSF began providing seed money through the University-Industry Cooperative Research Centers. By 1987, thirty-nine centers were being funded at over $120 million annually (Hoch 1990c, 44). The most important federal initiative began in 1983. As a result of a meeting between a small group of distinguished engineers and George Keyworth, the need for advances involving computer-aided design and manufacturing (CAD/CAM) became the subject of high-level discussion. At the time, Keyworth was the science adviser to the president and director of the Office of Science and Technology Policy. The discussion quickly broadened to include the potential for interdisciplinary contributions in engineering to America's industrial enterprise (*Interdisciplinary Research* 1990, ix). NSF's commitment strengthened with the launching of a new initiative supporting university-based "cross-disciplinary" Engineering Research Centers (ERCs) closely attuned to the needs of the nation. During his tenure as head of NSF, Erich Bloch gave the program strong support, stirring further debate on proportional allotments of funds for basic and applied science. In an event that became enshrined as a founding moment in the origin of new alliances, President Reagan heralded the formation of a new program, the Science and Technology Centers, in his 1987 State of the Union address (Friedman and Friedman 1988, 52–53).

The pace of change was daunting, paralleling the speed with which the new theory of plate tectonics transformed the earth sciences in a single decade. In 1981, as legal and policy changes were being put into place, Harvard president Derek Bok proclaimed publicly that the university had a civic duty to ally itself more closely with private industry in order to counteract foreign competition and improve productivity. Former military projects centered on MIT, Berkeley, and Stanford were adapted to the civilian economy (Gibbons et al. 1994, 53). By 1991 more than a thousand university-industry research centers were in place at about 450 universities, and forty-eight states were sponsoring university-industry programs, with annual expenditures totaling $550 million. This trend was evident across industrialized nations. New R&D framework programs, science parks, networks, and centers of excellence were launched in member countries of the European Union. In Sweden, for instance, new emphasis was placed on working more closely with the public sector (Florida and Kenney 1991, B1, B3).

The rhetoric of competitiveness has reshaped the traditional image of the university into the "major weapon in America's battle for global competitiveness." Universities are supplying technological breakthroughs and receiving significant commercial rewards in return. In many quarters the bridging of disciplinary, academic, industrial, and government boundaries is now viewed as essential for improving America's "economic malaise" (Florida and Kenney 1991, B1). In the process, the metaphor of a "partnership" between governments and research universities has been replaced by the metaphor of a "purchase order" (Clark 1995, 152) Coupled with the expansion of new alliances, this rhetoric reinforces the belief that a structural realignment of the knowledge system is under way.

The New Alliances

The argument for structural realignment is based on increases in the number and the kind of alliances that aid research. The range of forms and mechanisms appears here in order of formality and kind, with more familiar forms first (Dill 1990, 123, 126, 129; Etzkowitz 1983, 230–31; Etzkowitz and Peters 1988; Klein 1990b, 99; *New Alliances 1986,* 12–14; *Interdisciplinary Research* 1990, 22).

science and research parks
government laboratories
experiment stations
research centers and institutes

offices of technology transfer
industrial liaison programs
joint mergers and ventures
high-technology partnerships
small entrepreneurial firms

patent and licensing operations
research networks and consortia
industrial associate/affiliate programs
collaboration and teamwork
contract research

academic chairs of excellence
industrial appointments of academics
industrial support of individual projects
venture capital start-up financing for entrepreneurial faculty
university equipment projects
consulting by university faculty members
the simple flow of personnel across academic and industrial labs

The nature, strength, and scale of alliances vary by type. The Government-University-Industry Research Roundtable identified five major clusters of partnerships, with some overlaps between adjacent types. Type 1 comprises programs and centers that support multiple projects and are closely tied to academic research and teaching. Monsanto supports a Biomedical Research Program at Washington University's Medical School. Eastman Kodak, General Foods, and Union Carbide support Cornell University's Biotechnology Program. Exxon and MIT have a formal agreement. So do Hoechst-Roussel Pharmaceuticals and the Department of Molecular Biology at Massachusetts General Hospital. The department is a medical facility affiliated with Harvard. Research tends to be allied with the disciplinary interests of faculty and is "basic" in the sense of yielding publishable findings. Commercial product or process development is not involved, but sponsoring corporations may expect specific benefits and have a proprietary stake. Generally speaking, academic freedom is protected, though not without sensitivity to the interests of client-sponsors, who range from single companies to several companies or an industrial consortium (*New Alliances* 1986, 8–9, 12–14; *Interdisciplinary Research* 1990, 22).

Type 2 encompasses focused projects with well-defined practical objectives and intellectual goals. Research teams, often staffed by both academic and corporate scientists, work toward the common interests of faculty and sponsors. Academics in type 2 clusters tend to be in fields such as engineering, applied physics, and computer science. The relationship between IBM and Carnegie Mellon University aims at developing a computer system appropriate for a university. Many type 2 programs are supported by the Department of Defense. In contrast to the greater amount of faculty control in type 1 partnerships, in type 2 the client has a high proprietary stake in achieving specific results, whether the client is a corporation or a government agency. The academic reputations of key faculty are still a matter of concern, though, since projects represent a testing of their ideas. Projects of the second type have tended to be located in university departments or schools and in research institutes affiliated with universities.

Type 3 programs help commercialize faculty research. The incubator program at Rensselaer Polytechnic Institute (RPI) exemplifies this type. So does Case Western Reserve's University Technology Incorporation and Engenics, a firm associated with Stanford, the University of California at Berkeley, and the Center for Biotechnology Research at MIT. These organizations differ from traditional contract research in technical universities. Their purpose is to help faculty members implement the fruits of their labors. The activities, though, are still related. Route 128 companies were established by scientists and engineers who worked at MIT on contract research projects. Centocor and Neogen are freestanding, for-profit companies that turned to universities to identify and develop commercially promising research and technology.

Type 4 includes programs and institutions that provide services to industry or a government agency. They are organized outside the university in order to aid clients directly. The models include incubator programs and contract research laboratories. Although access to university faculty and equipment may be important, these programs tend to be conducted in laboratories located at an administrative distance from the university. Type 5 partnerships include freestanding research institutes linked to several universities, such as the Microelectronics Center of North Carolina and the Industrial Technology Institute of Michigan. They operate on their own and are staffed for the most part by their own employees. Distancing from university culture is deliberate. These operations resemble a corporate laboratory or a contract research facility, even though the parties involved still depend on part-time participation of university faculty and other university resources.

Control of research differs across types. In the alliance between Hoechst-Roussel Pharmaceuticals and Massachusetts General Hospital (MGH), hospital procedures and policies are of primary importance. This agreement allows open publication and collaboration with other academic institutions. The Advanced Technology Development Center at Georgia Institute of Technology is based on a different arrangement. The center has an incubator facility with a building on campus. It conducts several operations, including developing venture capital and training entrepreneurs in business practices and marketing. In the first case, MGH scientists wanted a state-of-the-art department of molecular biology. They control the research. In the second example, the state wanted Georgia Tech to establish a program to contribute to industrial development, especially in advanced technology (Etzkowitz 1983, 202; *New Alliances* 1986, 21–22).

Several degrees of coordination and integration occur. The stage of least control, and sometimes the initial stage, is contracting designated services. Because it preserves the autonomy of each party, contracting parallels the juxtaposition of disciplines characteristic of "multidisciplinary" research. The second stage is the consortium, an arrangement whereby two or more organizations enter into a legal compact to accomplish specified objectives. They still have autonomy. The consortium, though, enhances coordination, thereby increasing the possibility of greater interdependence. Over a period of two decades, NSF's University-Industry Cooperative Research Centers program promoted this model throughout the United States. The final stage is the merger, a legal fusion into a new organizational identity. Interim degrees of interdependency also exist, including licensing and flows of personnel across industry and academy (Epton, Payne, and Pearson 1983, 3–9; Klein 1990b, 56–63).

University culture is a major factor in defining relations. Arrangements involving basic research tend to be located in regular departments or schools and are closely allied with academic activity. Institutions with long-standing commitments to the liberal arts tradition customarily consider the sciences in terms of contributions to knowledge, not technology. They tend to favor relationships supporting basic research and insist that faculty retain significant control. In contrast, business incubator programs and institutes for contract research usually involve facilities outside the main academic organization. Most new alliances are located in parts of universities with strong applied interests, such as engineering and medical schools, and chemistry and computer science departments. Industrial sponsorship of basic research has tended to occur more often in fields where the lines between basic and applied research are already blurred—for example, in microelectronics, electrical engineering, and biotechnology (Etzkowitz 1983, 219). Universities with traditions of public service and industrial collaboration consider linking mechanisms consistent with their institutional mandates. Technical universities, such as MIT and RPI, have been more open to applied research and industrial funding (*New Alliances* 1986, 10–11).

Industrial culture also shapes the relationship. Companies with a strong research tradition have been more likely to invest in the long-term potential of work in particular fields. Even companies that are not seeking a window on a field have been willing to fund academic research in order to help maintain the scientific vitality of their industries and to ensure a supply of well-trained industrial scientists. Other companies, even if they could afford it, do not consider basic research a sound risk. They prefer alliances focused on work of immediate commercial potential. Others yet prefer to keep R&D in house so they can control its pace, its direction, and the division of economic gains. In some partnerships, corporate sponsors remain at a distance, only broadly defining what constitute legitimate inquiries at the time of funding. In other cases, for example type 1 programs, corporate representatives actually sit on the committees that screen, focus, and influence the direction of research (*New Alliances* 1986, 11–12).

Linking mechanisms are mutually beneficial. Industry gains a window on new advances and exclusive licenses or patents for new technology. This is especially true in biotechnology, which draws heavily on revolutionary advances, techniques, and instrumentation developed in universities. Alliances also provide an environment for risk taking, though emphasis on product payoff narrows the room for experiment that is integral to the growth of new knowledge (*New Alliances* 1986, ix, 6). On the university side, the most obvious gain is in funding. Industrial alliances also broaden the research perspectives of faculty while speeding transfer of scientific and technical advances into actual products. In addition, they provide favorable environments for interdisciplinary collaboration and problem-solving capabilities (*Interdisciplinary Research* 1990, 22).

Individuals have several motives. Some are seeking funding for certain kinds of research or equipment. Others report that greater access to corporate R&D has enhanced their own competence and knowledge while providing income through consulting and, in some cases, actual profits from sales of inventions. Some believe, in addition, that alliances enhance their students' employment opportunities. When affiliation is located in a center or institute, faculty are attracted by perquisites of travel money, secretarial support, twelve-month contracts, center membership, and greater opportunities for interdisciplinary collaboration and task orientation. Administrators have found alliances effective means of retaining or attracting prominent faculty while increasing institutional prestige. Some further justify them as a way of carrying out the mandate to provide public service, though altruism is not the overriding motive (*New Alliances* 1986, 10; Friedman 1978, 62).

Actual research output varies greatly, and any one firm may engage in more than one activity. Some produce significant quantities of particular products, such as industrial enzymes and integrated circuits. Private firms owned by academic scientists are currently producing substances and devices such as genetically engineered bacteria and new methods for locating mineral deposits. These products are sold, in turn, to other firms. Other firms produce small quantities of material for use in research, such as new cell lines and prototypes of integrated circuits. Consulting firms tend to produce reports, market surveys, recommendations, and other proprietary information. The distinctive historical character of these firms lies in the fact that they have all been initiated with the active participation of scientists who still hold academic appointments (Etzkowitz 1983, 202).

Centering Interdisciplinary Research

The entwined rhetoric of interdisciplinarity and competitiveness has revitalized the idea that centers and institutes are primary sites of knowledge production. Centers became a budget rubric at NSF in 1972. The earliest example, the Materials Research Laboratories, resulted from a program transfer from the DOD. Since then the number and variety have grown. The list now includes the Industry-University Cooperative Research Centers, Minority Research Centers of Excellence, Engineering Research Centers, Science and Technology Centers, an Earthquake Engineering Center, and the Biological, Behavioral, and Social Sciences Center. By 1988 funding had risen from 2.83 percent of the 1972 research budget to 5.8 percent. In dollars, that meant an increase from $34.2 to $79.50 million (Devon 1990). The most pertinent examples in the current debate are the NSF-funded Engineering Research Centers (ERCs) and the Science and Technology Centers (STCs).

The goal of the ERCs program is to establish interdisciplinary research centers that bring together engineering and scientific disciplines to address fundamental research issues regarded as crucial to the next generation of technological systems. They are also intended to provide a mechanism for educating the next generation of engineering students in team approaches to interdisciplinary problem solving. Their mission requires active participation and long-term commitments from industry and other user organizations. By design, center budgets range from $1.5 to $3 million per year, at an average of $2 million. After three years of operation, ERCs are evaluated for a five-year renewal or two-year phaseout. If renewed a second time, a center may have up to an eleven-year life cycle.

The six major emphases of the ERCs program are indicated in a sample of actual centers. Significantly, a number of them involve more than one institution: *design and manufacturing,* the Engineering Design Research at Carnegie Mellon University; *materials processing for manufacturing,* the Advanced Electronic Materials Processing at North Carolina State University and other North Carolina institutions; *optoelectronics and microelectronics,* Telecommunications Research at Columbia University; *biotechnology and bioengineering,* Biotechnology Process Engineering at MIT; *energy and re-*

source recovery, the Offshore Technology Center at Texas A&M and the University of Texas at Austin; *infrastructure,* the Hazardous Substances Control at UCLA (*ERCs* 1991).

Launched three years after the beginning of the ERCs program, the STCs program seeks to extend the competitive posture of the United States by maintaining preeminence in science and technology while assuring a requisite pool of scientists with the quality and breadth of experience to meet changing needs. The major objective is to exploit opportunities in science and technology where the complexity of research problems or the resources needed to solve them require advantages of scale, duration, or equipment and facilities that can be provided only by a stable campus-based research center with long-term funding. The STCs institutionalize hybrid communities of students, scientists, and engineers from a spectrum of organizations in academe, the nonprofit sector, and industrial and federal laboratories.

The science in question is expected to determine the functions of the center, though the focus must emphasize important research opportunities that involve external parties and students in rapid transfer of new knowledge. The intellectual collaboration that occurs crosses the multiple boundaries of types of science (basic and applied), modes of research (experimental, computational, and theoretical), and social sectors (industrial, government, and academic). Three models suggest possible structuring principles: an intellectual theme that requires a critical mass of researchers from within a single discipline or several disciplines; a common facility, set of experimental techniques, database, or research instruments; and a "center without walls," a network of research scientists at several institutions who interact frequently by electronic or other means (*Science and Technology Centers* 1987, 9–13).

Mindful of the controversy created by targeting specific areas, a review panel advised NSF that "it would be unfortunate if the Science and Technology Centers program induced able scientists to abandon important problems simply because they are not regarded as sufficiently crossdisciplinary to be funded under the program" (*Science and Technology Centers* 1987, 24). Early evaluations of the ERCs for the Government Accounting Office show that research quality has been the most important criterion in selecting a center, followed by industrial competitiveness and education. In-lab collaborations between university and industry scientists and engineers have been a minimal component, consisting primarily of document exchange and contacts. Interactions are increasing, but they have had little impact on the most vital segment for the future—students. Industrial partners reported that the type and quality of research were more important than its "cross-disciplinary" or joint nature, although 74 percent of industrial members reported the opportunity for "cross-disciplinary" research was moderately to extremely important (Devon 1990).

The United States is not alone in revitalizing the center concept. In the

Organization for Economic Cooperation and Development (OECD) countries of Europe stiff international competition in key science-related industries has stimulated comparable initiatives to link university science more closely with the demands of industrial innovation. In the United Kingdom, the counterpart of the ERCs and STCs is the university-based Interdisciplinary Research Centers (IRCs) program. There is a significant difference, though. What was envisioned as an avenue of expansion in the United States is a strategic rationalization in Britain. The IRCs more closely resemble the interdisciplinary electronics and materials research laboratories established after World War II at MIT and the University of Chicago (Hoch 1990c, 44). This is not the first effort to stimulate interdisciplinary research in Britain. In the late 1960s a Joint Committee of the Economic and Social Research Council (ESRC) and the Science Research Council of the U.K. promoted collaborations between physical and social scientists, managers and engineers. In a widely criticized move, the ESRC abandoned disciplinary committees in 1982 and encouraged more practical orientations. The IRCs formalized this intent (Hoch 1990a, 348).

The proposal for IRCs originated in a May 1987 proposal, *A Strategy for the Science Base.* It was issued by the U.K. counterpart of NSF, the Advisory Board for the Research Councils (ABRC). Their report rationalized redeployment of limited science resources to IRCs located at universities and focused on areas of potential strategic economic importance. ABRC emphasized that most major research growth over the past century has occurred at the "interdisciplinary borderlands" between established fields. Originally, six new IRCs were to be established each year for three years. By March 1990 seventeen had been established, including centers at Cambridge (high-temperature superconductivity), Oxford (molecular sciences and molecular medicine), Glasgow (engineering design), Liverpool (surface science), London (semiconductor materials), and Edinburgh (human communication). Original projections proved financially impossible. In 1990 the government called for a temporary pause and requested stringent review of existing centers (Hoch 1990b, 115).

The IRCs are controversial for several reasons. Their introduction coincided with the impact of funding cutbacks that began in the 1980s. Research capability in the United Kingdom is hampered by the decline of mobility within tenured grades of the university system, both horizontally between institutions and vertically between promotional levels. The ABRC proposal also called for a small number of core staff at each center. Dubbed a "research hotel" because the facility would be staffed by visiting research teams, this model is not without precedent. Large-particle accelerator laboratories in Europe and the United States, such as Brookhaven and CERN, have mobile staffs. They are not, however, mission oriented or preoccupied with applications. They also have sizable core staffs, protecting the continuity and coherence of research (Hoch 1990b).

The implications of new alliances and centers cannot be fully understood without considering an added theme in the debate, the changes in traditional disciplines that have resulted from new modes of knowledge production.

The Changing Picture of Knowledge

The picture of knowledge that emerges from recent descriptions of interdisciplinary science and problem-focused research is characterized by the exhilarating pace and number of developments. New ideas and methods born at the interfaces of disciplines are increasing the ability to address complex problems. New breakthroughs in high-temperature superconductivity have rapidly transformed several areas. New inventions such as the gene-splicing machine have provided powerful new instruments. New facilities such as supercomputer centers and networks are advancing research and training in new ways. New technologies such as high-speed electronics and optical communications and advanced medical instrumentation, as well as defense, energy, and environmental systems, have matured in only a few years after the physical discoveries they are based on (*Scientific Interfaces* 1986, 3–25).

The changes differ in scope and in kind. Some cut across several disciplines. Others affect only parts of disciplines. One of the clearest signs is the boundary between basic and applied research. The interplay between different forms of scientific and technological investigation and between investigative technique and product development has blurred the distinction even further (Clark 1995, 208). Advanced fundamental knowledge is becoming relevant to technological development in the near term, and product life cycles are becoming shorter (*New Alliances* 1986, x). The areas attracting the greatest attention are advanced engineering materials and methods, computer sciences and complex systems software, molecular biology, and biomedical specialties. Macroscopic manifestations of molecular structures require increasingly sophisticated combinations of physics, chemistry, biology, applied biology in medical settings, and engineering (Sproull and Hall 1987, 3). In engineering, traditional divisions of "civil," "mechanical," "chemical," and "electrical" still form the core of the engineering curriculum. Yet the dominant metaphor of description is "systems," a keyword that signifies the interaction of older core disciplines with economics, social values, and expanding technical and scientific knowledge (*Bioengineering Systems* 1987, 1–2).

Bioengineering illustrates the breadth of connections and the power of application. Bioengineering applies basic knowledge about the human body and other biological systems. In doing so, it makes use of virtually every traditional engineering discipline, in addition to the life sciences of biochemistry, biophysics, biology, medicine, public health, agriculture, mathematics, chemistry, and physics. Consequently the field has several names: bioengineering, genetic engineering, biotechnology, and biomedical and biochemical engineering. The most common term, bioengineering, is applied to a wide range of products and processes. Development of the first artificial heart valve required engineering research. Further refinement will require understanding of basic principles of fluid mechanics, physiology, and biomaterials. As anatomy, physiology, and pathophysiology are understood in new ways, less invasive diagnostic methods, replacement joints, organisms, and other processes and products that improve medical care are being developed (*Bioengineering Systems* 1987, 9, 78, 84–86).

The number of medical advances classed as "interdisciplinary" in the 1990 report *Interdisciplinary Research* is as striking as the variety. In the area of imaging in clinical medicine and surgery, advances been made in nuclear magnetic resonance imaging, ultrasonic imaging, and mammography. Quantitative analysis of biological processes has resulted in progress in the mathematics of DNA unfolding, the molecular basis of cataract disease, and the theory of control of enzyme action. Advances in medical and surgical devices and methods have led to cardiac pacemakers, laser surgery, renal dialysis, and heart-lung machines. In the area of synthetic biomaterials and artificial organs, the advances include artificial heart valves and blood vessels, intraocular lenses, hip joints, and synthetic and artificial skin (*Bioengineering Systems* 1987, 7–8).

New developments have altered traditional notions of what constitutes the core in a number of disciplines (Friedman and Friedman 1986, 85). They have also produced a greater density of discipline. In one research university the subject area "biology" is spread across thirteen discipline-based departments and seventeen interdisciplinary programs (Clark 1995, 142). Physics is also a prominent example. In the early 1900s the discipline was based in a quantum physics of solids and atomic theory. Between 1930 and 1960 it was reordered around two poles, a physics of solids and a physics of the atomic nucleus. By 1960, because of its applications to solid-state electronics and materials engineering, the field of solid-state physics was quantitatively and technologically the most important subfield of the discipline, even though it assumed intellectual and institutional identity only in 1945 (Hoch 1987, 210, 235). At that point physics was no longer a single discipline but a federation of disciplines, a "super-discipline" (Verhagen 1984, 95) that incorporated a range of subdisciplines, from optics and astronomy to nuclear and solid-state physics. Nuclear and solid-state physics, though, have more in common with chemistry and engineering than with traditional physics.

Since the 1960s, permeations of the boundaries dividing physics and other disciplines have displaced the notion of a single isolated discipline. In 1972 the Physics Survey Committee of the National Research Council (NRC) declared there was "no definable boundary" between physics and other disciplines (*Physics in Perspective,* 67). In 1986 the NRC issued a new series of reports compiled by prominent academic and industrial leaders. Interdisciplinary rhetoric reverberates across all eight volumes of *Physics through the 1990's.* Volume 8, *Scientific Interfaces and Technological Applications* (1986), highlights the interfaces of physics with other natural sciences, new scientific disciplines arising from those interfaces, the stimulus provided by applications of physics in advanced technology, and applications of physics to technology, medicine, and national defense. Situated at the site of new developments in physics, *Scientific Interfaces* is the counterpart of *Redrawing the Boundaries* in literary studies.

Almost all significant growth in research in recent decades, the committee concluded, has occurred at "the interdisciplinary borderlands" between established fields. The most prominent activities in fundamental research are in five areas: biological physics, materials science, the physics-chemistry interface, geophysics, and mathematical and computational physics. Boundary crossing is apparent all across the sciences of molecules and atoms, surfaces and interfaces, and fluids and solids. Physics has advanced to a level at which it is beginning to address the complexity of fundamental biological science at both molecular and many-body organizational levels. Computer science, geology, engineering, and materials sciences are "fully symbiotic," and mathematical and computational physics are influenced by powerful new machinery and concepts. The interface has been crossed "so often in both directions," the committee found, "that its exact location is obscure." Its passage is signaled more by gradual changes in language and approach than by sharp demarcations of content.

Current patterns of interaction differ from the traditional transfer of techniques or experimental and theoretical discoveries. *Scientific Interfaces* treats the new patterns as "true interdisciplinary science." Physicists laid the basic foundations in classical thermodynamics, quantum mechanics of atoms and molecules, X-ray crystallography, optical spectroscopy, and magnetic resonance. Both physicists and chemists built on these areas and enriched them to create new subfields. Chemists, for their part, often made fundamental discoveries that were taken up by physicists, such as statistical mechanics, irreversible thermodynamics, and some aspects of fluid mechanisms. Today new instrumentation has required chemists to develop their own instruments in the traditional manner of physicists. They are also working in close collaboration with physicists to address microscopic properties of complex molecules, materials, and interfaces. New complex materials displaying chemical and physical properties have forged alliances among coalitions of synthetic chemists, physical experimentalists, and theoretical physicists. These alliances occur far from the traditional interface and deep within their respective fields.

Materials science is widely regarded as a prototype of an interdisciplinary field. Over the past three decades, materials science has developed into an independent discipline that fuses metallurgy, chemistry, and ceramics engineering with aspects of condensed-matter physics. Interdisciplinary research centers have been influential in initiating and sustaining progress at the interface. The spectrum from basic problems to applications in technology is continuous. At their common boundary, materials science and condensed-matter physics are distinguished primarily by viewpoints transmitted in the curriculum. At present a great deal of attention is being paid to new materials, methods, and modes of analyzing materials based on new understanding and interpretations. Geophysics has also developed into an independent subfield of geology, though interactions with physics are based more on the conversion of individual physicists to geophysics and on adoption of physics-based methodologies than on the collaborative patterns characteristic of other interfaces. The notable exceptions include new interdisciplinary studies of turbulence and disordered nonlinear systems.

In the realm of technical applications, which are pivotal to large-scale industrial technology, there are six outstanding areas: microelectronics, optical technology, new instrumentation, the fields of energy and environment, national security, and medical applications. The pace of change in optical information technology is startling. Only two decades ago, in 1973, the first continuous room-temperature semiconductor laser was being operated. Today lasers may operate reliably for over one hundred years. Smaller than a grain of sand, they are capable of sending signals exceeding a billion bits of information per second. This capacity stems from work that emanated from molecular and atomic physics and optics, then supplemented the basic physics of the laser with the physics of materials and semiconductors. The laser is an excellent example of a device that has made physics research more precise while finding rapid application in other fields and in society at large.

New developments have blurred boundaries by reconfiguring the location of scientific and technological work away from discrete sites to complex problems and puzzles that are characterized by unpredictability, complexity, and quickening pace. In many areas of advanced technology, the intellectual boundary between engineering and physics is depicted as "vanishing," creating a continuum that speeds technology transfer and innovation. The postgraduate demands of most scientists and engineers involved in research and development are pulling them "inexorably" into the continuum, away from disciplinary boundaries (*Scientific Interfaces* 1986, 22–23). At major synchrotron facilities the cultures of physicists and chemists are merging. The boundaries between chemistry, physics, and to an extent biology are blurring in macromolecular research, while advances in spectroscopy link parts of chemistry and physics. University-affiliated centers for biophysics are revolutionizing research in materials science and in some areas of biology. Meanwhile, chemical physics has become an established component of most chemistry departments.

Even with these striking developments, claims of radical transformation are overstated. The celebrated synergistic interactions between physicists and chemists far from the traditional interface have usually occurred "in spite of department structures, not because of them" (*Scientific Interfaces* 1986, 67). Institutional structures, budgeting categories, and reward systems continue to favor institutionalized disciplinary categories. The limits of change are as pervasive as boundary crossings.

The Limits of Change

Impediments to change expose the gap between description and practice. New research patterns, however vital and important, however much they are transforming the character of contemporary disciplines, are not always readily accommodated by the existing support system. The institutional organization of education and funding in biophysics, for example, often impedes progress. Biophysics is incorporated into many biological science research programs, but few departments include it as a formal option. Few formal graduate school programs in biophysics are available, and many graduate students must acquire multidisciplinary training through experience or by pursuing multiple degrees. Similarly, conventional disciplinary pathways in chemistry, biology, and biophysics tend to limit funding and publication opportunities to particular areas. The principal funding routes in biophysics of the brain and nerves tend to favor institutionalized neurophysiology and the now fashionable fields of computer science, robotics, and automation. The conjunction of molecular biophysics and genetic biotechnology is a promising area for fundamental biophysical processes. Yet, at present the two fields are so disparate that progress in establishing contacts is slow (*Scientific Interfaces* 1986, 6, 49–51).

Similar limits impede product design. The ability to make biological products has created new research needs in bioprocess engineering. Future medical technology will require greater fundamental understanding at the organ, cell, and subcellular levels. Most likely this kind of research will be based on collaborative efforts in the biological and physical sciences. In contrast to the established relationship between chemistry and chemical engineering, however, no comparable level of association exists between biology and biochemical engineering. Developing this relationship is crucial to extending practical implementation of genetic engineering (*Bioengineering Systems Research* 1987, 87). Integrative systems analysis is also needed if the results of new discoveries are to be translated into effective therapies. The accelerating focus toward the molecular level in biological research threatens to leave vacant research areas at the subcellular, cellular, and organ levels. This concern surfaces in criticism of life scientists for not integrating molecular biology into systems biology (*Interdisciplinary Research* 1990, 11).

The cost of instrumentation has become a pressing concern. Instrumentation is becoming obsolete more rapidly than in the past, at the same time as most scientific research fields are increasingly dependent on advances in equipment that require, in turn, more support personnel with the skills to operate that equipment. Studies of OECD countries in the early 1980s revealed persistent skill shortages in areas of software design and development, systems analysis, and computer engineering (Gibbons et al. 1994, 126). Even maintaining laboratory equipment takes a significant amount of research time. The average age of lab equipment in engineering schools, for example, is roughly twenty-five years, and only 18 percent is up to state-of-the-art standards. One-fourth is completely obsolete. Researchers are also buying more computer equipment or using universitywide computer systems. By 1990 one major research institution, the University of Michigan, was spending over $160 million each year on information systems, amounting to 10 percent of its operating expenses (*Bioengineering Systems Research* 1987; *Federally Funded Research* 1991, 181).

Shared facilities and industrial gifts alleviate the instrumentation problem to an extent. Modifications of traditional academic and industrial restrictions, coupled with greater sanctioning of large multidisciplinary projects involving industry, have also eased the pressure. Yet policies still limit interaction on important matters of curriculum development, equipment loans, and personnel exchanges. Moreover, even though user groups share facilities and there is pedagogical value to building equipment that is too expensive to purchase, sophisticated facilities in the millions of dollars are needed at many locations in order to conduct even small-group research requiring molecular-beam and electron-microscopy apparatus (*Scientific Interfaces* 1986, 5–7). One proposed solution is greater cooperation with existing facilities that have collaborative research built into their missions.

Despite recent cutbacks, the U.S. Department of Agriculture's system of experiment stations and research labs remains in place. Intramural laboratories supported by NIH, NASA, and the Departments of Energy and Defense incorporate multidisciplinary approaches to problem solving and research tasks that would jeopardize normal career paths of graduate students and junior faculty. They also provide training models for graduate students and sabbatical visitors who are seeking new perspectives or directions. In addition, the Department of Energy's (DOE) Hollaender fellowships fund work in life, biomedical, and environmental sciences as well as related disciplines. In DOE programs, intramural and extramural funds are used to support collaborative research. This research, though, has been restricted to the mission of the DOE, and support of graduate students and postdoctoral fellows seeking interdisciplinary experience is not regularized (*Federally Funded Research* 1991, 119–21; *Interdisciplinary Research* 1990, 12–13, 28). Furthermore, problem-oriented research agencies that have historically addressed interdisciplinary projects—such as the U.S. Geological Survey, the Bureau of the Census, and the Bureau of Mines—have not been oriented toward basic research or able to attend to the needs and interests of emerging disciplines (Clark 1995, 125).

If new developments are to have long-term impact, four primary areas must be addressed: organizational structure, faculty development, education, and peer review. Initiatives in these areas are, in effect, reports from the front of institutional change.

Organizational Structure and Faculty Development Interdisciplinarity and collaboration are not synonymous, but in science and technology interdisciplinary research often entails collaborative work patterns. Collaboration derives from both top-down and bottom-up initiatives. One person or a group may have a problem requiring expertise from someone in another discipline. Or a particular gathering may bring together individuals who discover a shared interest and then formulate a cooperative program. Research ideas are also generated by bringing together ad hoc groups to discuss specific topics. One person may act as matchmaker or broker, or an agency may stimulate collaboration around a designated topic. In universities, collaboration often results from self-generated meetings of faculty members. In national laboratories and industry-sponsored collaboration, it usually emanates from the directorate and management. The critical elements in promoting collaboration are administrative and institutional support, adequate funding, open communication and collegiality, overlapping educational experience, and opportunities for practical application and technology transfer (*Interdisciplinary Research* 1990, 12).

Interdisciplinary research is incorporated into existing departments in three major ways: by creating categorical appointments in interdisciplinary fields, by gathering faculty into a department that represents a particular interdisciplinary expertise, and by setting up organized research units that carry an institutional commitment of space, money, and positions. Sponsoring interdisciplinary research in an established department ensures that the existing resources of faculty, laboratories, and graduate students will be brought to bear on a particular task or interest. The current faculty in those departments, however, are not always ready or willing to engage in pioneer collaborations. Sometimes a single member possesses the needed interdisciplinary capability. The likelihood of a large supply of such individuals, though, depends on long-term investment in faculty development and educational structure.

The ability to attract and to retain individuals in pertinent areas is becoming a competitive factor in institutional hiring. To accommodate them some biology and medical school departments have created categorical appointments in hybrid fields, such as biophysics, biomathematics, bioengineering, medical physics, and medical engineering. The "rolling appointment" system used at the Beckman Institute for Advanced Science and Technology at the University of Illinois Urbana-Champaign allows flexibility in research missions while providing security for faculty in departmental homes (*Federally Funded Research* 1991, 225). The question of what faculty members will teach always comes up. Their teaching obligations are fulfilled in several ways: by developing new discipline-based courses, through team teaching in interdisciplinary programs, and by teaching new and existing courses in their original disciplines. Individuals may still be vulnerable, though, to departmental control over the curriculum. Institutionalizing hybrid positions as tenured appointments, or at least long-term commitments of ten to fifteen years, provides a measure of security (*Interdisciplinary Research* 1990, 10–17).

When a new unit is created, whether it is a center or a department, the range of research needs must be carefully defined to ensure overlaps as well as constructive criticism. If the scope of a unit is defined too narrowly, it may conflict with broader-based needs of undergraduate and graduate curricula. Creating a new department, such as biomedical engineering or biophysics, depends on the nature of the institution and on available resources. Some institutions are hostile to nontraditional departments, others encourage them. The choice between a traditional and an integrative department is often resolved by creating a center, division, or laboratory. These units, to repeat an earlier lesson of hybrid communities, range from near departments to small-scale instruments for collaborative research. The more new units incorporate the structure and powers of established departments, the more stable and attractive they are (*Interdisciplinary Research* 1990, 20–21).

Lack of communication is the most persistent obstacle. The cultural imperatives created by different cognitive skills produce different approaches to problem solving, ways of arraying data, and methods of using technical language and mathematics. These differences manifest themselves, for example, in the way physical scientists and engineers focus on analysis, whereas life and health scientists stress observation and evaluation. They are also apparent in characteristic styles of argument in publication formats and modes of presentation. Physical scientists, for example, tend to prefer overhead transparencies in professional presentations; biological scientists prefer thirty-five-millimeter color slides. The shadow structure of study groups, retreats, lecture series, seminars, colloquiums, summer workshops, and conferences comprises vital forums for interdisciplinary communication, especially in new knowledge areas. The willingness of public and private agencies to fund such gatherings, however, shifts over time. Some scientific societies do provide homes for interdisciplinary interests. They include the Biophysical Society, the Radiation Research Society, the Biomedical Engineering Society, the American Association for the Advancement of Science, and Sigma Xi (*Interdisciplinary Research* 1990, 13–14, 20, 30).

Institutional commitments of space, money, and positions are the key to long-term investment in change. Local champions, especially respected administrators with interdisciplinary experience, can have a significant impact (Sproull and Hall 1987, 7). So can provisions for seed money, which stimulates collaboration that may lead to external funding and promote technology transfer. The current trend toward interinstitutional cooperation holds the triple promise of cost sharing, disseminating successful approaches, and devising new undergraduate curricula. In engineering the traditional model of reliance on government funding is being supplemented by a new strategy of promoting secondary and tertiary effects across institutions that usually compete for support. This strategy legitimates both interdisciplinary approaches to knowledge and new organizational structures. New funding initiatives, such as the Engineering Education Coalitions program, also enhance this effort. Yet to provide the full range of adequately trained personnel, technical colleges must be integrated into the effort (Devon 1990).

Even these promising initiatives will be undermined if the educational structure does not change.

Education Education, as usual, is the most earnestly invoked but persistently neglected component. Professional forums and popular books such as *Made in America* and *Retracking America* have heightened awareness of the need for a new generation of students, faculty, and researchers able to work effectively beyond the confines of a single discipline or profession. Most curricula, though, represent limited responses, if not outright impediments. The limitations Rustum Roy (1979) identified in an earlier study of materials science have eased in some areas, but they persist. Unless the education and training system serves new interests more extensively, changes will remain ad hoc, producing exceptional models but not long-term structural change or even a general lowering of barriers.

A number of new alliances provide for some degree of student participation. Both students and postdoctoral personnel are involved in research centers at Carnegie Mellon University. Students hold part-time jobs at Georgia Tech's Advanced Technology Development Center, and they are entering electronics and related disciplines through the Center for Integrated Systems at Stanford and the Microelectronics Center of North Carolina (*New Alliances* 1986, 30–31). These facilities mark a significant change. Students are now entering the workforce with training gained in educational models that stress research in units other than academic departments. The new models feature greater sharing of resources such as equipment and space as well as people, including doctoral students, nonfaculty researchers, and technicians. In addition, NSF-sponsored centers utilize models that entail research in units other than academic departments, research in nonacademic sectors, and nonresearch roles in academe (*Federally Funded Research* 1991, 222).

Even with these innovations, entry routes are narrow and preparedness levels limited. At present, researchers are entering interdisciplinary fields primarily through multiple career and educational paths. In the field of biomedical engineering, Ph.D. biomedical engineers constitute a primary source of personnel, though not the only one. Most current leaders are doctoral-level researchers in traditional engineering fields or individuals in medical specialties who became interested in applying their expertise to developing new knowledge, techniques, or equipment. Graduate programs in biophysics tend to attract students who concentrated in physics and mathematics as undergraduates and now wish to apply those disciplines to biological problems. Graduate programs in biomedical engineering tend to attract students with engineering degrees. These programs provide capable graduates the experience of working across disciplinary boundaries and exposure to collaborative patterns of thinking. At the same time, graduate students are pursuing biomedical problems in traditional engineering departments (*Bioengineering Systems Research* 1987, 107).

One of the important trends in interdisciplinary studies is the introduction of basic science cores in the undergraduate curriculum and in medical schools. They provide general education and greater exposure to a cross section of science disciplines and mathematical and computational skills. Specialized programs have also been developed, including a course in pathobiology for nonmedical scientists sponsored by the Josiah Macy Jr. Foundation. Except for targeted programs, though, opportunities for education outside a student's major are still meager (*Interdisciplinary Research* 1990, 14). Biochemical engineering students, for example, need better exposure to the biological sciences in order to improve their ability to manipulate and control cellular biosynthesis. They also need to be taught techniques and methods for solving large-scale bioprocess problems (*Bioengineering Systems Research* 1987, 108). Significantly, the period of education is being expanded to include mid- and late career. An established physicist, for example, might work on cardiac blood flow for several years, then turn to applications of scattering theory in medical imaging, before turning to problems of neural networks. To address those problems, the physicist will require knowledge of new developments and the skills required for using new instrumentation (*Interdisciplinary Research* 1990, 26).

To develop the full potential of new fields and interests, targeted support is under way in the form of new grant categories. In October 1989, NSF announced a new $4 million Research Training Grant Award to stimulate interdisciplinary research in ten U.S. universities (*Interdisciplinary Research*

1990, 31). Industrial support for academic research includes provisions for joining with federal and state agencies to provide matching grants for engineering curriculum development and initiation of research, as well as donating lab equipment and exchanging research personnel (*Bioengineering Systems Research* 1987, 8). New funds for interdisciplinary doctoral appointments and special cross-directorate sabbatical leave programs enable established researchers to gain education in a new discipline. In direct response to the growth of the biotechnology industry, NIH targeted a new predoctoral and postdoctoral training program in biotechnology. The program emphasizes engineering, mathematical, and physical research methods as well as analysis of biological processes. NIH also began soliciting proposals for interdisciplinary research in order to develop new technology for the Human Genome Project, with provisions for a training center. In 1989, working through the National Institute of General Medical Sciences, NIH opened the Lawton Chiles Fellowships program, a $2.8 million training program for applications of physical sciences and engineering to biotechnology (*Interdisciplinary Research* 1990, 5, 18 n. 19).

University-affiliated teaching hospitals are a unique site for interdisciplinary research, health care, and product design (Klein 1990b, 140–55). They present added boundary complexity, because interactions must be structured across separate units of two separate organizations, universities and hospitals (*Interdisciplinary Research* 1990, 2–3). Mounting concern that the number of research-oriented physicians is falling below the minimum desired, coupled with increasing use of sophisticated equipment in clinical practice, has exposed the need for changes in three major areas: upgrading training in mathematics and physics in premedical school and residency programs; narrowing the gap between traditional education and training in the use of modern devices; and increasing the number of joint M.D.–Ph.D programs that stress physical sciences, such as the joint program between Harvard and MIT (*Scientific Interfaces* 1986, 256).

Peer Review The earlier lessons of peer review repeat. The question of funding new developments brings to mind another old saw: Which came first, the chicken or the egg? Because few interdisciplinary research proposals from scientists are funded, few are submitted. Those that are often face dismissal on grounds of not fitting existing categories or not falling within the review expertise of the study groups and panels who control research dollars. Even when new initiatives are funded, the organizational structure of agencies by and large reinforces existing categories. Except for the National Institute of General Medical Sciences, NIH, for example, is organized for the most part into institutes focused on disease- or organ-specific research (*Interdisciplinary Research* 1990, 26).

When interdisciplinary work is funded, it is usually regarded as an exception or is dispersed across categories. Support for bioengineering, for example, is scattered across different units, offices, and programs within and across agencies, making it difficult to obtain an exact picture of the field or even to determine the extent of government support. The category of bioengineering is spread across NSF, NIH, DOE, and NIST (the National Institute of Standards and Technology, formerly the National Bureau of Standards), as well as the Veterans Administration, the Department of Agriculture, and the Defense Advanced Research Projects Agency (*Bioengineering Systems* 1987, 101). Even disciplinary research tends to overlap agencies, despite the categorical premise of assigning particular disciplines to particular agencies. High-energy physics is supported primarily by the DOE, for example, and astrophysics by NASA. Theoretical physics does not belong to a particular agency. In the "decade of the brain," neuroscience was supported by six institutes of NIH and ten other agencies (*Federally Funded Research* 1991, 149).

The critical mechanism in scientific peer review is the system of study sections. Because their members are primarily established researchers in the same or related disciplines, they have tended to be inherently conservative. There are notable exceptions. The Diagnostic Radiology Study Section at NIH is composed of chemists, physicists, and engineers as well as clinical radiologists and radiation biologists. It is not the norm, however. Authors of NRC's 1990 report *Interdisciplinary Research* heard repeated testimony about proposals that few or no members of study sections could adequately judge. When incommensurate knowledge and information are at stake, like can no longer be compared with like (*Federally Funded Research* 1991, 147). Typically, proposals are eliminated in the initial screening stage. Even when outside evaluation is solicited, they may still be assigned lower priority. The lessons of borderlands studies and plate tectonics come readily to mind. Familiar and better-established categories prevail. These problems do not invalidate the study section system, but they underscore the need for appraising its limitations.

Crossing agency boundaries is one solution. In the past there was no mechanism by which programs of NSF, NIH, NASA, and the National Bureau of Standards (NBS) were coordinated, even though all of them have programs or interests in bioengineering research. In response to the difficulties this dispersion created, NSF created an Office of Biotechnology Coordination. NIH has no such mechanism (*Bioengineering Systems Research* 1987, 79). Awareness of institutionalized impediments at NSF was heightened in July 1987 by the report of an internal task force on interdisciplinary research. Among other obstacles, the report called attention to the thorny problem of finding suitable reviewers and the powerful role that program officers play (*Interdisciplinary Research 1990*, 24–25). The recommendations included adding new study sections and joint operational units within existing sections, as well as creating new budget categories. Efforts to ease barriers, though, will not substantially change patterns of thinking unless clear and informed guidelines for evaluating interdisciplinary proposals are developed and shared across agencies.

The limitations of the public system of research support have rekindled hopes for industrial funding. During the 1930s and 1940s many corporate executives and prominent academics called for significant increases in funding basic research through corporate philanthropy. They never materialized. Large-scale external funding of academic research occurred only when the government assumed that role (*New Alliances* 1986, 40–45). Current trends suggest that private funding can play a valuable role in supporting new and risky projects that deviate from established guidelines in federal agencies. The Whitaker Foundation's biomedical engineering program of grants, for example, supports young investigators working at the interface between engineering and life sciences. The Pew Charitable Trusts has also taken an active role in endorsing the initial independent efforts of young collaborators in emerging areas of interdisciplinary research (*Interdisciplinary Research* 1990, 28–30).

Nevertheless, despite "heady projections" in the press and policy circles during the 1970s, industry's contribution to the public sector research system remains modest (Gibbons et al. 1994, 50). Industrial funding of university research has been more "selective" than "sweeping." During the 1980s it was "brisk," but by 1986 it still constituted only roughly 5 percent of all external funding. Because corporate research budgets are relatively small, the total proportion may never exceed 7 to 8 percent. Current projections suggest that royalty streams will remain relatively small compared with the total amount of research support at any university. Even with federal deficit reduction, the federal government is and likely will remain the primary patron of scientific research, differing though its commitment has been and will continue to be over time (*New Alliances* 1986, 1, 16–17, 38; Clark 1995, 152).

Implications, Old and New

Even factoring in limitations, impediments, and disincentives, current trends affirm the growing prominence of new alliances, work modes, and professional roles. The customary flow of academics into industry is being supplemented by the movement of industrial scientists into academic posts and by activities at new sites, beyond the older eminent models such as the Bell Laboratories. Contrary to the public image, most industrial funding of research on campus has been geared to generic, nonproprietary knowledge. Technology transfer, patenting, and commercial gains have not been primary motivations (*Federally Funded Research* 1991, 200–201).

The rhetoric of justification is complicated. To protect basic research, arguments about science often invoke the Newtonian vision of fundamental understanding of natural phenomena. Claims for pragmatic projects invoke the Baconian vision of a science yielding practical benefit. This division has never been absolute, though, especially when scientists are seeking public funding (Gieryn 1983, 789–91). Arguments vary by the nature of the research, the particular institutions, and the individuals who are involved. In the competitiveness debate, Newtonian and Baconian arguments are often joined in an implicit metaphor of investment banking that depicts academic science as the key to practical progress (*New Alliances* 1986, 6). Investing in basic research becomes a down payment on products and processes that will fuel economic growth and productivity (*Scientific Interfaces* 1986, 59, 229). As authors of the report on *Bioengineering Systems Research* put it, "The nation that leads in research has an edge in commercialization" (1987, 100).

The institution of science winds up carrying an impossible load of expectations. In its mammoth 1991 report on the capacity of the nation's research system, the Office of Technology Assessment reported the nation now expects that in addition to generating knowledge, science and engineering will contribute to U.S. prestige and competitiveness abroad, create new centers of research excellence, continue to provide unparalleled opportunities for education and training, and nurture a more diverse workforce (*Federally Funded Research* 1991, 3). Registering the weight of these expectations, the National Science Foundation is facing pressure to move beyond its traditional focus on investigator-initiated research to broader social and economic goals. Even before Congress trimmed NSF's growth profile in the 1993 budget, the agency was already being asked to fund a sizable portfolio of large instruments—such as radio telescopes, magnetic laboratories, and a laser gravity sensor—while expanding educational programs and technology projects such as the high-performance computing initiative. In 1992 Walter Massey, president of NSF, foresaw three options for the future: continuing the status quo, reducing ambitions, or broadening its mandate to include improving society. Even as objections were being raised to the threat that a closer relationship with industry poses for basic science, the 1993 appropriations bill for NSF included language from the Senate specifying more direct concern for the nation's economic strength (Gibbons et al. 1994, 142–44).

The strains are apparent in the flashpoints of debate.

Proprietary Knowledge

From a traditional perspective, the danger of blurring the boundaries separating industrial and academic research is that industrial problems and economic needs will define the direction of research. This danger surfaces in the conflicted status of propriety knowledge. Freedom to publish research findings and the open exchange of ideas and information are the epistemological equivalents of the first amendment. Industrial participation increases the likelihood that the body of knowledge produced in industrial alliances will be treated as privatized, confidential information because of its commercial value (Hoch 1990c, 46). One of the reasons American scientists opposed military control of atomic energy after World War II was their dislike of military-imposed secrecy during the Manhattan Project. The dislike was repeated decades later when some universities refused to engage in contractual military research or to allow the Institute of Defense Analysis to work on their campuses. The posture of scientists, however, has never been uniform. Others saw the Strategic Defense Initiative as a lucrative source of research funds and redirected their focus. Many issues in the competitiveness debate, the authors of a report on *New Alliances and Partnerships in American Science and Engineering* contend, came to the forefront when the Department of Defense began funding research in universities. In the latter half of the 1980s DOD support of research at universities exceeded industrial support. Some of that research was classified (1986, 27–28).

The commercial utilization of scientific research is not new. Raising research funds by selling results is an extension of, rather than a sharp departure from, the established practice of seeking research funds from patrons external to the university. What is new is the raising of private capital to establish a firm that will sell results of research as knowledge or as products for the private profit of a scientist or a university that is legally designated as its owner or coowner. In the current climate, many academic scientists no longer regard traditional constraints as "necessary or right" (Etzkowitz 1983, 198, 201, 210). The earlier development of solid-state physics as an object of commercial interest, though sizable, was not accompanied by the same innovations in institutional arrangements and professional careers that followed the development of molecular biology. Similarly, in the field of semiconductors, the engineers and physicists who established firms during the 1950s and 1960s did not play a major role in those firms while remaining within universities. Furthermore, in the past only specific fields were relevant to industrial investment for profit—namely, computer science, metallurgy, materials science, and chemistry. At present active and symmetrical alliances are occurring in many fields. The most notable are in two areas: between computer science departments in universities and computer corporations and between departments of biology in universities and firms in biotechnology. Significant numbers of the country's leading researchers in molecular genetics are affiliated with highly competitive biotechnology companies, many of which emerged from university research projects. In some cases appointments in private firms are becoming regarded as equal to university appointments (Etzkowitz 1983, 200–201, 217; *New Alliances* 1986, 7, 28).

These changes affirm Gibbons et al.'s theory of mode 2 knowledge production. Technology is no longer a simple commodity to be taken "off the shelf" or guaranteed through technology transfer or intellectual property agreements. The new competitive environment links commercial success with the ability to generate knowledge by using resources lacking in a given industrial firm. The necessary resources are distributed throughout a large and increasingly global network. In order to commercialize knowledge today, firms must play a part in its production. This means developing new types of links with universities, government laboratories, and other firms. In the older linear model, science led to technology and technology satisfied market needs. In many advanced sectors of science and technology today, knowledge is being generated *in* the context of application, not as a simple application and exploitation of existing knowledge. Mode 1 still provides many of the models and metaphors of technology transfer, yet they are strained by the new social contract between industry and academe. Intensified international competition has forced governments to reevaluate the function of science and technology investments and firms. As they become more active participants in the production of knowledge, competition becomes an essential part of discovery (Gibbons et al. 1994, 50–51, 54–55).

Who owns knowledge in the new social contract? Academic-industrial agreements typically delay publication to permit filing of patent applications. Universities tend to resist such constraints. Early reports indicate that corporate values generally do not hamper interchange. Active participants admit that commercial interests sometimes stand in the way of full disclosure of results. They justify the trade-off by pointing to increased availability of capital resources that accelerate research, thereby increasing the amount of knowledge produced. Biotechnology is a striking exception. The monetary stakes are high, and competition is fierce. This economic reality results in greater sanctioning of privatized knowledge. In a revealing example, Columbia University engineering faculty, especially computer scientists, objected to proposed rules regarding conflict of interest and participation in private firms. They feared bureaucratic interference. They did not object to sharing profits with the university but wanted to maintain their status as independent entrepreneurs by accepting stock and making consulting arrangements at their own discretion. In their view university participation infringed on academic freedom and curbed their competitive advantage over other universities and industries that allow consulting and other relations with private firms (Etzkowitz 1983, 224–25).

Even with greater sanctioning of entrepreneurial roles and self-interest, conflicts in cultural values are tenacious. Earning money beyond an academic salary, consulting, and financial profits from patents have acquired a modified legitimacy. Yet the boundary between "disinterested" and "interested" research has blurred, not dissolved. Industrial alliances heighten preexisting differences between those who produce knowledge that can be made the basis of business enterprises and those who do not. Many universities are using the one-fifth rule to limit consulting to one day a week. Infractions of this rule are increasing, but academic loyalties remain powerful sources of identity. The intellectual stimulation and social legitimation of a university appointment remain strong among entrepreneurial scientists. In recently formed innovation centers, most faculty members are still committed to university values and expectations. They are often ignorant of marketing and typically uninterested in assuming the traditional business role of product champion. Not all scientists have remained active in universities; some have left voluntarily, and others have been forced to resign (Etzkowitz 1983, 200, 221, 228).

Six major issues need to be addressed in establishing and conducting partnerships: preservation of academic initiatives and educational missions in cooperative ventures involving commercial concerns; freedom to publish research findings; freedom to collaborate with scientific colleagues; appropriate limits on consulting and entrepreneurial activity; establishment of policies and procedures to avoid real or perceived conflicts of interest; and establishment of policies that clarify patenting, licensing, and the ownership of intellectual property (*Interdisciplinary Research* 1990, 22–23). The working balance of the partnership is the result of testing the terms of relation, not unlike the testing of workable hypotheses that occurs in developing interdisciplinary intellectual fields.

Interdisciplinary Prospects

Like their poststructuralist counterparts in the humanities and social sciences, some proponents of new alliances would realign, if not jettison, the traditional department structure. Others would reinforce the trend toward greater legitimacy of alternative sites and practices. Historical patterns, coupled with early assessments, suggest the promise will be greater than the outcome. Generally speaking, patterns of work and outcomes in centers and institutes still exhibit unidisciplinary tendencies (Friedman and Friedman 1982, 1986, 1988). Locating interdisciplinary activity primarily at centers and alternative sites may lead to the same accommodationist politics that have plagued interdisciplinary studies in the curriculum. Separating them physically and socially from the main campus is a way of keeping industrial values at bay. The status of interdisciplinarity in the debate would be misunderstood if construed only in terms of a simple equation of interdisciplinarity and instrumentality. Interdisciplinarity is also caught in a larger debate about the growing collectivization and complexity of science.

During the 1960s the most prevalent unit of research production in the United States was a professor with two to six students working in a single discipline. By the 1990s a greater variety of research units existed, including large groups with many graduate students, nontenure-track researchers, postdoctoral fellows, and technicians working under one principal investigator (*Federally Funded Research* 1991, 33–35, 219–26). Large projects often involve multi- or interdisciplinary teams, heightening the need for collaborative skills and experience in teamwork. One of the potential victims of greater emphasis on large projects and megacenters is small-scale interdisciplinary research. Despite highly visible megaprojects and large groups, most physics research in the United States is still conducted in small university laboratories consisting of a few researchers and a total instrumentation inventory of less than $1 million. Research on this scale continues to produce a significant share of fundamental new science while training a large portion of scientific and technical personnel. Significant innovations in instrumentation also occur at this level (*Scientific Interfaces* 1986, 188, 195).

Nevertheless, the long-term structural trend has been in the direction of larger organizations. Collaborations in physics, astronomy, and oceanography often involve teams with complex divisions of labor. Biology and chemistry have been slower to change to a large-team model, but experiments in particle physics now involve from ten to two hundred collaborators, or more. International collaborations at CERN, the European high-energy physics facility, have involved as many as four hundred people on a single team (Stine 1992, 401–3). Projects are also increasingly undertaken by groups or teams that have limited control over resources and cannot claim personal responsibility for what is attempted or achieved. The value of individualism embodied in the traditional academic ethos diminishes as collective action becomes the norm, and science loses its distinct identity and place as an autonomous social segment (Ziman 1984, 138–39). Knowledge production becomes an instrument of deliberate societal actions taken by research administrators and policymakers. The most controversial aspect in the debate stems from the strategic targeting of research.

Previous funding programs focused on applying pieces of redefined disciplinary knowledge to a given problem, often through multidisciplinary trial and error. In contrast, the U.S. Science and Technology Centers and the British Interdisciplinary Research Centers attempt to isolate and develop elements of potential basic research foreseen to have strategic importance for the next generation of new technologies. As new technologies become more complex and science becomes more intensive, the older sequential progression of technological effort from R&D to manufacturing then marketing is strained by the increasing branching and complexity of knowledge (*Bioengineering Systems Research* 1987, 100). Governments, grappling with the need to address complex problems, make decisions that increase the likelihood of deinstitutionalization. Greater control of science passes to nonscientists, and science is reinstitutionalized as the mass focus passes out of disciplinary departments (Elzinga 1985). When interdisciplinarity is cast as a principal means of achieving targeted objectives, the outcome may be determined more by a power battle between disciplinary groupings and hybrid communities than by considerations of scientific validity, objectively demonstrable social need, or the legitimacy of integration and collaboration (Hoch 1990c, 45).

One of the major claims advanced in Gibbons et al.'s theory of mode 2 knowledge production is that conventional terms of the past—"applied science," "technological" or "industrial research," "technology transfer," "strategic research," "mission-oriented research," "research and development"—are inadequate to describe what is currently happening. "Technology interchange" has become a more appropriate phrase than "technology transfer." Interchange is an appropriate metaphor for the new complex of alliances, sites, and strategies. Production and distribution of knowledge are more closely related than in the past. As discovery and application become more closely integrated, contexts of application and use gain greater visibility as sites of challenging intellectual problems and opportunities for collaboration. Evidence of structural transformation exists in some institutions. Broadly speaking, though, current developments still amount to a shift of emphasis, not a historical break (Gibbons et al. 1994, 2, 9, 53, 87, 163).

Scientists will remain the driving force in proposing research in the foreseeable future. Science and higher education, however, have been drawn into fuller and more complicated relationships with patrons, especially national governments, which have their own agendas and expectations (Clark 1995, 3–4). A greater number of scientists, moreover, are also working on problems outside their traditional specialties, and they are entering into new social arrangements. As they do, definitions of a "good scientist" and "good science" become more pluralistic. Problem context heightens boundary crossing. Problem solvers, problem identifiers, and strategic brokers are working with knowledge resources held in government laboratories, consultancies, and other businesses. Managers in higher education are also beginning to operate in a similar mode. They are becoming more active partners in an arena that demands moving back and forth between environments that are at one moment collaborative, at another moment competitive (Gibbons et al. 1994, 23, 32, 37, 65, 76, 145).

The relation between excellence in science and international competitiveness is neither linear nor direct. But there is a strong relation, one that strains older notions of structure and authority. The organizations that carry projects at the forefront of science, technology, and high-value enterprises resemble a spiderweb more than a pyramid. Connections are being spun all the time. Problems in genetics, electronics, mathematics, and physics possess an intrinsic intellectual interest that is continuously nourished by the research and the practical interests of other users. As a new mode spreads, the norms and values traditionally associated with disciplinary research broaden and are reinterpreted. International competition has intensified a shift that was already under way, from vertical growth and linearity to horizontal growth, heterogeneity, and hybridity. Relationships within and between science and society have likewise changed. The changes are driven by the globalization of science and sources of R&D, the role that specialized knowledge is playing in technological innovation, and a greater diversity of knowledge producers from a wider range of specialties and fields, institutions, and geographic locations (Gibbons et al. 1994, 19, 34, 37, 44, 47–49, 81, 84, 124, 140, 147).

Interdisciplinarity is not the only variable, but it is a major one. Interdisciplinary problem-focused research gained prominence in World War II because it answered military needs. Subsequent support of defense needs, aerospace, and industrial products enhanced its legitimacy. The current push of high technology and international competition in key science-based industries has made "collaboration" and "teamwork," "competitiveness," "problem solving," "systems," and "complexity" new keywords in science. They are powerful warrants for interdisciplinary values. They have not rendered IDR central to the academy. Nonetheless, problem complexity, economic competition, federal deficit reduction, the costs of instrumentation and facilities, and the desire to transfer knowledge rapidly from laboratory to hospital and marketplace will continue to sanction new hybrid modes of knowledge production. The rhetoric of interdisciplinarity will remain the locus of claims about what is internal and external to science, technology, industry, and the nation.

CONCLUSION:

Interdisciplinary Futures

There is a crack, a crack in everything. That's the way light gets in.
Leonard Cohen, "Anthem," _The Future_, 1992

The degree to which academic and intellectual trends are causes for anxiety or calls to action depends in large part on how we explain them.
Barry Supple, "Economic History," 1981

Our theoretical and educational efforts will not be served by vague ideas, platitudes, and unfounded promises; nor will they be served either by criticism that is not to the point.
Joseph Kockelmans, "Science and Discipline," 1979

Over the course of the twentieth century, interdisciplinarity has developed from an idea into a complex set of claims, activities, and structures. It has become a challenge to orthodoxy and a force for change. It is now part of academic consciousness and is even regarded as essential to the vitality of work outside the academy (Salter and Hearn 1993). Yet obstacles and disincentives are pervasive. It takes little courage or originality, Ludwig Huber reminds us, to point out that a problem or issue can be addressed only in an interdisciplinary manner. Interdisciplinarity is on everyone's agenda; actually implementing it in institutional settings is a more difficult proposition (1992b, 285).

The argument that knowledge is increasingly interdisciplinary is sounded publicly while financial cutbacks curb and eliminate existing programs. This threat is not limited to interdisciplinary contexts. Both disciplinary and interdisciplinary futures are being determined by fiscal and political realities that enable some fields while impeding others. Interdisciplinary activities fall victim, in part, to the academic equivalent of last hired, first fired. Many of their underlying knowledge fields are newer than established disciplines. Ironically, though, given that the context is institutions devoted to knowledge, ignorance and confusion are greater obstacles. Interdisciplinary activities are undermined by misinformation, bias, and easy generalizations. Decisions are often made without a full airing of what is "basic" and "essential." This failure shortchanges both disciplinary and interdisciplinary development.

In this circumstance, knowledge of three issues—integrative process, criteria for judgment, and institutional strategies—is essential for informed decision making and action. Judgments about validity and quality cannot be made without understanding how interdisciplinary work gets done. Claims cannot be advanced without knowing and deploying strategies of institutionalization.

Process and Criteria

Criteria for judgment constitute the least understood aspect of interdisciplinarity, in part because the issue has been the least studied and in part because the multiplicity of tasks seems to militate against a single standard. The discussion is skewed from the start by portraying interdisciplinary activities as anomalies. Stephen Toulmin uses a rhetoric of negativity in classifying activities that do not measure up to "normal" disciplines. "Nondisciplinary" activities, in Toulmin's hierarchy of knowledge fields, tend to be directed by personal rather than communal or collective goals. They encompass goals for everyone, not a professional class of specialists or experts. They are often concerned with multivalued problems, and they do not necessarily lend themselves to analysis in abstract or general terms (1972, 379–80, 396). Beyond leaving the question of appropriate criteria unanswered, Toulmin's scheme contains debatable assumptions.

Are the disciplines of literary studies and sociology "nondisciplinary" because the problems they deal with are multivalued? Are the interdisciplinary fields of women's studies and science policy studies "nondisciplinable" because they examine excluded traits? Or are they "disciplinary" after all, because they have been institutionalized and their claims are advanced through disciplinelike strategies? Conversely, is even science, at the peak of the pyramid of rational criteria, nondisciplinary? Studies of scientific practices have revealed the personal, nonrational, and multilayered factors that operate in determining "science." Redefinition of disciplinary problems of the first kind as multidimensional problems of the second and third kinds reinforces the view that all disciplines should be concerned with their "nondisciplinable" dimensions, their consumers, and the effects of the knowledge they produce (Ellen Messer-Davidow pers. comm., 29 May 1994).

Like disciplinary and professional work, interdisciplinary work should be judged on how well the job is done. The conventional ideology of excellence, though, rests on the assumption of a standard body of knowledge or a fixed body of content. The basis of interdisciplinary work is different. Interdisciplinary work reconfigures disciplinary and professional knowledge and knowledge communities. Because the work is often sui generis, standard criteria have limited applicability. The appropriate approach to judging quality and success is not to impose standard assumptions but to insert into the ideology of excellence an interdisciplinary-specific discourse (Ellen Messer-Davidow pers. comm., 12 May 1995). Competing formulations of interdisciplinarity shape competing assumptions about quality. Designing a new transportation system is a different context from borrowing a concept or formulating a new field of knowledge. Each of these activities, though, requires integrative process. Interdisciplinary activities should be judged, then, on how well they accomplish the particularities of their tasks and how well they integrate knowledge.

Three interwoven issues have emerged from the analysis of boundary work: integrative process; the role of disciplines; and communicative action.

Integrative Process and the Role of Disciplines

Argument remains inescapable. When interdisciplinary work is conceived as part of the "natural" generation and gravitation of fruitful inquiries that will be located in the disciplinary system, assumptions about criteria tend to be strongly disciplinary. This view is prominent in science, where interdisciplinary research is often treated as one more form of the general division of labor in the production of knowledge (Whitley 1984, 22). Boundaries are crossed in order to understand the world, not in the interest of getting ahead professionally or politically (Pahre 1994, 16), advancing interdisciplinarity per se, or critiquing the disciplinary status quo. This formulation, though, sidesteps the question whether integrative process creates different demands and how, as a result of those demands, results are to be judged. In limiting interdisciplinarity to a developmental stage, it also denies the possibility of intrinsic property and epistemological ground (Eckhardt 1978, 11).

Instrumental claims differ. In focusing on external imperatives of problem solving, they locate criteria narrowly in the principle of use. In foregrounding efficacy and utility, they trade the short-term success of getting a job done for long-term reflection on ends and means. In critical interdisciplinarities, radical change is the goal. The "rhetoric of interpenetration" that is characteristic of critical interdisciplinarities does not simply enrich existing fields. It constructs new criteria and replaces them. It alters not only the *products* of research but the very *procedures* (Fuller 1993, xx, 37). The clearest distinction raised by competing formulations is the stance on organizational structure. In the first two formulations, making room for interdisciplinary work through programs, centers, and projects is an acceptable bridge-building strategy. The logic of making room clashes, however, with the raison d'être of critical interdisciplinarities. Accommodation becomes a subtle legitimation of the status quo (Ewell 1990, 45).

The more intricate distinction is the role of the disciplines. "Nondisciplinary" is a slippery notion. For Toulmin it is a negative judgment. For radical interdisciplinarians it is a position. Even radical activities that eschew the institution of disciplinarity, however, make use of disciplinary results and insights. Competing formulations meet in the question of how interdisciplinary work gets done. Process and criteria are implicated in each other. Appropriate criteria are not given or found, they are made. They are created in an ongoing process of discovery (Bechtel 1986b, 43) that opens up barriers and cross-fertilizes by replacing the dichotomy of either-or with the inclusive relationship of both-and. Root metaphors play a powerful role in shaping assumptions. Disciplinary work is signified by the metaphor of deepening along a vertical axis. Interdisciplinary work is usually depicted along the horizontal axis of breadth. The depth/breadth dichotomy, however, fails to acknowledge a crucial third element—synthesis ("Interdisciplinary Studies" 1990, 65).

Extending the visual metaphor, interdisciplinary work gets done by moving across the vertical plane of depth and the horizontal plane of breadth. Breadth connotes a comprehensive approach based in multiple variables and perspectives. Depth connotes competence in pertinent disciplinary, professional, and interdisciplinary approaches. Synthesis connotes creation of an interdisciplinary outcome through a series of integrative actions. Synthesis does not derive from simply mastering a body of knowledge, applying a formula, or moving in linear fashion from point A to point B. Recognized interdisciplinary approaches such as systems theory or feminism may be useful, but integrating knowledge is neither routine nor formulaic. It requires active triangulation of depth, breadth, and synthesis.

There is a crucial difference between the metaphors of mastery and of adequacy. The metaphor of mastery implies complete knowledge of a discipline. Adequacy shifts the role of the disciplines to another ground, the interdisciplinary task at hand. The difference between mastery and adequacy lies in the difference between learning a discipline in order to practice it and comprehending how that discipline characteristically looks at the world—its observational categories, key terms, and relevant methods and approaches (Newell 1992, 213; Petrie 1976). The "requisite disciplinary knowledge" needed to perform an interdisciplinary task must be treated "respectfully and respectably" (Vickers 1991, 27; Newell 1992, 212–13). Disciplines may be accepted without challenge in instrumental work or may be critiqued in critical interdisciplinarities, but they must be understood.

The discussion is incomplete if adequacy of disciplinary knowledge remains the primary focus. The notions of "depth" and "rigor" are usually equated with disciplinarity. In interdisciplinary activity, they are redefined. Depth in interdisciplinary work derives from competence in pertinent knowledges and approaches. Rigor derives from attention to integrative process.

Policy analysis and public management illustrate what the shift to interdisciplinary ground entails. The context is problem orientation, but the example has generic value because selection of relevant resources is an important part of integrative process.

Policy analysis, Joel L. Fleishman explains, is a framework designed to "fit around a problem" that lends itself to purposive individual or social action. Appropriate information must be identified and organized in order to define the problem and explore possible solutions. Well-constructed policy analysis specifies the analytic techniques needed for understanding underlying data, the decisions that must be made in order to accomplish desired results, their sequencing, and statistical techniques for estimating the probability of certain outcomes. "Policy analysis," Fleishman adds, "is not a discipline. Rather, it chooses the analytic methods, theories, and substantive knowledge generated by other fields that are useful to integrate into its own framework for application to particular problems at hand." Like other interdisciplinary activities, it differs from the disciplines it draws on (1991, 236).

The major disciplines in this case are political science and economics; both are predominantly descriptive and contemplative. Policy analysis, in contrast, is prescriptive and decisive. The two disciplines also tend toward a kind of orthodoxy by erecting boundaries around what is and what is not political science or economics. Policy analysis, in contrast, is "heterodox, eclectic, integrative, and inclusive." It attempts to be comprehensive by looking at the whole problem rather than looking at the parts each discipline isolates. Political scientists are often prescriptive, yet their basic orientation is toward explaining political institutions and forces. Economic theory does pay attention to normative and descriptive issues, but its normative framework is narrow. Policy analysis starts where economics and political science leave off. It builds on their descriptions and inferences in order to formulate alternative solutions and project likely consequences. In doing so, it incorporates only a small fraction of the contents of each underlying discipline. It selects fragments that appear relevant to solving the problem at hand and adds useful elements from the fields of statistics, operations research, and ethics (Fleishman 1991, 236–37).

Selecting relevant fragments and synthesizing them entails certain skills. In research, problem solving, and the curriculum an interdisciplinary approach encourages development of problem-posing and problem-solving capacities as well as an "integrative habit of mind" (Newell 1983, 245–46). The basic skills needed for all integrations are familiar ones: differentiating, comparing, contrasting, relating, clarifying, reconciling, and synthesizing (Klein 1990b, 183). Multilogical thinking occurs in defining the task at hand, determining how best to use available approaches, and devising a working metalanguage. The worldview or perspective embedded in each discipline must be extracted; its underlying assumptions must be identified, then compared when they conflict. The definition of intellectuality shifts from absolute answers and solutions to tentativeness and reflexivity. In all interdisciplinary activities, some time should be devoted to examining the philosophical underpinnings of the challenge they pose to disciplinary approaches. Good interdisciplinary work requires a strong degree of epistemological reflexivity, regardless of the position taken on epistemological critiques of disciplinarity (Robinson 1996).

In the curriculum, students gain a sense of confidence that conclusions can be achieved, or at least that intelligent and fruitful questions can be raised. They learn to apply and evaluate specific methodologies and the differing value patterns that influence reasoning. They learn to abstract and generalize from specific findings to a higher order of knowledge (conceptualization), perhaps even to the level of being able to organize several orders of concepts. By going beyond logical skills to being critically reflexive of self and discipline, an interdisciplinary approach promotes strong sense critical thinking (Hursh, Haas, and Moore 1983; Newell 1992, 220; Paul 1987).

Any course or program must be more than the pieces of the disciplines from which it is constructed. Self-synthesis, the assumption that students can integrate materials and ideas themselves, is inadequate. Synthesis does not occur by osmosis. Jonathan Z. Smith's iron law bears repeating: "Students shall not be expected to integrate anything the faculty can't or won't" (Gaff 1980, 54–55). In the context of general education, the breadth part of the triad of depth, breadth, and synthesis is often accentuated. This results in a weak synthesis that takes the form of enriching students' understanding of an issue or topic, defining the limitations of disciplinary perspectives and methods, and contextualizing contending ideologies and worldviews. These are appropriate goals in general education, and they constitute an important preliminary stage in the education process (Richards 1996). They are also necessary steps in integrative process but not the end point.

One dimension of criteria—assessment of learning—is especially pressing in the United States, where use of testing and faith in its validity are greater than in Europe (Huber 1992a, 198–99). The conceptual format for assessment is shaped by the premise that knowledge of established areas can be measured, usually through nationally normed tests. By their very nature, though, interdisciplinary programs tend to be unique, and acquisition of knowledge alone is a questionable measurement goal. Interdisciplinary context changes the process of thinking about outcomes: the range of knowledge and the amount of integration will be greater. The priority also shifts to analyzing, synthesizing, applying, and using for evaluation what has been learned in creative ways. The crucial "homework" for assessment is defining the subject and desired learning outcomes (Davis 1995, 55, 57, 70–73).

In the first comprehensive discussion of interdisciplinary assessment, Field, Lee, and Field (1994) report that some standardized tests are useful to interdisciplinary programs. The primary examples are the College Outcomes Measures Project of the American College Testing Program (ACT-COMP) and the General Intellectual Skills of the Educational Testing Service. Even relevant tests, though, must be matched to the goals of a particular curriculum and combined with multiple measures, including locally designed strategies. Lack of standard curricula, often seen as a disadvantage in interdisciplinary fields, may well be an advantage. They require an approach based in intellectual maturation and cognitive development, not a fixed body of information. Appropriate strategies include using relevant parts of existing instruments, portfolio analysis of student work, proactive attention to integrative process, employing qualitative measures such as entry and exit interviews, surveys, and contextualized use of quantitative measures, gathering data on graduate- and professional-school admissions, tracking progress through a defined sequence of learning experiences, and requiring capstone courses and culminating essays or projects.

Several models depict the operational elements of integrative process. Hursh, Haas, and Moore's (1983) model of an interdisciplinary solution to a given problem in general education identifies two levels: *clarification* of salient concepts and skills to be used in evaluating the concepts, then *resolution* of the differences identified in defining salient concepts. A course on U.S. energy policy, for example, may draw on the geology of coal and oil formation, the chemistry of energy storage, the physics of energy release and transformation in a power plant, the chemistry of air pollution, the biology of low-level ionizing radiation, the economics of energy pricing, and the politics of the oil market. The concept of efficiency is central to combining these insights into policy. Yet it is defined differently in physics, economics, and political science. Each discipline recognizes efficiency as a measure of output per unit but varies in what it includes as input and output. By contrasting the ambiguities and assumptions of different definitions, students can construct a higher-order comprehensive meaning that can accommodate discrepancies and integrate salient concepts. The worldview or perspective embedded in each disciplinary piece is extracted, compared, and evaluated for relevance. When conflicts are detected, they are clarified. They do not disappear, however, in a false unity that denies difference (Klein 1995; Klein and Newell 1996).

Maurice DeWachter's (1982) model of an interdisciplinary approach to a problem in bioethics substitutes a global question for Hursh, Haas, and Moore's notion of salient concepts. A global question is shaped by the immediate bioethical problem. The question is then translated into specific disciplinary languages, and the relevance of each answer is constantly checked. Achieving agreement on a final answer, which becomes the decision to be implemented, depends on integrating all the particular answers that are available. The crucial insight is the recognition that people do not start out working from an ideal model. They are usually unwilling to abstain from approaching the topic along lines of their own disciplinary and professional worldviews. Realistically, the best chance of succeeding lies in starting by translating a global question into the specific language of each participating discipline, then working back and forth in iterative fashion. This way a global question is formulated in a manner that acknowledges all relevant aspects. No one answer is privileged.

William Newell (1993) offers added insight from techniques he observed in the work of three socioeconomists: Kenneth Boulding, Robert Frank, and Amitai Etzioni. For Boulding, integrative process entailed *redefinition* and *extension.* After identifying what subjects have in common, conflicting assumptions may be placed on a *continuum* in order to identify the underlying common elements. Using this method, Boulding transformed the debate about whether human nature is selfish or altruistic into a choice of where, on a continuum of motivations, people fall in any given study. In his model of transfers, two separate but analogous and *interconnected* economies exist side by side, operating in parallel. Robert Frank and Amitai Etzioni transformed conflicting assumptions into *variables,* thereby pushing back original assumptions and expanding the scope of theory. In Etzioni's view, tension is preserved but conflict is eliminated. In discussing rational-empirical decision making versus normative-affective choices, he examined situations where the factors affecting choice are *interpenetrating* or *facilitating,* as well as those where one operates inside the *envelope* of boundaries set by the other.

Difference, tension, and conflict emerge as important parts of integrative process. They are not barriers that must be eliminated; they are part of the character of interdisciplinary knowledge. Their role underscores the importance of the third issue—communication. All interdisciplinary activities require translation and negotiation.

Interdisciplinarity as Communicative Action

Interdisciplinarity is not a monologue. Even individuals working alone must familiarize themselves with the problematics of the material and approaches being used. George Levine dubs failure to check on the accuracy and current validity of borrowed material and ideas "the quiet scandal of interdisciplinarity" (1991). Drawing on the experience of interdisciplinary teams at the Center for Interdisciplinary Research at the University of Bielefeld, Wilhelm Vosskamp (1994) suggests that the agreement/disagreement structure necessary for all communication shapes the conditions of dialogue among differing disciplines and bodies of knowledge. Consent/dissent (*Alterität*) requires accepting, from the outset, the unforeseeable and the productive role of misunderstanding. A sense of the new and the surprising is decisive in mutual exchange and dialogue. The result is not necessarily consensus or unity; dissent will remain a thorny issue. The "fallacy of eclecticism" is the naive faith that partial methods will add up to a complete picture of the phenomena rather than a microcosm of disciplinary struggles to colonize the phenomena (Fuller 1993, 42).

The communicative competence needed for interdisciplinary work is inextricably bound up with problems of language. Desertification, for example, is a complex problem in the field of natural resources that is ripe for interdisciplinary solution by climatology, soil science, meteorology, and hydrology as well as geography, political science, economics, and anthropology. The concept of desertification, though, is defined differently in disciplinary, national, and bureaucratic settings. Each emphasizes aspects that derive from conflicting special interests of climate, human factors, animals, soils, natural vegetation, and range management. The literature on desertification contains no fewer than a hundred definitions, leading to miscommunication among researchers and between researchers and policymakers within and between countries. Any interdisciplinary effort requires analyzing definitions and terminology in order to improve understanding and construct an integrated framework (Glantz and Orlovsky 1986, 215; Bennett 1986, 347).

Conditions of synthesis will vary according to the nature and scope of a given activity. Kelly (1996) and Van Dusseldorp and Wigboldus (1994, 96) distinguish "narrow interdisciplinarity" from "wide" or "broad interdisciplinarity." A narrowly defined instrumental project or a study among disciplines with similar paradigms and methods will have different communication dynamics than an activity that bridges a wider epistemological gap, such as that between the humanities and the sciences. The number of participating disciplines and organizations will also complicate communication. In each case, though, a common language and a shared sense of what is at stake must be created. A number of techniques aid this process (Klein 1990b, 119–55, 189–90).

In health-care teams, role negotiation and role clarification help individuals assess what they need and expect from one another while clarifying differences in methodology and ideology. By translating specialized knowledge into a proposed synthetic product, they act as filters for each other and consult experts as necessary. In problem-focused research, rotation of work assignments, internal and external reviews, and numerous rewrites of reports and joint publications promote an integrated outcome. Through iteration, assumptions are repeatedly checked. Returning to earlier stages encourages critical appraisal of individual contributions and collective resolution of differences. Peer editing of drafts increases the likelihood of moving beyond juxtaposition to integrated perspective. In an example of collaborative historical research, the Freedom and Southern Society Project, "score carding" was used to assess the relevance of disciplinary inputs (S. Miller 1992, 123). In Farming Systems Research in developing countries, the prospect of integration is enhanced by having all team members available at once. Some of the integration can take place in fieldwork. The quality of outcomes depends on the quality of the disciplinary building blocks and communication across component parts (Van Dusseldorp and Wigboldus 1994).

Systems engineering is a major example. The label "systems engineering" is used across a broad spectrum of activities centered on integrated problem solving. Within the aerospace industry, to cite a major instance, the term denotes management of research as well as development and production of complex high technology, defense, and aerospace systems. Systems engineering is client-centered: it relies on a structured, top-down iterative approach to problem solving. A hypothesis is formed and tested or a problem is solved in six steps: identification of goals and objectives; identification of alternative approaches that are ranked comparatively; synthesis of alternatives in order to discover new or better solutions; selection of the "best" solution; definition of steps to implement the chosen solution; definition and documentation of the process that led to the decision (Mar 1988).

The final and—from an interdisciplinary standpoint—crucial step is not always taken. Yet in specifying the importance of identifying alternative approaches and documenting the decision-making process, systems engineering creates a broader, more comprehensive approach to problem solving than traditional methods. Systems engineering can occur at any level, from macroscopic group management to individual projects. The key to implementation has been powerful, low-cost personal computers and accessible word processing equipment and software for data management. Computers aid in data management and provide micro- and macroscale testing of models through simulation. Specially designed computerized systems facilitate interdisciplinary work at different levels of complexity by constructing network representations of relations among particular ideas and elements. The context may be a single discussion, an entire project, or a field of knowledge.

Computers undeniably are valuable tools when dealing with aggregate data sources, multivariate databases, and archives. Yet even powerful software and proven techniques such as Delphi method, iteration, common data analysis, system simulation, and theory construction do not guarantee that synthesis will occur (Klein 1990–91, 39). Integration is a human action. The result, synthesis, is negotiated, situationally dependent, and contingent on the participants. If participants share the same habitus and the same position in time and space, communication is easier and knowledge more likely to be disseminated. This is not, however, the typical interdisciplinary situation.

For that reason, change of perspective and acquisition of multiple perspectives are built into the curriculum of the Oberstufen-Kolleg at the University of Bielefeld (Germany). Interdisciplinary process is grounded in social learning. "Changing one's perspective," faculty members Andrea Frank and Jürgen Schulert suggest, "is like entering another culture." Interdisciplinary work, in this respect, is a form of intercultural learning. The theoretical approach to interdisciplinarity in the Oberstufen-Kolleg underscores the importance of communication. If disciplinarity and interdisciplinarity are taken as different forms of communication, not dichotomized as institutional alternatives, criteria can be defined based on how knowledge and information are to be understood and appropriately organized (Frank and Schulert 1992, 223, 231, 235).

Members of the same teaching or research team tend to lack formal consensus on a definition of interdisciplinarity, and they rarely engage in philosophical discussion. Different operational and implicit definitions usually emerge from pragmatic discussions. In the curriculum, they center on what topics to cover, books to read, issues to raise, and sensibilities to develop in a particular course or degree program. At the School of Interdisciplinary Studies at Miami University, to illustrate, some courses draw on basic *concepts* that teachers contribute from disciplines (discourse communities from literature, marginal utility from economics, and old-field succession from biology). Other courses draw on *theories* (dependency theory from political science or plate tectonics from geology), *facts* (Avogadro's number from chemistry or the differential life changes of lower and middle classes from sociology), or *methods* (ethnography from anthropology or laboratory experiments from the physical sciences) (Newell 1992, 213).

Degrees of faculty interaction fall at different points along a continuum of collaboration that James Davis (1995) defines in terms of four criteria: planning, content integration, teaching, and evaluation. There is no one way to plan or to teach courses and no a priori logic for setting them up in a particular way. The participants create the boundaries of a course. Faculty are often preoccupied with "coverage," but "inventing the subject" is a more accurate image of what occurs in course design. Furthermore, Davis found in a recent study of team planning and teaching, the greater the level of desired integration, the higher the level of collaboration required. More minds are brought to the task of selecting or creating interesting objects of inquiry. Because more contrasting disciplinary perspectives are involved, facilitators skilled in methods of inquiry are crucial to the integrative process.

Davis's notion of "inventing the subject" underscores an important commonalty across activities, from problem solving and teaching to developing new categories of knowledge. Ultimately, the domain of interdisciplinarity is the domain of argument. Certain languages are useful, but there is no interdisciplinary Esperanto. Even when established vocabularies are used, they must be shaped to the particularities of the task at hand. The principle of appropriate criteria emerging in the process of doing interdisciplinary work is underscored by Barmarck and Wallen's (1980) chronicle of problems encountered in trying to impose systems theory and other global models on a large ecosystem research project in Sweden. Creating an integrated product, solution, or perspective requires moving from lower-level translation of disciplinary perspectives by "bootstrapping up," to use Steve Fuller's term, to higher levels of conceptual synthesis. Linguistic models are not imported intact from metamathematics, set theory, symbolic logic, or any particular disciplinary or interdisciplinary paradigm. They evolve in the creation of a trade language that, to recall, may develop into a pidgin, an interim tongue, or a creole, a new first language among a hybrid community of knowers (Fuller 1993, 45; Lowy 1992, 374; Galison 1992).

Bilingualism is a popular metaphor for interdisciplinary work, but it is inappropriate. Bilingualism implies a mastery of two complete languages that rarely if ever occurs. Pidgin and creole are the typifying forms of interdisciplinary communication. Quality depends on *richness* of language, not unity or fidelity to a prescribed metalanguage. Communicative competence is a condition for the possibility of interdisciplinary work, because the quality of outcomes cannot be separated from development of a language culture (Vosskamp 1994, 49–50). Studies of interdisciplinary communication reveal that most activities involve combining everyday language with specialist terms from pertinent domains. At a higher level of conceptual synthesis, new terminology and redeployed older terminology form the basis of a working metalanguage (Frey 1973). This also means that dialectic is the underlying method of interdisciplinary work. Like dialectic, integrative process entails clarifying and resolving differences in order to produce an integrated solution to a problem or conceptualization of an issue (Broido 1979; Davis 1978; and Fuller 1993 treat interdisciplinarity as dialectic.)

The importance of language is highlighted in a recent special issue of the journal *Social Epistemology* devoted to the topic "Boundary Rhetorics and the Work of Interdisciplinarity" (1995). Debra Journet (1995) coined the term "boundary rhetorics" to describe the rhetorical strategies that create interdisciplinary discursive space. They include establishing intertextual links between separate disciplines through citations, translating the findings of one discipline into the terminology of another, suppressing differences in order to emphasize points of contact, finding common enemies, and juxtaposing different research genres dialogically in the same textual space. In some instances writers may sublimate differences by not only articulating connections but also recasting the knowledge claims of one discipline into the generic forms of another. In a case study of *Tempo and Mode in Evolution*, Journet reveals how George Gaylord Simpson synthesized paleontology and genetics into a more inclusive narrative argument about evolutionary history. Narrative served both an epistemic and a rhetorical function. It was both a cognitive mode and a generic space in which new knowledge was constructed and communicated. (For a correlation of the notion of Journet's concept of boundary rhetoric with Galison's idea of trading zone and Fuller's notion of interpenetration of disciplines in a zone of interdependence, see Berkenkot-ter 1995.)

The older interdisciplinary ideal was a world in which differences were to be overcome. The reality is that differences matter. Even if negotiated and mediated, differences do not go away—they continue to create "noise." Misunderstandings, animosities, and competitions cannot be mitigated or glossed over. They must be taken seriously as attempts are made to spell out differences and their possible consequences. Interdisciplinarity conceived as communicative action does not trust that everything will work out if everyone will just sit down and talk to each other. Decades of scuttled projects and programs belie the naive faith that status hierarchies and hidden agendas will not interfere or that the individual with the greatest clout or loudest voice will not attempt to dominate.

The ideal speech situation assumes lack of coercion and equal access to dialogue at all points. The ideal speech situation, Jürgen Habermas con-tended (1987), is a valid critical standard against which all apparent consen-sus can be called into question and tested. The shamming of communicative relations, however, occurs in disciplinary relations as much as the interper-sonal and social relations on which Habermas based his theory of communi-cative action. Interdisciplinary work entails rhetorical, social, and political negotiation. Therefore close attention must be paid to language, group dy-namics, and the regroupings and redefinitions that arise in constructing shared knowledge. The ideal and the real are bridged through a process of discovery and testing that brings appropriate criteria into being.

The three core principles of interdisciplinary communicative action are *maturing and deepening, cooperation and interplay,* and *creativity.* These prin-ciples were embodied in Th. K. Van Lohuizen's (1948) vision of the unity of town planning, though Van Lohuizen's notion of "artistry" is transformed here into the general notion of "creativity." *Maturing and deepening* are analo-gous to Merleau-Ponty's concept of working toward excellence in stages. Progress does not derive from sequential movement along a fixed line; it is recursive and iterative. The guiding metaphors shift from foundation and structure, implying a fixed body of knowledge, to an evolutionary process in which the body of knowledge changes as modifications are made. *Coopera-tion and interplay* are comparable to J. Friedman's (1973) concept of mutual learning and Donald Schön's (1983) theory of action. The parties involved learn from each other as they work together. They seek each other out, they become aware of their own limits, and they create a shared sense of a situ-ation through testing individual dilemmas and the assumptions underlying those dilemmas. Maturing and deepening through cooperation and interplay utilizes feedback loops and is reflexive.

Creativity is embodied in the act of crafting multiple elements into an organic whole. The nature of the whole differs by the task at hand. In problem-focused projects, it may be devising a solution. In the curriculum, it may be constructing an explanatory framework. In a hybrid field of knowledge, it may be forging an integrative framework. In each case, though, individuals and groups draw from a repertoire of examples, images, understandings, and actions. The process is necessarily iterative and dynamic, because it starts with partial information. Insight develops through exploration and experimental application of familiar techniques to new situations. Objectives and approaches are modified in light of ongoing accomplishments, not a fixed definition or a final solution (after Van Dusseldorp and Wigboldus 1994).

David Sill (1996) has identified the links between creativity and integrative thinking. Most definitions of creativity point to the appearance of something new. The major characteristics of the creativity model for integrated thought are bisociation, ripeness, creative tension, preinventive structures, active imagination, iterative process, and complexity. Creativity is heuristic, not algorithmic. It relies on rules of thumb or incomplete guidelines to drive learning and discovery, not mechanical rules. It also draws from the richness of the subconscious in relying on nonlogical and nonlinear thought processes. Preinventive structures in the subconscious provide the raw material for creative combinations. These structures can be ideas, images, or concepts. Their ripeness encourages creative insights that tend to be ambiguous, novel, meaningful, incongruent, and divergent. They also contain emergent features.

Arthur Koestler's model of bisociation, Sill suggests, provides a model for understanding creativity as a form of synthetic thought. The disciplines represent independent matrices of thought. Bisociative thought works at the intersection of distinctly separate matrices, some cognitive and some social. When they contradict or conflict, tensions must be resolved through creation of a new order. The resolution is integrated thought. By its very nature, creativity violates the present order. Novelty brings about instability. Barthes's notion of a "mutation," Paulson's notion of "noise," Davis's notion of "inventing the subject," and Hursh, Haas, and Moore's emphasis on "disequilibrium" come together. Interdisciplinarity unsettles existing assumptions; something that makes sense in one matrix may not make sense in another. Making the subject or idea problematic makes it "absurd." It no longer makes sense. Because the creative process is complex as well as fluid, it is also iterative. Reconsideration, reformulation, and restating are vital activities.

The global model in figure 1 synthesizes the different aspects of integrative process in a generic model that treats interdisciplinarity as a form of communicative action (based on Klein 1990–91, 52).

The broken lines in the model emphasize the dual movement of interdisciplinary work across the vertical plane of requisite disciplinary knowledge and, on the horizontal plane, pertinent interdisciplinary approaches and integrative process. Communicative action accepts that two trade-offs will al-

CORE STEPS AND TYPES OF KNOWLEDGE   CONCEPTUAL FRAMEWORK AND SKILLS

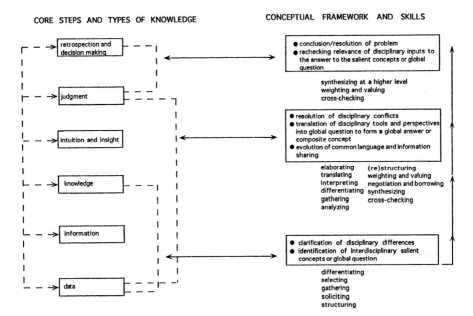

Figure 1. A generic model of integrative process

ways occur. The first trade-off is between all the knowledge that might be utilized and what is actually used by virtue of existing resources, both material and human. The sum total of information, needs, possibilities, and activities will never be available all at once. "Perfect knowledge," Thomas Murray warns, "is a chimera; imperfect knowledge our timeless condition" (1983, 305). The second trade-off is between the power of monodisciplinary inputs and the rigor of integrative process. Interdisciplinarity conceived as communicative action recognizes that differentiation and unity will coexist.

Differentiation provides for a plurality of facts, values, norms, and alternative courses of action. Unification provides for an integrated resolution of a problem (after Diesing 1962, 178) or at least agreement on a viable approach. The risks of segmentation should not be minimized. Yet the benefits of specialization—devising more powerful techniques, greater precision, a richer supply of data, and accumulation of knowledge—must be acknowledged as they are brought into dialogue with broader contexts, large questions, and general frameworks. Because achieving a working relationship between differentiation and unification is an ongoing task, the boundaries between stages also blur. Synthesis is not reserved for a final step. The possibilities are tested throughout, moving in zigzags (Wise 1978) and in fits and starts (Cassell 1977) as new knowledge becomes available and new possibilities and limits arise.

The overriding importance of process and communication means, finally, that interdisciplinary skills become forms of knowledge themselves:

> knowing how to structure a workable framework that is flexible enough to allow for shifting groupings
>
> knowing how to recognize ignorance of a particular area, then solicit and gather appropriate state-of-the-art information and knowledge
>
> knowing how to analyze the relationship among discrete pieces of elements of knowledge and weigh their relevance to the task at hand
>
> knowing how to balance depth and specificity with breadth and general connection
>
> knowing how to identify salient concepts and global questions, then using them in an integrative manner
>
> knowing how to clarify and present results for mutual revision

These skills are necessary in all interdisciplinary activities. Excellence is measured in terms not of fidelity to disciplinarity but of interdisciplinary originality. Disciplinary accuracy and clarity are important, but the clarity of interdisciplinary communication and the solution to a problem or the creation of new meaning are of primary importance. Criteria of interdisciplinary quality are also strategic because process—knowing how to do—is a fundamental part of interdisciplinary knowledge. Interdisciplinary work is most successful when it is most creative; when borders are constructively and constantly engaged; when, in Fuller's words, borders are seen as necessary evils that become more evil the more they are perceived as necessary. Interdisciplinary quality does not lie in the imposition of an epistemically superior discipline or a neutral repository of cognitive criteria (Fuller 1993, xx, 37).

Doing interdisciplinary work well requires an added form of knowledge. The most dangerous dichotomy is between knowledge and action. Whether they are accommodated in existing structures or form the basis of new structures, interdisciplinary activities take place in institutions. Knowledge of institutional strategies is as important as knowledge of process and criteria.

Institutional Strategies

Two and a half decades ago, French activists rallied to the cry "Soyons réalistes, demandons l'impossible!" Times have changed. The impossible is now part of the possible. The simple idealism of the 1960s and 1970s, however, has been lost (Squires 1992, 209). It has been replaced by an empirical realism about implementing interdisciplinary ideas (Papadopoulos 1985, 206). Part of the necessary know-how is knowing how to find pertinent resources. Until recently, the massive body of literature on conceptualization, models, and strategies was relatively invisible. Reliable bibliographies were not available until 1968 and even then were limited in scope. Core literatures have now been identified. (For starting points, see Chubin et al. 1986; Klein 1990a, 1990b, 231–325; Klein 1994; Klein and Newell 1996.) Experience also begets knowledge. Over two decades of work as a scholar, a teacher, and a consultant have convinced me that three sets of factors are crucial to advancing interdisciplinary claims: identity and visibility, the dynamics of institutional change, and knowledge and information.

Identity and Visibility

Recent reports on the climate for interdisciplinary research and education at Ohio State University (OSU), Wayne State University (WSU), the University of British Columbia (UBC), and the University of Alberta (Alberta) disclose a significant institutional reality. There will be more interdisciplinary activity on campus than initially assumed. This fact affirms the importance of what Klein and Newell call "listening to the system" (Newell and Klein 1996; Klein and Newell 1996). Mapping the results will reveal not only the overt presence of programs and centers but also the shadow structure of shared interests, theme- and topic-based teaching, and problem-focused research. Simplified views of complex academic enterprise only add to the problem of operation. Unifying images of knowledge and institutional simplicity are strained by realities that outrun old expectations, especially older definitions that view one part or function as the "essence" or "essential mission" (Clark 1995, 154).

Responses will differ. Some will oppose any interdisciplinary activities, branding them shallow and illegitimate. Others will insist that the best activities arise spontaneously. Tinkering with the system, in their view, will kill natural and spontaneous interactions. Others will pronounce the interdisciplinary revolution in knowledge complete, while some, even in the same department, condemn the stifling height of disciplinary walls. One respondent to the University of Alberta's request for campus views on interdisciplinary change contended, "All that is really necessary is for the Dean's office to indicate its support and urge department chairs to do whatever they can to encourage it" (Alberta 1990, 6). Even in a well-endowed department, this strategy is usually inadequate. Benign neglect can be a bigger threat than outright opposition.

The marginality of many programs is reinforced by their location in the spare building space and on the physical periphery of campus. Interdisciplinary activities need a place. Johnson C. Smith University (North Carolina) has a model set of facilities. Using external funding from the Mellon Foundation and a private gift, the university constructed two buildings with complementary missions side by side—an interdisciplinary center and a faculty-development center. Lack of a building need not be a deterrent: centers for teaching and learning provide excellent sites. So do offices with compatible missions, such as academic affairs, the graduate school, or research and sponsored programs. When new buildings and remodeling projects are in the development stage, provision for locating interdisciplinary activities should be included in planning discussions.

In some cases, establishing a separate department of interdisciplinary studies might make sense, in order to house a single program or a cluster of programs that cannot otherwise secure sound footing. This is often a controversial strategy, however. The important consideration is devising a suitable mechanism to ensure ongoing, coordinated support. Establishing a central office is an excellent strategy, especially in large universities. Names and formats vary, from an office of interdisciplinary studies or a division of interdisciplinary programs to an interdisciplinary activities committee that coordinates a network of faculty committees at local levels. At a small college, responsibility for oversight may be placed in the office of the dean, at a large university in the office of the provost or vice president for academic affairs. Central oversight provides a way of easing the confusion that results when separate offices and infrastructures use separate procedures, applications, report mechanisms, and evaluation criteria for funding, credit load, use of space, curriculum development, and research management (WSU 1993, 7, 9).

One of the earliest activities of a central office or organizational body should be an inventory of all interdisciplinary activities and interests. Existing facilities and equipment should also be assessed to determine the potential for sharing space and instrumentation. Based on the inventory, a directory of information can be compiled and made available both in print and in electronic form. With periodic updating, the directory will be a valuable data bank for programs and projects. Individual faculty members at different sites, such as sociology and biology, might be engaged in research or teaching on the subject of hunger, for instance. Without the inventory, their common interests and the potential for hunger-related coursework and research might go unrecognized.

As a result of the inventory, standard organizational charts should be amended to include all activities and track faculty participation. If a major part of knowledge production is occurring in structures and alliances that blur the lines of organizational charts, the charts ought to be changed. In short, the white space should be mapped, not left blank. When John Grace (1993), dean of the graduate school at the University of British Columbia, charted links between graduate faculty units and interdisciplinary activities on campus, he also calculated degrees of involvement on a scale of zero to three. The first category, institutes and centers, ranged from applied math, fisheries, and sustainable development to Asian research, applied ethics, and women's studies/gender relations. The second category, interdisciplinary programs, included clinical engineering, genetics, resource management science, and an individual interdisciplinary program. The third category, journals, accounted for work on *B.C. Studies, Canadian Literature,* and *Pacific Affairs.* The fourth category, new activities, recognized an institute of advanced studies, Green College (a residential graduate research center), and vocational rehabilitation counseling.

A central office can also serve as an information clearinghouse. By publishing a print newsletter and maintaining an electronic bulletin board, the office can keep the campus informed about pertinent funding sources and legislation, local curricula and research projects, activities, and national models and new initiatives. In conjunction with this effort, existing campuswide publications and publications at department and college levels can add regular or periodic columns featuring pertinent information. In addition, the office might host its own speakers' forum. Targeting annual themes or topics is a good way of stimulating dialogue campuswide. Either in conjunction with or instead of an independent forum, the office can also coordinate visits by external guests in departments and programs. Featured speakers in individual units often discuss state-of-the-art developments, many of them interdisciplinary in character. Their presence constitutes an important example of invisible interdisciplinary traffic on campus.

One of the most effective ways of stimulating dialogue is convening a task force or commission to study the campus climate for interdisciplinary teaching, research, and service work. Three types of individuals that are often overlooked should be involved from the very beginning: library personnel, who serve the information needs of a campus, and members of the development office and grants office, who identify and coordinate funding. Many interdisciplinary activities occur in alliances with government and industry as well as local, regional, national, and international communities. Representatives of those constituencies should also be involved in some fashion. When the group produces its final report, it should be strategically networked. An executive summary and pertinent parts may be distributed to individual members of the academic community (UBC 1993, 16). Using selected parts as discussion pieces is a sounder strategy than trusting that people will read the entire report when it appears in their crowded mailboxes. Follow-up events should be scheduled as well, including workshops and retreats on portions of the report that are of interest to particular groups.

The principle of public face underscores the link between visibility and legitimacy. Catalogs, bulletins, prospectuses, recruitment brochures, and advertisements are the first rank of institutional self-representation. All printed material should be scrutinized to determine how well interdisciplinary activities are represented. If they are not included at present, they should be added when publications are revised and reprinted. Good material will also aid in advising students effectively. A number of examples illustrate what can be done to enhance understanding of interdisciplinary missions.

To validate program claims, the School of Interdisciplinary Studies at Miami University and the Human Development and Social Relations Program at Earlham College include in printed material information on graduate-school and employment placement. To articulate their mission and recruit wider support, the University of Maryland, Baltimore County, devised an attractive booklet explaining its array of programs in environmental sciences. To counter continuing confusion among students, personnel managers, and graduate-school admissions officers, the Interdisciplinary Studies Program at Wayne State University developed a brochure that explains the meaning and purpose of interdisciplinary studies. The women's studies program at the University of British Columbia has a good model for illuminating surface and shadow structures. A loose-leaf annotated description of courses identifies three levels of presence. The first level is courses required for a major. The second level is courses that may count toward a major, and the third level lists courses and faculty that incorporate woman-centered topics and components. Rarely is the third level identified, although it constitutes an important part of the shadow structure and is often the site where students encounter the latest interdisciplinary research.

Research programs and centers also need to be fully identified. Few universities, even if they have directories of research centers, explain their interdisciplinary nature. Directors of programs and centers should also meet at least once a year, if not in a regular forum, to reflect on common problems. This meeting can be facilitated by a central interdisciplinary office or an appropriate administrative office. Directors and program coordinators are busy people. An enormous amount of energy is wasted, however, in struggling with problems that people in different fields on the same campus have solved. Between face-to-face meetings, targeted questions on campus e-mail can keep the conversation going. Electronic communication is an ideal forum for all directors and coordinators, planning committees, and research and teaching teams to use between meetings. It keeps the conversation going.

Institutional Change

None of these strategies exists in a vacuum. Each is subject to the dynamics of institutional change. "The intelligent management of change," Caroline Eckhardt observed, "is never easy, and it becomes particularly difficult at a time when change no longer implies an overall growth in size" (1978, 2–3). It is sobering to recall that Eckhardt made this statement almost twenty years ago. It rings even truer today, when academic institutions are being pressed to do more with less while serving a greater diversity of needs and demands. The best strategy will not be a matter of agreement. Echoing the difference between bridge building and restructuring, debate usually hinges on whether incremental or radical approaches are more appropriate. The incremental posture advocates small steps; the radical posture eschews piecemeal change. However correct the radical stance is in critiquing the inability of incremental approaches to effect long-term transformation, the bottom line is that in many institutions even piecemeal change may be a struggle. Some changes also enjoy greater capital than others. At a large research university, a molecular biology center with NIH support may perhaps have a greater chance of succeeding than a campuswide interdisciplinary approach to general education or a new cultural studies program.

Between motivations and actual structures, several intervening variables are at work in institutional change (Klein and Newell 1996):

> the nature of the institution (size, mission, financial base)
>
> institutional culture (past experience with reform, and new initiatives, patterns of interaction among faculty and administration, the nature of the academic community, assumptions about the learning styles of students and the importance of education)
>
> the level of the desired change (institutionwide, program, or course)
>
> the nature of the desired change (general education, interdisciplinary majors and concentrations, department and program enhancement, faculty development, hybrid research and teaching communities, research centers, megaprojects, a general loosening of structural barriers)
>
> faculty capabilities and interests
>
> knowledge cultures (disciplinary, professional, and interdisciplinary)

Institutional culture is a strong factor. In the United States especially, with its system of over 3,400 institutions of higher education, institutional cultures vary a great deal (Oakley 1992, 282). Questions about why an environmental studies program is desirable may never come up on one campus. On another they will remain permanent stumbling blocks. Released time, joint appointments, and cross-listing courses are common means of legitimating interdisciplinary activity. Yet on one campus they will be commonplace, on another campus impossible. Some institutions have strong traditions of interdisciplinary work. At others, institutional structure and disciplinary cultures inhibit even modest programs. Examining the institutional mission statement is an effective legitimating strategy.

The Human Development and Social Relations Program at Earlham College was founded in 1976 to provide interdisciplinary, value-oriented preparation for the helping professions. This goal was consistent with Earlham's commitment to service as a Quaker institution. The program also provides focused liberal education drawing on the social sciences and philosophy. Institutional mission also means the same type of program will look different from campus to campus. The University of Hartford's general education program seeks to place learning for students in a contextual framework that unites knowledge and human experience through courses called "Living in a Social Context" and "Living in a Scientific and Technological World." Bradford College seeks to link liberal and professional education and the world of work. Harvard's interdisciplinary general education core is scholarly in content, reflecting its commitment to preparation of a highly select student body (Casey 1994, 54, 59).

Size is an added factor. Departments in small colleges tend to correspond to disciplines defined at global levels. In addition, disciplines may already be combined, typically joining sociology and anthropology, philosophy and religion, and physics and astronomy. The most significant difference is the time it takes to implement change. In a large university, an innovation may take years to work its way through planning and policy committees. In a smaller institution change often comes more quickly. Even in a large institution, though, comprehensive change can occur on a short time scale. At Michigan State University (MSU), a large research institution, the shift from the quarter system to semesters provided a rare opportunity for recasting an older system of general education that had become the subject of wide dissatisfaction. The switchover to a semester system is a disruptive change, but it is also a golden opportunity for interdisciplinary initiatives. Everything in the institution has to be rethought. At Michigan State a new set of college-level centers of integrative studies in the social sciences, humanities, and sciences was devised. The centers are located within three core colleges of natural science, social science, and arts and letters. In addition to providing general education, the centers also foster faculty development (Casey 1994, 57).

The MSU example highlights an important qualifying circumstance—institutional history. The failure of past experiments can be a formidable impediment to new efforts, even if the details are misremembered through the fog of institutional amnesia. Some faculty members resisting new initiatives at the University of Alberta based their opposition on the failure of a faculty of interdisciplinary studies that never existed. Campuses would do well to learn from their own histories by putting misinformation to rest and analyzing how their own institutional culture deals with change (Alberta 1990, 4). As one anonymous administrator put it, remembering a prior effort to launch an interdisciplinary approach to general education, "If we fail this time, it will be twenty years before we have another chance." Attempting to promote interdisciplinarity and then faltering very often exacerbates any existing cynicism and bad faith.

Regardless of institutional size and mission, several questions should be addressed early in the planning stages:

> Does the program, course, or project require small, limited, localized, and incremental interventions or more global, comprehensive, or even radical actions?

Does it entail a modification of existing structures or the creation of
new ones?
Are existing material resources and personnel adequate for the change, or
is external consultation and financial support necessary?
Who are the key administrative and faculty personnel for the initial
development?
What is the appropriate administrative structure?

Targeted support and general loosening are not mutually exclusive. They
occur simultaneously. Large programs with significant student numbers and
research support exist alongside small programs for targeted populations,
shadow institutes, and informal networks. In a time of narrowing internal and
external funding, the system should be carefully examined for existing mechanisms that may be utilized or modified. In describing the final report of the
Interdisciplinary Task Force at Ohio State University, Paul Isaac, cochair of
the task force, admitted, "There are no home run balls here" (pers. comm.,
8 October 1993). Yet if enacted, they could lead to a cultural change.
A portfolio of small-scale events, pilot projects, and modest investments
can go a long way toward changing campus climates. A central office or an
individual program can allot $100 to pertinent departments for purchase of
books and journals and the social lubrication of informal gatherings. Brown
bag, pizza and sandwich lunches, as well as wine and cheese gatherings, are
effective forums for hosting speakers, discussing particular curricular and
research initiatives, and exploring pedagogical and intellectual issues. Some
campuses actually structure a free hour in the week that can be used for such
events campuswide or on a department and college level. At a more moderate
level, funds may be designated for patronage options such as graduate assis-
tantships, program operation costs (staff and supplies), seminars, workshops,
and colloquiums, and financial support for planning days in summer and
during the regular academic calendar. At a higher level, a percentage of in-
direct costs and overhead from grants may be channeled into facilities and
equipment, colloquiums and visiting professorships, incentive grants and
seed funds.
Existing development mechanisms may be tapped as well. Enrollment in
advanced courses and off-campus and on-campus sabbatical leaves enable
faculty to develop new capabilities, as do summer fellowships, travel to professional meetings, visits to other programs, and the opportunity to complete
advanced degrees. Even in a time of strained budgets, small-grant programs
for curriculum and research projects are still in place on most campuses. One
faculty member, listening to a litany of strategies for supporting a proposed
interdisciplinary general education program, suddenly realized that all the
strategies were already being used successfully by the chemistry department
on his campus. They already existed. From the standpoint of the new pro-

gram, however, they were inert. Here again, involving members of the development office pays off. They are aware of existing funds that may be tapped and potential gifts from donors who would be supportive of particular interdisciplinary interests.

The bottom line of legitimacy is the reward system. Interdisciplinary activities should be celebrated, not punished. In the words of one faculty member, "The university will receive what it rewards" (WSU 1993, narrative 21). According interdisciplinary activity a "legitimate place at the table" (Alberta 1900, 19) begins at the level of rewarding excellence in student and faculty work. Interdisciplinary activities can also be institutionalized through inclusion as a category in annual reports, program reviews, and budget lines. Most important, the "culture of evaluation" needs to be changed. Existing criteria should be broadened, the process of evaluation within departmental homes modified, and guidelines for evaluation devised by the departments participating in programs (Davis 1995, 149).

Faculty members should be involved in determining the criteria by which they are evaluated, and guidelines must be written down. Guidelines should cover what is involved and expected in regard to expertise, workload, and review for tenure, promotion, and salary increases. Matrix evaluation is a procedure for stipulating consultation with all pertinent units, sometimes even specifying the designated amount of credit from each unit. At the vital entry point, expectations and rewards need to be discussed in job interviews and written down in letters of hire. On unionized campuses, they should be stipulated in the bargaining agreement.

The most tenacious obstacle on most campuses is workload count. One solution, reliance on overload and voluntary participation, is a foolish strategy in the long run. It denies legitimacy and may ultimately generate more bad faith by burning out even the most dedicated faculty. There are options for handling credits. They may be split, rotated, or double counted. As incentive for participation, individual departments can receive credit accumulation and replacement funding for faculty time. Courses may also be cross-listed. In team-taught courses, load can be determined based on splitting enrollment credits. Some institutions use a point system. Points for participation can be applied to or converted to fractions of the courses that are used to determine load (Davis 1995, 143).

The most underrecognized site of interdisciplinary activity is the department. Reports on the undergraduate major from the Association of American Colleges and Universities' study-in-depth project confirm that disciplinary divisions are no longer self-evident. Contextual inquiry has redrawn boundaries, alternative tracks are offered in crowded fields, and hybrid departments have emerged from combinations of knowledge emanating from research. Generally speaking, though, departments still underrepresent these developments and connections among disciplines. They are also failing to develop the integrative skills students need for dealing with complex problems and issues (*Liberal Learning* 1990, vol. 2).

As a result, enriching the major has become a major theme in educational reform. Bridging the gap between research and teaching is imperative in reform at the undergraduate level. Failure to represent new research in the curriculum is a failure to represent knowledge. Some of the most invigorating curricular initiatives today involve students in actually *doing* science with researchers. To address these issues, department chairs and appropriate committees should ensure that faculty are kept aware of pertinent reports on higher education, the disciplines, and the professions. These reports not only recommend greater interdisciplinary focus in disciplinary and professional education, they point the way to program models and resources.

Finally, an enlightened posture toward institutional change foregrounds the importance of faculty development and the continuing education of all professional staff, which are vital to deep structuring. Lasting improvements, Jerry Gaff emphasizes, depend on creating a pervasive, deeper, and supportive structure (1991, 156). Deep structuring changes a campus culture by infusing values throughout the institution and creating a new generation of faculty who hold those values. The single most productive step is providing access to knowledge and information.

Knowledge and Information

The problem of fit resurfaces in serving the knowledge and information needs of activities that call into question the very verbal, numerical, and spatial systems we currently rely on (Searing 1992, 7). Interdisciplinary activities generate needs that span program administration, curriculum development, pedagogy and process, learning assessment and program review, and the intellectual contents of a staggering variety of interdisciplinary interests. Filling these needs is a formidable task. Resources are scattered across an expanse of books and articles, conference presentations, institutional working papers and internal reports, course syllabi, software, and audio and visual resources.

The importance of resource basing cannot be overstated. Resource basing begins with collecting pertinent literatures and materials. The major interdisciplinary literature should be available, as well as specialized literatures, program models, course syllabi and pedagogical material, research models and materials. Elsewhere I have defined a basic collection and strategies for electronic database searching and networking (Klein 1994). Interdisciplinary work puts a greater onus on networking, a complex activity that includes familiar person-to-person forms of social contacts (forged through corresponding, telephoning, and meeting in person) and electronic communication (ranging from interinstitutional conversations and viewing library holdings to downloading actual texts and conducting work on the rapidly expanding information highway).

A good resource bank will tap the vast fugitive literature—material of limited circulation, from internal memos, planning documents, and reports to organization newsletters and news columns in journals. Fugitive literature is often the only place that oral wisdom is shared beyond its immediate audience. A recent survey of women's studies researchers showed a surprising reliance on newsletters of women's organizations, even though action-oriented publications are rarely found in academic libraries (Searing 1992, 16). Professional organizations and interest groups also identify, and sometimes distribute, resources that may be difficult to track down through standard information-seeking strategies (Bingham 1994).

Being familiar with the latest recommendations of disciplinary learned societies and professional accrediting bodies is a powerful strategy for validating new initiatives. Reports from pertinent symposia and workshops should be gathered, as well as the multitude of published tools for teaching and research management. Several journals provide models of serving readers' interdisciplinary interests. *American Quarterly* codes its annual bibliography by disciplinary interests. Along with the *Journal of Interdisciplinary History* and *Signs: The Journal of Women in Society,* it also provides review essays on boundary-crossing themes and interests. In addition, *Signs* supplies updates on pertinent scholarship in various disciplines, and the *American Journal of Physics* publishes resource letters covering particular fields.

Because interdisciplinary activities exhibit both general and specific needs, careful thought should be given to locating resources. They may be housed in a central office, a central place in the library, or appropriate curriculum and research offices. Or they may be divided across a central location and pertinent sites. At the local level, the hybrid communities that form to teach courses, run programs, and conduct research need to engage in continuing development. During the regular academic year, weekly, bimonthly, or monthly meetings tend to be taken up with day-to-day business. At the end and the beginning of each academic year, there should be opportunities to engage in fuller review and reflection, preferably in a retreat setting or day-long meetings free of interruptions. Maintaining course, program, and project portfolios provides a second tier of resource basing. A portfolio is a large three-ring binder that contains all materials pertinent to an activity, such as syllabi and readings, instructor-designed handouts, support tools for research, and material on intellectual fields. Course, program, and research portfolios are in effect living laboratories where resources are placed, then shared. Anyone joining an activity should be given a complete copy, and an updated copy should always be on file where an activity is institutionally located.

Because interdisciplinary work drives information needs that differ dramatically from those of twenty years ago (Searing 1992, 7), serving those needs has become a theme in the professional library literature. This literature is yielding valuable ideas. In science, Julie Hurd (1992) suggests, broader divisional science libraries are better supportive of interdisciplinary needs than separate collections. Science libraries operating in decentralized environments can employ intracampus exchange programs to enable browsing of new journal issues or title pages. They can also provide photocopy services through campus mail, couriers, and telefax transmission for timely delivery of documents to dispersed sites. Electronic mail networks facilitate communication with remote libraries regarding reference questions, on-line search requests, book and journal delivery, circulation and interlibrary loan services. Early and ongoing consultations with library staff are vital for coordinating materials acquisition and developing support services for courses and programs, projects and centers (Searing 1992). Unfortunately, librarians once again are often the last to be consulted.

When does a different approach to research and teaching become a new approach to knowledge? When does a way of doing things differently become a trend? A revolution? The line is not always clear. Some changes have been sudden and dramatic. Others have occurred quietly. New words enter the vocabulary and old words take on new meanings, marking shifts in perspective and new ways of seeing (Suleiman 1980, 3). In its final report, the Commonwealth of Virginia's Commission on the University of the Twenty-first Century recalled the comment of one university president. That much exciting teaching and research is called "interdisciplinary," he lamented, is a mark of shame. Finding the disciplines are no longer adequate to what we know and the problems we must solve, the commission calls for nothing less than a basic transformation in the way Virginia thinks about higher education, the way colleges and universities think about their responsibilities, and the way faculties think about knowledge and their disciplines (*Case for Change* 2, 13).

This call echoes across academic systems worldwide. A loss of future is occurring in failure to serve interdisciplinary needs and interests. Part of the motivation is the eternal need to keep up. The reports of countless campus committees, learned societies, educational commissions, and research advisory bodies stress the importance of being competitive educationally, technologically, and culturally (OSU 1991, 59). One of the motivations identified by an advisory committee at the University of Alberta is the loss of job candidates who find their interdisciplinary interests better accommodated elsewhere. Significantly, the faculty members who were most precise and passionate about the intellectual rewards for students and faculty in pursuing interdisciplinary research and teaching had been hired within the past six to seven years. Economic retrenchment is a frequent argument for not changing. The costs of action, however, are more modest than the costs of inaction (Alberta 1990, 3, 6–7).

The greatest immediate threat is institutional downsizing. The fallacy of what Steve Fuller calls "the dean's razor" is a common solution. Because interdisciplinary programs consist of people trained in regular disciplines, presumably nothing essential is lost if programs are eliminated (1993, 52). Eliminating a program in the short run to save money, however, is a penny wise, pound foolish strategy. It is wiser to merge comparable units for survival than to eliminate them or trust that interdisciplinary interests will be protected, let alone developed, in departments. In larger universities, a trend toward combination is emerging. Separate African American, Chicano, and Asian American studies programs have been combined into larger ethnic studies programs that stress collaboration and comparative studies (Davis 1995, 241). Loss of identity is a real danger, but coalition building is a powerful political strategy. "It is easier to drum up support for abandoned children," Sproull and Hall aptly quip, "than for abandoned multidisciplinary programs" (1987, 9). One institution eliminated a program to save money, then several years later, responding to lingering discontent and new demands, restarted the program—a remarkable waste of time, energy, and start-up costs.

Retrenchment decisions that fall back on older notions of what is "basic" and "essential" are not enlightened decisions. They reflect the logic of either-or, not both-and. Administration bashing is an equally narrow tactic. Increasing numbers of administrators, even as they are caught in the squeeze play of financial exigency, are looking for ways to facilitate interdisciplinary work. The dean, moreover, is not the only player. Even faculty who go on record as supporting interdisciplinary activities undermine efforts by their own behavior. One member of a high-level task force, appointed to promote interdisciplinary activities, proclaimed at one meeting that the university was foolhardy not to move aggressively in that direction. At a later meeting he confessed that he advises Ph.D. candidates not to select interdisciplinary projects in order to be more competitive, though in the next breath he admitted his field has become interdisciplinary in nature.

In the present climate of retrenchment, collapsing separate departments into a new combined unit is perceived and even promoted as an interdisciplinary initiative. This strategy has obvious advantages of economy and may well stimulate new curricula and research. Simply joining units, however, does not ensure that interdisciplinary teaching and research will occur or, worse, even be understood. Carolyn Steedman sounds a warning about the dangers of enforced "cross-disciplinarity." Driven by economic hard times in Britain, combined curricular units teach a cheaper and more practical text-based form of historical inquiry that shortchanges archival research. This move has serious implications for the kind of historical work that is taught in schools. Proponents of cultural studies must look seriously at how "a proper historicity" is constructed in the interdisciplinary study of culture (1992, 618–21). Without enlightened action, both disciplinary and interdisciplinary objectives are shortchanged.

Delivering the presidential address to the Western Social Science Association, Marilyn Stember recalled Muzafer Sherif and Carolyn Sherif's earlier claim that interdisciplinarity has become irreversible (Stember 1991, 3; Sherif and Sherif 1969a, 5). Ample evidence validates the claim. The need for coherence and connectedness is everywhere. Yet interdisciplinary futures will be mixed. The rise of Green College, an interdisciplinary research institute at the University of British Columbia; the Tamaki campus of the University of Auckland, a wide-scale effort to promote interdisciplinary research and teaching; and new theme-based schools at McMaster University prove that new structures will continue to emerge. The demise of other programs and projects proves, with equal force, that some will fail and others will fall short on the critical-mass scale. New initiatives will revitalize one campus but never get off the ground at another site. Given the plurality of claims, interdisciplinarity will also continue to be alternately embraced, rejected as a false issue, and reformulated to meet new needs and demands.

The disciplines have not lost their power to generate new knowledge. Yet side by side other forces—propelled by new demands, interests, and technologies—have produced new subjects and new ways of looking at older subjects (Davis 1995, 132). Students and their teachers, researchers and scholars, workers and citizens live in a world in which problems require both specialized skills and the integrative skills to cope with complexity. They live at a time when a general weakening of all cultural boundaries is flattening hierarchies, blurring categories, and rendering organizational lines ambiguous. Often dubbed postmodernism (Muller and Taylor 1993; Stehr and Ericson 1992, 24–25), this process was under way long before "postmodern" became a household word. It has been occurring for nearly a century in the form of interdisciplinary activities that recontextualize disciplines, weaken boundaries, and alter identities. The lesson of boundary work is twofold. These activities will not escape the dynamics of the knowledge-power relation, because they will attract their own legitimations. Yet the recontextualizations they create have become as prominent a part of knowledge in the late twentieth century as the canons, codes, and categories they engage.

WORKS CITED

This list of cited works extends the basic literature already identified in two earlier sources:

Klein, Julie Thompson. 1990. "Selected Bibliography." In *Interdisciplinarity: History, Theory, and Practice,* 229–325. Detroit: Wayne State Univ. Press.
———. 1994. "Finding Interdisciplinary Knowledge and Information." In *Interdisciplinary Studies Today,* ed. Julie Thompson Klein and William Doty, 7–33. New Directions in Teaching and Learning 58. San Francisco: Jossey-Bass.

Abbott, Andrew. 1988. *The System of Professions: An Essay on the Division of Expert Labor.* Chicago: Univ. of Chicago Press.
Abdelal, Ahmed. 1986. Introduction to "The Coming Together of Biochemistry." In *Integrating Scientific Disciplines,* ed. William Bechtel, 55–58. Dordrecht: Martinus Nijhoff.
Abel, Elizabeth. 1981. "Editor's Introduction." *Critical Inquiry* 8, 2:173–78.
Abir-Am, Pnina. 1985. "Themes, Genres, and Orders of Legitimation in the Consolidation of New Scientific Disciplines: Deconstructing the Historiography of Molecular Biology. *History of Science* 23, 2:73–117.
———. 1987. "The Biotheoretical Gathering, Trans-disciplinary Authority and the Incipient Legitimation of Molecular Biology in the 1930's: New Perspective on the Historical Sociology of Science." *History of Science* 25:1–70.
———. 1988. "The Assessment of Interdisciplinary Research in the 1930's: The Rockefeller Foundation and Physico-chemical Morphology." *Minerva* 26, 2:153–76.
Abrams, Philip. 1980. "History, Sociology, Historical Sociology." *Past and Present* 87 (May): 3–16.
Addelson, Kathryn Pyne, and Elizabeth Potter. 1991. "Making Knowledge." In Hartman and Messer-Davidow 1991, 259–77.

Agger, Ben. 1989. *Socio(onto)logy: A Disciplinary Reading.* Urbana: Univ. of Illinois Press.

Alberta. 1990. "Final Report of the Dean's Advisory Committee on Interdisciplinary Studies." Faculty of Arts, Univ. of Alberta, Edmonton. November.

Alexander, E. R. 1984. "After Rationality, What? A Review of Responses to Paradigm Breakdown." *Journal of the American Planning Association* 50, 1:62–69.

Allan, George. 1986. "The Canon in Crisis." *Liberal Education* 72, 2:89–100.

Allen, Paula Gunn. 1992. "The Intersection of Gender and Color." In Gibaldi 1992, 303–19.

Almond, Gabriel A. 1989. *A Discipline Divided: Schools and Sects in Political Science.* Thousand Oaks, Calif.: Sage.

Amariglio, Jack, Stephen Resnick, and Richard Wolff. 1993. "Division and Difference in the 'Discipline' of Economics." In Messer-Davidow, Shumway, and Sylvan 1993b, 150–84.

Andranovich, Gregory, and Gerry Riposa. 1993. *Doing Urban Research.* Applied Social Research Methods Series 33. Newbury Park, Calif.: Sage.

Apostel, Leo, and Jaak Vanlandschoot. 1994. "Interdisciplinarity: The Construction of Worldviews and the Dissemination of Scientific Results." *Issues in Integrative Studies* 12:9–22.

Applebee, Arthur N. 1974. *Tradition and Reform in the Teaching of English: A History.* Urbana, Ill.: National Council of Teachers of English.

Arac, Jonathan. 1989. *Critical Genealogies: Historical Situations for Postmodern Literary Studies.* New York: Columbia Univ. Press.

Armstrong, Cheryl, and Sheryl I. Fontaine. 1989. "The Power of Naming: Names That Create and Define the Discipline." *WPA: Writing Program Administration* 13, 1–2:5–14.

Arnold, C. J. 1986. "Archaeology and History: The Shades of Confrontation." In *Archaeology at the Interface: Studies in Archaeology's Relationships with History, Geography, Biology, and Physical Science,* ed. J. L. Bintliff and C. F. Gaffney, 32–39. BAR International Series 300. Oxford: BAR.

Aronowitz, Stanley. 1991. "The Punishment of Disciplines: Cultural Studies and the Transformation of Legitimate Knowledge." In *Postmodern Education,* ed. Stanley Aronowitz and Henry Giroux, 136–56. Minneapolis: Univ. of Minnesota Press.

Atlan, Henri. 1983. "L'émergence du nouveau et du sens." In *L'auto-organisation: De la physique au politique,* ed. P. Dumouchel and J.-P. Dupuy, 115–30. Paris: Seuil.

Bahm, Archie J. 1980. "Interdisciplinology: The Science of Interdisciplinary Research." *Nature and System* 2, 1:29–35.

Bailis, Stanley. 1984–85. "Against and for Holism: A Review and Rejoinder to D. C. Phillips." *Issues in Integrative Studies* 3:17–41.

———. 1986. "Review of *Inter-disciplinarity Revisited.*" *Association for Integrative Studies Newsletter* 8, 1:1, 8–9.

———. 1993. "Holism, Pluralism and the Interdisciplinary Persuasion in American Studies." Paper presented at American Studies Association meeting. Boston, 5 November.

Bal, Mieke. 1990. "De-disciplining the Eye." *Critical Inquiry* 16, 3:506–31.

————. 1991. *Reading "Rembrandt": Beyond the Word-Image Opposition.* New York: Cambridge Univ. Press.

Bann, Stephen. 1989. "Art History in Perspective." *History of the Human Sciences* 2, 1:1–18.

Banta, Martha. 1991. "Working the Levees: Building Them up or Knocking Them Down?" *American Quarterly* 43, 3:375–91.

Barker, Randolph. 1982. "Farming Systems Research: Interdisciplinary Responses to Problems." In *Enabling Interdisciplinary Research: Perspectives from Agriculture, Forestry, and Home Economics,* ed. Martha Garrett Russell, Richard Sauer, and John Barnes, 101–4. Miscellaneous Publication 19. St. Paul: Agricultural Experiment Station, Univ. of Minnesota.

Barmarck, Jan, and Goran Wallen. 1980. "The Development of an Interdisciplinary Project." In *The Social Process of Scientific Investigation,* ed. K. D. Knorr, R. Krohn, and R. D. Whitley, 221–35. Dordrecht: D. Reidel. See also "Interaction of Cognitive and Social Factors in Steering a Large Interdisciplinary Project," in *Interdisciplinary Research Groups,* ed. Richard T. Barth and Rudy Steck, 180–90 (Vancouver: Interdisciplinary Research Group on Interdisciplinary Programs, 1979).

Barnes, Barry. 1974. *Scientific Knowledge and Sociological Theory.* London: Routledge.

Barnes, John M. 1982. "Regional Coordination of Scientists' Initiatives in Interdisciplinary Research." In *Enabling Interdisciplinary Research: Perspectives from Agriculture, Forestry, and Home Economics,* ed. Martha Garrett Russell, Richard Sauer, and John Barnes, 135–38. Miscellaneous Publication 19. St. Paul: Agricultural Experiment Station, Univ. of Minnesota.

————. 1988. "Challenges for Interdisciplinary Agricultural Research." In *Soybean Diseases of the North Central Region,* ed. T. D. Wylie and D. H. Scott, 1–2. St. Paul: American Phytopathological Society Press.

Baron, Dennis. 1992. "Language, Culture, and Society." In Gibaldi 1992, 28–52.

Barricelli, Jean-Pierre, and Joseph Gibaldi, eds. 1982. *Interrelations of Literature.* New York: Modern Language Association.

Barricelli, Jean-Pierre, Joseph Gibaldi, and Estella Lauter. 1990. *Teaching Literature and Other Arts.* New York: Modern Language Association.

Barthes, Roland. 1977. "From Work to Text." In *Image, Music, Text,* trans. Stephen Heath, 155–64. New York: Hill and Wang.

Bate, W. Jackson. 1982. "The Crisis in English Studies." *Harvard Magazine* 85: 46–53.

Bateson, Gregory. 1972. *Steps to an Ecology of Mind.* New York: Ballantine.

————. 1979. "The Pattern Which Connects." In *Mind and Nature: A Necessary Unity.* New York: Dutton.

Bathrick, David. 1992. "Cultural Studies." In Gibaldi 1992, 320–40.

Bazerman, Charles. 1988. *Shaping Written Knowledge: The Genre and Activity of the Experimental Article in Science.* Madison: Univ. of Wisconsin Press.

————. 1989. Introduction to "What Are We Doing as a Research Community?" *Rhetoric Review* 7, 2:223–25.

Beam, Robert D. 1983. "Fragmentation of Knowledge: An Obstacle to Full Utilization." In *The Optimum Utilization of Knowledge,* ed. Kenneth Boulding and Lawrence Senesh, 160–74. Boulder, Colo.: Westview Press.

Becher, Tony. 1987. "The Disciplinary Shaping of the Profession." In *The Academic Profession: National, Disciplinary, and Institutional Settings,* ed. Burton R. Clark, 271–303. Berkeley: Univ. of California Press.

———. 1989. *Academic Tribes and Territories: Intellectual Inquiry and the Cultures of Disciplines.* Milton Keynes, Eng.: Society for Research into Higher Education and Open Univ. Press.

———. 1990. "The Counter-culture of Specialization." *European Journal of Education* 25, 2:333–46.

———. 1994. "Esperantists in a Tower of Babel." *Issues in Integrative Studies* 12: 23–41.

Becher, Tony, and Ludwig Huber. 1990. "Editorial." *European Journal of Education* 25, 3:235–40.

Bechtel, William. 1986a. "Biochemistry: A Cross-disciplinary Endeavor That Discovered a Distinctive Domain." In *Integrating Scientific Disciplines,* ed. William Bechtel, 77–100, 101–6. Dordrecht: Martinus Nijhoff.

———. 1986b. "The Nature of Scientific Integration." In *Integrating Scientific Disciplines,* ed. William Bechtel, 3–52. Dordrecht: Martinus Nijhoff.

Bell, Daniel. 1984. "The Turn to Interpretation: An Introduction." *Partisan Review,* 215–19.

Bender, John. 1992. "Eighteenth-Century Studies." In Greenblatt and Gunn 1992, 79–99.

Bender, Thomas. 1984. "The Erosion of Public Culture: Cities, Discourses, and Professional Disciplines." In *The Authority of Experts,* ed. Thomas Haskell, 84–106. Bloomington: Indiana Univ. Press.

———. 1986. "Wholes and Parts: The Need for Synthesis in American History." *Journal of American History* 73, 1:120–36.

Bennett, John. 1986. "Summary and Critique: Interdisciplinary Research on People-Resources Relations." In Dahlberg and Bennett 1986, 343–72.

Bennett, Tony. 1992. "Putting Policy into Cultural Studies." In Grossberg, Nelson, and Treichler 1992, 23–34.

Benson, Oliver, and Charles Bonjean. 1970. "The *Social Science Quarterly,* 1920–1970: A Case History in Organizational Growth." *Social Science Quarterly* 50, 4:806–25.

Bercovitch, Sacvan, and Myra Jehlen, eds. 1987. *Ideology and Classic American Literature.* Cambridge: Cambridge Univ. Press.

Berger, Guy. 1972. "Opinions and Facts." In *Interdisciplinarity: Problems of Teaching and Research in Universities* 1972, 21–74.

Berger, Peter, and Thomas Luckmann. 1967. *The Social Construction of Reality.* New York: Doubleday.

Bergeron, Katherine. 1992. "Prologue: Disciplining Music." In Bergeron and Bohlman 1992, 1:9.

Bergeron, Katherine, and Philip Bohlman, eds. 1992. *Disciplining Music: Musicology and Its Canons.* Chicago: Univ. of Chicago Press.

Bergonzi, Bernard. 1990. *Exploding English: Criticism, Theory, Culture.* Oxford: Clarendon Press.

Berk, Richard. 1981. "On the Compatibility of Applied and Basic Sociological Research: An Effort in Marriage Counseling." *American Sociologist* 16, 4: 204–11.

Berkenkotter, Carol. 1995. "Theoretical Issues Surrounding Interdisciplinary Interpenetration." *Social Epistemology* 9, 2:175–87.

Berkhofer, Robert F., Jr. 1989. "A New Context for a New American Studies?" *American Quarterly* 41, 4:588–613.

Berkin, Carol. 1991. "'Dangerous Courtesies': Assault Women's History." *Chronicle of Higher Education,* 11 December, A44.

Berman, Art. 1988. *From the New Criticism to Deconstruction: The Reception of Structuralism and Poststructuralism.* Urbana: Univ. of Illinois Press.

Bhabha, Homi K. 1992. "Postcolonial Criticism." In Greenblatt and Gunn 1992, 437–65.

Binder, Arnold. 1987. "Criminology: Discipline or Interdiscipline?" *Issues in Integrative Studies* 5:41–68.

Bingham, Nelson. 1994. "Organizational Networking: Taking the Next Step." In Klein and Doty 1994, 85–91.

Bingham, Richard D., Gary T. Henry, and John P. Blair. 1981. "Urban Affairs Graduate Programs: A Ranking of U.S. Colleges and Universities." *Urban Affairs Quarterly* 16, 3:355–68.

Bintliff, J. L. 1986. "Archaeology at the Interface: An Historical Perspective." In *Archaeology at the Interface: Studies in Archaeology's Relationships with History, Geography, Biology, and Physical Science,* ed. J. L. Bintliff and C. F. Gaffney, 4–31. BAR International Series 300. Oxford: BAR.

Bioengineering Systems Research in the United States: An Overview. 1987. Washington, D.C.: National Academy Press.

Birnbaum, Norman. 1969. "The Arbitrary Disciplines." *Change: The Magazine of Higher Learning,* July–August, 10–21.

Bizzell, Patricia, and Bruce Herzberg, eds. 1990. *The Rhetorical Tradition.* Boston: Bedford.

Bledstein, Burton J. 1976. *The Culture of Professionalism.* New York: Norton.

Bligh, P. H. 1977. "Territorial Physics." *Physics Bulletin* 28:73.

Blume, Stuart. 1985. "After the Darkest Hour: Integrity and Engagement in the Development of University Research." In *The University Research System: The Public Policies of the Home of Scientists,* ed. Bjorn Wittrock and Aant Elzinga, 139–63. Stockholm: Almqvist and Wiksell International.

Bogue, Allan G. 1990. "The Quest for Numeracy: Data and Methods in American Political History." *Journal of Interdisciplinary History* 21, 1:89–116.

Boisot, Marcel. 1972. "Discipline and Interdisciplinarity." In *Interdisciplinarity: Problems of Teaching and Research in Universities* 1972, 89–97.

Boulding, Kenneth. 1977. "Peace Research." *International Social Science Journal* 29, 4:601–14.

"Boundary Rhetorics and the Work of Interdisciplinarity." 1995. Special issue of *Social Epistemology* 9, 2.

Bourdieu, Pierre. 1993. *The Field of Cultural Production: Essays on Art and Literature,* ed. Randal Johnson. New York: Columbia Univ. Press.

Boxer, Marilyn J. 1982. "For and about Women: The Theory and Practice of Women's Studies in the United States." *Signs* 7, 3:661–95.

Boyer, Ernest. 1981. "The Quest for Common Learning." In *Common Learning: A Carnegie Colloquium on General Education,* 3–21. Washington, D.C.: Carnegie Foundation.

Brantlinger, Patrick. 1990. *Crusoe's Footprints: Cultural Studies in Britain and America.* New York: Routledge.

Broido, Jonathan. 1979. "Interdisciplinarity: Reflections on Methodology." In Kockelmans 1979, 244–305.

Bucher, R., and A. Strauss. 1961. "Professions in Process." *American Journal of Sociology* 66:325–34.

Bulick, Stephen. 1982. *Structure and Subject Interaction.* New York: Marcel Dekker.

Burchell, R., and J. Hughes. 1979. "Planning Theory in the 1980's—a Search for Future Directions." In *Planning Theory in the 1980's,* ed. R. Burchell and G. Sternlieb. New Brunswick, N.J.: Center for Urban Policy Research.

Burke, Peter. 1991. "Overture: The New History, Its Past and Its Future." In *New Perspectives on Historical Writing,* ed. Peter Burke, 1–23. University Park: Pennsylvania State Univ. Press.

Buttigieg, Joseph. 1987a. "Introduction: Criticism without Boundaries." In *Criticism without Boundaries: Directions and Crosscurrents in Postmodern Critical Theory,* ed. Joseph A. Buttigieg, 1–22. Notre Dame: Univ. of Notre Dame Press.

———. 1987b. *Criticism without Boundaries: Directions and Crosscurrents in Postmodern Critical Theory.* Notre Dame: University of Notre Dame Press.

Buttimer, Anne. 1969. "Social Space in Interdisciplinary Perspective." *Geographical Review* 59, 3:417–26.

Cabrese, Andrew M. 1987. "Social Science Discourse: Issues in Scholarly Communication." Paper presented at Speech Communication Association meeting, Boston, 5–8 November. Available as ERIC microfiche ED 295223.

Cain, William E. 1985. "English in America Reconsidered: Theory, Criticism, Marxism, and Social Change." In *Criticism in the University,* ed. Gerald Graff and Reginald Gibbons, 85–104. Evanston, Ill.: Northwestern Univ. Press.

Caldwell, Lynton K. 1983. "Environmental Studies: Discipline or Metadiscipline?" *Environmental Professional* 5:247–59.

Calhoun, Craig. 1992. "Sociology, Other Disciplines, and the Project of a General Understanding of Social Life." In Halliday and Janowitz 1992, 137–95.

Campbell, Colin. 1986. "Scholarly Disciplines: Breaking Out." *New York Times,* 25 April, A18.

Campbell, Donald. 1969. "Ethnocentrism of Disciplines and the Fish-Scale Model of Omniscience." In *Interdisciplinary Relationships in the Social Sciences,* ed. Muzafer Sherif and Carolyn Sherif, 328–48. Chicago: Aldine.

Carby, Hazel V. 1989. *Reconstructing Womanhood: The Emergence of the Afro-American Woman Novelist.* New York: Oxford Univ. Press.

The Case for Change, n.d. Richmond: Commonwealth of Virginia, Commission on the University of the Twenty-first Century.

Casey, Beth A. 1986. "The Quiet Revolution: The Transformation and Reintegration of the Humanities." *Issues in Integrative Studies* 4:71–92.

———. 1994. "The Administration of Interdisciplinary Programs." In Klein and Doty 1994, 53–67.

Cassell, Eric J. 1977. "How Does Interdisciplinary Work Get Done?" *In Knowledge, Value, and Belief,* ed. H. T. Englehardt and D. Callahan, 35–61. New York: Hastings Center.

Certeau, Michel de. 1984. *The Practice of Everyday Life.* Trans. Steven F. Rendall. Berkeley: Univ. of California Press.

The Challenge of Connecting Learning. 1990. See *Liberal Learning and the Arts and Sciences Major.* 1990.

Chen, Robert S. 1981. "Interdisciplinary Research and Integration: The Case of CO_2 and Climate." In *Social Science Research and Climate Change: An Interdisciplinary Appraisal,* ed. Robert S. Chen, Elise Boulding, and Stephen H. Schneider, 230–48. Dordrecht: D. Reidel, 1983. Also available in *Climatic Change* 3, 4 (1981): 429–48.

Chubin, Daryl. 1976. "The Conceptualization of Scientific Specialties." *Sociological Quarterly* 17:448–76.

———. 1983. *Sociology of Sciences: An Annotated Bibliography on Invisible Colleges, 1972–1981.* New York: Garland.

———. 1990. "Scientific Malpractice and the Contemporary Politics of Knowledge." In *Theories of Science in Society,* ed. Susan E. Cozzens and Thomas F. Gieryn, 144–63. Bloomington: Indiana Univ. Press.

Chubin, Daryl E., Alan Porter, and Frederick Rossini. 1984. "'Citation Classics' Analysis: An Approach to Characterizing Interdisciplinary Research." *Journal of the American Society for Information Science* 35, 6:360–68.

Chubin, Daryl E., A. L. Porter, F. A. Rossini, and T. Connolly, eds. 1986. *Interdisciplinary Analysis and Research: Theory and Practice of Problem-Focused Research and Development.* Mount Airy, Md.: Lomond.

Clark, Burton R. 1983. *The Higher Education System: Academic Organization in Cross-National Perspective.* Berkeley: Univ. of California Press.

———. 1995. *Places of Inquiry: Research and Advanced Education in Modern Universities.* Berkeley: Univ. of California Press.

Clarke, Adele. 1990. "A Social Worlds Research Adventure." In *Theories of Science in Society,* ed. Susan Cozzens and Thomas Gieryn, 15–45. Bloomington: Indiana Univ. Press.

Claval, Paul. 1988. "Geography: A Crossroads Science." International Social Science Council. Unpublished manuscript, cited in Dogan and Pahre 1990, 93–94, 167.

Clayton, Keith. 1984. Remarks at international seminar on "Interdisciplinarity Revisited." Linköping, Sweden, 5 October.

———. 1985. "The University of East Anglia." In Levin and Lind 1985, 189–205.

Clifford, James, and George E. Marcus, eds. 1986. *Writing Culture: The Poetics and Politics of Ethnography.* Berkeley: Univ. of California Press.

Clough, Stanley B. 1970. "A Half-Century in Economic History: Autobiographical Reflections." *Journal of Economic History* 30:4–17.

Cohen, Walter. 1992. "Marxist Criticism." In Greenblatt and Gunn 1992, 320–48.

Cohn, Bernard S. 1980. "History and Anthropology: The State of Play." *Comparative Studies in Sociology and History* 22, 2:198–221.

———. 1981. "Anthropology and History in the 1980's." *Journal of Interdisciplinary History* 12, 1:227–52.

Collin, Robert. 1989. "Shifting Paradigms and Interdisciplinarity: A Case Study." Unpublished manuscript. Available from the author.

Collins, Patricia Hill. 1991. "Learning from the Outsider Within: The Sociological Significance of Black Feminist Thought." In Hartman and Messer-Davidow 1991, 40:65.

"Comment and Debate: Historical Sociology and Social History." 1987. *Social Science History* 11, 1:17–62.

Connors, Robert J. 1989. "Rhetorical History as a Component of Composition Studies." *Rhetoric Review* 7, 2:230–40.

Cornell, L. L. 1987. "Reproduction, Production, Social Science, and the Past: A Dissenting Review." *Social Science History* 11, 1:43–52.

Costanza, Robert. 1990. "Escaping the Overspecialization Trap: Creating Incentives for a Transdisciplinary Synthesis." In *Rethinking the Curriculum: Toward an Integrated, Interdisciplinary College Education,* ed. Mary E. Clark and Sandra A. Wawrytko, 95–106. Contributions to the Study of Education, no. 40. New York: Greenwood.

Coyner, Sandra. 1991. "Women's Studies." *NWSA Journal* [National Women's Studies Association] 3, 3:349–54.

Craige, Betty Jean. 1992. *Laying the Ladder Down: The Emergence of Cultural Holism.* Amherst: Univ. of Massachusetts Press.

Crane, Diana. 1972. *Invisible Colleges.* Chicago: Univ. of Chicago Press.

Crane, Diana, and Henry Small. 1992. "American Sociology since the Seventies: The Emerging Identity Crisis in the Discipline." In Halliday and Janowitz 1992, 197–234.

Crane, R. S. 1967. "History versus Criticism in the Study of Literature." In *The Idea of Humanities and Other Essays,* ed. Wayne Booth. Chicago: Univ. of Chicago Press.

"The Crisis in Discipline." 1982. Special issue of *Art Journal* 42, 2.

Crow, Thomas. 1985. "Codes of Silence: Historical Representation and the Art of Watteau." *Representations* 12:2–14.

Culler, Jonathan. 1982. "Literature and Linguistics." In Barricelli and Gibaldi 1982, 1–24.

———. 1992. "Literary Theory." In Gibaldi 1992, 201–35.

Cutcliffe, Stephen. 1989. "Science, Technology, and Society: An Interdisciplinary Academic Field." *National Forum* 69, 2:22–25.

Dahlberg, Ingetraut. 1994. "Domain Interaction: Theory and Practice." *Advances in Knowledge Organization* 4:60–71.

Dahlberg, Kenneth. 1986. "The Changing Nature of Natural Resources." In Dahlberg and Bennett 1986, 11–35.

Dahlberg, Kenneth, and John Bennett, eds. 1986. *Natural Resources and People: Conceptual Issues in Interdisciplinary Research.* Boulder, Colo.: Westview Press.

Darden, Lindley, and Nancy Maull. 1977. "Interfield Theories." *Philosophy of Science* 44 (March): 43–64.

Davis, James. 1995. *Interdisciplinary Courses and Team Teaching: New Arrangements for Learning.* American Council on Education Series on Higher Education. Phoenix, Ariz.: Oryx Press.

Davis, Natalie Z. 1981. "Anthropology and History in the 1980's." *Journal of Interdisciplinary History* 12, 2:267–75.

Davis, Walter. 1978. *The Act of Interpretation: A Critique of Literary Reason.* Chicago: Univ. of Chicago Press.

DeBie, Pierre. 1968. Introduction to special section on "Multidisciplinary Problem-Focused Research." *International Social Science Journal* 20, 2:192–210.

Delkeskamp, Corinna. 1977. "Interdisciplinarity: A Critical Appraisal." In *Knowledge, Value, and Belief,* ed. H. T. Engelhardt Jr. and D. Callahan, 324–54. Foundations of Ethics and Its Relationship to Science 2. Hastings-on-Hudson, N.Y.: Hastings Center.

Denzen, Norman K. 1992. *Symbolic Interactionism and Cultural Studies: The Politics of Interpretation.* Cambridge, Mass.: Blackwell.

Dermer, Jerry. 1988. "Intraorganizational Interdisciplinary Projects: Design Issues." INTERSTUDY *Bulletin* 9, 19. Reprint of paper presented at Fifth International Conference on Interdisciplinary Research Groups, Manchester, UK, 13–15 July.

Derrida, Jacques. 1983. "The Principle of Reason: The University in the Eyes of Its Pupils." *Diacritics,* fall 1983, response section 3–20.

Deutsch, Karl W., Andrei S. Markovits, and John Platt. 1986. *Advances in the Social Sciences, 1900–1980: What, Who, Where, How?* Cambridge, Mass.: Univ. Press. of America.

Devon, Tonia. 1990. "Trends in Interdisciplinarity and Institutional Collaboration in Engineering: Building the Infrastructure for University-Industry Relations." INTERSTUDY *Bulletin* 11, 23:4–10.

DeWachter, Maurice. 1982. "Interdisciplinary Bioethics: But Where Do We Start? A Reflection on Epochē as Method." *Journal of Medicine and Philosophy* 7, 3: 275–87.

Dhareshwar, Vivek. 1990. "The Predicament of Theory." In *Theory between the Disciplines: Authority/Vision/Politics,* ed. Martin Kreiswirth and Mark A. Cheetham, 231–50. Ann Arbor: Univ. of Michigan Press.

Diesing, P. 1962. *Reason in Society.* Urbana: Univ. of Illinois Press.

Dill, David. 1990. "University/Industry Research Collaborations: An Analysis of Interorganizational Relationships." *R&D Management* 20, 2:123–29.

Dillon, George L. 1991. *Contending Rhetorics: Writing in Academic Disciplines.* Bloomington: Indiana University Press.

"Divisions and Discussion Groups." 1993. *PMLA* 108, 4:649–58.

Dogan, Mattei, and Robert Pahre. 1990. *Creative Marginality: Innovation at the Intersections of Social Sciences.* Boulder, Colo.: Westview Press.

Doornkamp, J. S., and K. Warren. 1980. "Geography in the United Kingdom, 1976–80: Report to the Twenty-fourth International Geographical Congress in Tokyo, Japan, in August 1980." *Geographical Journal* 146, 1:94–110.

Doty, William. 1991. "The Disciplinary Discourses as Institutionalizations of Authority in a Post-/Non-/Trans-disciplinary Era." In *Curricular Reform: Narratives of Interdisciplinary Humanities Programs,* ed. Mark E. Clark and Roger Johnson Jr., 73–88. Chattanooga: Southern Humanities Press.

Douglas, Mary. 1986. *How Institutions Think.* Syracuse: Syracuse Univ. Press.

Dressel, Paul. 1970. *The Confidence of Crisis: An Analysis of University Departments.* San Francisco: Jossey-Bass.

Dreyfus, Hubert L., and Paul Rabinow. 1983. *Michel Foucault: Beyond Structuralism and Hermeneutics.* 2d ed. Chicago: Univ. of Chicago Press.

Dubin, Robert. 1969. "Contiguous Problem Analysis: An Approach to Systematic Theories about Social Organization." In Sherif and Sherif 1969b, 65–76.

Dubois, Carol Ellen, et al. 1987. *Feminist Scholarship: Kindling in the Groves of Academe.* Urbana: Univ. of Illinois Press.

Easton, David. 1991a. "The Division, Integration, and Transfer of Knowledge." In Easton and Schelling 1991, 7–36.

———. 1991b. "Political Science in the United States: Past and Present." In Easton and Schelling 1991, 37–58.

Easton, David, and Corinne Schelling, eds. 1991. *Divided Knowledge: Across Disciplines, across Cultures.* Newbury Park, Calif.: Sage.

Eckhardt, Carolyn D. 1978. *Interdisciplinary Programs and Administrative Structures: Problems and Prospects for the 1980's.* University Park: Center for the Study of Higher Education, Pennsylvania State Univ.

"Editor's Introduction." 1992. *Urban Studies* 29, 3–4:341.

Eisel, Ulrich. 1992. "About Dealing with the Impossible: An Account of Experience in Landscape Planning Courses." *European Journal of Education* 27, 3: 239–55.

Elam, Diane. 1990. "Ms. en Abyme: Deconstruction and Feminism." *Social Epistemology* 4, 3:293–308.

Elbow, Peter. 1990. *What Is English?* New York: Modern Language Association.

Elder, Charles. 1992. Internal university memorandum. Wayne State University. 7 August.

Elias, Norbert. 1982. "Scientific Establishments." In *Scientific Establishments and Hierarchies,* ed. Norbert Elias, Herman Martins, and Richard Whitley, 3–70. Dordrecht: D. Reidel.

Elzinga, Aant. 1985. "Research, Bureaucracy and the Drift of Epistemic Criteria." In *The University Research System,* ed. B. Wittrock and A. Elzinga, 191–220. Lund, Sweden: Research on Higher Education Program.

Epton, S. R., R. L. Payne, and A. W. Pearson. "Multidisciplinary, Interdisciplinary: What Is the Difference?" In *Managing Interdisciplinary Research,* ed. S. R. Epton, R. L. Payne, and A. W. Pearson, 3–9. Chichester, Eng.: Wiley.

The ERCs: A Partnership for Competitiveness. 1991. Report of a Symposium, February 28–March 1, 1990. Washington, D.C.: National Science Foundation.

Esch, Deborah. 1992. "Deconstruction." In Greenblatt and Gunn 1992, 374–91.

Etzkowitz, Henry. 1983. "Entrepreneurial Scientists and Entrepreneurial Universities in American Academic Science." *Minerva* 21, 2–3:198–233.

Etzkowitz, Henry, and Lois Peters. 1988. "Organizational Innovation in the University for Knowledge Transfer." Paper presented at international meeting of the International Association for the Study of Interdisciplinary Research, Manchester, U.K., 13–15 July.

Evans, Colin. 1990. "A Cultural View of the Discipline of Modern Languages." In *European Journal of Education* 25, 3:273–82.

Ewell, Barbara C. 1990. "Empowering Otherness: Feminist Criticism and the Academy." In *Reorientations: Critical Theories and Pedagogies,* ed. Bruce Henricksen and Thais E. Morgan, 43–62. Urbana: Univ. of Illinois Press.

Faber, Malte, and John L. R. Proops. 1985. "Interdisciplinary Research between Economists and Physical Scientists: Retrospect and Prospect." *Kyklos* 38, 4: 599–614.

Federally Funded Research: Decisions for a Decade. 1991. Washington, D.C.: Office of Technology Assessment, United States Congress.

Fedoseyev, P. N. 1984. "Philosophy and the Integration of Knowledge." In *Integration of Science and the Systems Approach,* ed. A. Javurek, A. D. Ursul, and J. Zeman, 13–31. Prague: Academia.

Ferguson, P. P., P. Desan, and W. Griswold. 1988. "Mirrors, Frames, and Demons: Reflections on the Sociology of Literature." *Critical Inquiry* 14:421–30.

Field, Michael, Russell Lee, and Mary Lee Field. 1994. "Assessing Interdisciplinary Learning." In Klein and Doty 1994, 69–84.

Finegan, Edward. 1992. "Linguistics." In Gibaldi 1992, 1–27.

Finestone, Harry, and Michael F. Shugrue, eds. 1973. *Prospects for the 70's: English Departments and Multidisciplinary Study.* New York: Modern Language Association.

Fiscella, Joan B. 1989. "Access to Interdisciplinary Information: Setting the Problem." *Issues in Integrative Studies* 7:73–92.

Fischer, Michael M. J. 1992a. Comment. "Knowledge Collaborations in the Arts, the Sciences, and the Humanities. Part 3: The Humanities and Social Sciences." *Knowledge* 14, 1:124–28.

———. 1992b. "Edited Excerpts from a Smithsonian Seminar Series. Part 3: The Humanities and the Social Sciences." *Knowledge* 14, 1:110–32.

Fish, Stanley. 1983. "Profession Despise Thyself: Fear and Self-Loathing in Literary Studies." *Critical Inquiry* 10 (December): 349–64.

———. 1989a. "Being Interdisciplinary Is So Very Hard to Do." *Profession 89: A Publication of the MLA,* 1989, 15–22.

———. 1989b. "Don't Know Much about the Middle Ages: Posner on Law and Literature." In *Doing What Comes Naturally: Change, Rhetoric, and the Practice of Theory in Literary and Legal Studies,* 294–311. Durham, N.C.: Duke Univ. Press.

Fisher, C. A. 1973. "The Contribution of Geography to Foreign Area Studies: The Case of Southeast Asia." In *Geographers Abroad: Essays on the Problems and Prospects of Research in Foreign Areas,* ed. Marvin Mikesell. Chicago: Univ. of Chicago Press.

Fisher, C. S. 1973. "Some Social Characteristics of Mathematicians and Their Work." *American Journal of Sociology* 75, 5:1094–1118.

Fisher, David Hackett. 1981. "Climate and History: Priorities for Research." In *Climate and History: Studies in Interdisciplinary History,* ed. Robert I. Rotberg and Theodore K. Rabb, 241–50. Princeton: Princeton Univ. Press.

Fisher, Donald. 1990. "Boundary Work and Science: The Relation between Power and Knowledge." In *Theories of Science in Society,* ed. Susan Cozzens and Thomas Gieryn, 98–119. Bloomington: Indiana Univ. Press.

————. 1993. *Fundamental Development of the Social Sciences: Rockefeller Philanthropy and the United States Social Science Research Council.* Ann Arbor: Univ. of Michigan Press.

Fiske, John. 1992. "Cultural Studies and the Culture of Everyday Life." In Grossberg, Nelson, and Treichler 1992, 154–73.

Flax, Jane. 1987. "Postmodernism and Gender Relations in Feminist Theory." *Signs* 12, 4:621–43.

Fleishman, Joel L. 1991. "A New Framework for Integration: Policy Analysis and Public Management." In Easton and Schelling 1991, 219–43.

Flenley, R. 1953. "History and Its Neighbors Today." *Canadian Historical Review* 4, 4:324–38.

Flexner, Hans. 1979. "The Curriculum, the Disciplines, and Interdisciplinarity in Higher Education." In *Interdisciplinarity and Higher Education,* ed. Joseph Kockelmans, 93–122. University Park: Pennsylvania State Univ. Press.

Florida, Richard, and Martin Kenney. 1991. "It Is a Mistake to Push Universities into Becoming Research-and-Development Units of Corporations." *Chronicle of Higher Education,* 10 July, B1, B3.

Foucault, Michel. 1972. *The Archaeology of Knowledge and the Discourse on Language.* Trans. A. M. Sheridan Smith. New York: Pantheon.

————. 1973. *The Order of Things: An Archaeology of the Human Sciences.* New York: Vintage.

————. 1979. *Discipline and Punish: The Birth of the Prison.* Trans. Alan Sheridan. New York: Vintage.

————. 1980. *Power/Knowledge: Selected Interviews and Other Writings, 1972–1977.* Ed. Colin Gordon. Trans. Colin Gordon, Leo Marshall, John Mepham, and Kate Sopher. New York: Pantheon.

Fox-Genovese, Elizabeth. 1990. "Between Individualism and Fragmentation: American Culture and the New Literary Studies of Race and Gender." *American Quarterly* 42, 1:7–34.

Fox-Keller, Evelyn. 1993. "Fractured Images of Science, Language, and Power: A Postmodern Optic or Just Bad Eyesight?" In Messer-Davidow, Shumway, and Sylvan 1993b, 54–69.

Frank, Andrea, and Jürgen Schulert. 1992. "Interdisciplinary Learning as Social Learning and General Education." *European Journal of Education* 27, 3:223–37.

Frank, Roberta. 1988. "'Interdisciplinary': The First Half-Century." In *WORDS: For Robert Burchfield's Sixty-fifth Birthday,* ed. E. G. Stanley and T. F. Hoad, 91–101. Cambridge: D. S. Brewer.

Frey, Gerhard. 1973. "Methodological Problems of Interdisciplinary Discussions." *RATIO* 15, 2:161–82.

Friedman, J. 1973. *Retracking America: A Theory of Transactive Planning.* Garden City, N.Y.: Anchor Doubleday.

Friedman, Renee. 1978. "Centers and Institutes: The State of the Art." In *Policy Research Centers Directory,* ed. S. Nagel and W. Neef, 60–74. Urbana: Univ. of Illinois Policy Studies Organization.

Friedman, Robert, and Renee Friedman, with the assistance of K. Mortimer, S. Bragg, and F. Sherman. 1982. *The Role of University Organized Research Units in*

Academic Science. University Park: Center for the Study of Higher Education, Center for the Study of Science Policy and Institute for Policy Research and Evaluation, Pennsylvania State Univ.

Friedman, Robert, and Renee Friedman. 1988. "Science American Style: Three Cases in Academe." *Policy Studies Journal* 17, 1:43–61.

Friedman, Robert, and Renee Friedman, with the assistance of Cindy Parsons. 1986. *Sponsorship, Organization and Program Change at One Hundred Universities.* University Park: Center for the Study of Science Policy, Institute for Policy Research and Evaluation, Pennsylvania State Univ.

Frye, Northrop. 1957. *Anatomy of Criticism: Four Essays.* Princeton: Princeton Univ. Press.

Fuller, Steve. 1988. *Social Epistemology.* Bloomington: Indiana Univ. Press.

———. 1993. *Philosophy, Rhetoric, and the End of Knowledge,* Madison: Univ. of Wisconsin Press.

Gaff, Jerry. 1980. "Avoiding the Potholes in General Education." *Educational Record* 61, 4:50–59.

———. 1989. "The Resurgence of Interdisciplinary Studies." *National Forum* 69, 2: 4–5.

———. 1991. *New Life for the College Curriculum: Assessing Achievements and Furthering Progress in the Reform of General Education.* San Francisco: Jossey-Bass.

Galison, Peter. 1992. Image and Logic. Unpublished manuscript.

Galtung, Johan. 1981. "Structure, Culture, and Intellectual Style: An Essay Comparing Saxonic, Teutonic, Gallic, and Nipponic Approaches." *Social Science Information* 20, 6:817–56.

Gaonkar, Dilip Parameshwar. 1990. "Rhetoric and Its Double: Reflections on the Rhetorical Turn in the Human Sciences." In *The Rhetorical Turn: Invention and Persuasion in the Conduct of Inquiry,* ed. Herbert W. Simons, 341–66. Chicago: Univ. of Chicago Press.

Gates, Henry Louis. 1992. "African American Criticism." In Greenblatt and Gunn 1992, 303–19.

Geertz, Clifford. 1980. "Blurred Genres: The Refiguration of Social Thought." *American Scholar* 42, 2:165–79. Reprinted in *Local Knowledge: Further Essays in Interpretive Anthropology,* 19–35 (New York: Basic Books, 1983).

Geiger, Roger. 1986. *To Advance Knowledge: The Growth of the American Research Universities, 1900–1940.* New York: Oxford Univ. Press.

Geisler, Cheryl, and Susan C. Jarratt. 1989. "The Research Network 1988: Impressions from the Floor." *Rhetoric Review* 7, 2:289–93.

Gellner, Ernest. 1990. "The Stakes in Anthropology." *American Scholar,* winter, 17–30.

Gerholm, Tomas. 1990. "On Tacit Knowledge in Academia." *European Journal of Education* 15, 3:263–71.

"Germanistik as German Studies. Interdisciplinary Theories and Methods." 1989. Special issue of *German Quarterly* 62, 2.

Gerson, Elihu. 1983. "Scientific Work and Social Worlds." *Knowledge* 4, 3:357–77.

Gerstenberger, Donna, and Carolyn Allen. 1977. "Women's Studies/American Studies, 1970–1975." *American Quarterly* 29 (bibliography issue) 262–79.

Gibaldi, Joseph, ed. 1981. *Introduction to Scholarship in Modern Languages and Literatures.* New York: Modern Language Association.

———. 1992. *Introduction to Scholarship in Modern Languages and Literatures.* 2nd ed. New York: Modern Language Association.

Gibbons, Michael, et al. 1994. *The New Production of Knowledge: The Dynamics of Science and Research in Contemporary Societies.* London: Sage.

Gieryn, Thomas. 1983. "Boundary-Work and the Demarcation of Science from Nonscience: Strains and Interests in Professional Ideologies of Scientists." *American Sociological Review* 48:781–95.

———. 1995. "Boundaries of Science." In *Handbook of Science and Technology Studies,* ed. Sheila Jasanoff et al., 383–443. Thousand Oaks, Calif.: Sage.

Giroux, H., D. Shumway, and J. Sosnoski. 1984. "The Need for Cultural Studies: Resisting Intellectuals and Oppositional Public Spheres." *Dalhousie Review* 64 (summer): 472–86.

Glantz, Michael, and Nicolai Orlovsky. 1986. "Desertification: Anatomy of a Complex Environmental Process." In Dahlberg and Bennett 1986, 213–29.

Goldman, Harvey. 1995. "Innovation and Change in the Production of Knowledge." *Social Epistemology* 9, 3:211–32.

Golley, Frank B. 1986. "Ecosystems and Natural Resource Management." In Dahlberg and Bennett 1986, 281–99.

Gottdiener, M., and Joe Feagin. 1988. "The Paradigm Shift in Urban Sociology." *Urban Affairs Quarterly* 24, 2:163–87.

Grace, John. 1993. "Graduate Faculty Units and Their Linkages." In UBC 1993, 24, table 3.

Graff, Gerald. 1985. "The University and the Prevention of Culture." In *Criticism in the University,* ed. Gerald Graff and Reginald Gibbons, 62–84.

———. 1987. *Professing Literature: An Institutional History.* Chicago: Univ. of Chicago Press.

Graff, Gerald, and Reginald Gibbons. 1985. Preface to *Criticism in the University,* ed. Gerald Graff and Reginald Gibbons, 7–14. Evanston, Ill.: Northwestern Univ. Press.

Graff, Gerald, and Bruce Robbins. 1992. "Cultural Criticism." In Greenblatt and Gunn 1992b, 419–36.

Greenblatt, Stephen. 1988. *Shakespearean Negotiations: The Circulation of Social Energy in Renaissance England.* Berkeley: Univ. of California Press.

Greenblatt, Stephen, and Giles Gunn. 1992a. Introduction to Greenblatt and Gunn 1992b, 1–11.

———. eds. 1992b. *Redrawing the Boundaries: The Transformation of English and American Literary Studies.* New York: Modern Language Association.

Green, Jon. 1993. "Integrative Studies Core Program at Michigan State." *Association for Integrative Studies Newsletter* 15, 1:1–4.

Greenwood, E. 1982. "Attributes of a Profession." In *Man, Work and Society,* ed. Sigmund Nosow and William H. Form, 207–18. New York: Basic Books.

Grossberg, Lawrence, Cary Nelson, and Paula Treichler, eds. 1992. *Cultural Studies.* New York: Routledge.

Gunn, Giles. 1992a. "Interdisciplinary Studies." In Gibaldi 1992, 239–61.

———. 1992b. *Thinking across the American Grain: Ideology, Intellect and the New Pragmatism.* Chicago: Univ. of Chicago Press.

Gunnell, John S. 1983. "Political Theory: The Evolution of a Sub-field." In *Political Science: The State of the Discipline,* ed. Ada Finifter, 3–45. Washington, D.C.: American Political Science Association.

Gusfield, Joseph R. 1992. "Listening for the Silences: The Rhetorics of the Research Field." In *Writing the Social Text: Poetics and Politics of Social Science Discourse,* ed. Richard Harvey Brown, 117–34. New York: Aldine.

Habermas, Jürgen. 1987. *The Theory of Communicative Action.* Vol. 2, *Lifeworld and System: A Critique of Functionalist Reason.* Trans. Thomas McCarthy. Boston: Beacon.

Habib, Hedi Bel. 1990. *Towards a Paradigmatic Approach to Interdisciplinarity in the Behavioral and Medical Sciences.* Karlstad, Sweden: Center for Research in the Humanities, University of Karlstad.

Hagendijk, Rob. 1990. "Structuration Theory, Constructivism, and Scientific Change." In *Theories of Science in Society,* ed. Susan Cozzens and Thomas Gieryn, 43–66. Bloomington: Indiana Univ. Press.

Hagstrom, W. O. 1974. "Competition in Science." *American Sociological Review* 39: 1–18.

Hall, Stuart. 1979. "Cultural Studies and the Center: Some Problematics and Problems." In *Culture, Media, Language: Working Papers in Cultural Studies,* ed. Stuart Hall et al., 16–47. London: Hutchison.

———. 1992. "Cultural Studies and Its Theoretical Legacies." In Grossberg, Nelson, and Treichler 1992, 270–94.

Halliday, Terence. 1992. "Introduction: Sociology's Fragile Professionalism." In Halliday and Janowitz 1992, 3–42.

Halliday, Terence, and Morris Janowitz, eds. 1992. *Sociology and Its Publics: The Forms and Fates of Disciplinary Organization.* Chicago: Univ. of Chicago Press.

Hanisch, Thor E., and Wolfgang Vollman, eds. 1983. *Interdisciplinarity in Higher Education.* Bucharest: European Center for Higher Education. UNESCO. Available as ERIC microfiche ED 249 864.

Harth, Phillip. 1981. "Clio and the Critics." In *Studies in Eighteenth-Century Culture,* 10:3–16. Madison: Univ. of Wisconsin Press for American Society for Eighteenth-Century Studies.

Hartman, Joan E. 1991. "Telling Stories: The Construction of Women's Agency." In Hartman and Messer-Davidow 1991, 11–39.

Hartman, Joan E., and Ellen Messer-Davidow, eds. 1991. *(En)Gendering Knowledge: Feminists in Academe.* Knoxville: Univ. of Tennessee Press.

Harvey, John H. 1981. Preface to *Cognition, Social Behavior, and the Environment,* ed. John H. Harvey, xv. Hillsdale, N.J.: Erlbaum.

Hayles, N. Katherine. 1990. *Chaos Bound: Orderly Discourse in Contemporary Literature and Science.* Ithaca: Cornell Univ. Press.

Heckhausen, Heinz. 1972. "Discipline and Interdisciplinarity." In *Interdisciplinarity: Problems of Teaching and Research in Universities,* 83–89. Paris: Organization for Economic Cooperation and Development.

Henderson, Nancy. 1994. "Scholarly Hybrids." *U.S. News and World Report,* 30 December, 73–75.

Hermand, Jost, and Evelyn Torton Beck. 1968. *Interpretive Synthesis: The Task of Literary Scholarship.* New York: Ungar.

Hershberg, Theodore. 1981. "Prologue," "The New Urban History: Toward an Interdisciplinary History of the City," and "Epilogue: Sustaining Interdisciplinary Research." In *Philadelphia: Work, Space, Family, and Group Experience in the Nineteenth Century. Essays toward an Interdisciplinary History of the City,* ed. Theodore Hershberg, v–xvi, 3–35, 492–95. New York: Oxford Univ. Press.

———. 1988. "The Fragmentation of Knowledge and Practice: University, Private Sector and Public Sector Perspectives." *Issues in Integrative Studies* 6: 1–20.

Hiley, David R., James Bohman, and Richard Shusterman, eds. 1991. *The Interpretive Turn: Philosophy, Science, and Culture.* Ithaca: Cornell Univ. Press.

Hillocks, George. 1989. "The Need for Interdisciplinary Studies on the Teaching of Writing." *Rhetoric Review* 7, 2:257–72.

Himmelfarb, Gertrude. 1987. *The New History and the Old.* Cambridge: Harvard Univ. Press.

Hoagland, Sarah. 1978. "On the Reeducation of Sophie." In *Women's Studies: An Interdisciplinary Collection,* ed. Kathleen O'Connor Blumhagen and Walter Johnson, 13–20. Westport, Conn.: Greenwood.

Hoch, Paul. 1987a. "Institutional versus Intellectual Migrations in the Nucleation of New Scientific Specialties." *Studies in History and Philosophy of Science* 18, 4:481–500.

———. 1987b. "Migration and the Generation of New Scientific Ideas." *Minerva* 25, 3:209–37.

———. 1990a. "Institutional Mobility and the Management of Technology and Science." *Technology Analysis and Strategic Management* 2, 4:341–56.

———. 1990b. "Interdisciplinary Research Centers: A Problem in Strategy and Management." *R and D Management* 20, 2:115–21.

———. 1990c. "New UK Interdisciplinary Research Centers: Reorganization for New Generic Technology." *Technology Analysis and Strategic Management* 2, 1:39–48.

Hoddeson, Lillian. 1981. "The Discovery of the Point-Contact Transistor." *Historical Studies in the Physical Sciences* 12, 1:41–76.

Hohendahl, Peter U. 1989. "Interdisciplinary German Studies: Tentative Conclusions." *German Quarterly* 62, 2:227–34.

Horn, T. C. R., and Harry Ritter. 1986. "Interdisciplinary History: A Historiographical Review." *History Teacher* 19, 3:427–48.

House, J. S. 1977. "The Three Faces of Social Psychology." *Sociometry* 40:161–77.

Howard, Jean, and Marion O'Connor. 1987. *Shakespeare Reproduced: The Text in History and Ideology.* New York: Methuen.

Howe, Florence. 1978. "Breaking the Disciplines." In *The Structure of Knowledge: A Feminist Perspective,* ed. Beth Reed, 1–10. Ann Arbor, Mich.: Great Lakes Colleges Association Women's Studies Program.

Huber, Ludwig. 1990. "Disciplinary Cultures and Social Reproduction." *European Journal of Education* 25, 3:241–61.

———. 1992a. "Editorial." *European Journal of Education* 27, 3:193–99.

———. 1992b. "Toward a New *Studium Generale:* Some Conclusions." *European Journal of Education* 27, 3:285–301.

Huerkamp, Claudia, et al. 1981. "Criteria of Interdisciplinarity." In *Center for Interdisciplinary Research, the University of Bielefeld: Annual Report 1978 and Supplement 1979–1981,* 23–24. Bielefeld, West Germany: Center for Interdisciplinary Research.

"Humanities Research Centers." 1992. *PMLA* 107, 4:992.

Hurd, Julie. 1992. "Interdisciplinary Research in the Sciences: Implications for Library Organization." *College and Research Libraries,* July, 283–97.

Hursh, Barbara, Paul Haas, and Michael Moore. 1983. "An Interdisciplinary Model to Implement General Education." *Journal of Higher Education* 54:42–59.

Hutchison, Ray. 1993. "The Crisis in Urban Sociology." In *Urban Sociology in Transition: Research in Urban Sociology,* ed. Ray Hutchison, 3:3–26. Greenwich, Conn.: JAI.

Hutkins, Steve. 1994. "The Materialization of an Idea: Interdisciplinarity as Ideology." Paper presented at Association for Integrative Studies meeting, Pittsburgh, 30 September.

Hyman, S. E. 1955. *The Armed Vision: A Study in the Methods of Modern Literary Criticism.* Rev. ed. New York: Vintage.

Ikenberry, Stanley, and Renee Friedman. 1972. *Beyond Academic Departments.* San Francisco: Jossey-Bass.

Interdisciplinarity: Problems of Teaching and Research in Universities. 1972. Paris: Organization for Economic Cooperation and Development.

Interdisciplinarity: A Report by the Group for Research and Innovation. 1975. London: Group for Research and Innovation, Nuffield Foundation.

Interdisciplinary Research: Promoting Collaboration between the Life Sciences and Medicine and the Physical Sciences and Engineering. 1990. Washington, D.C.: National Academy Press.

"Interdisciplinary Studies." 1990. In *Reports from the Fields,* 61–76. Washington, D.C.: Association of American Colleges.

Intriligator, Michael. 1985. "Interdependence among the Behavioral Sciences." Paper presented at World Congress of Political Science, Paris.

"Introduction." 1993. *Urban Studies* 30, 2:229–36.

Jameson, Frederic. 1981. *The Political Unconscious: Narrative as a Socially Symbolic Act.* Ithaca: Cornell Univ. Press.

Jantsch, Erich. 1972. "Towards Interdisciplinarity and Transdisciplinarity in Education and Innovation." In *Interdisciplinarity: Problems of Teaching and Research in Universities,* 97–121.

———. 1980. "Interdisciplinarity: Dreams and Reality." *Prospects* 10, 3:304–12.

Jardine, Alice A. 1985. *Gynesis: Configurations of Woman and Modernity.* Ithaca: Cornell Univ. Press.

Jay, Martin. 1990. "Name-Dropping or Dropping Names? Modes of Legitimation in the Humanities." In Kreiswirth and Cheetham 1990, 19–34.

Jennings, E. 1970. *Science and Literature: New Lenses for Criticism.* Garden City, N.Y.: Anchor Doubleday.

Johnson, Chalmers. 1975. "Political Science and East Asian Studies." In *Political Science and Area Studies: Rivals or Partners?* ed. Lucien Pye, 78–97. Bloomington: Indiana Univ. Press.

Jordanova, L. 1986. Introduction to *Languages of Nature: Critical Essays on Science and Literature,* 15–47. New Brunswick: Rutgers Univ. Press.

Journet, Debra. 1995. "Synthesizing Disciplinary Narratives: George Gaylord Simpson's *Tempo and Mode in Evolution.*" *Social Epistemology* 9, 2:113–50.

Kaes, Anton. 1989. "New Historicism and the Study of German Literature." *German Quarterly* 62, 2:210–19.

Kain, Daniel. 1993. "Cabbages—and Kings: Research Directions in Integrated/Interdisciplinary Curriculum." *Journal of Educational Thought* 27: 312–31.

Kann, Mark. 1979. "The Political Culture of Interdisciplinary Explanation." *Humanities in Society* 2, 3:185–200.

Kaplan, Ann. 1991. Model presented at meeting on "What Use Are Humanities Centers?" New Haven, 27 April.

Kearney, Michael. 1991. "Borders and Boundaries of State and Self at the End of Empire." *Journal of Historical Sociology* 4, 1:52–74.

Kedrov, B. 1974. "Concerning the Synthesis of the Sciences." *International Classification* 1, 1:3–11.

Kelley, James. 1996. "Wide and Narrow Interdisciplinarity: The Role of the Humanities in Integrative Education." *Journal of General Education* 45, 2.

Kemper, Robert. 1991a. "Trends in Urban Anthropological Research: An Analysis of the Journal *Urban Anthropology,* 1972–1991." *Urban Anthropology* 20, 4: 373–84.

———. 1991b. "Urban Anthropology in the 1990's: The State of Its Practice." *Urban Anthropology* 20, 3:211–23.

Kenshur, Oscar. 1991. "Incursions, Excursions, and the Paradoxes of Interdisciplinarity." Conference on Interdisciplinarity: Science, Literature, and the University. Bloomington, Ind., 7–10 February.

Kerber, Linda. 1989. "Diversity and the Transformation of American Studies." *American Quarterly* 41, 3:415–31.

Kernan, Alvin. 1990. *The Death of Literature.* New Haven: Yale Univ. Press.

Kertzer, David I., Darrett B. Rutman, Sydel Silverman, and Andrejs Plakans. 1986. "History and Anthropology: A Dialogue." *Historical Methods* 19, 3: 119–28.

Klein, Julie Thompson. 1990a. "Bibliography." In *International Research Management: Studies in Interdisciplinary Methods from Business, Government, and Academia,* ed. Philip Birnbaum-More, Frederick Rossini, and Donald Baldwin, 179–207. New York: Oxford Univ. Press.

———. 1990b. *Interdisciplinarity: History, Theory, and Practice.* Detroit: Wayne State Univ. Press.

———. 1990–91. "Applying Interdisciplinary Models to Design, Planning, and Policy Making." *Knowledge and Policy* 3, 4:29–55. Published in Europe in *Managing Knowledge for Design, Planning, and Decision Making,* ed. W. F. Schut and C. W. W. Van Lohuizen, 29–52 (Delft: Delft Univ. Press, 1990).

———. 1992. "Text/Context: The Rhetoric of the Social Sciences." In *Writing the Social Text: Poetics and Politics in Social Science Discourse,* ed. Richard Harvey Brown, 9–27. New York: Aldine.

———. 1993. "Blurring, Cracking, and Crossing: Permeation and the Fracturing of Discipline." In Messer-Davidow, Shumway, and Sylvan 1993b, 185–211.

———. 1994. "Finding Interdisciplinary Knowledge and Information." In Klein and Doty 1994, 7–33

———. 1995. "Interdisciplinarity and Adult Learners." *Journal of Graduate Liberal Studies* 1, 1:113–26.

Klein, Julie Thompson, and William Doty, eds. 1994. *Interdisciplinary Studies Today.* New Directions in Teaching and Learning 58. San Francisco: Jossey-Bass.

Klein, Julie T., and William Newell. 1996. "Interdisciplinary Studies." In *Handbook on the Undergraduate Curriculum,* ed. Jerry Gaff and James Ratcliffe. San Francisco: Jossey-Bass.

Klein, Julie T., and Alan Porter. 1990. "Preconditions for Interdisciplinary Research." In *International Research Management: Studies in Interdisciplinary Methods from Business, Government, and Academia,* ed. P. Birnbaum-More, F. Rossini, and D. Baldwin, 11–19. New York: Oxford Univ. Press.

Kluver, Jürgen, and Jorn Schmidt. 1990. "The Disciplinary Realization of Cognitive Education." *European Journal of Education* 25, 3:305–17.

Knapp, Peter. 1984. "Can Social Theory Escape from History? View of History in Social Sciences." *History and Theory* 23:34–52.

"Knowledge Collaborations in the Arts, the Sciences, and the Humanities." 1991–92. *Knowledge: Creation, Diffusion, Utilization:* part 1: "The Arts," 13, 2 (1991): 193–215; part 2: "The Sciences," 13, 4 (1992): 399–409; part 3: "The Humanities and Social Sciences," 14, 1 (1992): 110–32; part 4: "Collaboration, for Better or for Worse," 14, 1 (1992): 133–42.

Kockelmans, Joseph, ed. 1979a. *Interdisciplinarity and Higher Education.* University Park: Pennsylvania State Univ. Press.

———. 1979b. "Science and Discipline: Some Historical and Critical Reflections." In Kockelmans 1979a, 12–48.

———. 1979c. "Why Interdisciplinarity." In Kockelmans 1979a, 124–60.

Kraft, Selma. 1989. "Interdisciplinarity and the Canon of Art History." *Issues in Integrative Studies* 7:57–71.

Kreiswirth, Martin, and Mark A. Cheetham. 1990a. "Introduction: 'Theory-Mad Beyond Redemption'?" In Kreiswirth and Cheetham 1990b, 1–16.

———, eds. 1990b. *Theory between the Disciplines: Authority, Vision, Politics.* Ann Arbor: Univ. of Michigan Press.

Krieger, M., ed. 1987. *The Aims of Representation: Subject/Text/History.* New York: Columbia Univ. Press.

Kroker, Arthur. 1980. "Migration across the Disciplines." *Journal of Canadian Studies* 15 (fall): 3–10.

Kubler, George. 1975. "History—or Anthropology—of Art?" *Critical Inquiry* 1, 4: 757–67.

Kuhn, Thomas. 1970. *The Structure of Scientific Revolutions.* 2d ed. Chicago: Univ. of Chicago Press.

LaCapra, Dominick. 1987. "Criticism Today." In Krieger 1987, 235–55.

Lambert, Richard. 1991. "Blurring the Disciplinary Boundaries: Area Studies in the United States." In Easton and Schelling 1991, 171–94.

Lambert, Richard, et al. 1984. *Beyond Growth: The Next Stage in Language and Area Studies.* Washington, D.C.: Association of American Universities.

Landau, Martin, Harold Proshansky, and William Ittelson. 1962. "The Interdisciplinary Approach and the Concept of Behavioral Sciences." In *Decisions, Values, and Groups,* ed. N. Washburne, 7–25. New York: Pergamon Press.

LaPonce, J. A. 1980. "Political Science: An Import-Export Analysis of Journals and Footnotes." *Political Studies* 28, 3:401–19.

Lauer, Janice. 1983. "Studies of Written Discourse: Dappled Discipline." Address to the Rhetoric Society of America, thirty-fourth meeting of the Conference on College Composition and Communication. Detroit, Mich., 17 March.

Lebow, Richard. 1988. "Interdisciplinary Research and the Future of Peace and Security Studies." *Political Psychology* 9, 3:507–25.

Leitch, Vincent. 1988. *American Literary Criticism from the Thirties to the Eighties.* New York: Columbia Univ. Press.

Lemaine, Gerard, et al. 1976. "Introduction: Problems in the Emergence of New Disciplines." In *Perspectives on the Emergence of Scientific Disciplines,* ed. G. Lemaine et al., 1–23. Paris: Mouton.

Lemert, Charles C. 1989. "The Shallowness of Depth." *Liberal Education* 75, 7:12–13.

———. 1990. "Depth as a Metaphor for the Major: A Postmodernist Challenge." Paper presented at meeting of Association of American Colleges, San Francisco, 11 January.

Lenoir, Timothy. 1993. "The Discipline of Nature and the Nature of Disciplines." In Messer-Davidow, Shumway, and Sylvan 1993b, 70–102.

Lenz, Gunther H. 1982. "American Studies—Beyond the Crisis? Recent Redefinitions and the Meaning of Theory, History, and Practical Criticism." *Prospects, Annual of American Cultural Studies* 7:53–113.

Lepenies, Wolf. 1976. "History and Anthropology: A Historical Appraisal of the Current Contact between the Disciplines." *Social Science Information* 15, 2–3:287–306.

———. 1978. "Toward an Interdisciplinary History of Science." *International Journal of Sociology* 8, 1–2:45–69.

Lerner, Gerda. 1979. *The Majority Finds Its Past: Placing Women in History.* New York: Oxford Univ. Press.

Levin, Lennart, and Ingemar Lind, eds. 1985. *Inter-disciplinarity Revisited: Re-assessing the Concept in the Light of Institutional Experience.* Stockholm: Organization for Economic Cooperation and Development, Swedish National Board of Universities and Colleges, Linköping University.

Levine, George. 1987. Introduction and epilogue to *One Culture: Essays in Science and Literature,* ed. George Levine, 3–32, 339–42. Madison: Univ. of Wisconsin Press.

————. 1991. Remarks at a meeting on "What Use Are Humanities Centers?" New Haven, 27 April.

————. 1992. "Victorian Studies." In *Redrawing the Boundaries: The Transformation of English and American Literary Studies,* ed. Stephen Greenblatt and Giles Gunn, 130–53. New York: Modern Language Association.

Levine, George, et al. 1989. *Speaking for the Humanities.* ACLS Occasional Paper 7. New York: American Council of Learned Societies.

Liberal Learning and the Arts and Sciences Major. 1990. Washington, D.C.: Association of American Colleges and Universities. Vol. 1: *The Challenge of Connecting Learning;* Vol. 2: *Reports from the Fields.*

Likens, G. E. 1992. *Excellence in Ecology* Vol. 3, *The Ecosystem Approach: Its Use and Abuse.* Oldendorf/Luhe, Germany, Ecology Institute.

Lind, Ingemar. 1984. Remarks at "Inter-disciplinarity Revisited" international seminar, Linköping. Sweden, 3 October.

Livingston, Eric. 1993. "The Disciplinarity of Knowledge at the Mathematics-Physics Interface." In Messer-Davidow, Shumway, and Sylvan 1993b, 368–93.

Lohdahl, J. B., and G. Gordon. 1972. "The Structure of Scientific Fields and Functioning of University Graduate Departments." *American Sociological Review* 37:57–72.

Lotchin, Roger. 1983. "The New Chicano History: An Urban History Perspective." *History Teacher* 16, 2:229–47.

Lowy, Ilana. 1992. "The Strength of Loose Concepts—Boundary Concepts, Federative Experimental Strategies and Disciplinary Growth: The Case of Immunology." *History of Science* 30, 4, 90:371–96.

Lyon, Arabella. 1992. "Interdisciplinarity: Giving up Territory." *College English* 54, 6:681–93.

Lyotard, Jean-François. 1988. *The Postmodern Condition: A Report on Knowledge.* Trans. G. Bennington and B. Massumi, with foreword by F. Jameson. Minneapolis: Univ. of Minnesota Press.

Mar, Brian. 1988. "System Engineering." Unpublished manuscript. Available from the author.

Marcell, David. 1977. "Characteristically American: Another Perspective on American Studies." *Centennial Review* 21, 4:388–400.

Marcus, George, and Fischer, Michael. 1986. *Anthropology as Cultural Critique: An Experimental Moment in the Human Sciences.* Chicago: Univ. of Chicago Press.

Marshall, Donald G. 1992. "Literary Interpretation." In Gibaldi 1992, 159–82.

Mason, R. O., and I. Mitroff. 1981. *Challenging Strategic Planning Assumptions.* New York: Wiley.

Mathiesen, Werner Christie. 1990. "The Problem-Solving Community: A Valuable Alternative to Disciplinary Communities?" *Knowledge: Creation, Diffusion, Utilization* 2, 4:410–27.

McPhee, John. 1981. *Basin and Range.* New York: Farrar.

McQuade, Donald. 1992. "Composition and Literary Studies." In Greenblatt and Gunn 1992, 482–519.

Mechling, Jay, Robert Meredith, and David Wilson. 1973. "American Culture Studies: The Discipline and the Curriculum." *American Quarterly* 25, 4:363–89.

Meredith, Robert. 1968. "Introduction: Theory, Method, and American Studies." In *American Studies: Essays on Theory and Method,* ed. Robert Meredith, i–xi. Columbus, Ohio: Charles E. Merrill.

Merton, R. L. 1973. "The Normative Structure of Science." In *The Sociology of Science,* ed. R. K. Merton. 2d ed. Chicago: Univ. of Chicago Press.

Messer-Davidow, Ellen. 1991. "Know-how." In Hartman and Messer-Davidow 1991, 281–309.

Messer-Davidow, Ellen, David R. Shumway, and David Sylvan. 1993a. Preface and "Introduction: Disciplinary Ways of Knowing." In Messer-Davidow, Shumway, and Sylvan 1993b, vii–viii, 1–21.

————, eds. 1993b. *Knowledges: Historical and Critical Studies in Disciplinarity.* Charlottesville: Univ. Press of Virginia.

Middleton, Anne. 1992. "Medieval Studies." In Greenblatt and Gunn 1992, 12–40.

Mikesell, Marvin. 1969. "The Borderlands of Geography." In Sherif and Sherif 1969, 227–48.

Miller, J. Hillis. 1988. "The Function of Rhetorical Study at the Present Time." In *Teaching Literature: What Is Needed Now,* Cambridge: Harvard Univ. Press.

————. 1991. "The Role of Theory in the Development of Literary Studies in the United States." In Easton and Schelling 1991, 118–38.

————. 1992. *Illustration.* Cambridge: Harvard Univ. Press.

Miller, Raymond. 1982. "Varieties of Interdisciplinary Approaches in the Social Sciences." *Issues in Integrative Studies* 1:1–37.

Miller, Steven. 1992. Comment. "Knowledge Collaborations in the Arts, the Sciences, and the Humanities. Part 3: The Humanities and Social Sciences." *Knowledge* 14, 1:121–24.

Milliken, Jennifer. 1990. "Traveling across Borders: A Response." *Social Epistemology* 4, 3:317–21.

Minnich, Barbara. 1990. *Transforming Knowledge.* Philadelphia: Temple Univ. Press.

Minshull, Robert. 1973. "Functions of Geography in American Studies." *Journal of American Studies* 7, 3:267–78.

Mitchell, W. J. T. 1990. "Against Comparison: Teaching Literature and the Visual Arts." In *Teaching Literature and Other Arts,* ed. J.-P. Barricelli, J. Gibaldi, and E. Lauter, 30–37. New York: Modern Language Association.

Montrose, L. W. 1989. "Professing the Renaissance: The Poetics and Politics of Culture." In *The New Historicism,* ed. H. A. Vesser, 15–36. New York: Routledge.

Morris, Meaghan. 1992. "'On the Beach.'" In Grossberg, Nelson, and Treichler 1992, 450–73. See also comments in response to Graeme Turner, ibid., 651, 653.

Mulkay, M. 1969. "Some Aspects of Cultural Growth in the Social Sciences." *Social Research* 36:22–52.

————. 1972. *The Social Process of Innovation.* London: Macmillan.

————. 1974. "Conceptual Displacements and Migration in Science." *Science Studies* 4:205–34.

————. 1977. "The Sociology of the Scientific Research Community." In *Science, Technology, and Society,* ed. I. Spiegel-Rosing and D. de Solla Price. London: Sage.

Mulkay, M. J., and D. O. Edge. 1973. "Cognitive, Technical, and Social Factors in the Growth of Radio Astronomy." *Social Science Information* 12:25–61.

Muller, Johan, and Nick Taylor. 1993. "The Gilded Calabash: Schooling and Everyday Life." Paper presented at the Kenton-at-Olwandle Conference, University of Natal, Durban.

Mullins, Nick. 1973. "The Development of Specialties in Social Science: The Case of Ethnomethodology." *Science Studies* 3:245–73.

Murray, Thomas. 1983. "Partial Knowledge." In *Ethics, the Social Sciences, and Policy Analysis,* ed. Daniel Callahan and Bruce Jennings, 305–31. New York: Plenum.

Nelson, Cary, Paul Treichler, and Lawrence Grossberg. 1992. "Cultural Studies: An Introduction." In Grossberg, Nelson, and Treichler 1992, 1–22.

Nelson, John S., A. Megill, and D. N. McCloskey, eds. 1987. *The Rhetoric of the Human Sciences: Language and Argument in Scholarship and Public Affairs.* Madison: Univ. of Wisconsin Press.

New Alliances and Partnerships in American Science and Engineering. 1986. Washington, D.C.: National Academic Press.

Newell, William H. 1983. "The Role of Interdisciplinary Studies in the Liberal Education of the 1980s." *Liberal Education* 69, 3:245–55.

———. 1988. "Interdisciplinary Studies Are Alive and Well." *Association for Integrative Studies Newsletter* 10, 1:1, 6–8. Reprinted in *AAHE Bulletin* 40, 8 (1988): 10–12, and in *National Honors Report* 9, 2 (1988): 5–6.

———. 1990. "What to Do Next: Strategies for Change." In *Rethinking the Curriculum: Toward an Integrated, Interdisciplinary College Education,* ed. Mary E. Clark and Sandra A. Wawrytko, 253–60. Contributions to the Study of Education 40. New York: Greenwood.

———. 1992. "Academic Disciplines and Undergraduate Interdisciplinary Education: Lessons from the School of Interdisciplinary Studies at Miami University, Ohio." *European Journal of Education* 27, 3:211–21.

———. 1993. "Transcending Dichotomies: Theory and Practice in Socio-economics and Interdisciplinary Studies. Paper presented at the Society for the Advancement of Socio-economics meeting on Incentives and Values as Foundations for Social Order. New York City, 26–28 March.

———, ed. and comp. 1986. *Interdisciplinary Undergraduate Programs: A Directory.* Oxford, Ohio: Association for Integrative Studies.

Newell, William, and Julie Thompson Klein. 1996. "Interdisciplinary Studies into the 21st Century." *Journal of General Education.* 45, 2.

Newton, J. L. 1989. "History as Usual? Feminism and the 'New Historicism.'" In *The New Historicism,* ed. H. A. Veeser, 152–67. New York: Routledge.

Oakley, Francis. 1992. "Against Nostalgia: Reflections on Our Present Discontents in American Higher Education." In *The Politics of Liberal Education,* ed. Darryl Gless and Barbara Herrnstein Smith, 267–89. Durham: Duke Univ. Press.

Olson, Gary, and Irene Gale. 1991. *(Inter)views: Cross-disciplinary Perspectives on Rhetoric and Literacy.* Carbondale: Southern Illinois Univ. Press.

OSU. Ohio State University Task Force for Interdisciplinary Research and Graduate

Education. 1991. *Report on Recommendations for Fostering Interdisciplinary Research and Graduate Education.* Columbus, Ohio. 19 April.

Pagels, Heinz. 1988. *The Dream of Reason: The Computer and the Rise of the Sciences of Complexity.* New York: Simon.

Pahre, Robert. 1994. "Symbolic Discourse and Crossdisciplinary Communities." Paper presented at Group for Research into the Institutionalization and Professionalization of Knowledge Production meeting. Minneapolis, 14–17 April.

———. 1995. "Positivist Discourse and Social Scientific Communities: Towards an Epistemological Sociology of Science." *Social Epistemology,* 9, 3:233–55.

Pantin, C. F. A. 1968. *The Relations between the Sciences.* Cambridge: Cambridge Univ. Press.

Papadopoulos, George S. 1985. "Concluding Remarks." In Levin and Lind 1985, 206–8.

Parsons, Talcott. 1970. "Theory in the Humanities and Sociology." *Daedalus,* spring, 495–523.

Patterson, Annabel. 1992. "Historical Scholarship." In Gibaldi 1992, 183–200.

Paul, R. W. 1987. "Critical Thinking and the Critical Person." In *Thinking: The Second International Conference,* ed. D. Perkins, J. Lochhead, and J. Bishop, 383–403. Hillsdale, N.J.: Erlbaum.

Paulson, William. 1988. *The Noise of Culture: Literary Texts in a World of Information.*

———. 1991. "Literature, Complexity, Interdisciplinarity." In *Chaos and Order: Complex Dynamics in Literature and Science,* ed. N. Katherine Hayles, 37–53. Chicago: Univ. of Chicago Press.

Paxson, Thomas. 1996. "Modes of Interaction between Disciplines." *Journal of General Education,* 45, 2.

Pearson, A. W., R. L. Payne, and H. P. Gunz. 1979. "Communication, Coordination, and Leadership in Interdisciplinary Research." In *Interdisciplinary Research Groups,* ed. R. T. Barth and R. Steck, 112–27. Vancouver: International Group on Interdisciplinary Programs.

Peck, Jeffrey M. 1989. Introduction and "There's No Place Like Home? Remapping the Topography of German Studies." *German Quarterly* 62, 2:141–42, 178–87.

Perper, Timothy. 1989. "The Loss of Innovation: Peer Review in Multi- and Interdisciplinary Research." *Issues in Integrative Studies* 7:21–56.

Peston, M. 1978. "Some Thoughts on Evaluating Interdisciplinary Research." *Higher Education Review* 10, 2:55–60.

Peterson, Russell. 1990. "Why Not a Separate College of Integrated Studies." In *Rethinking the Curriculum: Toward an Integrated, Interdisciplinary College Education,* ed. Mary E. Clark and Sandra A. Wawrytko, 215–26. Contributions to the Study of Education 40. New York: Greenwood.

Peterson, V. Spike 1993. "Disciplining Practiced/Practices: Gendered States and Politics." In Messer-Davidow, Shumway, and Sylvan 1993b, 243–67.

Petrie, Hugh G. 1976. "Do You See What I See? The Epistemology of Interdisciplinary Inquiry." *Journal of Aesthetic Education* 10 (January): 29–43.

Physics in Perspective. 1972. Washington, D.C.: National Academy of Sciences.

Pickering, Andrew. 1993. "Anti-discipline or Narratives of Illusion." In Messer-Davidow, Shumway, and Sylvan 1993b, 103–22.

Pickett, Steward T. A., Jurek Kolasa, and Clive G. Jones. 1994. *Ecological Understanding: The Nature of Theory and the Theory of Nature.* San Diego: Academic Press.

Pilet, Paul-Emile. 1981. "The Multidisciplinary Aspects of Biology: Basic and Applied Research." *Scientia* 116:629–36.

Pinch, Trevor. 1990. "The Culture of Scientists and Disciplinary Rhetoric." *European Journal of Education* 25, 3:295–304.

Popenoe, David. 1965. "On the Meaning of 'Urban' in Urban Studies." *Urban Affairs Quarterly* 1, 1:17–33.

Posner, Roland. 1988. "What Is an Academic Discipline?" In *Gedankenzeichen,* ed. Regina Claussen and Roland Daube-Schacket, 165–85. Festschrift for Klaus Oehler. N.p.: Stauffenburg.

Preziosi, Donald. 1993. "Seeing through Art History." In Messer-Davidow, Shumway, and Sylvan 1993b, 215–31.

Pring, Richard. 1971. "Curriculum Integration." *Proceedings of the Philosophy of Education Society of Great Britain.* suppl. 5, 2:170–200.

Pye, Lucien. 1975. "The Confrontation between Discipline and Area Studies." In *Political Science and Area Studies: Rivals or Partners?* ed. Lucien Pye, 5–22. Bloomington: Indiana Univ. Press.

Rabb, Theodore K. 1981. "Coherence, Synthesis, and Quality in History." *Journal of Interdisciplinary History* 12, 2:315–22.

———. 1983. "The Historian and the Climatologist." In *The New History: The 1980's and Beyond, Studies in Interdisciplinary History,* ed. Theodore K. Rabb, Robert I. Rotberg, and Thomas Glick, 251–58. Princeton: Princeton Univ. Press.

Ransom, John Crowe. 1938. "Criticism, Inc." In *The World's Body,* 330–36. New York: Scribner's.

Reiger, Henry A. 1978. *A Balanced Science of Renewable Resources, with Particular Reference to Fisheries.* Seattle: Washington Sea Grant, distributed by Univ. of Washington Press.

"Review of the Joint Committee on Chinese Studies (JCSS) of the American Council of Learned Societies (ACLS) and the Social Science Research Council (SSRC)." 1990. Available from ACLS.

Rich, Daniel, and Robert Warren. 1980. "The Intellectual Future of Urban Affairs: Theoretical, Normative, and Organizational Options." *Social Science Research* 17, 2:53–66.

Richards, Donald G. 1996. "Meaning and Relevance of 'Synthesis' in Interdisciplinary Studies." *Journal of General Education,* 45, 2.

Rigney, Daniel, and Donna Barnes. 1980. "Patterns of Interdisciplinary Citation in the Social Sciences." *Social Science Quarterly* 61:114–27.

Rittle, H. W. J., and M. M. Webber. 1973. "Dilemmas in a General Theory of Planning." *Policy Sciences* 4:167–69.

Robbins, Bruce. 1987. "Poaching off the Disciplines." *Raritan* 6, 4 (spring): 81–86.

Robinson, John B. 1996. "Falling between Schools: Some Thoughts on the Theory and Practice of Interdisciplinarity." In Salter and Hearn 1996.

Roederer, Juan G. 1988. "Tearing down Disciplinary Barriers." *Astrophysics and Space Science* 144:659–67.

Ross, Dorothy. 1991. *The Origins of American Social Science.* Cambridge: Cambridge Univ. Press.

Rouse, William B. 1982. "On Models and Modelers: N Cultures." *IEEE Transactions on Systems, Man and Cybernetics* SMC-12, 5:605–10.

Rowe, John Carlos. 1992. "Postmodernist Studies." In Greenblatt and Gunn 1992, 179–208.

Roy, Rustum. 1979. "Interdisciplinary Science on Campus: The Elusive Dream." In *Interdisciplinarity and Higher Education,* ed. Joseph Kockelmans, 161–96. University Park: Pennsylvania Univ. Press.

Ruscio, Kenneth. 1985. "Specializations in Academic Disciplines: 'Spokes on a Wheel.'" Paper presented at Association for the Study of Higher Education meeting. Chicago, 15–17 March. Available as ERIC microfiche ED 259643.

Russell, Martha Garrett. 1982. "Introduction and Overview." In Russell, Sauer, and Barnes 1981, 1–8.

Russell, Martha Garrett, Richard Sauer, and John M. Barnes, eds. 1982. *Enabling Interdisciplinary Research: Perspectives from Agriculture, Forestry, and Home Economics.* Miscellaneous Publication 19. St. Paul: Agricultural Experiment Station, Univ. of Minnesota.

Ryan, Michael. 1988. "Cultural Studies: A Critique." Cited in in Leitch 1988, 404, 438 n. 34.

Said, E. 1979. "Reflections on Recent American 'Left' Literary Criticism." *Boundary 2,* 8, 11–30. Also in *The World, the Text, and the Critic* (Cambridge: Harvard Univ. Press, 1983).

Salomon, Nanette. 1991. "The Art Historical Canon: Sins of Omission." In Hartman and Messer-Davidow 1991, 222–36.

Salter, Liora, and Alison Hearn, eds. 1996. *Outside the Lines: Issues and Problems in Interdisciplinary Research.* Montreal: McGill-Queens Press.

Salzman-Webb, Marilyn. 1972. "Feminist Studies: Frill or Necessity." *Feminist Studies V,* ed. Rae Lee Siporin. Pittsburgh: Know.

Schachterle, L. 1987. "A Review Essay: Contemporary Literature and Science." *Modern Language Studies* 17, 2:78–86.

Schmandt, Henry J., and George D. Wendel. 1988. "Urban Research 1965–1987: A Content Analysis of *Urban Affairs Quarterly.*" *Urban Affairs Quarterly* 24, 1:3–32.

Schneider, Stephen N. 1977. "Climate Change and the World Predicament: A Case Study for Interdisciplinary Research." *Climatic Change* 1:21–43.

Schön, Donald. 1983. *The Reflective Practitioner: How Professionals Think in Action.* New York: Basic Books.

Schor, Naomi. 1992. "Feminist and Gender Studies." In Gibaldi 1992, 262–87.

Schriver, Karen A. 1989. "Theory Building in Rhetoric and Composition: The Role of Empirical Scholarship." *Rhetoric Review* 7, 2:272–88.

Schütze, Hans G. 1985. "Interdisciplinarity Revisited: Introduction to a New Debate on an Old Issue." In Levin and Lind 1985, 9–14.

Schwartz, Benjamin I. 1980. "Presidential Address: Area Studies as a Critical Discipline." *Journal of Asian Studies* 40:15–25.

Schwartz, Mildred. 1987. "Historical Sociology in the History of American Sociology." *Social Science History* 11, 1:1–16.

Science and Technology Centers: Principles and Guidelines. A Report by the Panel on Science and Technology Centers. 1987. Washington, D.C.: National Academy of Sciences.

Scientific Interfaces and Technological Applications. 1986. Physics through the 1990's. Washington, D.C.: National Academy Press.

Scott, Peter. 1984. *The Crisis of the University.* London: Croom Helm.

Searing, Susan E. 1992. "How Librarians Cope with Interdisciplinarity: The Case of Women's Studies." *Issues in Integrative Studies* 10:7–25.

Semmes, Clovis E. 1981. "Foundations of an Afrocentric Social Science: Implications for Curriculum-Building, Theory, and Research in Black Studies." *Journal of Black Studies* 12, 1:3–17.

Serr, Ronnie. 1991. "The End-of-History." *Issues in Integrative Studies* 9:91–97.

Sewell, William H. 1989. "Some Reflections on the Golden Age of Interdisciplinary Social Psychology." *Social Psychology Quarterly* 52, 2:88–97.

Shapin, Steven. 1989. "The Invisible Technician." *American Scientist* 77:554–63.

———. 1992. "Discipline and Bounding: The History and Sociology of Science as Seen through the Externalism-Internalism Debate." *History of Science* 30, 4:333–69.

Sherif, Muzafer, and Carolyn D. Sherif. 1969a. "Interdisciplinary Coordination as a Validity Check." In Sherif and Sherif 1992b, 3–20.

———, eds. 1969b. *Interdisciplinary Relationships in the Social Sciences.* Chicago: Aldine.

Showalter, Elaine. 1977. *A Literature of Their Own: British Women Novelists from Brontë to Lessing.* Princeton: Princeton Univ. Press.

———. 1981. "Feminist Criticism in the Wilderness." *Critical Inquiry* 8, 2:179–205.

Shumway, David. 1988. "The Interdisciplinarity of American Studies." Unpublished manuscript. Available from the author.

Shumway, David, and Ellen Messer-Davidow. 1991. "Disciplinarity: An Introduction." *Poetics Today* 12, 2:201–25.

Sigma Xi. 1988. *Removing the Boundaries: Perspectives on Cross-disciplinary Research.* New Haven: Sigma Xi.

Sill, David J. 1996. "Integrative Thinking, Synthesis, and Creativity in Interdisciplinary Studies." *Journal of General Education,* 45, 2.

Simon, Elaine, and Judith G. Goode. 1989. "Constraints on the Contribution of Anthropology to Interdisciplinary Policy Studies: Lessons from a Study of Saving Jobs in the Supermarket Industry." *Urban Anthropology* 18, 2:219–39.

Simons, Herbert W., ed. 1989. *Rhetoric in the Human Sciences.* London: Sage.

Sklar, Robert. 1975. "The Problem of an American Studies 'Philosophy': A Bibliography of New Directions." *American Quarterly* 27, 3:245–61.

Smirnov, S. N. 1984. "The Main Forms of Interdisciplinary Development of Modern Science." In *Integration of Science and the Systems Approach,* ed. Z. Javurek, A. D. Ursul, and J. Zeman, 65–84. Prague: Academia.

Soja, Edward. 1989. *Postmodern Geographies: The Reassertion of Space in Critical Social Theory.* London: Verso.

Sproull, Robert, and Harold Hall. 1987. *Multidisciplinary Research and Education Pro-*

grams in Universities: Making Them Work. Washington, D.C.: Government-University-Industry Research Roundtable, National Academy Press.

Squires, Geoffrey. 1992. "Interdisciplinarity in Higher Education in the United Kingdom." *European Journal of Education* 27, 3:201–9.

Stafford, Barbara. 1988. "The Eighteenth-Century: Towards an Interdisciplinary Model." *Art Bulletin* 70, 1:6–24.

Star, S. Leigh, and James R. Griesmer. 1988. "Institutional Ecology, 'Translations' and Boundary Objects." *Social Studies of Science* 19:387–420.

Steedman, Carolyn, 1992. "Culture, Cultural Studies, and the Historians." In Grossberg, Nelson, and Treichler 1992, 613–22.

Stehr, Nico, and Richard V. Ericson. 1992. Introduction to "Part 2: Theoretical Perspectives." In *The Culture and Power of Knowledge: Inquiries into Contemporary Societies,* ed. Nico Stehr and Richard V. Ericson, 23–27. Berlin: De Gruyter.

Stember, Marilyn. 1991. "Advancing the Social Sciences through the Interdisciplinary Enterprise." *Social Science Journal* 28, 2:1–14.

Stimpson, Catherine R. 1978. "Women's Studies: An Overview." *University of Michigan Papers in Women's Studies,* May, 14–26.

———. 1992. "Feminist Criticism." In Greenblatt and Gunn 1992b, 251–70.

Stine, Jeffrey K. 1992. Comment. "Knowledge Collaborations in the Arts, the Sciences, and the Humanities. Part 2: The Sciences." *Knowledge* 13, 4:400–409.

Stocking, George W., Jr., and David E. Leary. 1986. "History of Social Scientific Inquiry." *Items* 40:53–57.

Stoddard, Ellwyn. 1982. "Multidisciplinary Research Funding: A 'Catch 22' Enigma." *American Sociologist* 17:210–16.

———. 1986. "Border Studies as an Emergent Field of Scientific Inquiry: Scholarly Contributions of U.S.–Mexico Borderlands Studies." *Journal of Borderlands Studies* 1 (spring): 1–33.

———. 1991. "Frontiers, Borders, and Border Segmentation: Toward a Conceptual Clarification." *Journal of Borderlands Studies* 6, 1:1–22.

———. 1992. "Legitimacy and Survival of a Professional Organization: The Association of Borderlands Scholars." *Journal of Borderlands Studies,* spring.

Stone, James H. 1969. "Integration in the Humanities: Perspectives and Prospects." *Main Currents in Modern Thought* 26, 1:14–19.

Suleiman, Susan. 1980. "Introduction: Varieties of Audience-Oriented Criticism." In *The Reader in the Text: Essays on Audience and Interpretation,* ed. Susan Suleiman and Inge Crosman, 3–45. Princeton: Princeton Univ. Press.

Swoboda, Wolfram. 1979. "Discipline and Interdisciplinarity: A Historical Perspective." In Kockelmans 1979a, 49–92.

Tabor, David. 1990. "Interdisciplinary Research Centers." *Interdisciplinary Science Reviews* 15, 1:9–10.

Tate, Thad. 1991. "Statement for the Whitney Humanities Center Conference." New Haven, Conn., April.

Taylor, Alistair. M. 1969. "Integrative Principles and the Educational Process." *Main Currents in Modern Thought* 25, 5:126–33.

Teich, Albert. 1979. "Trends in the Organization of Academic Research Performance:

The Role of ORU's and Full-Time Researchers." In *Interdisciplinary Research Groups,* ed. R. T. Barth and R. Steck, 244–59. Vancouver: International Group on Interdisciplinary Programs.

Thomas, Brook. 1991. *The New Historicism and Other Old-Fashioned Topics.* Princeton: Princeton Univ. Press.

Thornton, Russell. 1977. "American Indian Studies as an Academic Discipline." *Journal of Ethnic Studies* 5 (fall): 1–15.

Thorpe, James, ed. 1963. *The Aims and Methods of Scholarship in Modern Languages and Literatures.* New York: Modern Language Association.

———. 1967. *Relations of Literary Study: Essays on Interdisciplinary Contributions.* New York: Modern Language Association.

———. 1970. *The Aims and Methods of Scholarship in Modern Languages and Literatures.* 2d ed. New York: Modern Language Association.

Tichi, Cecelia. 1992. "American Literary Studies to the Civil War." In Greenblatt and Gunn 1992b, 209–31.

Tilly, Charles. 1991. "How (and What) Are Historians Doing?" In Easton and Schelling 1991, 86–117.

Tompkins, Jane P. 1980. "The Reader in History: The Changing Shape of Literary Response." In *Reader-Response Criticism: From Formalism to Post-structuralism,* ed. Jane P. Tompkins, 185–232. Baltimore: Johns Hopkins Univ. Press.

Toulmin, Stephen. 1972. *Human Understanding: The Collective Use and Evolution of Concepts.* Princeton: Princeton Univ. Press.

Turner, Bryan. 1990. "The Interdisciplinary Curriculum: From Social Medicine to Postmodernism." *Sociology of Health and Illness* 12:1–23.

Turner, Graeme. 1992. "'It Works for Me': British Cultural Studies, Australian Cultural Studies, Australian Film." In Grossberg, Nelson, and Treichler 1992, 640–53.

Turner, Ralph H. 1991. "The Many Faces of American Sociology: A Discipline in Search of Identity." In Easton and Schelling 1991, 59–85.

UBC. 1993. "Between Disciplines." A Report on the UBC Joint-Faculties Symposium on Interdisciplinarity. University of British Columbia. Vancouver, British Columbia. August.

UNESCO. 1994. First World Congress on Transdisciplinarity. Setúbal, Portugal, 2–7 November. Cosponsored by the Group of Transdisciplinary Studies at UNESCO, the International University of Lisbon, and the Centre International de Recherches et Études Transdisciplinaires.

The University and the Community: The Problems of Changing Relationships. 1982. Paris: Organization for Economic Cooperation and Development.

Van den Daele, Wolfgang, and Peter Weingart. 1975. "Resistance and Receptivity of Science to External Direction: The Emergence of New Disciplines under the Impact of Science Policy." In *Perspectives on the Emergence of Scientific Disciplines,* ed. Gerald Lemaine et al., 247–76. The Hague: Mouton.

Van Dusseldorp, Dirk, and Seerp Wigboldus. 1994. "Interdisciplinary Research for Integrated Rural Development in Developing Countries: The Role of Social Sciences." *Issues In Integrative Studies* 12:93–138.

Van Lohuizen, Th. K. 1948. "The Unity of Town Planning." Address upon taking office as Professor Extraordinary for Town Planning Research in the Delft Technological University. February.

Van Valen, Leigh. 1972. "Laws in Biology and History: Structural Similarities of Academic Disciplines." *New Literary History* 3, 2:409–19.

Veeser, H. A. 1989. Introduction to *The New Historicism,* ed. H. A. Veeser, ix–xvi. New York: Routledge.

Verhagen, D. J. D. M. 1984. "Some Characteristics of Multi- and Interdisciplinary Activities." In *Problems in Interdisciplinary Studies,* ed. R. Jurkovich and J. H. P. Paelinck, 94–103. Issues in Interdisciplinary Studies 2. Aldershot, Hampshire: Gower.

Veysey, Laurence R. 1965. *The Emergence of the American University.* Chicago: Univ. of Chicago Press.

Vickers, Jill. 1991. "Where Is the Discipline in Interdisciplinarity?" Paper presented at Rob McDougall Symposium on Interdisciplinarity, June.

Vlachy, Jan. 1982. "Interdisciplinary Approaches in Physics: The Concepts." *Czechoslovak Journal of Physics* B3:1311–18.

Vosskamp, Wilhelm. 1986. "From Scientific Specialization to the Dialogue between the Disciplines." *Issues in Integrative Studies* 4:17–36.

———. 1994. "Crossing of Boundaries: Interdisciplinarity as an Opportunity for Universities in the 1980's?" *Issues in Integrative Studies* 12:43–54.

Walters, Ronald. 1970. "The Discipline of Black Studies." *Negro Educational Review* 21, 4:138–44.

Warrick, Richard A., and William I. Riebsame. 1981. "Societal Response to CO_2-Induced Climate Change: Opportunities for Research." *Climatic Change* 3: 387–428.

Weber, Samuel. 1987. *Institution and Interpretation.* Minneapolis: Univ. of Minnesota Press.

Welchman, John, ed. 1996. *Rethinking Borders.* Minneapolis: Univ. of Minnesota Press.

White, James Boyd. 1985. *Heracles' Bow: Essays on the Rhetoric and Poetics of the Law.* Madison: Univ. of Wisconsin Press.

Whitley, Richard. 1976. "Umbrella and Polytheistic Scientific Disciplines and Their Elites." *Social Studies of Sciences* 6:471–97.

———. 1984. "The Rise and Decline of University Disciplines in the Sciences." *Problems in Interdisciplinary Studies,* ed. R. Jurkovich and J. H. P. Paelinck, 10–25. Issues in Interdisciplinary Studies 2. Aldershot, Hampshire: Gower.

Wilderson, Paul. 1975. "Archaeology and the American Historian: An Interdisciplinary Challenge." *American Quarterly* 27, 2:115–32.

Williams, Raymond. 1983. *Keywords: A Vocabulary of Culture and Society.* Rev. ed. New York: Oxford Univ. Press.

Wilson, Elizabeth. 1988. "A Short History of a Border War: Social Science, School Reform, and the Study of Literature." *Poetics Today* 9, 4:711–35.

Winkler, Karen. 1987. "Interdisciplinary Research: How Big a Challenge to Traditional Fields?" *Chronicle of Higher Education,* 7 October, A1, 14–15.

Winsborough, Halliman. 1992. "Sociology Departments and Their Research Centers: An Essential Tension?" In Halliday and Janowitz 1992, 269–95.

Wise, Gene. 1978. "Some Elementary Axioms for an American Culture Studies." *Prospects: The Annual of American Cultural Studies* 4 (winter): 517–47.

Wolff, Janet. 1992. "Excess and Inhibition: Interdisciplinarity in the Study of Art." In Grossberg, Nelson, and Treichler 1992, 706–18.

Wolfle, Dael L. 1981. "Interdisciplinary Research as a Form of Research." *SRA: Journal of the Society of Research Administrators* 13:5–7.

"Women's Studies." 1990. In *Liberal Learning and the Arts and Sciences Major. V. II. Reports from the Fields,* 207–24.

Woolgar, Steve, and Dorothy Pawluch. 1984. "Ontological Gerrymandering: The Anatomy of Social Problems Explanations." *Social Problems* 32, 3:214–27.

WSU. 1993. "Report of the Commission on Interdisciplinary Studies." Detroit: Wayne State Univ.

Ziman, John. 1984. *An Introduction to Science Studies: The Philosophy and Social Aspects of Science and Technology.* Cambridge: Cambridge Univ. Press.

INDEX

Academic departments, 7; and centers, 29; declining control of science, 206–7; defined, 29, 53–54; and disciplines, 54; importance, 145–46; and interdisciplinary research, 195; of interdisciplinary studies, 226; and new interdisciplines, 196; as sites of interdisciplinary activity, 227, 232–33; strains on, 54

ACLS (American Council of Learned Societies): report on China studies, 110–11; report on humanities, 31

African American studies, 119, 164; and cultural studies, 130; and Native American studies, 118; and women's studies, 116, 118. *See also* Interdisciplinary studies

Agriculture: and natural resources, 97–98; and problem-focused research, 175; U.S. Department of, 9, 194

American Association of Colleges and Universities, 232

American studies: as a field, 140, 163–67; in humanities centers, 30; and interdisciplinary studies, 32; myth and symbol school, 95, 163; programs, 33; and women's studies, 116. *See also* Interdisciplinary studies

Anthropology: and American studies, 164; biological anthropologists, 45–46; in cultural studies, 123, 125–26; departmental reorganization, 55; and geography, 40–41; and history, 73–74, 78; and literary studies, 154, 156, 158; policy research, 61; as synoptic discipline, 40; urban research, 93

Area studies: in centers, 28; field of, 107–15; and interdisciplinary studies, 32; and medieval studies, 156; ologizing, 113; and problem-focused research, 175. *See also* Interdisciplinary studies

Art history: boundaries of, 172; and cultural studies, 130–31; current status, 44; problem of interpretation, 70–71

Artificial intelligence, 44

Assessment of learning, 214–15. *See also* Criteria of quality

Barthes, Roland, 84, 172
Bateson, Gregory, 84, 162
Becher, Tony, 55–56, 70

Printed in the United States
52838LVS00005B/26

9 780813 916798